The Role of Courts in Transitional Justice

Bringing together a group of outstanding judges, scholars and experts with first-hand experience in the field of transitional justice in Latin America and Spain, this book offers an insider's perspective on the enhanced role of courts in prosecuting serious human rights violations and grave crimes, such as genocide and war crimes, committed in the context of a prior repressive regime or current conflict. The book also draws attention to the ways in which regional and international courts have come to contribute to the initiation of national judicial processes. All of the contributions evince that the duty to investigate and prosecute grave crimes can no longer simply be brushed aside in societies undergoing transitions.

The Role of Courts in Transitional Justice is essential reading for practitioners, policy-makers and scholars engaged in the transitional justice processes or interested in judicial and legal perspectives on the role of courts, obstacles faced and how they may be overcome. It is unique in its ambition to offer a comprehensive and systematic account of the Latin American and Spanish experience and in bringing the insights of renowned judges and experts in the field to the forefront of the discussion.

Jessica Almqvist is a Lecturer in Public International Law at the University Autonóma of Madrid, specializing in international law of human rights and criminal justice. She has published *Human Rights, Culture and the Rule of Law* and *Justicia Transicional en Iberoamérica* (co-edited with Carlos Espósito).

Carlos Espósito is a Professor of Public International Law at the University Autónoma of Madrid. He has published widely, including the books *Inmunidad del Estado y derechos humanos* (2007) and *La jurisdicción consultiva de la Corte Internacional de Justicia* (1996).

The Role of Courts in Transitional Justice

Voices from Latin America and Spain

Edited by Jessica Almqvist and Carlos Espósito

Routledge
Taylor & Francis Group
LONDON AND NEW YORK

First published 2012
by Routledge
2 Park Square, Milton Park, Abingdon, Oxon OX14 4RN

Simultaneously published in the USA and Canada
by Routledge
711 Third Avenue, New York, NY 10017

Routledge is an imprint of the Taylor & Francis Group, an informa business

British Library Cataloguing in Publication Data
A catalogue record for this book is available from the British Library

Library of Congress Cataloging in Publication Data
The role of courts in transitional justice : voices from Latin America and Spain / [edited by] Jessica Almqvist, Carlos Espósito.
p. cm.
Includes bibliographical references and index.
1. Transitional justice—Latin America. 2. Justice, Administration of—Latin America. 3. Courts—Latin America. 4. Transitional justice—Spain. 5. Justice, Administration of—Spain. 6. Courts—Spain. 7. International criminal law. I. Almqvist, Jessica. II. Espósito, Carlos D.
KG495.R65 2011
347.8—dc23 2011022317

ISBN 978–0–415–60137–5 (hbk)
ISBN 978–0–203–15502–8 (ebk)

Typeset in Garamond
by Keystroke, Station Road, Codsall, Wolverhampton

MIX
Paper from responsible sources
FSC www.fsc.org FSC® C004839

Printed and bound in Great Britain by
CPI Antony Rowe, Chippenham, Wiltshire

Contents

Acknowledgements

This book is the outcome of an international expert roundtable discussion on the role of courts in transitional justice contexts (*El papel de los tribunales en contextos de justicia transicional: Oportunidades y desafíos actuales en la región Iberoamericana*), organized by the Centre for Political and Constitutional Studies in Madrid between 6 and 8 May 2008. The roundtable, which was kindly sponsored by the Spanish Agency of International Co-operation (*Agencia Española de Cooperación Internacional para el Desarrollo*), brought together judges, prosecutors, consultants and scholars who are extensively engaged in transitional justice processes in Latin America and Spain. The objective of the meeting was to reflect upon some of the recent advances made by the courts in these countries and also to engage in a constructive discussion on the challenges facing several of these courts in the process of delivering justice in transitional societies.

The meeting turned out to be extremely productive. Even if there is nowadays much talk about transitional justice in the international setting, including on the role of courts, it still seems relatively rare that judges, prosecutors, lawyers and civil society actors from different countries, albeit with similar legal systems, are brought together to talk about how to achieve justice in the light of the immense difficulties, including legal ones, commonly faced in this process. The discussion also revealed that the question of how to respond to these difficulties remains partly contested and debated. In our view, the reality of disagreement on the limits to criminal justice is not to be brushed aside. Thus, while most of the contributions are permeated by a conviction that criminal justice must have a special or privileged place in transitional justice processes—what we in this book call the canon of criminal law—also included are dissenting opinions on the prevalence of limits that cannot be ignored.

We are most indebted to the judges, consultants and scholars who have contributed to this book and it has been a true pleasure and, above all, a great honour to collaborate with them. We express special gratitude to Judge Antonio Cançado Trindade, who accepted our invitation to write a foreword on his experience with massacres while on the bench of the Inter-American Court of Human Rights. We immediately realized that these recollections of Judge Cançado Trindade were so rich and much more than a foreword and, thus, we finally decided to include his contribution as the opening chapter of this book.

We are thankful to the Centre of Political and Constitutional Studies; without its support, this book and its previous Spanish version (*Justicia transicional en Iberoamérica*, Madrid: CEPC, 2009) would never have become a reality. The majority of the chapters of the present book stem from that publication. This book, however, is not just a translation. Indeed, most of the chapters have been thoroughly revised and updated, and new chapters have been added. Chapters 2, 9, 10, 12 and 13 were originally written in English by their authors; the remaining chapters have been translated into English by the editors. Alejandra Torres Camprubí ably helped us in the editing process and we are grateful for her assistance.

We would like to acknowledge that the chapter of Naomi Roht-Arriaza and Almudena Bernabeu stems from an article published in the *Chicago Journal of International Law* vol. 79 (2008) pp. 79–106.

Furthermore, we want to emphasize and express our gratitude for the constructive comments received from the external reviewers of Routledge and to our editor Katie Carpenter who helped us to refine the focus and the contents of the book.

Most of all, we thank our families—Carlos, Sebastian and Rebecca, and Irene, Federico and Pablo—for their love and patience.

Notes on contributors

Jessica Almqvist Lecturer in Public International Law, Faculty of Law, Autónoma University in Madrid. She has also worked as Research Associate, the Project on International Courts and Tribunals, New York University, and the Centre for Political and Constitutional Studies, Madrid.

Alejandro Aponte Professor of Criminal Law, Faculty of Law, University Javeriana, Bogotá, Colombia. Consultant of the *Centro Internacional de Toledo para la Paz* in Madrid and Chief of the Area of Justice of this centre's Observatory of Demobilization, Justice and Peace, Bogotá.

Almudena Bernabeu Transitional Justice Program Director and International Attorney at the Center for Justice and Accountability. She is lead counsel on the Spanish Genocide case since 2006.

Antônio Augusto Cançado Trindade Former President of the Inter-American Court of Human Rights; Judge of the International Court of Justice; Emeritus Professor of International Law of the University of Brasilia; Member of the *Curatorium* of the Hague Academy of International Law, and of the *Institut de Droit International*.

Javier Chinchón Álvarez Lecturer in Public International Law and International Relations at the University Complutense of Madrid, and one of the leading Spanish scholars in the field of transitional justice.

Carlos Espósito Professor of Public International Law, Autónoma University in Madrid. Former Deputy Head of the International Law Department of the Spanish Ministry for Foreign Affairs (2001 to 2004) and Senior Researcher at think-tank *Fundación para las Relaciones Internacionales y el Diálogo Exterior* (FRIDE) (2004 to 2005). Collaborator with the *Consejo para la Consolidación de la Democracia*, Argentina (1988 to 1989).

Roberto Garretón Chilean lawyer and consultant on human rights. Member of the UN Secretary General's Advisory Committee on Genocide Prevention since 2006. Former representative of the UN High Commissioner for Human Rights for Latin America and the Caribbean. Lawyer at the *Vicaría de la Solidaridad* (1974 to 1990).

Alicia Gil Gil Senior Lecturer of Criminal Law, Spanish Open University (UNED) and Sub-director of the General Gutiérrez Mellado University Institute in Madrid.

Ricardo Gil Lavedra Congressman, Argentinian Congress. Lawyer and Associate Professor of Criminal Law at the University of Buenos Aires and former Judge of the Federal Appeals Court, Chamber on Criminal and Correctional Matters (1984 to 1987).

Felipe González Morales Professor of International Law at Diego Portales University, Santiago de Chile, and Member and Former President of the Inter-American Commission on Human Rights.

Susan Kemp Member of the UN Team of Experts on Sexual Violence in Armed Conflict, Department of Peace-Keeping Operations at the United Nations in New York. She has also worked for the Guatemalan NGO CALDH, bringing cases before the Inter-American Human Rights system and co-ordinating field investigations for a domestic prosecution of former Guatemalan heads of state and the armed forces representing genocide survivors of the *Associacion de Justicia y Reconciliacion*. She was an investigator with the International Criminal Court on Darfur, remaining in The Hague as Legal Adviser to Dutch non-profit Impunity Watch.

Yván Montoya Vivanco Professor of Human Rights and Criminal Law, Pontificia Universidad Católica del Peru, Lima.

Elizabeth Odio Benito Judge of the International Criminal Court and former Judge of the ad hoc International Criminal Tribunal for the Former Yugoslavia (1993 to 1998).

Naomi Roht-Arriaza Professor of Law, University of California, Hastings College of the Law. Member of the Legal Advisory Council of the Center for Justice and Accountability in San Francisco and a member of the legal team involved in the Spanish Genocide case litigation since 2006.

Paul Seils General Counsel of the International Center for Transitional Justice in New York since October 2010. He has also been Chief of the Rule of Law Section at the Office of the High Commissioner for Human Rights in Geneva, Chief of Analysis at the International Commission against Impunity in Guatemala and Head of the Unit for the Analysis of Situations of the Office for the Prosecutor of the International Criminal Court.

1 Introduction

Jessica Almqvist and Carlos Espósito

This book examines the role of courts in transitional justice. It brings into focus and analyzes the extent to which national courts in Latin America and Spain have come to investigate, prosecute and sanction serious human rights violations or grave crime perpetrated on a massive or considerable scale in the context of transitions and post-transitional settings. The book discusses what are in the view of the judges, lawyers and consultants in the field the key factors that have contributed to this development. Special attention will be afforded to the architectural design of the emerging system of international criminal justice, the progress made in terms of international legal codification and classification of the crimes in focus as well as the contributions by regional and international tribunals in terms of progressive interpretations of international human rights and criminal law with a view to govern judicial action in relation to "radical evil".[1]

In our view, the body of international and transnational law that is emerging and which is now meant to govern the role of courts in times of transitions and their aftermaths is driven by a desire to give full recognition in international law to what is present throughout the book as a *canon of criminal law*. This canon refers to a set of principles or rules of conduct for judges and prosecutors, mandating or dictating the investigation and prosecution of all crime, including grave crime, without any exception. The canon, as we understand it, really changes the axis of the discussion of how we should deal with grave crime in transitional justice. Several obstacles have been encountered in the process of implementing this canon. The challenges that are especially recurrent for the courts in transitional justice include amnesty laws, the principle of legality, statutory limitations and the prohibition against the retroactive application of criminal law to the detriment of the accused, as well as the absence of effective schemes of transnational judicial co-operation. How the courts have dealt with these matters and the extent to which they may be overcome are questions that lie at the heart of this book. Also considered are non-legal obstacles, such as the lack of judicial independence and the presence of strong political and military

1 Nino, C S, *Radical Evil on Trial*, New Haven: Yale University Press, 1998.

opposition, which tend to postpone the arrival of the courts and judges into the framework of transitional justice.

1.1 Transitions judicialized

A book dedicated to these themes takes on renewed importance in the light of the universe of international criminal justice initiatives that have developed since the end of the Cold War and which seek to ensure the investigation and prosecution of grave crime. The UN Security Council has been, and continues to be, a critical actor in this process. Especially significant is its repeated recourse to its mandatory powers under Chapter VII of the UN Charter declaring situations of grave crime as amounting to international security threats and as requiring the introduction of international judges and prosecutors to investigate, prosecute and punish the perpetrators of such crime. To this end, it has created two ad hoc international criminal tribunals for the former Yugoslavia (ICTY—1993)[2] and Rwanda (ICTR—1994),[3] and has requested the UN Secretary-General to ensure that internationalized or hybrid tribunals be established or authorized by the Special Representatives of UN transitional administrations to act in its place on this matter through the establishment of panels composed of international judges.[4] Even more significant is the parallel development in the post-Cold War period towards the establishment of an International Criminal Court (ICC) that is institutionally independent, at least formally speaking, from the organs of the United Nations and with competences to try crimes against humanity, war crimes and genocide. In spite of the misgivings about the efficacy or legitimacy of a court of this kind, its advocates and supporters have already managed to attract 115 states to ratify its Statute and join its Assembly. And, several cases are by this time at the pre-trial and trial stages.[5] The creation of the ICC means that for the first time in history there is a permanent international judicial institution with competences to investigate, prosecute and sanction the crimes in focus.

The international institutional advances over the last 20 years bear witness to a growing international conviction that grave crime cannot go unpunished and that courts have a crucial role to play in times of transition, including in conflict situations, and to the establishment of the basic conditions for lasting peace in a given country or region. At the same time, although this development has placed the question about the role of international judges and prosecutors

2 UN Security Council Resolution 827 of 25 May 1993.

3 UN Security Council Resolution 955 of 8 November 1994.

4 See, e.g. Romano, C, Nollkaemper, A and Kleffner, J (eds), *Internationalized Criminal Courts. Sierra Leone, East Timor, Kosovo, and Cambodia*, Oxford: Oxford University Press, 2004.

5 The Rome Statute establishing the International Criminal Court, signed on 17 July 1998 and in force since 1 July 2002. As of 12 October 2010, there are 114 States Parties to the Rome Statute.

at the forefront of contemporary international debates, a study of the architectural design of the emerging system of international criminal justice indicates that national courts and judges are expected to assume the main burdens of bringing this contemporary aspiration and ambition into effect. Especially telling is the introduction of the complementarity principle into the ICC framework. According to this principle, the ICC can only investigate or prosecute a case if the national courts with territorial or universal jurisdiction competences over the same case are unwilling or unable to do so.[6] The first Prosecutorial Strategy that was adopted by the ICC Chief Prosecutor in September 2006 stressed the exceptional character of the ICC-led investigations and prosecutions and ICC action considered as a last resort. As it noted, from the standpoint of the ICC Office of the Prosecutor, emphasis will be placed on the need for the *national* courts of States Parties, rather than the ICC itself, to shoulder the task of investigating and prosecuting the perpetrators of these crimes.[7] The second Prosecutorial Strategy (2009 to 2012) states that the ICC Office of the Prosecutor is committed to a positive approach to complementarity, which is defined as a "proactive policy of cooperation aimed at promoting national proceedings" and which means that the office "will encourage genuine national proceedings where possible, including in situation countries, relying on its various networks of cooperation, but without involving the Office directly in capacity building or financial or technical assistance".[8] The trend to assist and empower national judiciaries and thus seek to embed UN criminal justice-initiatives in the national judiciaries of affected societies is also reinforced by the policies emanating from the Rule of Law section of the UN Office of the High Commissioner for Human Rights as well as the policies of the UN Security Council in collaboration with the Secretary-General.[9]

6 Note the distinction between negative and positive complementarity. With regard to the notion of positive complementarity, see Burke-White, W W, "Proactive Complementarity: The International Criminal Court and National Courts in the Rome System of International Justice", *Harvard International Law Journal*, vol 49, no 1, 2008, pp 53–108.

7 The International Criminal Court, Office of the Prosecutor, *Report on Prosecutorial Strategy* (Ref-RP20060914-OTP), 14 September 2006. Indeed, the promotion of a primary role for national courts is not confined to the ICC framework, but is also a key element in the completion strategies of the two ad hoc international criminal tribunals. See completion strategies of each tribunal as presented in UN Security Council resolutions S/RES/1503 of 28 August 2003; S/RES/1534 of 26 March 2004; and S/2007/323 of 31 May 2007. In addition, attention should be given to the seminal report of the UN Secretary-General on *The rule of law and transitional justice in conflict and post-conflict societies*, UN Doc S/2004/616, 23 August 2004, according to which international institutions that seek to assist in peace-building efforts must focus on the building of national court capacities in order to ensure respect for the rule of law, which includes the investigation and the prosecution of the crimes in question.

8 See Prosecutorial Strategy 2009–2012, ICC Office of the Prosecutor, 1 February 2010, p 5.

9 For further information, see resources of the Rule of Law section, UN Office of the High Commissioner for Human Rights, available online at www2.ohchr.org/english/issues/rule_of_law/democracy.htm.

The recent international criminal justice initiatives are no doubt critical sources of inspiration and provide an important impetus for judicial action in national settings. However, from the standpoint of the national courts, of equal significance are the outcomes of international law-making processes towards the international legal codification of grave crime, including the duty of states and their courts to investigate and prosecute such crime, as well as the progressive development of the bulk of international law that is meant to govern and inform their conduct in times of transition more generally. To be sure, the ambition to draft something like an international penal code has been present ever since the end of the Second World War and the organization of the Nuremberg and Tokyo Trials. Even so, it took until 1998 and the adoption of the Rome Statute of the International Criminal Court before it could be said that the international community has a multilateral treaty in force the contents of which are akin to such a code. During the Cold War period, the principal successful law-making initiatives in the field were case-based and consisted of the adoption of treaties that recognized especially horrendous abuses as amounting to crimes under international law and also reinforced the obligation of states and their courts to prevent and punish such crime. Thus, prior to the adoption of the Rome Statute in 1998, the international criminalization of the crime of genocide, war crimes and crimes against humanity was partial and scattered and some crimes had been only partially defined. The first significant achievement in the field was the adoption of the UN Convention on the Prevention and Punishment of the Crime of Genocide (1948).[10] A year later, war crimes were thereafter defined in the four Geneva Conventions (1949). The two Additional Protocols to these Conventions define attacks against civilian populations as war crimes, but were not adopted until 1977. Before the adoption of the Rome Statute, the crimes against humanity had only been defined in the London Charter of the International Military Tribunal (1945), the application of which was limited to times of war and to prosecution of perpetrators belonging to the Axis Powers, as well as the ICTY and ICTR Statutes, the application and enforcement of which were limited to a given conflict situation. The crime of torture was recognized in the UN Convention against Torture and Other Cruel, Inhuman or Degrading Treatment or Punishment (1984), but is limited to public officials as perpetrators.[11] Finally, the crime of enforced disappearance was defined as late as 2006 in the UN Convention on the Protection of Persons from Enforced Disappearance and has so far achieved 25 ratifications.[12]

To this must be added the significant contributions made by international and regional courts and tribunals to the progressive development of inter-

10 UN Convention on the Prevention and Punishment of the Crime of Genocide, UNGA Res 260 (III)A of 9 December 1948.

11 UN Convention against Torture and Other Cruel, Inhuman or Degrading Treatment or Punishment, UNGA Res 39/46 of 10 December 1984.

12 UN Convention on the Protection of Persons from Enforced Disappearances, UNGA Res 61/177 of 20 December 2006.

national law meant to govern the role of courts in transitions.[13] To begin with, regional human rights courts have derived rather specific obligations and duties of states related to investigation and prosecution from rather generally held provisions of the human rights treaties that they have been given the authority to interpret. Thus, the Inter-American Court of Human Rights (IACtHR) has interpreted the international legal obligation of the States Parties to the Inter-American Convention of Human Rights to "ensure the free and full exercise of the rights recognized by the Convention to every person subject to its jurisdiction" as implying the duty of these states to prevent human rights violations, including serious ones, to investigate them, to identify the victims and the perpetrators, to impose sanctions and to afford reparations.[14] Additionally, it has ruled that amnesty laws, such as the Peruvian or Uruguayan laws, are contrary to international law even if democratically adopted and confirmed by referenda.[15] In a similar manner, the European Court of Human Rights (ECtHR) has contributed to an interpretation of the European Convention on Human Rights that fosters a role for criminal justice in response to grave crime, a role that in its view does not vanish even when more than 50 years have passed since the time of its commission.[16]

Finally, attention must be paid to recent international litigations before the International Court of Justice. The court has come to adjudicate controversies related to matters of criminal justice with the effect of advancing the body of international law in this field, including the meaning and scope of the duty of states to investigate or prosecute (the principle of *aut dedere aut punire*);[17]

13 For a consideration of international judicial law-making, see Ginsburg, T, "Bounded Discretion in International Judicial Law-making", *Virginia Journal of International Law*, vol 45, 2005, 631 ff.

14 IACtHR, case of *Velásquez Rodríguez v Honduras*, Series C No 4, Judgment of 29 July 1988, para 166.

15 IACtHR, case of *Barrios Altos v Peru*, Series C No 75, Judgment of 14 March 2001; IACtHR, case of *Gelman v Uruguay*, Series C No 221, Judgment of 24 February 2011. See also IACtHR, case of *Almonacid Arellano v Chile*, Series C No 154, Judgment of 26 September 2006. But compare with the decision of the Supreme Court of Brazil rejecting the challenge to *Lei da Anistia*, no 6683/79, which gave amnesty to political crimes in Brazil between 2 September 1961 and 15 August 1979. See Supremo Tribunal Federal, case CBFP 153, reporting judge Eros Grau, decided in plenary session on 10 April 2010 and published on 6 August 2010, available online at www.stf.jus.br/portal/jurisprudencia/listarJurisprudencia.asp?s1=%28ADPF%24.SCLA.+E+153.NUME.%29+OU+%28ADPF.ACMS.+ADJ2+153.ACMS.%29&base=baseAcordaos. For an analysis of transitional justice in Uruguay, see Errandonea, J. "Justicia transicional en Uruguay", *Revista Instituto Interamericano de Derechos Humanos*, vol. 47, 2008, pp. 13–70.

16 ECtHR, case of *Kononov v Latvia*, Application 36376/04, Judgment of 24 July 2008.

17 On 19 February 2009, the Belgian application to the International Court of Justice to institute proceedings against Senegal was made public. It originates as a result of Senegal's lack of compliance with the principle of *aut dedere aut punire* in relation to the former President of Chad, Hissène Habré. See *Proceedings instituted by the Kingdom of Belgium against the Republic of Senegal (Belgium v Senegal)*. Furthermore, the principle is also studied by the International Law Commission. See the report prepared by Zdizlaw Galic, *Second Report on the Obligation to Extradite or Prosecute (aut dedere aut judicare)*, 14 UN Doc A/CN.4/585 (11

questions concerning the terms and conditions of immunity from jurisdiction for government officials;[18] and the international obligation to co-operate on matters pertaining to criminal justice.[19] The judges of international criminal tribunals must also be seen as critical judicial actors in the furthering of the substantial contents of the canon of international criminal law. The recognition of gender-specific crimes of the two ad hoc criminal tribunals is especially telling as this achievement led to their inclusion in the Rome Statute.[20]

1.2 The basic elements of transitional justice

One may have a broad or narrow definition of transitional justice.[21] This book adopts a relatively narrow view of transitional justice as it is concerned with the propriety of judicial responses to the question of how society should deal with an evil past or conflictive present. Thus, we reject the contention that the answer to this question is subject to national political judgment based exclusively on strategic calculations on how to maximize the prospects for peace and stability in the light of the specific circumstances prevailing in each case. In its place, it sets forth an alternative and competing claim about the prevalence of a substantive notion of transitional justice enforceable by the judicial branch, which purports to constrain and inform the political options available for national governments in transitions and their aftermaths.

June 2007). For a comprehensive account of the principle, see also Cherif Bassiouni, M and Wise, E M (eds), *Aut Dedere Aut Judicare: The Duty to Extradite or Prosecute in International Law*, Dordrecht: Martinus Nijhoff, 1995.

18 See International Court of Justice, case of *Certain Criminal Proceedings in France (Republic of the Congo v France)*, which was initiated on 9 December 2002, although it was removed from the docket of this court on 16 November 2010 as a result of a letter dated 5 November 2010 and received in the court's registry the same day on which the Agent of the Republic of the Congo informed the court that his government "withdraws its Application instituting proceedings".

19 See International Court of Justice, case of *Certain Questions of Mutual Assistance in Criminal Matters (Djibouti v France)*, Judgment of 4 June 2008.

20 See the contribution of Judge Elizabeth Odio Benito included in this book.

21 For legally informed accounts of transitional justice, see Teitel, R G, *Transitional Justice*, Oxford: Oxford University Press, 2000, p 1; and Teitel, R G, "Transitional Justice Genealogy", *Harvard Human Rights Journal*, vol 16, 2003, p 69. In the latter article, Teitel defines the notion of transitional justice as a "conception of justice associated with periods of political change, characterized by legal responses to confront the wrongdoing of repressive predecessor regimes". See also Roht-Arriaza, N, "The New Landscape of Transitional Justice", in Roht-Arriaza, N and Mariezcurrena, J (eds), *Transitional Justice in the Twenty-first Century*, Cambridge: Cambridge University Press, 2006, p 2, who, when defining the purpose of this book, adopts an understanding of transitional justice as including "that set of practices, mechanisms and concerns that arise following a period of conflict, civil strife or repression, and that are aimed directly at confronting past violations of human rights and humanitarian law".

The elaboration of a substantive notion of justice breaks with the idea of transitions and transitional politics, largely inspired by the experiences in the Southern European hemisphere in the 1970s. In the field of political science, these experiences, and the Spanish one in particular, were converted into models to be followed by other countries when seeking to tackle similar situations. The Spanish transition is still seen as particularly successful, as it managed to secure a relatively peaceful move from a dictatorship to a democratic form of government. On the other hand, hardly any attention was paid to the fate of those who had suffered from serious human rights violations or grave crime committed during these dictatorships. Instead, in the Spanish case, an Amnesty Law was adopted in 1977, a law that has gained public support until this very day; and, until recently, there were no reparations given to the victims. As the Spanish Constitutional Court had pronounced, the measures were adopted as a matter of grace and not as reflecting any legal obligation to do so.[22] Although this stance has changed somewhat as a result of the adoption of the so-called Historic Memory Law in December 2007, at least in terms of reparation, as manifested by the fervent judicial reactions from the Supreme Court to the opening by Judge Baltasar Garzón of criminal investigations into the violations and crimes of the past in 2008, the Spanish model remains rather intact and consistent. However, in the light of the developments in Argentina, Chile, Peru and Colombia, the Spanish experience is slowly converting itself into an exception or an anomaly that does not necessarily meet the general expectations of international law in the field.[23]

In the initial stages of elaborating on a competing account of how transitions are to be realized in order to meet substantive standards of justice, most attention was paid to the fate of victims and their interests in accessing the truth of what had happened during the repressive regime, not only to their loved ones, who had disappeared, been illegally detained, tortured and murdered, but also what sorts of policies and actions of the repressive government had authorized or legitimized the commission of these crimes, and who had actually executed them. The idea of truth commissions emerged as a response to such concerns and the South African Truth and Reconciliation Commission, while not actually the first one to be organized, came to be promoted as a model and source of inspiration for other societies finding themselves in the process of tackling an evil past. However, since that time, remarkable developments have taken place in the international setting in terms of articulating a much more comprehensive notion of justice applicable to transitions, including a range of measures meant to give effect to its basic requirements. Though counting as soft law, strictly speaking, the Basic Principles and Guidelines on

22 See Tribunal Constitucional de España (Spanish Constitutional Court), STC 361/1993, Judgment of 3 December 1993.

23 For a more detailed analysis of the Spanish transition, see the contributions of Alicia Gil Gil and Javier Chinchón Álvarez included in this book.

the Right to a Remedy and Reparations for Victims of Gross Violations of International Human Rights Law and Serious Violations of International Humanitarian Law, adopted by the UN General Assembly on 16 March 2005 ("Basic Principles") has become a standard reference in the field when advising transitional governments and judiciaries what to do (and not to do) when responding to such violations.[24] According to this instrument, any such response must include not only ensuring that persons who claim to be the victims of a violation of this kind are given equal and effective access to justice as well as effective remedies, including reparations, but also that the violations in question are investigated "effectively, promptly, thoroughly and impartially", and that governments "where appropriate, take action against those allegedly responsible in accordance with domestic and international law".

The right to reparation is defined in broad terms as entailing the rights to restitution, compensation, rehabilitation, satisfaction and guarantees of non-repetition. The provisions related to the measures meant to meet the obligation of states to afford satisfaction to the victims of gross and systematic human rights violations or violations of international humanitarian law are especially relevant to the field of transitional justice, as these include: truth-seeking activities; the searching for the whereabouts of disappeared persons and the bodies of those killed; public apologies; and commemoration and tributes to the victims. According to the Basic Principles, the imposition of judicial and administrative sanctions against persons liable for the violations as modes of giving satisfaction is also relevant. Finally, consideration should also be given to the measures meant to give effect to the right to guarantees of non-repetition, as the relevant provisions refer to institutional reform, including of national judicial organs, and extend to: "ensuring that all civilian and military proceedings abide by international standards of due process, fairness and impartiality"; the strengthening of the independence of the judiciary; and reviewing and reforming laws contributing to or allowing gross violations of international human rights law and serious violations of international humanitarian law.

While the Basic Principles do not set forth a claim that investigations and prosecutions would be mandatory and in this sense represent a softer version of the UN Report of Diane Orentlicher,[25] it is clear that national courts are expected to participate in significant ways in the actual enforcement of these measures. It is equally clear that contemporary international human rights law purports to define the contents of justice that is to inform and constrain the actions of transitional governments and judiciaries. It thus seeks to work in tandem with and reinforce the obligations created in the field of international criminal law as well as situating these obligations in a broader international legal framework for action.

24 UNGA Resolution 60/147 (A/RES/60/147) of 16 December 2005.

25 Diane Orentlicher, *UN Report of the independent expert to update the set of principles to combat impunity*, UN Doc E/CN.4/2005/102, 18 February 2005.

1.3 Outstanding issues

The advances that have taken place in the realms of international human rights and criminal law in the last two decades towards the full recognition of the canon of criminal law in international law presuppose the possibility of courts—all courts—to administrate justice in periods of transition and post-transition, including in relation to grave crime, in spite of the large numbers of perpetrators and victims involved, and even if committed by political leaders or military powers. The international legal framework that is emerging indicates that, from the standpoint of justice and the law, there is nothing extraordinary or exceptional about such periods that would legitimize the derogation of law altogether or the adoption of a version of justice that has been heavily watered down. In an important sense, it represents an internationalized reaction to the fact that the law and thus a role for the courts have often been swept aside in moments of political upheaval, crisis and stability in favour of political judgments based on prudential grounds. Insisting on a role for the law and the courts is an attempt to limit the space for political will and strategic calculation and rests on a belief that the question of how to respond to grave crime is a matter of criminal justice, essentially legal in nature, which prompts the investigation, prosecution and sanctioning by impartial and independent courts.

The strengthening of the penal canon in international law has implied a change in the spirit of the international discussions devoted to transitional justice. More specifically, it has entailed a move away from a considerable preoccupation with the question as to whether judges and courts are actually bound to administrate justice in periods of transition or post-transitional contexts to a new set of unprecedented questions related to effective judicial action. Especially troublesome are the range of obstacles confronting courts and judges when seeking to meet new expectations and obligations. We believe that it is the recurrence and magnitude of some obstacles in times of transition (as opposed to settled periods) that legitimize the study of the role of the courts in transitional justice as a topic deserving to be studied in its own right. In most cases, their magnitude generates inevitable postponements and delays in the delivery of criminal justice. As the contributions in this book evince, criminal justice is not carried out in times of political reconfiguration or transformation, but is rather a phenomenon that belongs to post-transitional settings. Of primary interest in this book is to explore what these obstacles are, the extent to which they can be overcome and, if so, how. Also under consideration is whether some of the obstacles in focus are actually better understood as representing legitimate limits and constraints upon judicial action in relation to an evil past or conflictive present. In what follows is an outline of the kinds of obstacles we have in mind.

A possible obstacle for the national courts is the absence of clear national legal basis for judicial action or recognized court competences to investigate and prosecute perpetrators of specific categories of crimes. Most often the absence of a legal basis is the result of a deliberate effort of political branches of government to adopt laws or decrees meant to give immunity from jurisdiction (amnesties) for certain persons or specific crimes. This obstacle has come to raise outstanding questions about the possibility of courts to overrule or sidestep such laws or decrees and how courts may legitimize such action. In some cases, it has also come to prompt a consideration of the potential need to weigh the importance of conducting criminal investigations and prosecutions against the legitimacy of democratically adopted laws restricting the role of the courts.

A somewhat different problem related to the absence of a national legal basis for judicial action and which is often encountered in times of transition and, indeed, in post-transitional settings, is the non-inclusion into the national penal codes of the crimes of genocide, crimes against humanity, including the crime of enforced disappearance, torture and summary executions as well as gender-specific crimes. From the standpoint of the courts, the fact that the conduct to be sanctioned was not criminalized at the time of its commission raises critical issues of how to balance or mediate the dictates of the criminal law canon with the principle of legality and the prohibition against the retroactive application of criminal law to the detriment of the accused, which may be constitutionally entrenched. Also under consideration in this context is the passage of time and the consequent need to address the question of statutory limitations.[26]

A second category of obstacles is extra-legal in character and refers to a cluster of different factors. The first thing to note here is that the national courts in societies that seek to tackle an evil past often lack independence from political branches of government, which is especially evident when the judges were elected and their functions fully controlled by the previous repressive regime, and no lustration was ever carried out. Also relevant in the context of transitions from repressive regime to democratic form of government is that of the unequal power balance that tends to prevail between different sectors of government, including the strength of military opposition against judicial action. Finally, when it comes to transitions from conflict to peace, additional obstacles come into play, including the existence of good faith compromises and restrictions imposed on how the courts are to administrate justice in a manner that increases the prospects of bringing the conflict to an end.

1.4 Method

Our book collects distinguished perspectives, experiences and wisdoms of direct relevance to the objective of deepening our understanding of the challenges confronting the courts and to the articulation of well-informed responses in reaction to them. In particular, it includes narratives of exceptional national judges who have sat in courtrooms where proceedings related to the crimes in

26 See the Convention on the Non-Applicability of Statutory Limitations to War Crimes and Crimes Against Humanity. UNGA Res 2391 (XXIII), 26 November 1968. As of 25 April 2011, it had 54 States Parties.

focus have been conducted and where attempts have been made to mediate between the canon and its competing claims (legality, statutory limitations or non-retroactivity) or realities on the ground (strength of military opposition, etc). Also included are accounts of judges from international and regional courts, including the ICC and the Inter-American Court of Human Rights. In this context, attention is also given to the contributions of the Inter-American Commission of Human Rights because of its special status in the Inter-American system. Also considered are the views of lawyers with experience of how to develop strategies to overcome the obstacles often faced in judicial settings. In this manner, the book seeks to cover a diversity of informed perspectives which, taken together, deepen our understanding of the role of the courts in transitions, obstacles confronted and possible strategies to overcome them.

The study is limited to courts that have sought to take action in times of transition or post-transitional settings in relation to an evil past or a conflictive present. It thus includes the courts of Argentina, Chile, Colombia, Peru and Spain (including the exercise of universal jurisdiction in relation to Guatemala). It also considers the positive contributions made by the Inter-American Court of Human Rights, and international criminal justice to the advancement of the bulk of international human rights and criminal law meant to govern judicial action in relation to an evil past or an ongoing conflict. Having made this selection, we do not thereby assume that the increase of judicial activities in reaction to grave crime represents a linear and uniform development across Latin America and Spain that necessarily leads to positive results.

While the universe of courts that is relevant to respond to our more general queries is certainly not limited to courts with a direct impact on transitional processes in Latin America and Spain, it is our contention that this region hosts a wealth of judicial and legal knowledge that has still not been explored fully, and which should be extremely relevant to courts in transitional societies of other regions. However, because of linguistic and cultural hurdles, there is still limited accessibility of different judicial experiences from Latin America and Spain that reveal how their courts came to exercise their judicial functions, the time it actually took, the factors that contributed to this development and the obstacles faced. From this perspective, our book also purports to facilitate access to intellectual and empirical resources that allow the possibility of comparisons of judicial experiences, not only across Latin America and Spain, but also with other regions, with a view to improving our understanding of what it takes to bring effect to the canon and what seem to be the inevitable limits faced in concrete settings.

1.5 Outline of chapters

The first two chapters of the book focus on the *contributions of the Inter-American system of human rights* in developing concepts, rules and principles meant to govern and inform judicial action in transitional and post-transitional contexts.

The contribution of Antônio Augusto Cançado Trindade, currently judge of the International Court of Justice, can be read as part of his overall commitment to elucidate and give effect to the "new *ius gentium* of our times, the international law for the human person and, ultimately, for humankind". He presents his recollections of the cases concerning massacres which were brought to the Inter-American Court of Human Rights during his prominent tenure as a judge of that court. Building on the jurisdictionalization of international law and the growing pre-eminence of the rule of law, the conceptual construction of transitional justice, truth commissions and apologies, as well as "the legitimacy of the concern of the international community as a whole with the conditions of leaving of the population everywhere", he asserts the existence of true crimes of states and underscores the expansion of the international jurisdiction centred on the victims of these crimes. According to Judge Cançado Trindade, true crimes of state involve the complementary relationship between international responsibility of the state and the international criminal responsibility of the individuals concerned.

In Chapter 3, Felipe González Morales, former President of the Inter-American Commission on Human Rights, directs attention to the crucial role performed by the Inter-American system in transitional justice processes in Latin America. Indeed, as his chapter demonstrates, the Inter-American Commission and Court of Human Rights have established and reinforced the claim about the existence of international obligations to investigate and prosecute massive violations, obligations that are of a peremptory character. These institutions have set forth an interpretation of international human rights law that is radically different from the previously endorsed doctrine according to which the democratic state had broad discretion to decide on these matters. While the real impact of these pronouncements is uneven, as the author contends, it has meant that states that are now grappling with problems related to transitional justice can hardly avoid taking these obligations seriously.

The following five chapters of the book are devoted to *national judicial experiences*. Of main interest is to analyze the extent to which selected national courts in Latin America and Spain have opened investigations and conducted criminal proceedings in relation to perpetrators of serious human rights violations or grave crime, and the most prevalent challenges confronted in this process. In particular, the goal is to find out how the progressive interpretation of international human rights and criminal law meant to govern judicial action in periods of transition has become a crucial tool for national courts in finding solutions to the challenges faced. Among these challenges are the lack of a clear national legal basis for judicial action resulting from the existence of an amnesty law blocking such action or the non-criminalization of grave crime (genocide, crimes against humanity or war crimes) in national penal codes, the broad competences of military tribunals, the prohibition against the retroactive application of criminal law to the detriment of the accused and statutory limitations. Other challenges contemplated include the lack of political will to end impunity, the absence of judicial independence and the scarcity of resources, as well as modest social mobilization.

In Chapter 4, Ricardo Gil Lavedra, one of the judges in the *Military Junta* trial, provides a comprehensive and vivid account of how Argentinean courts have been able to adjudicate the broad range of serious human rights violations that were committed by militaries during the dictatorship, and how a variety of obstacles confronting the courts have been overcome. He also considers the challenges that the courts are still facing in seeking to deliver justice in relation to these violations. In order to stress the immediate relevance of the political and legal contexts of adjudication of these kinds of violations, the author distinguishes between two periods. The first period is characterized in terms of a tense political climate with the militaries still in power, and the absence of a firm international legal basis for court action. While these constraints did not block investigations and prosecutions altogether, their presence made it much more difficult for the judiciary to perform their functions in a satisfactory manner. The second period, in contrast, is defined by 20 years of uninterrupted democratic regime and a well-advanced international jurisprudence according to which states are obliged to investigate and prosecute serious human rights violations. These two factors have facilitated a more prominent position for Argentinean courts. As Gil Lavedra notes, however, for courts to be effective, practical issues must be anticipated, such as case management and a good organization of the collected evidence.

In the chapter that follows, Roberto Garretón, a key human rights lawyer during the Pinochet dictatorship, takes stock of the Chilean experience. Unlike the Argentinean case, no domestic trials were conducted at the time of the transition or in its immediate aftermath; in fact, nothing was done prior to the arrest of Pinochet in London on 17 October 1998 to face charges of genocide and terrorism in Spain. As Garretón explains, the absence of any judicial initiatives prior to that date must be understood in the light of how the dictatorship secured complete loyalty of the Chilean courts, the absence of court lustrations in the transitional period, and the governmental disinterest in derogating the Amnesty Law of 1978. However, the arrest of Pinochet caused an immediate judicial awakening resulting in the rapid commencement of national trials against militaries for serious human rights violations that had been committed during the dictatorship; it also led to arguments for derogating the Amnesty Law and the government changing its attitude. By now, the great majority of judges in Chile accept the legal argument in favour of investigation and prosecution. Factors that explain this situation include the persistency of the cause of the human rights organizations that were created in the wake of the transition, the progressive development of international human rights law, and continuous pressure exerted by the international community. Garretón also points to continued difficulties of applying international human rights law in domestic proceedings, and an all-too narrow definition of transitional justice—in order to overcome impunity, it is essential to tackle not only its criminal, but also moral, political and historical dimensions.

The author of the next chapter, Senior Lecturer Alicia Gil Gil, critically examines the recent developments in Spain regarding human rights violations committed during the Civil War and the Francoist dictatorship. She provides a concise account of the different transitional justice mechanisms envisioned in the Historic Memory Law of 2007, including the extension of benefits and reparations to the victims, the exhumation of mass graves, as well as the annulment and condemnation of Francoist laws. She then shifts the focus onto the role of criminal justice, emphasizing the insurmountable legal and practical obstacles encountered in this context; in particular, she considers the problems pertaining to the court order of Judge Baltasar Garzón of 16 October 2008 related to crimes committed between 1936 and 1951, not least in the light of Spanish law concerning the legality principle, rules regarding time limits and the amnesty law. The author concludes that these are the overriding concerns that must govern any decisions of Spanish courts in relation to the massive crimes that took place.

Chapter 7 is also devoted to the Spanish case, although with a different view. In it, Lecturer Javier Chinchón Alvárez analyzes in minute detail the recent proceedings concerning the Francoist crimes before the *Audiencia Nacional* and the Supreme Court between 2006 and 2010. The chapter narrates the experiences of Spanish civil society and how victims' associations have come to turn to Spanish courts with their grievances, without having a proper response. He explains that the aim of the victims with their turn to court is not an attempt to hold the perpetrators of the grave crimes committed in the context of the Spanish Civil War and the Francoist dictatorship to account. Rather, the Spanish courts are thought of as a very last resort to initiate investigations into the whereabouts and final destiny of persons who disappeared during these periods for the purpose of exhumation and dignified burial.

Professor Yván Montoya Vivanco presents in Chapter 8 a study of the Peruvian transitional justice experience. According to him, the role of criminal justice in Peru and the obstacles impeding judicial action in response to massive human rights violations must take into account the internal armed conflict (1980 to 1992) and 10 years of authoritarian regime under Fujimori (1990 to 2000). Montoya identifies the mechanisms of impunity during the armed conflict, including the lack of judicial independence, lack of co-operation by the military, statutory limitations, and the absence of security of judges and prosecutors. With the coming into power of Fujimori, impunity became institutionalized through the adoption of two amnesty laws in 1995. As a result, all of the cases were filed away. In 1999, Peru even decided to withdraw unilaterally from the contentious jurisdiction of the Inter-American Court of Human Rights. The process towards the end of impunity is explained in the light of the continued resistance of civil society movements; the pressure of international institutions, and democratic reforms undertaken following Fujimori's escape from Peru in November 2000.

The five remaining chapters slightly shift the main focus onto the role of courts located outside the territorial jurisdiction where the crimes occurred. The countries concerned are Colombia and Guatemala. The courts involved are the Spanish *Audiencia Nacional* and the International Criminal Court.

Consequently, issues of complementarity, subsidiarity and judicial co-operation are brought to the forefront of the analysis, as well as the discussion on best judicial strategies.

In Chapter 9, Professor Naomi Roht-Arriaza and Counsel Almudena Bernabeu, both members of the multinational legal team representing Guatemalan victims of genocide before the Spanish *Audiencia Nacional*, first briefly describe the background of the Guatemalan conflict and the evolution of the transnational cases against the military high command. The chapter then focuses on some of the legal strategy issues involved and on the gains and losses of this transnational networking approach to combating impunity. In particular, it looks at how the multinational legal team, working simultaneously in the Spanish and Guatemalan courts on different aspects of the case, has allowed for learning and training opportunities for the lawyers involved, forced local courts to engage with international law, and tried to use the power of foreign courts to leverage domestic processes. It also considers the content and impact of the Guatemalan and Spanish jurisprudence generated by the case and its current prospects. It then describes the mandate and goals of the International Commission against Impunity in Guatemala and concludes with some thoughts on how these initiatives might complement each other.

In Chapter 10, transitional justice expert Susan Kemp deals with the effects of choices and decisions made at the investigative stage on the choice of jurisdiction, extradition proceedings, international co-operation and even the overall criminal policies applied in different states across the globe to mass atrocities. A vast array of people are nowadays involved in campaigning for, planning, funding and carrying out investigations into grave crime and using their results to build prosecutions and judge guilt or innocence of suspects. Yet, investigations, sometimes by necessity, grow in piecemeal fashion and suffer from gaps, obstructions and under-funding. The existence of multiple forums where victims can present their case adds to the complex challenges. Who, where, what and when should we prosecute? In countries dealing with a violent past and moving through transitions to democracy or trying to overcome a conflict, these decisions can markedly affect the transition itself. Kemp emphasizes the importance of investing time, resources and thought in the preparation, planning and conduct of the investigation, and highlighting the consequences of mapping, crime classification and hypotheses, evidence sharing and strategy co-ordination for subsequent crucial decisions about choice of forum.

Chapter 11 is dedicated to the Colombian experience. Professor Alejandro Aponte notes that in contrast to the Argentinean, Chilean and Peruvian experiences, the Colombian courts are expected to investigate and prosecute grave crime perpetrated in the context of an ongoing conflict and within a democratic framework. These particularities raise doubts about the accuracy of understanding the Colombian case as an instance of transitional justice. Even so, Colombian courts have upheld that the basic national legal framework for investigating and prosecuting these crimes—the Justice and Peace Law of 2005—must be interpreted in the light of objectives and standards of transitional justice. While recognizing the undue influence exerted by the Colombian Government on the judicial process, such as the extradition of some perpetrators to the United States to face trial for drug crimes, Aponte also demonstrates how the Colombian judiciary has managed partially to counter diverse political interests. Indeed, Colombian courts have reaffirmed the right of the victims to reparation, insisted on a broad understanding of perpetrators, and restricted the possibility of extraditing crime suspects. At the same time, as Aponte contends, a deep tension exists between law and massive violence, which limits the actual prospects of criminal justice.

Paul Seils, currently General Legal Counsel with the International Center for Transitional Justice (ICTJ), is the author of Chapter 12. He considers that the different judicial developments require a conceptual rupture with dominant understandings of transitional justice for their lack of sufficient attention to the role of courts and criminal justice. Seils articulates the claim that criminal justice, in fact, occupies a privileged position within the transitional justice framework and that this argument is legal in character. The Rome Statute is the most straightforward manifestation of this point. This claim, however, does not mean that criminal justice must be given priority. Indeed, from a practical perspective, it usually takes time before courts are able to act in relation to an evil past or present, and these timing issues are made more complicated by the provisions of the Rome Statute and the position adopted by the current ICC Prosecutor. In addition, Seils criticizes the simplistic understanding of criminal justice as mainly retributive in character. For him, this approach rests on a simplified and mistaken understanding of the policy goals sought to be achieved through criminal justice. It is partly about giving reparations to the victims, but perhaps most significantly about restoring the confidence and trust of the citizens in the key institutions of their state.

In Chapter 13, ICC judge Elizabeth Odio Benito focuses on some possible contributions of international criminal justice to national processes of transitional justice and in particular of the Rome Statute to the furthering of a more prominent position for courts in Latin America. Special attention is paid to the progressive advancement of international criminal law with regard to gender-specific crime perpetrated predominantly against women. Odio Benito stresses the need for their formal and real inclusion into the national penal codes as well as the urgency of a gender perspective on both democracy and justice in Latin America.

Chapter 14 concludes with a selection of key ideas of the book. These ideas, born out of painful experiences in Latin America and Spain, include the claim about the existence of a canon of criminal law built into the concept of transitional justice, the practical and legal importance of the passage of time and timing issues in dealing with radical evil in a judicial context, the problems and prospects attached to the goal of seeking truth through judicial proceedings, and the obstacles and challenges posed to the role of courts in transitional justice.

2 Recollections of the international adjudication of massacre cases

Its relevance for transitional justice and beyond

Antônio Augusto Cançado Trindade

2.1 Introduction

It is with particular satisfaction that I accede to the kind invitation to write the opening chapter to the present book: *The Role of Courts in Transitional Justice: Voices from Latin America and Spain* (co-edited by Dr Jessica Almqvist and Professor Carlos Espósito). I do so in the form of my recollections of the international adjudication, of historical relevance, by the Inter-American Court of Human Rights (IACtHR), of the cycle of cases of massacres, and of its relevance for transitional justice and beyond. I propose to embark on my reflections within a wider conceptual framework, that of what I perceive as conforming with the advent of the new *jus gentium* of our times, the international law for the human person, and ultimately, for humankind.[1] To this end, I propose to identify, to begin with, a conjunction of factors, which, throughout the last three decades, has emerged and marked presence in the international scenario.

2.2 The phenomena of our age in temporal dimension

It may at first be identified as one of the phenomena of our age: the *jurisdictionalization* of international law itself, evidenced by the creation and coexistence of multiple contemporary international tribunals.[2] I regard this phenomenon as a particularly reassuring one, as it enlarges and secures *access to*

1 For my own conceptual framework, see Cançado Trindade, A A, *International Law for Humankind: Towards a New Jus Gentium*, The Hague/Leiden: The Hague Academy of International Law/Martinus Nijhoff, 2010.

2 See, e.g. Société Française pour le Droit International (SFDI), *La juridictionnalisation du droit international (Colloque de Lille de 2002)*, Paris: Pédone, 2003, pp 3–545; Cançado Trindade, A A, "The Merits of Coordination of International Courts on Human Rights", *Journal of International Criminal Justice*, vol 2, 2004, pp 309–312; and Cançado Trindade, A A, "Le développement du Droit international des droits de l'homme à travers l'activité et la jurisprudente des Cours européenne et interaméricaine des droits de l'homme", *Revue universelle des droits de l'homme*, 2004, vol 16, pp 177–180.

justice at the international level to a growing number of "*justiciables*". Secondly, it is not surprising that the theme of the rule of law ("*preéminence du droit*"), at both national and international levels, has lately attained the status as one of the items of the United Nations General Assembly itself (from 2006 onwards), where it has been attracting increasing attention to date.[3]

Thirdly, successive conflicts that have erupted and been overcome throughout the last three decades, mostly in the interior of various countries (at *intra*-state level), have propitiated the conceptual construction of *transitional justice*, keeping in mind post-conflict reconciliation. Also related to this latter can be found, fourthly, the work undertaken, in the same period, by numerous *Truth Commissions*,[4] each one of them with characteristics of its own, which, like the experiences of transitional justice, do not lend themselves to generalizations.

Fifthly, still within the last three decades, a new phenomenon has emerged, namely, that of *apologies*, at *intra*-state as well as *inter*-state levels.[5] It has emerged in such a remarkable way that there are those who behold our times as conforming with the *age of apologies*.[6] Sixthly, in the 1990s and the beginning of the twenty-first century, the recent *cycle of the World Conferences of the United Nations*—in some stages of which I had the fortune and privilege to participate actively—presented, as common denominator, as I perceive it, the

3 Concerning the issue of "The rule of law at the national and international levels", see UNGA Res 61/39, The rule of law at the national and international levels, Doc A/RES/61/39, adopted on 4 December 2006; UNGA Res 62/70, The rule of law at the national and international levels, A/RES/62/70, adopted on 6 December 2007; UNGA Res 63/128, The rule of law at the national and international levels, A/RES/63/128, adopted on 11 December 2008; UNGA Res 64/116, The rule of law at the national and international levels, A/RES/64/116, adopted on 16 December 2009; and UNGA Res 64/32, The rule of law at the national and international levels, A/RES/65/32, adopted on 6 December 2010. See also International Court of Justice, case concerning *Questions Relating to the Obligation to Prosecute or Extradite*, Order on 28 May 2009, Dissenting Opinion of Judge A A Cançado Trindade, paras 55 and 101.

4 See, e.g. Hayner, P B, *Unspeakable Truths—Transitional Justice and the Challenge of Truth Commissions*, 2nd edn, New York/London: Routledge, 2011; Godwin Phelps, T, *Shattered Voices—Language, Violence and the Work of Truth Commissions*, Philadelphia: University of Pennsylvania Press, 2004; and Sanford, V, *Buried Secrets—Truth and Human Rights in Guatemala*, New York: Palgrave, 2003.

5 See Cançado Trindade, A A, "Responsabilidad, Perdón y Justicia como Manifestaciones de la Conciencia Jurídica Universal", *Revista de Estudios Socio-Jurídicos*, vol 8, 2006, pp 15–36. For a general study, see Griswold, Ch L, *Forgiveness—A Philosophical Exploration*, Cambridge: Cambridge University Press, 2007. And, on the tensions between apologies and the struggle against impunity, see Ricoeur, P, *La mémoire, l'histoire, l'oubli*, Paris: Éd du Seuil, 2000, pp 423, 434, 609, 615 and 620; Abel, O et al (eds), *Le pardon—Briser la dette et l'oubli*, Paris: Éd du Seuil/Éds Autrement, 1991; Barkan, E, *The Guilt of Nations—Restitution and Negotiating Historical Injustices*, New York/London: W W Norton & Co, 2000; and Vaneigem, R, *Ni pardon ni talion—La question de l'impunité dans les crimes contre l'humanité*, Paris: Ed La Découverte, 2009.

6 Gibney, M et al (eds), *The Age of Apology—Facing up to the Past*, Philadelphia: University of Pennsylvania Press, 2008; and Lind, J, *Sorry States—Apologies in International Politics*, Ithaca/London: Cornell University Press, 2008.

legitimacy of the concern of the international community as a whole with the *conditions of living* of the population everywhere.[7]

Each one of those factors reveals a particularly rich dimension, and its aptitude for analysis in distinct areas of human knowledge. The *temporal dimension*, to evoke one example, appears to be present in the endeavours of transitional justice, as well as in the work of Truth Commissions, covering periods of years, or even of decades, in post-conflict situations of varying complexity. The temporal dimension, also present in the phenomenon of apologies, can here project itself in a period of decades or even centuries.[8]

2.3 The interdisciplinary optics

The factors have been studied in recent years, not only by jurists, but also by scholars of international relations, political scientists, sociologists and, in the case of apologies, also by historians and theologians.[9] Having made a point of counting, in my years as President of the Inter-American Court of Human Rights, on the testimonies of expert-witnesses—in public hearings before the court—of distinct background formation, such as psychologists and anthropologists, among others, I understand that their contribution can be better appreciated from an interdisciplinary optics. Unlike positivists, I do not think that law is self-sufficient; we all have to learn from each other, in whichever domain of human knowledge we happen to operate.

This brings me briefly to an additional point, also calling for an interdisciplinary optics. All of the aforementioned phenomena have attracted the attention of scholars of international law, sensitive to the central position nowadays occupied in its ambit by the human person. Yet, those phenomena identified above are being approached, each one in its own conceptual universe (still in construction), without sufficient attention being given to their interrelationships. It is advisable to keep one's mind open also to such interrelationships. With this point in mind, I purport now to move on to the

7 For a study on this point, see Cançado Trindade, A A, "Sustainable Human Development and Conditions of Life as a Matter of Legitimate International Concern: The Legacy of the U.N. World Conferences", in Japanese Association of International Law and Nisuke Ando (eds), *Japan and International Law—Past, Present and Future* (Symposium of the Centennial of the Japanese Association of International Law), The Hague: Kluwer, 1999, pp 285–309. See also International Court of Justice, *Accordance with International Law of the Unilateral Declaration of Independence in respect of Kosovo*, Advisory Opinion on 22 July 2010, Separate Opinion of Judge A A Cançado Trindade, paras 138–240.

8 Commissione Teologica Internazionale,Vaticano, *Memoria e Riconciliazione—La Chiesa e le Colpe del Passato: Il Papa Chiede Perdono—Purificare la Memoria*, Rome: Piemme, 2000, pp 131–180; Mpisi, J, *Les papes et l'esclavage des Noirs—Le pardon de Jean-Paul II*, Paris: L'Harmattan, 2008; and fn 9 below.

9 See, e.g. John Paul II, *Crossing the Threshold of Hope*, New York: Knopf, 2004, pp 63–66; Dalai Lama and Chan, V, *The Wisdom of Forgiveness*, New York: Riverhead Books, 2004, pp 234–236; and Accattoli, L, *Quando o Papa Pede Perdão*, São Paulo: Ed Paulinas, 1997.

international adjudication by the IACtHR of the cycle of massacre cases; I leave on the records of this opening chapter some of my condensed recollections[10] (below) on the basis of my own experience as a former Judge and former President of that international human rights tribunal.

2.4 The cycle of the class of massacres brought before the IACtHR

In recent years, the IACtHR was faced with a new cycle of cases concerning *massacres*—particularly in the period 2001 to 2008—wherein circumstances varied from case to case, but the aggravating elements of intentionality, of premeditation or planning, added to the particular gravity or seriousness of the damages perpetrated, appeared to be always present. In some cases there was a plurality of identified victims, in others there was such a considerable number of them that the exact total of victims and their identity were not entirely known. The monopoly of force misused by states—in a most regrettable distortion of the ends of the state—victimized groups of persons under their respective jurisdictions, who often happened to be the most vulnerable persons, in situations of defencelessness. States here incurred into grave violations of human rights that conformed, in some instances, in my understanding, to true *crimes of state*.[11]

This cycle of cases with aggravating circumstances in which grave violations of human rights (beginning with the fundamental right to life) were planned and perpetrated in pursuance of state policies of a *systematic* practice of extermination of human beings, started with the landmark judgment of the Inter-American Court in the case of the massacre of *Barrios Altos* concerning Peru (14 March 2001).[12] This leading case was followed by the court's judgments in the cases related to the massacres of the *Caracazo* concerning Venezuela (29 September 2002),[13] of *Plan de Sánchez* pertaining to Guatemala (29 April 2004),[14] of the *19 Tradesmen* against Colombia,[15] of the *Moiwana Community* concerning Suriname, of *Mapiripán* pertaining to Colombia, of *Ituango* also concerning Colombia, of *Montero Aranguren and Others (Detention*

10 For my systematized recollections, in full, see, recently, Cançado Trindade, A A, *El Ejercicio de la Función Judicial Internacional: Memorias de la Corte Interamericana de Derechos Humanos*, Belo Horizonte/Brazil: Ed Del Rey, 2011.

11 On this point, see Cançado Trindade, A A, "Complementarity between State Responsibility and Individual Responsibility for Grave Violations of Human Rights: The Crime of State Revisited", in Ragazzi, M (ed), *International Responsibility Today—Essays in Memory of O. Schachter*, Leiden: M Nijhoff, 2005, pp 253–269; and International Court of Justice, *Jurisdictional Immunities of the State* (Germany versus Italy), Counter-claim, Order of 6 July 2010, Dissenting Opinion of Judge A A Cançado Trindade, paras 142–145 and 151–153.

12 IACtHR, case of *Barrios Altos v Peru*, Series C No 75, Judgment of 14 March 2001.

13 IACtHR, case of *Caracazo v Venezuela*, Series C No 95, Judgment of 29 August 2002.

14 IACtHR, case of *Plan de Sánchez v Guatemala*, Series C No 105, Judgment of 29 April 2004.

15 IACtHR, case of *19 Tradesmen v Colombia*, Series C No 109, Judgment of 5 July 2004.

Centre of Catia) concerning Venezuela,[16] of *La Cantuta*, concerning Peru,[17] and of the *Prison Castro-Castro* also pertaining to Peru.[18] To these one can add the cases of assassinations planned at the highest level of the state power and executed by order of this latter, such as that of *Myrna Mack Chang*.[19]

This period coincided with the substantial changes introduced (in 1999 to 2004) by the IACtHR in its *interna corporis* (particularly its historical fourth Regulations, which entered into force in 2001),[20] added to its notable jurisprudential construction from 1998 until 2004, which left its mark[21] for the subsequent handling of cases of the kind by the court. The IACtHR became well equipped to handle the challenges raised in those cases pertaining to human collectivities and disclosing aggravating circumstances: the new cycle of the so-called "massacre cases".

Article 23 of the Rules of Court,[22] providing for direct access to international justice (paragraph 1) and participation of the alleged victims in the whole procedure before the court, provided with foresight, in its paragraph 2, that: "When there are several alleged victims, next-of-kin or duly accredited representatives, they shall designate a common intervener who shall be the only person authorized to present pleadings, motions and evidence during the proceedings, including the public hearings."

This provision—together with paragraph 1 of Article 23—proved to be of timely importance for the court's handling of the aforementioned cases concerning human collectivities, enabling it to conduct the proceedings in a reasonable—and feasible—manner. The right of individual petition turned out to be quite effective also for the adjudication of such cases concerning members of human collectivities.[23] Two particular legal issues may be singled out in those cases of massacres: first, the determination of the aggravated responsibility

16 IACtHR, case of *Montero Aranguren and Others (Detention Centre of Catia) v Venezuela*, Series C No 150, Judgment of 5 July 2006.

17 IACtHR, case of *La Cantuta v Peru*, Series C No 162, Judgment of 29 November 2006.

18 IACtHR, case of *Prison Castro-Castro v Peru*, Series C No 160, Judgment of 25 November 2006.

19 IACtHR, case of *Myrna Mack Chang v Guatemala*, Series C No 101, Judgment of 25 November 2003.

20 Rules of Procedure of the IACtHR, adopted by the IACtHR on 24 November 2000.

21 Cançado Trindade, A A, "Une ère d'avancées jurisprudentielles et institutionnelles: souvenirs de la Cour interaméricaine des droits de l'homme", in Hennebel, L and Tigroudja, H (eds), *Le particularisme interaméricain des droits de l'homme*, Paris: Pédone, 2009, pp 7–73.

22 Cançado Trindade, fn 21.

23 Cançado Trindade, A A, *El Acceso Directo del Individuo a los Tribunales Internacionales de Derechos Humanos*, Bilbao: University of Deusto, 2001; Cançado Trindade, A A, "El Nuevo Reglamento de la Corte Interamericana de Derechos Humanos (2000) y Su Proyección Hacia el Futuro: La Emancipación del Ser Humano como Sujeto del Derecho Internacional", in Secretaría General, Subsecretaría de asuntos jurídicos, *XXVIII Curso de Derecho Internacional Organizado por el Comité Jurídico Interamericano y la Secretaría General de la OEA en agosto de 2001*, Washington, DC: Inter-American Court of Human Rights, 2002, pp 33–92.

of the state concerned (aggravating circumstances of the wrongs perpetrated); and, secondly, the determination of the condition of *victim* in such cases.

2.5 The determination of the aggravated responsibility of the state

Under the American Convention on Human Rights (ACHR), the cycle of cases of massacres led the IACtHR to establish the *aggravating circumstances* of the violations at issue.[24] Those cases raised the question—acknowledged by the IACtHR—of the *aggravated* international responsibility of the respondent states. As demonstrated in the case of the *Massacre of Plan de Sánchez*,[25] the crimes committed in the course of the execution, by military operations, of a state policy of *tierra arrasada*, including the massacre itself of Plan de Sánchez (perpetrated on 18 July 1982), were intended to destroy wholly or in part the members of indigenous Maya communities. In its aforementioned judgment of 29 April 2004, the IACtHR determined that those violations "gravely affected the members of the *maya-achí* people in their identity and values", and, insofar as they occurred within a "pattern of massacres", they had "an aggravated impact" in the establishment of the international responsibility of the state.[26]

24 See the following judgments of the IACtHR: case of *Barrios Altos v Peru*, Series C No 75, Judgment of 14 March 2001; *Plan de Sánchez v Guatemala*, Series C No 105, Judgment of 29 April 2004; case of *19 Tradesmen v Colombia*, Series C No 109, Judgment of 5 July 2004; case of *Mapiripán Massacre v Colombia*, Series C No 134, Judgment of 15 September 2005; case of *The Moiwana Community v Suriname*, Series C No 124, Judgment of 15 June 2005; case of *The Ituango Massacres v Colombia*, Series C No 148, Judgment of 1 July 2006; case of *Montero-Aranguren et al (Detention Center of Catia) v Venezuela*, Series C No 150, Judgment of 5 July 2006; and case of *Prison of Castro-Castro v Peru*, Series C No 160, Judgment of 25 November 2006.

25 IACtHR, case of *Plan de Sánchez v Guatemala*, Series C No 105, Judgment of 29 April 2004.

26 *Plan de Sánchez v Guatemala*, Series C No 105, Judgment of 29 April 2004, para 51. The court ordered reparations in its subsequent judgment in the case. See case of *Plan de Sánchez v Guatemala*, Series C No 116, Judgment of 19 November 2004. In turn, earlier on, the Guatemalan Commission for the Historical Clarification, in its report *Guatemala—Memoria del Silencio*, had established the occurrence of 626 massacres committed by the forces of the state during the armed conflict, mainly the army, supported by paramilitary structures; 95 per cent of them had been perpetrated between 1978 and 1984 (with violence intensified in 1981 to 1983), and in this period 90 per cent had been executed in areas inhabited predominantly by the Maya people. The acts of extreme violence, in the assessment of that Commission, disclosed the characteristics of "acts of genocide", specifically against members of the peoples *maya-ixil*, *maya-achi*, *maya-k'iche'*, *maya-chuj* and *maya-q'anjob'al*, in four regions of the country. See la Comisión para el Esclarecimiento Histórico, *Guatemala—Memoria del Silencio*, vol III, Guatemala: CEH, 1999, pp 316–318, 358, 375–376, 393, 416 and 417–423. In the view of the Guatemalan Truth Commission, the grave and massive human rights violations engaged both the individual responsibility of the "intellectual or material authors" of the "acts of genocide" as well as the "responsibility of the State", as

There were other cases wherein the IACtHR reiterated its assertion of the "aggravated" international responsibility of the state, such as, for example, its judgments in the cases pertaining to the Pinochet regime in Chile (case of *Almonacid Arellano*)[27] and to the Stroessner regime in Paraguay (case of *Goiburú and Others*).[28] In my lengthy separate opinions to both of these judgments, I developed my personal reflections on the *crimes of state*, bearing in mind above all the horrors of the sinister *Operation Condor*.[29] The lessons that can be extracted from those two historical cases are clear.[30] At a conceptual level, the *objective* international responsibility of the state continues to coexist with its international responsibility *aggravated* by the *intentionality* (*mens rea*).

Following those two judgments, in the case of *La Cantuta* concerning Peru (judgment on 29 November 2006)[31] under the Fujimori regime, the victims (one professor and a group of students) were kidnapped from the premises of the University of La Cantuta, Lima, by security forces of the respondent state, after midnight, in the small hours of 18 July 1992, were "disappeared", and some of them promptly and summarily executed; following that, the facts were not duly investigated. In the earlier case of *Barrios Altos* (judgment on 14 March 2001),[32] the victims had been members of trade unions.

In the case of *Goiburú and Others* concerning Paraguay, occurring in a context of unlawful and prolonged detentions (in the mid-1970s) of the victims by state agents, the victims remained *incommunicado*, were tortured and murdered, and their mortal remains were hidden—all as a result of their opposition to the dictatorial regime of President A Stroessner. The IACtHR established the grave violations of human rights that took place, in the context of the so-called *Operation Condor*, in which security agents of the states of the Southern Cone of South America "co-operated" to exterminate political opponents of the repressive regimes of those days.

In the case of the *Massacre of Mapiripán* concerning Colombia,[33] which occurred between 15 and 20 July 1997, 100 members of the paramilitary forces

most of those acts were the product of a state "policy pre-established by a superior command to its material authors" (*Guatemala—Memoria del Silencio*, p 422).

27 IACtHR, case of *Almonacid Arellano et al v Chile*, Series C No 154, Judgment of 26 September 2006.

28 IACtHR, case of *Goiburú et al v Paraguay*, Series C No 153, Judgment of 22 September 2006.

29 Cançado Trindade, A A, *Évolution du Droit international au droit des gens—L'accès des particuliers à la justice internationale: le regard d'un juge*, Paris: Pédone, 2008, pp 121–184.

30 Which victimized more than 30,000 Latin Americans, in their great majority, young innocent people who were kidnapped, tortured and "disappeared", many having been thrown alive from airplanes into the sea, for "there no longer being place" for their mortal remains in clandestine cemeteries.

31 IACtHR, case of *La Cantuta v Peru*, Series C No 162, Judgment of 29 November 2006.

32 IACtHR, case of *Barrios Altos v Peru*, Series C No 75, Judgment of 14 March 2001.

33 IACtHR, case of *Mapiripán Massacre v Colombia*, Series C No 134, Judgment of 15 September 2005.

(*Autodefensas Unidas de Colombia*), counting on "the collaboration and acquiescence" of state agents, unlawfully detained, tortured and murdered at least 49 civilians in the town of Mapiripán, and then destroyed their bodies and sent their mortal remains into the river Guaviare. The case of the *Massacres of Ituango* (judgment on 1 July 2006)[34] fits into the same pattern of chronic violence in Colombia,[35] involving directly state agents (together with the paramilitary against the guerrillas) in the murders of the victims. And in the case of the *Moiwana Community* concerning Suriname,[36] on 29 November 1986, the armed forces attacked the members of the community, murdered many of them and the survivors were forcefully displaced from their traditional lands (of the Ndjuka Maroon Community, in the small town of Moiwana), unable to rebuild their communal *modus vivendi*.

In such cases of massacres, I insisted in my Separate Opinions on my view that the facts disclosed therein made it impossible to deny the existence of true *crimes of state*, entailing all their juridical consequences: in this context, I upheld the *complementarity* of the international responsibility of the state and the international criminal responsibility of the individuals concerned—as, for example, in the case of the *Massacre of Mapiripán* against Colombia[37] and, earlier on, in the case of the *Massacre of Plan de Sánchez* against Guatemala.[38] In its judgments in the cases of the *Massacre of Mapiripán* and of the *Massacre of the Moiwana Community*, the IACtHR ordered a series of measures of reparations (comprising indemnities as well as non-pecuniary reparations of distinct kinds), including measures to foster the voluntary return of the displaced persons to their original lands and communities, in Colombia and Suriname, respectively.

2.6 The determination of the condition of victim in cases of massacres

There have been cases, in the cycle considered herein, when the IACtHR has had to face the already mentioned difficulty of determining the condition of victim in the aforementioned massacre cases. The criteria it has adopted for

34 IACtHR, case of *The Ituango Massacres v Colombia*, Series C No 148, Judgment of 1 July 2006.

35 In the case of the *Massacres of Ituango*, the facts occurred in June 1996 and as from October 1997: the raids in the town of Ituango (Department of Antioquia) were undertaken by paramilitary groups of *Autodefensas Unidas de Colombia*, which, counting on the "omission, acquiescence and collaboration" on the part of the security forces of the state, murdered defenceless persons, deprived them of their goods, and generated terror and forced displacement.

36 IACtHR, case of *The Moiwana Community v Suriname*, Series C No 145, Judgment of 8 February 2008.

37 IACtHR, case of *Mapiripán Massacre v Colombia*, Series C No 134, Judgment of 15 September 2005.

38 IACtHR, case of *Plan de Sánchez v Guatemala*, Series C No 105, Judgment of 29 April 2004 (merits) and Series C No 116, Judgment on 19 November 2004 (reparations).

such determination in such cases have disclosed the awareness that the American Convention on Human Rights, like all other human rights treaties, is essentially *victim-oriented*. The fact is that the recent cycle of cases whereby the court has been seized has led to a new jurisprudential development as to the determination of the condition of victim.

The case of the *Caracazo* concerning Venezuela pertained to the street riots that occurred in the city of Caracas in February and March 1989, which, as a result of the indiscriminate and disproportional use of force by the state, caused the deaths of no less than 276 people. The problem of identifying the victims arose from the very start of the submission of the case—a true massacre—to the Inter-American Court by the Inter-American Commission of Human Rights (IACHR). In the complaint it lodged with the court, it referred to the hiding of evidence (clandestine graves). The IACHR was able to identify no more than 44 victims of the *Caracazo* disturbances. The court, in turn, in its judgment on 29 August 2002 concerning reparations, in determining the beneficiaries of these latter, saw it fit to single out distinct "categories of victims".

The 44 victims in the *Caracazo* case were thus classified by the IACtHR's judgment: 35 victims of extra-judicial executions, engaging the direct responsibility of the state; two forcefully disappeared persons by state agents; three victims of violations of the right to personal integrity; and four victims of breach of judicial protection and guarantees, in the context of the facts of the case.[39] The complexity of the *Caracazo* case illustrates the difficulties faced by the IACtHR in a case of a massacre with a great number of victims, and a prolonged lapse of time between the occurrence of the facts and the decision of the court.[40]

In another case of massacre, that of *Montero Aranguren and Others (Detention Centre of Catia) v Venezuela*,[41] the IACtHR faced yet an additional difficulty, namely, that of the coexistence of two versions of the facts.[42] Be that as it may, the court proceeded to the determination of the victims and of their relatives, displaying its concern not to leave outside the scope of its judgments (for the purpose of reparations) any of the victims of the massacres perpetrated, even after

39 IACtHR, case of *Caracazo v Venezuela*, Series C No 95, Judgment of 29 August 2002, para 67. The court added that the relatives of the 44 victims were also beneficiaries of reparations for violation of Arts 8 and 25 of the ACHR (judicial protection and guarantees) (paras 67–73); they were regarded also as "direct victims" (of violation of Arts 8 and 25) in their own right (para 74).

40 *Caracazo v Venezuela*, Series C No 95, Judgment of 29 August 2002, para 72.

41 IACtHR, case of *Montero Aranguren et al (Detention Centre of Catia) v Venezuela*, Series C No 150, Judgment of 5 July 2006. The case pertained to the killing of approximately 63 detainees by the guards of the Detention Centre of Catia, which took place between 27 and 29 November 1992, in addition to 28 disappeared people and 52 injured people (para 60.18).

42 *Montero Aranguren et al (Detention Centre of Catia) v Venezuela*, Series C No 150, Judgment of 5 July 2006, paras 60.16–60.17.

a lengthy lapse of time. To this end, the IACtHR considered, in such cases, as alleged victims, besides the persons *identified* (by the IACHR) in the petition lodged with it, *those who could be identified subsequently*, given that the difficulties found in their individualization led to presume that there were still victims pending of determination (court's judgments in the cases of the *Massacres of Plan de Sánchez, Mapiripán* and *Ituango*).[43] To overcome such difficulties, the Court considered as alleged victims some whose names derived from documents[44] other than the petition originally presented to it by the IACHR.[45]

The Court, furthermore, ordered the respondent state *to individualize and to identify* the victims and their relatives for the purpose of reparations.[46] The IACtHR took these measures in the light of the applicable law, that is, the American Convention on Human Rights and its Regulations, bearing in mind the complexities of each case, making sure that the right of defence of the parties had been respected (at the corresponding procedural moment), and that the alleged victims subsequently identified kept relation with the facts described in the (original) petition and the evidence produced before it.[47]

43 See the following judgments of the IACtHR: case of *Plan de Sánchez v Guatemala*, Series C No 105, Judgment of 29 April 2004 (reparation), para 48; case of *Mapiripán Massacre v Colombia*, Series C No 134, Judgment of 15 September 2005, paras 183 and 305; and the case of *The Ituango Massacres v Colombia*, Series C No 148, Judgment of 1 July 2006, para 92.

44 Incorporated into the *dossiers* of the cases.

45 IACtHR, case of *The Ituango Massacres v Colombia*, Series C No 148, Judgment of 1 July 2006, para 94. The court has on more than one occasion requested the Commission to correct such defects by providing lists of alleged victims *identified subsequently* to the presentation of the petition. See the following judgments of the IACtHR: case of *Aloeboetoe et al v Suriname*, Series C No 15, Judgment of 10 September 1993 (reparations), paras 39, 64, 66 and 69; case of *El Amparo v Venezuela*, Series C No 28, Judgment of 14 September 1996 (reparations), paras 39 and 42; case of *Caballero-Delgado and Santana v Colombia*, Series C No 31, Judgment of 29 January 1997, paras 13 and 38; and the case of *The "Juvenile Reeducation Institute" v Paraguay*, Series C No 112, Judgment of 2 September 2004, paras 107 and 111.

46 IACtHR, *Mapiripán Massacre v Colombia*, Series C No 134, Judgment of 15 September 2005, paras 305–306; and IACtHR, case of *The "Street Children" (Villagrán-Morales et al) v Guatemala*, Series C No 77, Judgment of 26 May 2001, para 17.

47 IACtHR, case of *Goiburú et al v Paraguay*, Series C No 153, Judgment of 22 September 2006, para 33; and case of *The Ituango Massacres v Colombia*, Series C No 148, Judgment of 1 July 2006, para 95. In this way, the court has taken the initiative of correcting, by means of its own analysis and assessment of the evidence produced by the parties, eventual gaps or defects in the identification of the alleged victims in the petition presented by the Commission, even when the parties themselves have admitted that some persons "by mistake were not included in the lists of alleged victims". See IACtHR, case of *Acevedo-Jaramillo et al v Peru*, Series C No 144, Judgment of 7 February 2006, para 227; and the case of *Aloeboetoe et al v Suriname*, Series C No 15, Judgment of 10 September 1993 (reparations), para 66, originally presented before the court. In the exercise of its duty of protection, the court has deemed it fit to proceed in this way, in cases disclosing a plurality of alleged victims, above all in the recent cycle of cases of massacres.

2.7 The existence of crimes of state

The recent cycle of massacre cases has brought the IACtHR to acknowledge clearly the existence of particularly *aggravating* circumstances—conforming in my view to true crimes of state, whether or not segments of doctrine wish to admit it. There have been instances in which the respondent states themselves have recognized their international responsibility for the atrocities and criminal policies pursued and criminal acts perpetrated. Segments of contemporary legal doctrine still try to circumvent the issue, but, with the awakening of human conscience, and the disclosure nowadays of atrocities which in the past did not reach international justice, it becomes increasingly more difficult for those petrified by state sovereignty to deny the existence and repeated occurrence of crimes of state.

Crimes of state have occurred in a sustained pattern of extermination of human beings, prolonged in time. No one can deny that this was precisely what happened in cases like, for example, those of the *Massacre of Plan de Sánchez* (one among 626 massacres, which occurred mainly between 1978 and 1984, as established by the Guatemalan Truth Commission), and of *Goiburú and Others v Paraguay* (one among so numerous other atrocities committed by the so-called *Condor Operation* in the Southern Cone of South America over three decades ago). They have victimized numerous defenceless persons, and denied investigation of the facts and access to justice to numerous other human beings. The relatives of the victims have, at last—after many years—found justice before an international human rights tribunal: the IACtHR.

In its interpretation of the judgment of 2 August 2008 in the case of the *Prison Castro-Castro* against Peru, the Court addressed, *inter alia*, with regard to reparations, the measures of guarantee of non-repetition of the wrongful and harmful acts.[48] In my lengthy Separate Opinion in this judgment,[49] I examined that same issue, together with the right of direct access to justice (national and international) as the right to the *realization* itself of justice, and as an imperative of *jus cogens*.[50] In my understanding, contemporary international legal doctrine will gain much credibility when it ceases to circumvent the issue, and proceeds to determine the juridical consequences of the perpetration of state crimes. To that end, it can now count, for example, on the recent case law of an international human rights tribunal such as the IACtHR, which has been seized of cases disclosing such crimes and has adjudicated them: it is indeed reassuring that even

48 IACtHR, case of *The Miguel Castro-Castro Prison v Peru*, Series C No 181, Judgment of 2 August 2008, paras 44–52.

49 *The Miguel Castro-Castro Prison v Peru*, Series C No 181, Judgment of 2 August 2008, paras 1–158.

50 For recent studies on these points, see Cançado Trindade, A A, *Évolution du Droit international au droit des gens—L'accès des particuliers à la justice internationale: le regard d'un juge*, Paris: Pédone, 2008, pp 1–188; and Cançado Trindade, A A, *El Derecho de Acceso a la Justicia en Su Amplia Dimensión*, Santiago, Chile: CECOH/Librotecnia, 2008, pp 61–407.

victims of massacres and crimes of state and their close relatives, laying in utter defencelessness, have in our days had their cases adjudicated by the IACtHR, wherein they finally achieved the realization of justice at the international level.

2.8 The expansion of international jurisdiction centred on the victims

The current and reassuring coexistence of international tribunals of human rights and international criminal tribunals brings to the fore other related themes deserving of close attention in contemporary life, such as, for example, that of the consolidation of the subjectivity (active as well as passive, respectively) of the individual in contemporary international law, and that of the approximation between restorative justice and retributive justice in our times.

The same phenomenon of the reassuring *multiplicity of contemporary international tribunals* comes to enlarge the access to justice (*lato sensu*, formal and material) nowadays, and to contribute to put an end to impunity, with the attainment of rule of law (*Estado de Derecho*, *État de Droit*) in a democratic society. The central position is occupied by the *justiciables*, those who seek justice. The approach is oriented towards the victims. In pursuance of this outlook, the reassuring advances achieved in recent years, in the determination of the *distinct forms of reparation due to the victims*, mainly in the rich case law of the IACtHR in this regard, are not surprising.

Although violations of human rights continue to subsist, the reactions to them are nowadays immediate and far more effective. The aforementioned conjunction of factors verifiable today—the phenomena of our age (above)—has operated to the effect of securing the prevalence of justice. And justice has now been achieved even in cases in which the victims or their close relatives found themselves in the most complete vulnerability or adversity, if not defencelessness. This would hardly have been anticipated a few years or decades ago, for example, in the legislative phase of human rights treaties and instruments. The fact that this is nowadays a reality is telling of the advances of international justice, which have taken place since then despite so many obstacles and difficulties, gradually overcome.

A few years or decades ago, no one could imagine that *grave* violations of human rights and of international humanitarian law were to be adjudicated by international tribunals, as they have been in recent times. No one could imagine, a few years or decades ago, that cases of *massacres*, of true *crimes of state*, were to be adjudicated by international tribunals, as they have been. I had the honour to have participated actively in the recent adjudication of the cycle of massacre cases lodged with the IACtHR, which I shall never forget: the IACtHR thereby rendered justice to the relatives of the fatal victims, thus alleviating their sufferings for the irreparable damages they endured, and helping them to recover their faith in human justice.

Another lesson that I extract therefrom points towards the *unity* of the law: not seldom, the international adjudication of those cases—true human tragedies—disclosed the approximations and convergences between the international human rights law and international humanitarian law (as in, for example, the case of *Bámaca Velásquez v Guatemala*,[51] within a pattern of massacres, or else the approximations and convergences between the international law of human rights and international refugee law (as in, for example, the case of the massacre of the *Moiwana Community v Suriname*).[52]

In successive Separate and Concurring Opinions that I appended to judgments of the IACtHR, I have sustained the *complementarity* (also including, in given circumstances, the concomitant application) of the relevant norms of the international human rights law, of international humanitarian law and of the international refugee law. On this particular point, may I refer to my Separate Opinion in the case of *Las Palmeras v Colombia*,[53] my Separate Opinion in the case *Bámaca Velásquez v Guatemala*,[54] my Concurring Opinion in the case of the *Indigenous People Kankuamo v Colombia*,[55] my Concurring Opinion in the case of the *Community of Peace of San José of Apartadó v Colombia*[56] and my Separate Opinion in the case of the *Prison Castro-Castro v Peru*,[57] among others.

But that is not all: such approximations and convergences are also noticeable today insofar as the international law of human rights and international criminal law are concerned, in their relationships. Thus, in a massacre case, that of the *Prison Castro-Castro v Peru*,[58] I saw it fit to point out, in my Separate Opinion, that whilst in the past retributive justice and restorative justice appeared to have been approached in a rather compartmentalized way, recent developments seemed to indicate that they do not exclude, but rather complement, each other, as there is a convergence between the search for justice by means of the investigation of the facts and the sanction of those responsible for grave breaches of human rights, and the endeavours towards the rehabilitation of the victims of those breaches.[59]

In the same line of reasoning, I have moreover sustained, as already indicated, the need to explore further and promote the *complementarity* between the international responsibility of the state and the international criminal responsibility

51 IACtHR, case of *Bámaca-Velásquez v Guatemala*, Series C No 70, Judgment of 25 November 2000 (merits); and Series C No 91, Judgment of 22 February 2002 (reparations).
52 IACtHR, case of *The Moiwana Community v Suriname*, Series C No 124, Judgment of 15 June 2005 (merits); and Series C No 145, Judgment of 8 February 2006 (interpretation of judgment).
53 IACtHR, case of *Las Palmeras v Colombia*, Series C No 67, Judgment of 4 February 2000.
54 IACtHR, case of *Bámaca-Velásquez v Guatemala*, Series C No 70, Judgment of 25 November 2000.
55 IACtHR, case of *Indigenous People Kankuamo v Colombia*, Order of 5 July 2004.
56 IACtHR, case of *Peace Community of San José of Apartadó v Colombia*, Order of 15 March 2005.
57 IACtHR, case of *Prison Castro-Castro v Peru*, Series C No 181, Judgment of 2 August 2008 (interpretation of judgment).
58 *Prison Castro-Castro v Peru*, Series C No 181, Judgment of 2 August 2008.
59 *Prison Castro-Castro v Peru*, Series C No 181, Judgment of 2 August 2008, para 97.

of the individual,[60] so as to clarify further the present-day confluence between the international law of human rights and contemporary international criminal law.[61] I trust these brief recollections may foster the interest in the study of transitional justice—in an enlarged conceptual framework—among scholars of the new generations.

60 In this sense I have pronounced myself, e.g. in my Separate Opinions in the following cases: IACtHR, case of *Myrna Mack Chang v Guatemala*, Series C No 101, Judgment of 25 November 2003; *Plan de Sánchez v Guatemala*, Series C No 105, Judgment of 29 April 2004; *Goiburú et al v Paraguay*, Series C No 153, Judgment of 22 September 2006; *Almonacid Arellano et al v Chile*, Series C No 154, Judgment of 26 September 2006, among others.

61 e.g. by means of the presence and participation of the victims in the corresponding international procedures.

3 The progressive development of the international law of transitional justice

The role of the Inter-American system

*Felipe González Morales**

3.1 Introduction

The transition from dictatorial regimes and civil wars to democratic systems in Latin American countries has placed several of its governments in front of new dilemmas. One of the most important questions that have come to surface as a result of transitions is what a government is required to do in terms of tackling the grave violations that were committed in a systematic manner and on a great scale by a preceding regime. The violations in focus are genocide, forced disappearances, extrajudicial executions and torture.

What is novel about this dilemma in the Latin American context derives from the fact that although historically the region has experienced numerous dictatorships, they usually did not commit abuses of the magnitude as those in more recent decades; neither did the region experience simultaneous processes of transition to democratic government as happens now. Furthermore, the current dilemma has been produced in a context in which the Cold War was debilitated and finally left behind, a factor that also has been conducive to processes of transition. A further factor that must be taken into account is the rise of significant pressure groups. In some Latin American countries—such as in Argentina and Chile—the victims and their families have managed to organize themselves and to foster a presence in public life that they never had before.

Indeed, the question of how to tackle grave human rights violations is now a preoccupation, not only for many contemporary democratic governments, but also for the human rights organs making up the Inter-American system: the Inter-American Commission on Human Rights (IACHR) and the Inter-American Court of Human Rights (IACtHR). This development has also generated an interesting conceptual debate in which the issues such as the

* The opinions expressed in this chapter are the author's and do not compromize the institutions to which he belongs.

relationship between these violations and the emergence of a democratic system, the role of judges and the scope of fundamental rights, have been discussed. In focus of this study are the most important aspects of this debate.

3.2 The development of a response by the Inter-American system

Throughout the 1980s, before the massive processes of transition to democracy in Latin America began, that is, while a series of dictatorships subsisted and several civil wars were taking place, the Inter-American Commission delivered some pronouncements concerning amnesty norms which intended to leave grave human rights violations without any sanction. In this period, the Commission adopted an approach that was sensitive to the type of political regime that promulgated the norms in question.

Thus, in the case of self-amnesty norms that had been issued by authoritarian regimes, the Commission considered that such norms were contrary to international law as they consisted of a decision of the perpetrators themselves to leave their abuses without sanction. In relation to such amnesty norms, the Commission affirmed that "the amnesties decreed previously by those responsible for the violations has [*sic*] no juridical validity".[1]

In contrast, the Commission delivered a different pronouncement—which was of a general character and so not delimited to one state or concrete case—in relation to amnesty norms (or their equivalents) that had been adopted by democratic regimes installed following a dictatorship. In relation to these norms, the Commission stipulated that democratic regimes possessed a legitimate discretion to decide whether or not to adopt amnesty norms, assuming that when they did adopt such norms they did so to pacify the country or to guarantee stability in the emerging democracy. Thus, reflecting its dominant stance during the 1980s, this organ held that:

> A difficult problem that recent democracies have had to face has been the investigation of human rights violations under previous governments and the possibility of sanctions against those responsible for such violations. The Commission recognizes that this is a sensitive and extremely delicate issue where the contribution it—or any other international body for that matter—can make is minimal. The response, therefore, must come from the national sectors that are themselves affected, and the urgent need for national reconciliation and social pacification must be reconciled with the ineluctable exigencies of an understanding of the truth and of justice.[2]

1 IACHR, Annual Report 1985–86, OEA/Ser.L/V/II.68, 26 September 1986, p 205.
2 IACHR, Annual Report 1985–86.

And, the Commission added that:

> Only the appropriate democratic institutions—usually the legislature—with the participation of all the representative sectors, are the only ones called upon to determine whether or not to decree an amnesty of the scope thereof.[3]

Nevertheless, towards the end of the 1980s, the Inter-American Court had to deliver two judgments in response to two cases that had come before it: those of *Manfredo Velázquez Rodríguez* and *Saúl Godínez Cruz*—both against Honduras.[4] While none of the cases referred to amnesty norms, but rather to grave human rights violations, the court came to make references to the scope of state obligations to respect and guarantee rights in the context of such violations and these references came to serve as a base for articulating the jurisprudence by the Inter-American system in relation to amnesty norms which then followed.

First of all, in these cases, the Inter-American Court held that the foundation for the obligation to respect human rights is found in the notion according to which "the exercise of public authority has certain limits which derive from the fact that human rights are inherent attributes of human dignity and are, therefore, superior to the power of the state".[5] Furthermore, in interpreting the obligation to guarantee the exercise of human rights, the court emphasized the active role (that is, positive obligations) that are incumbent on the state, including in situations in which the civil and political rights of persons are affected. In this regard, the court also made an explicit reference to the importance of the function of the judicial power in making human rights effective human rights, maintaining that the obligation to ensure the free and full exercise of human rights "implies the duty of States Parties to organize the governmental apparatus and, in general, all the structures through which public

3 IACHR, Annual Report 1985–86. The Commission added that: "Independently of the problem of proving guilt, which in every case must be determined individually and with due process guarantees by a pre-existing court which applies the law in force at the time the crime was committed, one of the few matters that the Commission feels obliged to give its opinion on in this regard is the need to investigate the human rights violations committed prior to the establishment of the democratic government". It then concluded that: "Every society has the inalienable right to know the truth about past events, as well as the motives and circumstances in which aberrant crimes came to be committed, in order to prevent repetition of such acts in the future. Moreover, the family members of the victims are entitled to information as to what happened to their relatives. Such access to the truth presupposes freedom of speech, which of course should be exercised responsibly; the establishment of investigating committees whose membership and authority must be determined in accordance with the internal legislation of each country, or the provision of the necessary resources, so that the judiciary itself may undertake whatever investigations may be necessary."

4 IACtHR, case of *Velásquez Rodríguez v Honduras*, Series C No 4, Judgment of 29 July 1988; and case of *Godínez Cruz v Honduras*, Series C No 5, Judgment of 20 January 1989.

5 *Velásquez Rodríguez v Honduras*, Series C No 4, Judgment of 29 July 1988, para 165.

power is exercised, so that they are capable of juridically ensuring the free and full enjoyment of human rights".[6]

Likewise, the court underlined that the sole act of passing an adequate piece of legislation, that is, a piece of legislation that reflects international standards, is not sufficient for a state to comply with its international obligations, but "it also requires the government to conduct itself so as to effectively ensure the free and full exercise of human rights".[7] In consequence, the obligations to respect and guarantee human rights was in these cases understood as entailing a duty of the state to "prevent, investigate and punish any violation of the rights recognized by the Convention and, moreover, if possible attempt to restore the right violated and provide compensation as warranted for damages resulting from the violation".[8] In addition, the court added that the duty to investigate "must be undertaken in a serious manner and not as a mere formality preordained to be ineffective". In the event that the violation goes unpunished and the victim ends up without compensation, there has also been a violation of the duty to guarantee the exercise of rights.[9] In this context, the court also pronounced that investigation is an obligation of means to an end and not an obligation of result in the sense that what matters is that the investigation is carried out in a serious manner.

In the beginning of the 1990s, the Commission came to receive a number of cases concerning the amnesty norms that had been issued by the democratic governments of Argentina and Uruguay, and which impeded the prosecution of the massive and systematic human rights violations that had taken place in these countries during their respective military dictatorships of the 1970s and the beginning of the 1980s. The cases concerned the rights of victims of grave abuses or their families who had been hindered from litigating their complaints before national courts as a result of the amnesty norms. While the cases presented important similarities in that both the Argentinean and the Uruguayan amnesties had been adopted by supervening democratic governments, the cases also manifested important differences considering the distinct social processes that had brought about their adoptions.

In Argentina, the transition to democracy was aided by the defeat in the Malvinas/Falkland Islands war that had been initiated by the military dictatorship in 1982. The new democratic government led by Raúl Alfonsín therefore found itself in a situation that was favourable to the settling of accounts with the past. First of all, the Argentinean Government established a Truth Commission in 1983, a measure that at the time had practically no precedent in the global context. The Truth Commission was tasked with the investigation of different types of abuses that had been committed and its findings were

6 *Velásquez Rodríguez v Honduras*, Series C No 4, Judgment of 29 July 1988, para 166.
7 *Velásquez Rodríguez v Honduras*, Series C No 4, Judgment of 29 July 1988, para 167.
8 *Velásquez Rodríguez v Honduras*, Series C No 4, Judgment of 29 July 1988, para 166.
9 *Velásquez Rodríguez v Honduras*, Series C No 4, Judgment of 29 July 1988, paras 176–177.

presented in a report only six months after its creation.[10] In addition, the Argentinean Parliament annulled the amnesty law decree that the military junta had dictated and this act enabled the initiation of proceedings concerning human rights violations.[11] Nevertheless, as the military pressures intensified, the Argentinean Government came to adopt a successive number of laws—the Law of Due Obedience and the Law of Full Stop—destined to close the investigations and which, from the standpoint of the effects in focus in this chapter, are equivalent to the adoption of amnesty norms in response to grave violations of human rights.

The Argentine experience provoked a doctrinal discussion about how to tackle violations of the past. Given that some legal philosophers, such as Carlos Nino and Jaime Malamud-Goti had been advisors to the Government of Raúl Alfonsín on these matters, they came to occupy a central role in this debate.[12] However, as this debate developed towards the end of the 1980s and the beginning of the 1990s, there were already other Latin American countries that had had their own experiences of transitions, and the debate developed into a more general one.

In contrast with the Argentinean dictatorship, the Uruguayan one (1973 to 1985) had not suffered a military defeat. While at the end of 1980 it did suffer a defeat, it was of a different nature: an electoral defeat which had its origin in an attempt of the Uruguayan military regime to ensure a transition under guardianship through the holding of a popular referendum. Its aim was to establish a political system that would preserve strong authoritarian elements, ensuring in particular a significant role for the armed forces. Although the military lost in this referendum, as there were no alternatives, they came to maintain their power de facto during four additional years. Finally, once the militaries had been assured that there would be no attempt to open proceedings against them, they opened the way to transition to democracy. As predicted, the initial context of the transition was much more restricted in comparison with the Argentinean one. The sole measure that was adopted was the establishment of a Commission concerning the Disappeared, a measure that was clearly insufficient considering the thousands of people who had been victims of torture. According to the report it issued, the Uruguayan disappeared detainees totalled 164, out of which approximately 80 per cent were victims

10 See Pasqualucci, J M, "Whole Truth and Nothing but the Truth: Truth Commissions, Impunity and the Inter-American Human Rights System", *Boston University International Law Journal*, vol 12, 1994, pp 321–370, especially pp 336 ff. See also Elster, J, *Closing the Books: Transitional Justice in Historical Perspective*, Cambridge: Cambridge University Press, 2004, pp 81–83.

11 See also Chapter 4 by R Gil Lavedra included in this book.

12 Malamud-Goti, J, "State Terror and Memory of What?", *University of Arkansas Review*, vol 21, 1998, pp 107–118; and Nino, C, "The Duty to Prosecute Past Abuses of Human Rights Put into Context", *Yale Law Journal*, vol 100, 1991, pp 2619–2640.

of the Argentinean dictatorship while they found themselves in exile in this country.[13]

However, at the margins of the agreements reached between the dominant political parties and the militaries in Uruguay, the affected began to interpose a massive number of denunciations before the courts. These actions led to the adoption of legislation in 1986 known as the Caducity Law (*Ley de Caducidad de la Pretensión Punitiva del Estado*), which impeded the investigation of the crimes that had been committed. The Uruguayan Constitution contemplated a mechanism of referendum to derogate laws and for such referendum to be held, it was necessary to collect the signatures of 25 per cent of the citizens in support of the referendum. This percentage was reached and the referendum took place in which the majority of the citizens approved the Caducity Law (with effects equivalent to amnesty norms).

Once the proceedings before the Inter-American Commission had been opened in relation to Argentina and Uruguay, Argentina argued that its original intention had been to prosecute those who were responsible for the abuses, but that extreme circumstances (military pressure) had led it to dictate the amnesty norms. Uruguay, in contrast, maintained that a measure of this nature lay within its discretion and that the Caducity Law had been legitimated by popular will.[14]

In response to these arguments, the Commission held that none of the states could self-exempt themselves from their international obligations, and that the amnesty norms that they had adopted infringed Articles 1.1, 8 and 25 of the American Convention. In this regard, the Commission linked the obligation of respecting and guaranteeing human rights (Article 1.1) with the right to a fair trial (Article 8) and the right to judicial protection (Article 25). The argumentation of the Commission manifested that the amnesties that the two countries had put into place deprived these states and the victims of an exhaustive judicial investigation. This deprivation amounts to a violation of both the right to judicial protection and the right to an effective judicial protection, which render it impossible to respect and guarantee human rights.[15]

The governments of the two countries contested the performance of the Commission. Uruguay reacted most forcefully, disqualifying the Commission's pronouncement, and criticizing it especially for not having taken into account its argument that the Caducity Law had been adopted following a democratic

13 Zalaquett, J, "Procesos de Transición a la Democracia y Derechos Humanos en América Latina", available at www.cdh.uchile.cl/articulos/Zalaquett/IIDH_paper_final.pdf, p 10. See also Elster, fn 10 above, p 85.

14 Observations of the Government of Uruguay to the Annual Report of the Inter-American Commission on Human Rights, OEA/Ser.G/CP/doc.2376/93, 18 May 1993 (on file with author).

15 IACHR, Report 34/91, Case Nos 10.147, 10.181, 10.240, 10.262, 10.309 and 10.311 (Argentina), 4 October 1991, concerning the effects of the law Nos 23.492 and 23.521 and Decree No 1002/89 (corresponding to the Laws of Final Stop, Law of Due Obedience and the Presidential Pardon); Report 29/92 (Uruguay), Case Nos 10.029, 10.036, 10.305, 10.372, 10.373, 10.374 and 10.375.

procedure (i.e. the popular referendum).[16] The negative reactions produced a paralysis in the Commission. As a result of the exculpatory arguments that were put forth by the two countries, the Commission held onto its reports concerning Uruguay and Argentina for more than one year without publishing them, an event without any precedent in the practice of this organ.[17]

To be exact, the Commission does mention the Uruguayan referendum in its report, although it does so only in a summarized manner and without making explicit its balancing act of the different goods at stake. In the words of the Commission:

> As for the domestic legitimacy and "the approval of the Caducity Law by a popular referendum" it should be noted that it is not up to the Commission to rule on the domestic legality or constitutionality of the national laws. However, application of the Convention and examination of the legal effects of a legislative measure, either judicial or of any other nature, insofar as it has effects incompatible with the rights and guarantees embodied in the Convention or the American Declaration, are within the Commission's competence.[18]

The same year as the Commission published its reports concerning the amnesty norms of Argentina and Uruguay, it also issued a report in response to the complaints set forth in relation to the amnesty norm that had been dictated in El Salvador (the *Massacre in Las Hojas*). The case concerned an amnesty norm that had been promulgated in order to leave 74 extra-judicial executions of the country's armed forces without any sanction. As the Commission noted:

> Decree No. 805, passed by the Legislative Assembly on October 27, 1987, provides in that part pertinent to the present case, in Article 1 that "Full and absolute amnesty is granted in favor of all persons, whether nationals or foreigners, who have participated directly or indirectly or as accomplices, in the commission of political crimes or common crimes linked to political crimes or common crimes in which the number of persons involved is no less than twenty, committed on or before October 22 current year"; and that as a result, the passage of the amnesty, even after an arrest warrant had been

16 Letter dated 7 May 1993, from the Permanent Mission of Uruguay to the President of the Permanent Council of the Organization of American States, copy of this letter on file with the author. In a passage, the letter points out: "no insignificant lack of sensitivity is manifested when the Commission disregards the approval of the Caducity Law through popular referendum as an exemplary expression of direct democracy of the Uruguayan people, for which the Commission owes, at least, consideration and respect", p 21.

17 The final reports, containing the defences of the governments and their refutation by the IACHR, were published on 2 October 1992. See Report No 28/92 (Argentina), Case Nos 10.147, 10.181, 10.240, 10.262, 10.309 and 10.311; and Report No 29/92, fn 15 above.

18 Ibid. IACHR, Report No 29/92, para 31.

> issued to Armed Forces officers, legally eliminated the possibility of an effective investigation and the prosecution of the responsible parties, as well as proper compensation for the victims and their next-of-kin by reason of the civil liability for the crime committed.[19]

Furthermore, according to the Commission, the decree in question contravenes international law considering that: "Article 27 of the Vienna Convention on the Law of Treaties prohibits a state from unilaterally invoking national law as a justification for failing to comply with legal obligations imposed upon it by the Convention".[20]

Even if the pronouncements of the Commission did not have any immediate practical impact in the two countries concerned, the findings had resonance at the international level. As a matter of fact, it is possible to observe how, in the years following these decisions, the UN human rights organs began to develop their positions on the matter in a similar direction, reformulating their interpretation of the relevant norms. This development is especially notable in the work of the Independent Expert, Louis Joinet, appointed by the UN Human Rights Commission. During the 1990s, Joinet publicized first a provisional study in 1993 on the matter (elaborated together with El Hadji Guissé).[21] Their study was followed by a final report in 1997, which affirms in substance the criteria of the Inter-American Commission. In particular, it recalls that the obligations of states in relation to grave violations committed in the past consist of the establishment of criminal responsibility, the publicity of judicial actions, the reparation to the victims and the formulation of guarantees of non-repetition of the crimes.[22]

In the 1990s, the Commission made a pronouncement concerning the amnesty law decree of Chile in three reports on the merits in which it accumulated a series of cases, declaring its incompatibility with the obligations of the American Convention. On the three occasions, it emitted the same *dictum*, observing that:

> The recognition of responsibility by the Government, the partial investigation of the events and the subsequent payment of compensation are not,

19 IACHR, Report 26/92, Case No 10.287 (El Salvador), 24 September 1992, para 11.

20 IACHR, Report 26/92, para 12.

21 See UN Human Rights Commission, Sub-Commission on Prevention of Discrimination and Protection of Minorities. The Question of Impunity of Authors of Human Rights Violations (Civil and Political), *Provisional Report Concerning the Question of Impunity of the Authors of Human Rights Violations*, prepared by Mr Guissé and Mr Joinet, in compliance with Resolution 1992/23 of the Sub-Commission, E/CN.4/Sub.2/1993/6, 19 July 1993.

22 UN Human Rights Commission, Sub-Commission on the Prevention of Discrimination and the Protection of Minorities, *The Question of Impunity of the Perpetrators of Human Rights Violations (Civil and Political)*, Final report, elaborated and revised by Mr Joinet in application of decision 1996/119 of the Sub-Commission, E/CN. 4/Sub.2/1997/20/Rev.1, 2 October 1997.

> in themselves, sufficient to comply with the obligations set forth in the Convention. As provided in Article 1.1 of that document, the state has the obligation to investigate any violations that have been committed within the sphere of its jurisdiction in order to identify the persons responsible, impose pertinent penalties on them and ensure adequate reparation for the victim.[23]

In addition, it adds that: "By adopting the *de facto* Decree Law on self-amnesty, the State of Chile failed to comply fully with the obligation stipulated in Article 1.1 and violated the rights recognized by the American Convention, to the detriment of the plaintiffs."[24]

Thereafter, the Inter-American Commission addressed in another case the amnesty promulgated in El Salvador following the end of the Civil War in this country. The Commission in 1999 emitted the Report on the Merits regarding the matter. The Commission had already delivered one pronouncement concerning another amnesty of El Salvador in the case *Las Hojas*, which has been referred to above. The principal difference was that in the case of *Las Hojas* what was at stake was an amnesty dictated during the war and in the other case an amnesty following a war. As a matter of fact, it was promulgated immediately after the assignments of the Truth Commission created by the United Nations had been finalized, which had formulated a series of recommendations in relation to grave human rights violations that had taken place in El Salvador.[25]

Thus, the Truth Commission issued its Report on 15 March 1993 and three days later the Executive Power proposed a legal body that established the amnesty, which, according to the President of the Republic at the time, Alfredo Cristiani, aimed at "erasing, eliminating and forgetting the past in its entirety" and reiterated "the call to all of the country's forces to support a general and absolute amnesty, in order to turn that painful page of our history and seek a better future for our country".[26] The amnesty was adopted in a speedy manner two days after it had been proposed, on 20 March 1993.

In accordance with what had been pointed out by the Inter-American Commission in its Report on the Merits in analyzing the amnesty law of El Salvador:

23 IACHR, Report on the Merits No 34/96, Case Nos 11.228, 11.229, 11.231 and 11.282 (Chile), 15 October 1996, para 76. This text is reproduced in identical terms in the Report on the Merits 36/96 (Chile) Case No 10.843, 15 October 1996, para 77; it is also in the Report on the Merits 25/98, Case Nos 11.505, 11.532, 11.541, 11.546, 11.549, 11.569, 11.572, 11.573, 11.583, 11.585, 11.595, 11.652, 11.657, 11.675 and 11.705, 7 April 1998, para 70.

24 IACHR, Report 34/96 and Report 36/96, para 77; and Report 25/98, para 71.

25 See Brody, R, "The United Nations and Human Rights in El Salvador: 'Negotiated Revolution'", *Harvard Human Rights Journal*, vol 8, 1995, pp 153–178, in particular pp 165 ff.

26 Both references can be found in IACHR, Report 1/99, Case No 10.480 (El Salvador), 27 January 1999, para 5.

> This law nullified the recommendations of the Truth Commission with regard to the crimes investigated, eliminating the possibility of legal sanction against the persons implicated in perpetrating the acts of violence described in its report, and eliminated their corresponding civil liability. In short, it left unpunished all crimes committed by agents of the state between 1980 and 1992, including those being examined in the present report, and ignored the legitimate rights to compensation for victims and their relatives.[27]

The Commission adds that the effect of the mentioned amnesty covers, among others, crimes of summary executions, torture and forced disappearances of persons realized by agents of the states. The Commission also refers to a series of instruments that manifests the gravity of these crimes, which includes specific measures so as to ensure that such crimes do not remain without sanction, such as universal jurisdiction and the non-applicability of statutory limitations. In this sense, the Inter-American Commission mentions the American Convention to Prevent and Punish Torture (1985) and the Inter-American Convention on Forced Disappearance of Persons (1994), which establish universal jurisdiction over the crimes referred to in these conventions. It also invokes the UN Convention against Torture and Other Cruel, Inhuman or Degrading Treatment or Punishment (1984), which stipulates that the criminal actions and the sanctions judicially imposed shall not be subject to prescription. In the light of all of these considerations, the IACHR concluded that the amnesty of El Salvador must be seen as incompatible with the American Convention on Human Rights.

At last, the Inter-American Court of Human Rights had the occasion to pronounce itself on the question about amnesties in the case of grave violations, first in the case of *Barrios Altos* against Peru in 2001[28] and later in the case of *Almonacid* against Chile in 2006.[29] On both occasions the Court relied upon the reasoning of the Commission. Also, in two other cases (*Goiburú and Others v Paraguay* in 2006 and *Masacre de La Rochela v Colombia* in 2007), while not dealing with amnesties, the Court delivered judgments that are relevant to the matter in focus. When this chapter was about to be sent to press, this jurisprudence was reaffirmed by the Court regarding an amnesty law from Brazil.[30]

The case of *Barrios Altos* referred to two amnesties dictated by the authoritarian government headed by Alberto Fujimori in Peru, destined to leave without any sanction the extrajudicial sanction of 15 people and the serious

27 IACHR, Report 1/99, para 6.

28 IACtHR, case of *Barrios Altos v Peru*, Series C No 75, Judgment of 14 March 2001.

29 IACtHR, case of *Almonacid-Arellano v Chile*, Series C No 154, Judgment of 26 September 2006.

30 IACtHR, case of *Gomes-Lund et al (Guerrilha do Araguaia) v Brazil*, Series C No 219, Judgment of 24 November 2010.

harms of four other people caused by agents of the state.[31] Once the responsibility of the Peruvian state had been established, and it did not comply with its recommendations, the Commission presented a complaint before the Inter-American Court. Peru thus proceeded with the withdrawal of its recognition of contentious jurisdiction of the Court, an act that was considered improper by the Court, which continued with the procedure.[32] While the case was pending before the Court, the Government of Fujimori fell and was replaced by another in a transition to democracy, headed by Valentín Paniagua. This second government recuperated the recognition of contentious jurisdiction of the Inter-American Court, and recognized its responsibility as set forth in the complaint. Notwithstanding this recognition, given the importance of the issue at stake, the Court provided its own fundamentals (although it did so in a summarized manner) to establish the responsibility of the Peruvian state.

Thus, the Court considered that:

> All amnesty provisions, provisions on prescription and the establishment of measures designed to eliminate responsibility are inadmissible, because they are intended to prevent the investigation and punishment of those responsible for serious human rights violations such as torture, extra-judicial, summary or arbitrary execution and forced disappearance, all of them prohibited because they violate non-derogable rights recognized by international human rights law.[33]

The Court added that the obstacles imposed by the mentioned Peruvian amnesties on the families of the victims and surviving victims from being heard by a judge violated Articles 8.1 and 25 of the American Convention, transgressing also Article 1.1 of the same instrument, which upholds the obligation to respect and guarantee human rights, and Article 2, which recognizes the obligation to adjust the domestic law to said Convention.

At a more fundamental level, the Court established that "self-amnesty laws lead to the defenselessness of victims and perpetuate impunity; therefore, they are manifestly incompatible with the aims and spirit of the Convention", adding that as a consequence of this incompatibility, "said laws lack legal effect and may not continue to obstruct the investigation of the grounds on which this case is based or the identification and punishment of those responsible, nor can they have the same or a similar impact with regard to other cases that have occurred in Peru".[34]

31 The first of these amnesties concerned the actual executions. The second one, dictated once a judge who was investigating the case declared the first amnesty unconstitutional, disposed explicitly that the first amnesty was not revisable by the judiciary.

32 The court pronounced that the American Convention on Human Rights as a whole could be denounced in accordance with Art 78, but it does not release Peru from the recognition of contentious jurisdiction.

33 See IACtHR, case of *Barrios Altos v Peru*, fn 28 above, para 41.

34 IACtHR, case of *Barrios Altos v Peru*, paras 43 and 44.

Finally, the only aspect in which the judgment of the Court differs from the claim of the Commission is in relation to the right to the truth. The Commission had considered that the failure to respect this right constituted an additional infringement of the American Convention by Peru: according to the Commission, Article 13, which upholds the right to search and receive information, implied in the concrete case an obligation of a positive character for the state to guarantee essential information to preserve the rights of the victims, to ensure transparency in public administration and the protection of human rights.

The Court, in contrast, maintained that being:

> ". . . evident that the surviving victims, their next of kin and the next of kin of the victims who died were prevented from knowing the truth about the events that occurred in Barrios Altos, in the circumstances of the instant case, the right to the truth is subsumed in the right of the victim or his next of kin to obtain clarification of the events that violated human rights and the corresponding responsibilities from the competent organs of the state, through the investigation and prosecution that are established in Articles 8 and 25 of the Convention".[35]

The Court has thereafter returned to these themes in other cases, first, in two almost simultaneous judgments, both in September 2006, falling back on, as we will show, in a Paraguayan case and another Chilean case and, in the year thereafter, in a Colombian case.

In the first of these, the case of *Agustín Goiburú and Otros v Paraguay*, even though an amnesty had not been dictated in the state in question, but rather that there had been no judicial investigations on the merits in a series of cases, the Court considered it necessary to formulate some specifications with regard to the obligations of the Convention in relation to forced disappearances. In this regard, it pointed out that:

> As may be deduced from the preamble to the aforesaid American Convention, faced with the particular gravity of such offenses and the nature of the rights harmed, the prohibition of the forced disappearance of persons and the corresponding obligation to investigate and punish those responsible has attained the status of *jus cogens*.[36]

35 IACtHR, case of *Bámaca-Velásquez v Guatemala*, Series C No 70, Judgment of 25 November 2000.

36 IACtHR, case of *Agustín Goiburú y Otros v Paraguay*, Series C No 153, Judgment of 22 September 2006, para 84. A footnote included in the sentence has been eliminated in the citation.

Explaining this point in more detail, the Court added:

> The prohibition of torture and forced disappearance of persons . . . are included among the conducts deemed to harm essential values and rights of the international community and entail the activation of national and international measures, instruments and mechanisms to ensure their effective prosecution and the sanction of the authors, so as to prevent them and avoid them remaining unpunished. Consequently, faced with the gravity of certain offenses, the norms of international customary and treaty-based law establish the obligation to prosecute those responsible. This acquires particular relevance in cases such as this, because the facts occurred in a context of the systematic violation of human rights—both offenses constituting crimes against humanity—and this gives rise to the states' obligation to ensure that such conduct is criminally prosecuted and the perpetrators punished.[37]

The Court concludes by holding that:

> Having established the broad scope of the international obligations *erga omnes* against the impunity of grave human rights violations, the Court reiterates that, in the terms of Article 1(1) of the American Convention, the states are obliged to investigate human rights violations and prosecute and punish those responsible.[38]

The second judgment on the issue, which was delivered in September 2006, was in the case of *Almonacid* and represents the most substantiated judgment regarding amnesties which has been delivered until now. The case referred to the extrajudicial execution of Mr Almonacid, brought about by the agents of the state during the first months of military dictatorship in Chile in 1973. The judgment analyzes successively the following aspects: whether or not the extrajudicial execution of Mr Almonacid constituted a crime against humanity; in the event that the response to that question is affirmative, whether said crime could or could not be amnestied; whether or not the Chilean amnesty law decree—promulgated by the dictatorship itself—included said crime and, if so, violated the American Convention; and, finally, whether or not the application of said law decree by the Chilean judges represents a transgression of Articles 8 and 25 of the American Convention.

In order to address the first of these questions, that is, whether the extrajudicial execution of Mr Almonacid constituted a crime against humanity, the

37 IACtHR, case of *Agustín Goiburú y Otros v Paraguay*, Series C No 153, Judgment of 22 September 2006, para 128.

38 IACtHR, case of *Agustín Goiburú y Otros v Paraguay*, Series C No 153, Judgment of 22 September 2006, para 129.

Inter-American Court, basing itself in the statutes of the military tribunals of Nuremberg and Tokyo, as well as subsequent developments—including diverse records of the United Nations—pointed out that "crimes against humanity include the commission of inhuman acts, such as murder, committed in a context of generalized or systematic attacks against civilians".[39] Basing itself on these considerations, the Court establishes that the annotated norm had an imperative character at the international legal level already in 1973. According to the Court, "crimes against humanity is a *ius cogens* rule, and the punishment of such crimes is obligatory pursuant to the general principles of international law".[40] In addition, the Court observes that in the year of 1998—when the amnesty law decree was applied by the Chilean courts in the present case—the statutes of the ad hoc International Criminal Tribunals for the Former Yugoslavia and Rwanda had already been adopted, events that reaffirm what has been said before.

In accordance with what has previously been said, the Court upholds that it is not possible to leave crimes against humanity without sanction through the adoption of an amnesty law as "according to the International Law *corpus iuris*, a crime against humanity is in itself a serious violation of human rights and affects mankind as a whole".[41] Besides referring to the statutes of the two ad hoc international criminal tribunals, the judgment relies upon a series of resolutions adopted by the UN General Assembly and the UN Security Council. The case finally determines that: "States cannot neglect their duty to investigate, identify, and punish those persons responsible for crimes against humanity by enforcing amnesty laws or any other similar domestic provisions. Consequently, crimes against humanity are crimes which cannot be susceptible of amnesty."[42]

With regard to the scope of the Chilean amnesty law decree, the judgment establishes that it turns out to be inadequate, as the law in question stipulates an amnesty of a general character, which not only does not exclude crimes such as the extrajudicial executions in question, forced disappearances and torture, but also has as its principal objective to amnesty the crimes against international law committed by the military regime. On the basis of this finding, the judgment establishes that the amnesty law decree lacks juridical effects and cannot continue to be an obstacle to the investigation or sanction of the present case, nor in others.

When it comes to the fourth and final question of interest in this chapter, the Inter-American Court holds that "the above mentioned legislative obligation

39 IACtHR, case of *Almonacid-Arellano v Chile*, Series C No 154, Judgment of 26 September 2006, para 96.

40 IACtHR, case of *Almonacid-Arellano v Chile*, Series C No 154, Judgment of 26 September 2006, para 99.

41 IACtHR, case of *Almonacid-Arellano v Chile*, Series C No 154, Judgment of 26 September 2006, para 105.

42 IACtHR, case of *Almonacid-Arellano v Chile*, Series C No 154, Judgment of 26 September 2006, para 114.

established by Article 2 of the Convention is also aimed at facilitating the work of the Judiciary so that the law enforcement authority may have a clear option in order to solve a particular case". It thereafter adds that:

> When the Legislative Power fails to set aside and / or adopts laws which are contrary to the American Convention, the Judiciary is bound to honor the obligation to respect rights as stated in Article 1(1) of the said Convention, and consequently, it must refrain from enforcing any laws contrary to such Convention.[43]

Recently, in the case of the *Rochela Massacre* (Colombia), the Inter-American Court observed that:

> In order for the State to satisfy its duty to adequately guarantee the range of rights protected by the Convention, including the right to judicial recourse, and the right to know and access the truth, the State must fulfill its duty to investigate, try, and, when appropriate, punish and provide redress for grave violations of human rights. To achieve this objective, the State should observe due process and guarantee the principles of expeditious justice, adversarial defense, effective recourse, implementation of the judgment, and the proportionality of punishment, among other principles.[44]

The Inter-American Court also noted that:

> States have the duty to initiate *ex officio*, without delay, and with due diligence, a serious, impartial and effective investigation designed to fully establish responsibility for violations. In order to achieve this objective, it is necessary, *inter alia* that an effective system exist to protect judicial branch officials, as well as victims and their next of kin. Moreover, when necessary, it is important to expose the existence of complex criminal structures and their connections, which made the violations possible. In this sense, dispositions that impede the investigation and punishment of those responsible for grave violations are inadmissible.[45]

Finally, as regards the proportionality of the sanction, the Court emphasizes "that the punishment which the State assigns to the perpetrator of illicit conduct should be proportional to the rights recognized by law and the culpability with

43 IACtHR, case of *Almonacid-Arellano v Chile*, Series C No 154, Judgment of 26 September 2006, para 123.

44 IACtHR, case of the *Rochela Massacre v Colombia*, Series C No 163, Judgment of 11 May 2007, para 193.

45 IACtHR, case of the *Rochela Massacre v Colombia*, Series C No 163, Judgment of 11 May 2007, para. 194. The footnote references contained in the judgment have been eliminated.

which the perpetrated [sic] acted, which in turn should be established as a function of the nature and gravity of the events".[46]

The progressive international legal interpretation in the Inter-American system has had a central role in the establishment of an international way of responding to massive and systematic human rights violations.[47] In particular, the foundations articulated in this regional system contributed to the development of similar standards at the UN level.

Nevertheless, within the domestic level of American states, the effect of the jurisprudence set forth by the Commission and the Court has been varied. As has already been noted, in Argentina and Uruguay, this effect was produced years after the resolutions of the Commission and with a greater impact in the first case compared with the second one. The compliance of the judgment in the case of *Barrios Altos* was facilitated by the fact that the Peruvian state itself smoothed the claim that had been interposed before this Court. Even so, there has been a series of debates in Peru with regard to the effects of this judgment in relation to other cases, something that the Court also had pointed out. In what concerns the judgment in the case of *Almonacid*, the Chilean Government has manifested publicly—through the President of the Republic—its disposition to conform to the sentence, but this has still not happened.

The impact, in any case, must be evaluated, not only with regard to the reaction of the states the conduct of which is being condemned in resolutions by the Commission and the Court, but must go much further. In other words, it is relevant to determine also the extent to which this jurisprudence has modified the actions of other American states. Although such a precise determination of this question would require an empirical study which lies outside the scope of this work, what is indeed clear is that the jurisprudence emanating from the Inter-American system—and its corresponding pronouncements in the United Nations—has placed the issue of confrontation of massive and systematic violations, and the question of amnesty as a way of tackling them, at centre stage. Thus, in each process of transition to democracy or pacification that has occurred in Latin America in more recent years, this theme has been at the centre of the agenda and public discussions. While the established jurisprudence has not always been followed, the treatment of the question is no longer seen as something that lies exclusively within the discretion of the states. Even when the jurisprudence has not been followed, governments have sought to set forth justifications as to why they have taken a different road.

46 IACtHR, case of the *Rochela Massacre v Colombia*, Series C No 163, Judgment of 11 May 2007, para 196.

47 See Cassel, D, "Lessons from the Americas: Guidelines for International Responses to Amnesties for Atrocities", *Law and Contemporary Problems*, vol 59, no 4, 1996, pp 197–230.

3.3 The scope of the fundamental rights involved

The development that has taken place in the Inter-American system regarding confrontation of grave violations committed by previous governments has evolved in the absence of legal specific and explicit parameters. Thus, through the exercise of international legal interpretation of some international norms, a tendency to maintain that these norms require the states to take initiative to back such confrontation has been consolidated.

In legal terms, the pivotal point lies in how international legal interpretation of the scope of these norms has led to the recognition of specific fundamental rights. As has been noted, in the case of the Inter-American system of Human Rights, as a result, a pioneering *corpus iuris* has been developed regarding especially two fundamental rights upon which the jurisprudence has come to focus, in relation to human rights: that concerning judicial guarantees and that relating to judicial protection. The organs of the Inter-American system have analyzed these rights in relation to Article 1.1 of the American Convention related to general human rights obligations of states.

The right to judicial guarantees is upheld in Article 8.1 of the mentioned international instrument. In this article, the right is explicitly mentioned as one that is not susceptible to suspensions in states of constitutional exception when these guarantees are indispensible for the protection of other rights that are not susceptible to suspension.[48] In one of its first Advisory Opinions in the 1980s, the Inter-American Court does not indicate in an explicit manner which the indispensable judicial guarantees are; through a systematic interpretation of various rules of this instrument, it concluded that:

> . . . judicial guarantees essential for the protection of the human rights not subject to derogation, according to Article 27(2) of the Convention, are those to which the Convention expressly refers in Articles 7(6) and 25(1), considered within the framework and the principles of Article 8, and also those necessary to the preservation of the rule of law, even during the state of exception that results from the suspension of guarantees.[49]

Article 8.1 establishes that "every person has the right to a hearing, with due guarantees and within a reasonable time, by a competent, independent, and

48 The expression "suspension of rights" is an unfortunate one as it induces the idea that in certain circumstances some rights can be left without effect, when in reality the provision refers to temporal delimitations that bind these rights, additional to those which can be made in a context of constitutional normalcy. The term is used in this chapter only as it is understood in international instruments so as to avoid any confusion.

49 IACtHR, Advisory Opinion OC-9/87 of 6 October 1987 concerning Judicial Guarantees in States of Emergency, para 38. See also Medina Quiroga, C, *La Convención Americana: Teoría y Jurisprudencia (Vida, Integridad Personal, Libertad Personal, Debido Proceso y Recurso Judicial)*, Santiago, Chile: Centro de Derechos Humanos Facultad de Derecho Universidad de Chile, 2005, especially pp 380 ff.

impartial tribunal, previously established by law, in the substantiation of any accusation of a criminal nature made against him or for the determination of his rights and obligations of a civil, labor, fiscal, or any other nature". The Court has pointed out that the subheading of Article 8 "judicial guarantees" (in the English text "right to a fair trial") "may lead to confusion because the provision does not recognize any judicial guarantees, strictly speaking. Article 8 does not contain a specific judicial remedy, but rather the procedural requirements that should be observed in order to be able to speak of effective and appropriate judicial guarantees under the Convention".[50] The Court adds that what the rule does is to uphold the right to due process of law, "which includes the prerequisites necessary to ensure the adequate protection of those persons whose rights or obligations are pending judicial determination".[51]

A first reading of this provision could lead to the conclusion that it concerns only the guarantees afforded to the accused in a criminal law context. As a matter of fact, however, in several domestic legal systems the state possesses the monopoly over criminal justice action in relation to the majority of crimes. The problem was noticed at the moment when the Inter-American Commission had to rule in relation to the Uruguayan amnesty law. It is not a coincidence that this law is denominated "The Caducity Law for the Penal State Action", as in this country the state possesses monopoly to initiate criminal justice proceedings. The Government of Uruguay argued that its procedural system does not contemplate the right for individuals to present a criminal complaint as the criminal justice action is public and only in exceptional circumstances permits individuals to intervene. As a result of this argument, the only consequence of the Caducity Law would be that the state renounced the exercise of public criminal justice action.

But the Commission centred itself in the impact of the law on cases of grave human rights violations by prohibiting by law that the state brings these cases forward and highlighting that what the law does is to hinder all investigations as the individuals could not—in accordance with domestic law—take an initiative that would have any such effect.

Nevertheless, the scope of the article concerning the right to judicial guarantees (right to fair trial) has come to be interpreted in a broad sense to include also the plaintiffs and the denouncers on criminal matters. In the case of grave human rights violations, the right shall extend to the victims of these crimes or their families. One way of arriving at this conclusion within the framework of the American Convention is to refer to the final part of Article 8.1, as it

50 IACtHR, Advisory Opinion OC-9/87 of 6 October 1987, para 27.

51 IACtHR, Advisory Opinion OC-9/87 of 6 October 1987, para 28. The court observes that this conclusion is confirmed with the meaning that Art 46.2(a) gives to this same expression, establishing that the duty to interpose and exhaust domestic judicial remedies is not applicable when "the domestic legislation of the State concerned does not afford due process of law for the protection of the right or rights that have allegedly been violated".

stipulates that the guarantees in question shall also be recognized in determination of a person's rights and obligations of any other nature.

It is pertinent to mention that contemporary criminal procedural law accepts the claim that the state has the monopoly of criminal proceedings in the majority of crimes and that it enjoys a certain margin of discretion when taking the decision regarding whether or not to prosecute them. What the Inter-American Commission and Court determine is that this discretion ought not to affect the investigation of crimes in the field of human rights. In the Uruguayan cases, the Commission specifies that:

> It is not taking issue with the public and official nature of criminal proceedings. However, in Uruguay the victim or injured party does have a right to participate in the criminal proceeding beyond the indictment. The Uruguayan Code of Criminal Procedure authorizes the injured party to request, during the summary proceedings, all measures that may be useful in ascertaining the crime and determining those responsible (Article 80). Consequently, in systems that allow it, the victim of the crime has access to the courts because of a citizen's fundamental right, which becomes particularly important as a dynamic of the criminal process.[52]

The right to judicial protection is regulated in Article 25 of the American Convention. According to this provision the right refers to "simple and prompt recourse, or any other effective recourse, to a competent court or tribunal for protection against acts that violate his fundamental rights recognized by the constitution or laws of the state concerned or by this Convention . . .". In consequence, the right must be understood to entail recourses such as those of *habeas corpus* or constitutional relief (*amparo*), without prejudice to the fact that the provision in question is extended to other possible recourses. In relation to amnesty norms, Inter-American jurisprudence has sometimes focused on the first (such as when these simple or prompt recourses become inoperative) and, at times, the second, when it is the possibility to take legal action (through criminal, civil or other channels), which has seen itself as being impeded by these norms.

The connection advanced in the jurisprudence of the Inter-American system of mentioned rights to judicial guarantees and to judicial protection with the scope of the obligations of states recognized in Article 1.1 of the American Convention is likewise relevant.

As the Inter-American Court established in the judgment in the case of *Velázquez*, the human rights obligations of states include prevention, investigation and sanction. It also pointed out that the obligation to investigate requires that it be serious so as to avoid mere formality or appearance of investigation.

52 IACHR, Report No 29/92, para 41.

But the Court also assumes the task to specify that the obligation to investigate does not imply that it must always lead to satisfactory results. Can this pronouncement be understood as opening a space for amnesty norms? The Court has denied this possibility. It is one thing if in a specific case because of circumstances that the state cannot be held responsible for, it becomes impossible to reach satisfactory results (for example, when the evidence of the crime has disappeared without the state having participated either directly or indirectly—through tolerance or acquiescence—in this disappearance); it is another thing when because of amnesty norms the state impedes *a priori* that the domestic courts realize a complete investigation.[53]

One final relevant aspect relates to the fact that neither the Commission nor the Court has incorporated explicitly a balancing of goods in its argumentation in the cases involving amnesties for grave violations. In this respect, it is sufficient to note that Article 32 of the American Convention makes a reference to the correlation between rights and duties, establishing in its second paragraph that "the rights of each person are limited by the rights of others, by the security of all, and by the just demands of the general welfare, in a democratic society". It was precisely the survival of a democratic society that the Governments of Argentina and Uruguay invoked in defence of their amnesty norms that had been dictated by democratic regimes.

When it comes to the correlation between rights and duties to which Article 32 of the Convention refers, strictly speaking, regardless of the existence of an explicit rule, the correlation would exist given that the hermeneutic task in the case of conflicting rights consists of balancing them adequately as has been latently developed in the modern theory of rights.[54]

It is sufficient to note that, in relation to other rights, but as a general assertion, the Inter-American Court has pointed out that Article 32.2 is not "automatically and equally applicable to all the rights which the Convention protects, including especially those rights in which the restrictions or limitations that may be legitimately imposed on the exercise of a certain right are specified in the provision itself". In this regard, the Court adds that the article in question "contains a general statement that is designed for those cases in particular in which the Convention, in proclaiming a right, makes no special reference to possible legitimate restrictions".[55] The latter statement is directly

53 On this issue, see Méndez, J, "Accountability for Past Abuses", *Human Rights Quarterly*, vol 19, 1997, pp 255–282, especially pp 264 ff.

54 See, e.g. Alexy, R, *A Theory of Constitutional Rights* (translated into English by Julian Rivers), Oxford: Oxford University Press, 2002, pp 50 ff, containing illustrative examples from German jurisprudence. See also Dworkin, R, *Taking Rights Seriously*, Cambridge, Massachusetts: Harvard University Press, 1977, pp 72 ff.

55 Both citations are from the IACtHR, Advisory Opinion OC-5/85, on Compulsory Membership in an Association Prescribed by Law for the Practice of Journalism (Arts 13 and 29 American Convention on Human Rights), Series A No 5, 13 November 1985, para 65.

related to the situation of the fundamental rights at stake in the case of amnesty norms as neither Article 8 which concerns judicial guarantees, nor Article 25 which recognizes the right to judicial protection, establishes limitations on these rights in an explicit manner.

The jurisprudence of the international human rights organs, including the Commission and the Inter-American Court, have consistently sustained that there is no absolute or abstract hierarchy among the rights recognized in treaties and declarations. In other words, the human rights catalogue does not entail an order according to which some rights would be subordinated to others.[56] On this point, the organs in question follow the tendencies in modern philosophy of rights, such as that of Alexy, who (speaking of a particular German case law) holds that:

> This tension [between principles] was not to be resolved by giving one of these duties absolute precedence, for neither principle enjoyed precedence *per se*. On the contrary, the conflict was to be resolved by balancing the conflicting interests. The question of this balancing process was which of the requirements having equal status in the abstract had the greater weight in the concrete cases.[57]

Dworkin also emphasizes the dimension of weight or importance of the principles at stake in concrete cases and, given the absence of an exact mediation, "the judgment that a particular principle or policy is more important than another will often be a controversial one".[58] Given the absence of an absolute hierarchy between rights, it is necessary to make a balancing act. The question is whether in the cases of general amnesties we are faced with a conflict between principles in this strict sense. In my judgment, Dworkin would respond negatively to this question, as for him the principles must be feasible to orient them to individual rights in order to recognize them as "competing rights", that is, "only the rights of other members of the society as individuals"—an assertion that Dworkin illustrates, saying that "the laws that provide a certain level of quiet in public places, or that authorize and finance a foreign war, cannot be thought to rest on individual rights".[59] These types of collective goods would be analogous to those invoked by Argentina and Uruguay in their defences of amnesty norms before the Inter-American system.

On this point, Alexy disagrees with Dworkin, recuperating the possibility that collective goods operate as limitations upon those rights, which, as a

56 On this issue, see Medina, C, "El Derecho Internacional de los Derechos Humanos", in Medina, C and Medina, J (eds), *Sistema Jurídico y Derechos Humanos*, Santiago, Chile: Facultad de Derecho Universidad Diego Portales, Cuadernos de Análisis Jurídico Serie Publicaciones Especiales, 1996, pp 27 ff.

57 Alexy, fn 54 above, p 51.

58 Dworkin, fn 54 above, p 26.

59 Dworkin, fn 54 above, pp 194–195.

consequence, can be balanced, adding that "without doubt, the distinction between individual rights and collective interests is important. But it is neither necessary nor desirable to tie the concept of a principle to that of an individual right".[60] He also mentions a cluster of collective goods that can operate as principles and come into conflict with specific individual rights, among them, public health, the security of the Republic, and most important for the issue at hand, the protection of the democratic order.

On the other hand, as we have pointed out, the American Convention itself (Article 32) refers to the balancing of goods, including some of collective character. With regard to the issue in question, neither the domestic legal systems based on the idea of the Rule of Law nor the international human rights system operates in the manner that Dworkin proposes. Both the political constitutions and the international instruments resort to the use of general provisions delimitating rights.

The developments experienced in the theory of law in the second half of the twentieth century made an important contribution, in that they afforded greater clarity to the functioning of general provisions in a legal system.[61] From a legal positivist perspective, the mutual charges put forth in the disputes between legal positivism and natural law have obscured the question of the function discharged by general provisions in law. As a result, the positivists have relegated them to a very secondary role. The posture of Kelsen is illustrative in this regard when he speaks of a kind of inevitability of having to resort to general provisions and legal principles (which he placed on a par with the first ones), as in some way they introduced an unsettling element in the purity of his understanding of the legal system. For Kelsen, it meant leaving it to the judges and the administrative functionaries to fill these principles and provisions with content.[62]

As noted by theorists such as Neumann,[63] the use made by totalitarian regimes of general provisions is unsettling, such as in the case of the general part of the Nazi Criminal Code.[64] However, as Kaufmann notes, what happens in reality in the example of the Nazi legislation is the use of a general provision that turns out to be incompatible with the Rule of Law, as it surpasses the theory of different types of crimes, which, instead of actually resolving the problem associated with the lack of legal precision, appears to be furnishing it, without it being a proper characteristic of all general provisions. For Kaufmann, the

60 Alexy, fn 54 above, p 66.

61 Engisch, K, *Einführung in das juristische Denken*, 10th edn, Stuttgart: Kohllhamer W, 2005.

62 Kelsen, H, *Pure Theory of Law*, Berkeley: University of California Press, 1967.

63 Neumann, F, *El Estado Democrático y el Estado Autoritario*, Buenos Aires: Editorial Paidós, 1968, pp 36 ff.

64 A similar situation was experienced in Latin America when leaving the dictatorial regimes behind and some put forth the idea about the necessity to eliminate the constitutionally entrenched states of exception clauses in the light of the historical abuses that had been made of them in this region.

formulation of general provisions appears to be an unavoidable part of the process of legal realization.[65]

What happens instead with general provisions concerning the "protection of the democratic system" is that it produces an apparent paradox given that it is presented as a limitation on specific rights of the persons while, at the same time, their objective is to ensure the stability required for the adequate exercise of such rights.

The point is that, without prejudice of the claim that there is a necessary connection between a democratic system and human rights,[66] when it operates as a general clause that delimits one or more rights within a Rule of Law framework, it is appropriate to interpret it in restrictive terms. In effect, even if the democratic system is destined to protect the rights of persons, at the same time, it is also understood as a limitation of these rights in the international instruments, political constitutions and national codes. For this reason, it is essential to distinguish between the kind of tension that is produced between a general clause that delimits rights and specific human rights from the other one that is produced when two specific human rights are in conflict with each other.

As already noted, with regard to human rights that come into conflict with each other, it is not possible to construe an absolute hierarchical order between such rights, as these are limited in a reciprocal manner that must be balanced in the concrete case. In contrast, the tension between a general clause that delimits rights and specific human rights is not a tension between equal rights, but rather a situation in which said clause is subordinated to human rights.

In the international context, it has been sufficiently clarified that, with regard to restrictions placed on human rights, general clauses that do not refer to the upholding of specific rights must be interpreted in a restrictive manner and in the light of these rights. This has been stated repeatedly by distinct international systems of protection. The Siracusa Principles on the Limitation and Derogation of Provisions in the International Covenant on Civil and Political Rights establishes that "all limitation clauses shall be interpreted strictly and in favor of the rights at issue" (principle 3) and that "the burden of justifying a limitation upon a right guaranteed under the Covenant lies with the state" (principle 12).[67]

However, in the case of amnesties of the type that we are analyzing in this study, the issue entails at least three additional edges: the first referring to the authenticity of the claim about the need to protect the democratic system (a

65 Kaufmann, A, *Analogía y naturaleza de la cosa*, Santiago, Chile: Editorial Jurídica, 1976, pp 42 ff.

66 See Habermas, J, *Between Facts and Norms*, Cambridge, Massachusetts: MIT Press, 1996.

67 See UN Economic and Social Council, UN Sub-Commission on Prevention of Discrimination and Protection of Minorities, *Syracuse Principles on the Limitation and Derogation of Provisions in the International Covenant on Civil and Political Rights*, Annex, UN Doc E/CN.4/1984/4 (1984).

question of fact), the second referring to the general character of such amnesties, and the third concerning the types of violations.

As regards the first question, it is important to note that it is one of empirical fact. The critical point is that, as has been manifested in a series of countries, rather than a genuine protection of the democratic system, the challenge is anti-democratic pressures of the perpetrators of violations who maintain certain degree of de facto power which produce distortions precisely at the moment when efforts are being made to establish the bases of the new political system.

With regard to the second question, amnesties of a general character affect human rights in a profound manner to the point of deforming them, and this is in relation to especially grave kinds of violations that they are meant to govern. This appears to be a critical aspect to ensure that the international human rights organs do not make explicit in their lines of reasoning a balancing of goods as it does not concern, as in the cases of balancing that are ordinarily performed by organs with constitutional jurisdiction, of a situation that refers uniquely to a specific case, but rather an enormous list of cases, which would be marginalized from all prospects of judicial action if legal validity is given to amnesty norms. One expression regularly used in the Anglo-Saxon world to refer to these norms is that of "blanket amnesties", which is very eloquent in the sense that such amnesties throw a mantle over a great volume of human rights violations, usually thousands or hundreds of thousands, which are then hidden and in a situation of impunity.

When it comes to the third and final question that has been formulated in this study— the one referring to the types of violations, even if as we have seen earlier, the international human rights organs have refuted the possibility to construct a hierarchical order between different types of rights, in all fairness, some types of violations have been considered for a long time as more grave than others. This is also reflected in the resolutions of these organs with regard to the amnesties cited in this study, such as when the Inter-American Court points out in a peremptory manner that the prohibition against the adoption of amnesties in case of violations of human rights that cannot be suspended,[68] in case of crimes against humanity,[69] or in case of grave human rights violations.[70] Furthermore, recent years bear witness to a process of crystallization of the notion of crimes against humanity in such a manner that today the concepts of "grave violations" of human rights and "crimes against humanity" are made ever more similar. This development has been reflected in the more recent cases before the Inter-American Court, in which it establishes the norm that obliges states to investigate and sanction perpetrators of crimes against humanity as

68 IACtHR, case of *Barrios Altos v Peru*, fn 28 above.

69 IACtHR, cases of *Almonacid-Arellano v Chile*, Series C No 154, Judgment of 26 September 2006; *Agustín Goiburú y Otros v Paraguay*, Series C No 153, Judgment of 22 September 2006; and *Rochela Massacre v Colombia*, Series C No 163, Judgment of 11 May 2007.

70 IACtHR, case of *Gomes-Lund et al (Guerrilha do Araguaia) v Brazil*, Series C No 219, Judgment of 24 November 2010.

having the character of *ius cogens*. This third aspect is also crucial to understand why the international organs have omitted to realize a balancing act of goods in relation to the amnesties that have been adopted to respond to these violations.

3.4 Conclusion

The treatment of grave violations of human rights has experienced a notable evolution over the last 15 years in terms of the way in which international human rights organs have come to respond to them. The mechanisms of the Inter-American system performed a crucial role in this process. This development has gone in the direction of establishing in a peremptory manner a series of state obligations in relation to the types of abuses in question, in opposition to the criterion that prevailed before that and according to which the democratic states possessed a wide discretion on these matters.

This development does not imply that the states have enforced the international standards in question in a homogenous manner. Some have advanced much more than others. Nevertheless, there is one aspect in common, derived from the growing attention afforded by international human rights organs, and that is that in practically all states currently coming out of periods of grave human rights violations, the question about how to tackle them is situated at the centre of public debate without there being any alternative to put them aside as happened only some years ago.

In the end, the construction of new democratic systems requires the reinforcement of the importance of recognizing and protecting human rights. This includes the prevention of the commission of grave violations and endeavouring that the citizens coexist as equals within the democratic system.

4 The possibility of criminal justice

The Argentinean experience

Ricardo Gil Lavedra

4.1 Introduction

The criminal prosecution of the massive human rights violations that occurred during the military dictatorship in power between 1976 and 1983 in Argentina has been neither uniform nor continuous. It is possible to divide the entire process up into two main periods. The first one, commencing towards the end of 1983 and lasting until the end of 1989, is characterized by the recuperation of democracy when those in the military who had been convicted during this period or were still in the process of being tried were pardoned.[1] The second period is the one that prevails until now. It was formally initiated[2] with the judgment of the Supreme Court in 2005 declaring the Laws of "Final Stop"[3] and "Due Obedience"[4] to be unconstitutional and null,[5] and resulting in the reopening of a couple of hundred cases in court, more denunciations, some condemnations and a procedure the financing of which is of governmental concern. Between these periods, however, one may include an intermediate one (1990 to 2005), in which some budding manifestations of a growing need to continue investigating and prosecuting massive human rights violations begin to develop and are revealed fully in the third period.

The two main periods correspond to two very distinct political and legal settings. The first series of investigations and prosecutions unfold in the immediate aftermath of the dictatorship followed by 50 years of alternation between civil and military governments in Argentina and with a significant

1 Presidential Decree of Pardon no 1002/89 of 7 October 1989, *Boletín Oficial*, 7 July 1989.

2 Note that the second period was initiated prior to the decision of the Supreme Court on 14 June 2005. As will be shown later in this chapter, the second period began with the so-called "truth proceedings", followed by the adoption of Law no 25.799 of 2 September 2003 annulling the Laws of "Full Stop" (Law no 23.492) and "Due Obedience" (Law no 23.521) (*Declaración de nulidad de las leyes de obediencia debida y punto final*).

3 Law no 23.492 of 23 December 1986, *Boletín Oficial*, 29 December 1986.

4 Law no 23.521 of 8 June 1987, *Boletín Oficial*, 9 June 1987.

5 Corte Suprema de Justicia de la Nación (Supreme Court of Argentina) (CSJN), Case No 17.768, *Nulidad Ley de Obediencia Debida y Punto Final (Simón, Julio y otros)*, Judgment of 14 June 2005.

number of repressors maintaining their functions in the military and the security forces. Also important to bear in mind is that these investigations and prosecutions were conducted in the absence of relevant rules of international human rights law, which began to develop more rigorously in the beginning of the 1990s. The second period, in contrast, takes place entirely within the "transitional justice" framework, which is defined by a set of principles that have been established by supranational organizations, the work of which is dedicated to international human rights protection, and which diminishes the range of options available for states in seeking to tackle massive human rights violations. This period is also situated within a fully consolidated democratic regime in which at least free and fair elections are guaranteed and which represents more than 20 years of uninterrupted exercise of popular sovereignty.

In spite of their remarkably different political and legal contexts, both periods are of great interest when analyzing the question of the role and function of courts in times of transition, their experiences and positive contributions as well as the difficulties that they may face, including their successes and failures, when new democracies seek to tackle massive human rights violations committed by a previous military dictatorship. In order to facilitate the possibility of comparison with experiences in other countries, including the "lessons learned", this chapter will begin with a concise account of the historical background to the investigations and prosecutions of massive human rights violations which have taken place and are still taking place in Argentina with the objective of extracting the most important contributions of the courts, as well as the inconveniences and obstacles that have been and are still being confronted by the national judiciary until this day.

4.2 The judgments and the beginning of democracy

4.2.1 The first steps

The military defeat in the frustrated attempt to recuperate the Malvinas/Falkland Islands in 1982, leading to a situation of economic and social deterioration, impeded somehow the military dictatorship to abandon the "agreement" to transfer its power to the entering democratic government (as was occurring in other neighbouring countries). This development must be taken into account when considering the question of how Argentinean courts came to tackle the human rights violations that had been committed in the 1970s with the objective of suppressing the guerrillas.

During the electoral campaign of 1983 resulting in the election of Raúl Alfonsín, who received 52 per cent of the votes, a promise was made to initiate proceedings against those who had violated human rights in the repression of the guerrillas, although it was also announced that the prosecution would not be complete, but limited.[6] However, the realization of this commitment confronted two serious obstacles, at least if the foreseen proceedings were to be conducted in accordance with the laws in force at that time.[7] First of all, just before abandoning power, the military regime had adopted Law no 22.924 of 23 March 1983,[8] which declared as extinct all criminal actions aimed at repressing activities with a terrorist or subversive purpose, and all those crimes that had been committed in order to prevent or plot against them. Secondly, the rules of the Code of Military Justice established jurisdiction for military tribunals over ordinary crimes that had been committed in military locations or as instances of acts while in service. Thus, if the repression of the guerrillas had been accomplished through official orders, as was suspected, and if the detainees had been lodged in military establishments, all actions of the military lay within the competence of military tribunals according to the laws in force.

A few days after coming to power, President Alfonsín, in his role as military chief of the armed forces, dictated Decree no 158 of 13 December 1983 ordering the subjection of the members of the three first military juntas that seized power, to proceedings before the *Consejo Supremo de las Fuerzas Armadas* ("Supreme Council of the Armed Forces"),[9] for crimes of homicide, illegal deprivation of liberty and the use of torture against the detainees, without prejudice of other crimes that they may additionally be held accountable for.[10] Simultaneously, the Executive Branch passed a bill to Congress that would thereafter become Law no 23.049,[11] which modified the Code of Military Justice insofar as it restricted the scope of military jurisdiction to crimes of essentially military character,[12]

6 The proposal set forth in the campaigns distinguished between three levels of responsibility: those who gave the orders, those who exceeded them and those who complied with them. In reality, orders that implied the commission of abhorrent crimes could never be considered as excessive acts.

7 Today, however, neither self-amnesty law nor military jurisdiction constitute any kind of bar to prosecution. See, e.g. the Inter-American Convention on Forced Disappearance of Persons (adopted on 6 September 1994), Arts VII and IX.

8 Law no 22.924, *Ley de Pacificación Nacional (Autoamnistía)*, 23 March 1983, *Boletín Oficial*, 27 March 1983.

9 According to Art 179 of the Code of Military Justice of 1951 (*Código de Justicia Militar*, Ley 14.029, 4 July 1951, *Boletín Oficial*, 6 August 1951), superior officials may only be submitted to proceedings following an order dictated by the Chief Commander. (The Code of Military Justice was derogated on 6 August 2008. See Law no 26394, *Boletín Oficial*, 9 August 2008.) The Argentinean Constitution grants to the President of the Republic the power as chief of all armed forces. See Art 86(15) of the Constitution in force at that time of the military dictatorship (i.e. the Constitution of 1853 as reformed in 1972), as well as Art 99(12) of the Constitution, in force since the reform of 1994.

10 Also note Presidential Decree no 157/83 of 13 December 1983, according to which the most responsible for the guerrilla organizations were to be submitted to prosecution. In this way, the government intended to appear as a neutral actor in relation to the violence, even if this position, known as the "theory of the demons", carried the risk of placing crimes that are in essence not comparable on a par with each other.

11 Law no 23.049 of 13 February 1984, *Boletín Oficial*, 15 February 1984 (concerning modifications of the Code of Military Justice).

12 That is, military jurisdiction was restricted to crimes that can only be committed by militaries on the basis of their condition as such, and civil judges would adjudicate the ordinary crimes.

while at the same time maintaining the competence of military tribunals for ordinary crimes that had occurred during the repression of the guerrillas during the dictatorship. It also recognized a right of appeal to the *Cámaras Federales de Apelaciones* ("Federal Courts of Appeals") in the respective territories where the different crimes had been committed. Furthermore, the bill contemplated an interpretation of Article 514 of the Code of Military Justice,[13] in the light of which it was assumed that in the absence of evidence to the contrary the subordinated had acted with "insuperable error" with regard to the legitimacy of the order. This interpretation was clearly intended to exclude the responsibility of the inferior commanders.

Congress approved the bill, albeit with two modifications that came to be of great relevance to the events that followed. The final formulation of Law no 23.049 included a provision stating that the Supreme Council was obliged to inform the Federal Appeals Court within six months about the progress made in the judicial process. This report could lead to a consideration of the case by the Appeals Court if the actions of the Supreme Council had turned out to suffer unjustified or negligent delays.[14] In addition, the law exempted the possibility of invoking "due obedience" in the case of atrocious or abhorrent crimes, an exemption that impeded the governmental strategy to exculpate inferior commanders. Simultaneously, Congress accepted Law 23.040, declaring thus the "self-amnesty" law that had been imposed by the military regime to be null and void.[15]

In this way, the scheme was completed. Insisting on the need to respect the *habeas corpus* guarantees of the crime suspects,[16] they were secured a right to first instance before the military judges. Nonetheless, they could lose that right if acting in bad faith or in a negligent manner. Furthermore, in accordance with the procedure laid down by the Code of Military Justice, there was a possibility of revising the decisions of the military tribunals by means of appeal to civil court.[17] The exemption of due obedience, initially intended to limit the number of people charged, did not protect the inferior commanders who had received illegitimate orders since, as came to be demonstrated later on, all crimes turned out to be atrocious and abhorrent.

13 Military Justice Code, Art 514, establishing that: "When a crime has been committed as a result of the execution of a service order, the superior who has given the order is the sole responsible, and the inferior shall only be considered as a complicit when he has exceeded in compliance with that order" (unofficial translation).

14 Law no 23.049 of 13 February 1984, Art 10.

15 Law no 23.040 of 27 December 1983, *Boletín Oficial*, 29 December 1983.

16 Recognized in Art 18 of the Constitution of 1853 as reformed in 1860, 1866, 1890, 1957 and 1972, according to which: "No inhabitant of the nation may be . . . prosecuted for special crimes or crimes adopted by the judges designated by law before the fact of the crime" (unofficial translation).

17 The initial strategy was based on the supposition that it would be the army officers themselves who would carry out the purges by signalling who had committed crimes. In this manner, the Armed Forces would "democratize" themselves. However, reality

There was also an important parallel development. Faced with the complaints from human rights organizations, and the section of Congress that was calling for the creation of a parliamentary commission to investigate what had happened, the Executive Branch dictated Decree 187/83 that created the *Comisión Nacional sobre la Desaparación de Personas*—CONADEP ("National Commission concerning Disappeared Persons").[18] Within a very short period (six months), CONADEP, composed of personalities of recognized prestige in society,[19] came to deliver a report that clarified the crimes related to the disappeared persons.[20]

4.2.2 *The proceedings of the military junta*

4.2.2.1 The evocation

In pursuance of Decree 158/83,[21] the Supreme Council of the Armed Forces opened a proceeding in accordance with the rules of the Code of Military Justice concerning the members of the first governmental juntas that integrated the Chief-in-Command of each band. In the first months of 1984, the Council came to dictate a rigorous preventive detention for General Videla and Admiral Massera. As indicated in Law 23.049,[22] within six months, a report was sent to the Criminal Chamber of the Federal Court of Appeals in the city of Buenos Aires, drawing attention to the advances made in the judicial process that had been made. The court returned the file with indications as to how the investigations ought to be conducted, pointing out that they ought to be directed towards the clarification as to whether there had existed an illegal method of combating terrorism and whom among the ex-commanders were to be held accountable. The court also requested a new report within 30 days.

thereafter contravened this expectation in a brutal manner. The equilibrium that the transition actually required is reflected in the words of President Alfonsín: "The beginning of democratic life in Argentina demanded that society took into consideration . . . the repression exercised by the state and bringing those responsible for the violence before the courts. But one had to do this without losing sight of the fragile nature of the democracy. Many times I have asked myself if the defence of those whose human rights had been violated did not put into risk the human rights in the future. That is, if one was not risking democratic stability and the security of the citizens" (unofficial translation). See Alfonsín, R, *Memoria Política*, Buenos Aires: Fondo de Cultura Económica, 2004, p 36.

18 Decree no 187/83, *Comisión Nacional sobre la Desaparición de Personas*, 15 December 1983, *Boletín Oficial*, 19 December 1983.

19 CONADEP was presided over by the writer Ernesto Sábato. Curiously enough, legislators of the "*Partido Justicalista*" and many human rights organizations refused to integrate into it because they doubted the intention of those who promoted its creation.

20 CONADEP was the first truth commission and has been followed by others in Chile, El Salvador, Haiti, Guatemala, South Africa and Peru.

21 Decree no 185/83, *Juicio Sumario ante el Consejo Supremo de las Fuerzas Armadas*, 13 December 1983, *Boletín Oficial*, 14 December 1983.

22 Law no 23.049 of 13 February 1984.

In September 1984, the CONADEP delivered its final report to President Alfonsín, which came to be known globally as "*Nunca Más*" ("Never Again"),[23] and which collects the testimonies of thousands of victims and witnesses, and describes the terrible methodology utilized by the armed forces to fight against the guerrillas, including the kidnappings, torture methods, clandestine centres and disappearances.

In the midst of the public shock caused by the CONADEP report,[24] the Supreme Council delivered a new report to the Federal Court of Appeals affirming that the orders that had been given in the fight against subversion were "unobjectionable" and that it could not foresee any early termination of the process. Immediately afterwards, in the beginning of October 1984, the Federal Court of Appeals resorted to the remedy that was vested in it by virtue of Law no 23.049, assuming thus the substantiation of the process, and removing it from the jurisdiction of military judges.[25] The defence counsels of those who had been charged appealed to the Supreme Court, claiming that there had been a violation of *habeas corpus*, an allegation that was rapidly refuted by that Court in the judgment delivered by it in December 1984.[26]

4.2.2.2 The organization of the proceeding

The way in which the process was organized came to be a decisive factor on the ability of the Federal Appeals Court in moving it forward in a successful manner. It was a process the objective of which was nothing less than the realization of an investigation of all of the crimes of the dictatorship, the responsibility for which would be attributed to the commanders. The crimes were those envisaged in the ordinary Penal Code (homicide, illegal deprivation of liberty, torture, etc). The procedure was military, with norms that turned out to be largely inapplicable,[27] as they were destined to regulate a procedure for infringements committed in the battlefield and not for massive human rights violations.

23 CONADEP, *Nunca Más—Informe CONADEP*, September 1984, available online at www.desaparecidos.org/nuncamas/web/investig/articulo/nuncamas/nmas0001.htm.

24 Argentinean society found itself segmented as large sections of the population sincerely believed the official version that had been given during the dictatorship, i.e. that there had been no disappearances and that there were only some regrettable and isolated cases of excessive actions during the repression.

25 In this manner, the intent of the military to prosecute its own officials failed.

26 CSJN, Case No XX, *Causa originariamente instruida por el Consejo Supremo de las Fuerzas Armadas en cumplimiento del decreto 158/83 del Poder Ejecutivo Nacional*, Sentencia (Decision) of 27 December 1984. In this case, the Supreme Court considered that the constitutional prohibition related to the prosecution by "special commissions", i.e. tribunals established *ex post facto*, but did not extend to permanent organs of the judicial power. Furthermore, no one had the constitutional right to be prosecuted in accordance with determined rules since the new regulations did not affect the right of defence.

27 The norms regulating proceedings in times of peace slackened in times of war (Code of Military Justice, Art 503). They consisted of a few rules, according to which the trial must be oral and brief (Code of Military Justice, Art 482). The procedure must include the

The Federal Court of Appeals adopted thus several important decisions. It maintained the basic scheme of procedure, in particular with regard to the realization of an oral and public hearing so as to produce the evidence, extending all of the deadlines for reasonable periods of time so as to permit the realization of an effective defence. The procedure was notably accusatorial in that it placed the responsibility of determining the crimes and the burden of proof upon the prosecutor. It also deferred the consideration of all possible exceptions and the numerous lines of argumentation of the defence counsels to the time of the final judgment, impeding the proceedings by delaying them unnecessarily.

As regards the procedural object, the eventual accountability of those who had been charged depended on a correlation of factors. On the one hand, it was essential to show that the commanders had effectively ordered in a general manner to each of its bands to repress the guerrillas, resorting to methods that lay outside the legal framework. Also of quintessence was to demonstrate that the concrete crimes corresponded to the actual use of that method. Considering that the reproach of culpability is personal and concerns specific illegal acts, the prosecution also had to prove the specific commission of the crimes.

However, it is worth noting that when it comes to massive crimes, it is not essential to prove each one of them, given the risk that the total duration of the process will become absolutely unreasonable. Time is a variable of great importance for retroactive justice,[28] especially when the judicial actions take place in a political context that is highly confused by the tension created by the prosecution of military officials who are still maintaining their positions. Prosecutor Julio Strassera thus chose a group of 709 paradigmatic cases that represented what had happened during the dictatorship, and reflected what had taken place in each band and in all the territory of the country.[29] These cases were attributed individually to the accused persons as a result of the criminal strategy that had been enforced. A great majority of these cases, although not all of them, emerged from the certified bundles of documents that had been delivered by the CONADEP. Indeed, its records, aimed at clarifying the truth of what had happened, turned out to be useful in order to move the judicial process forward.

conduct of an oral hearing where the evidence is received, the judges hearing without delay the prosecution and the defence, and delivering the sentence (Code of Military Justice, Arts 490, 498 and 500). The time limits were stated in terms of hours (e.g. Code of Military Justice, Art 497).

28 When comparing the trials realized in Greece by Karamanlis and what happened in Argentina, Samuel Huntington understands the delays of the trials of the military junta as conspiring against the politics of the government. See Huntington, S, *The Third Wave: Democratization in the Late Twentieth Century*, Oklahoma: University of Oklahoma Press, 1991, pp 193 ff.

29 The prosecutor followed the experience of the European Court of Human Rights in the well-known case of *Northern Ireland v United Kingdom*, App no 5310/71, Judgment of 18 January 1978.

4.2.2.3 The hearing

On 22 April 1985, the oral and public hearing contemplated in Article 490 of the Code of Military Justice began. The court dictated rules to regulate access to the hearing by the media and the public in general.[30] The hearings took place on all days of work from 3 pm onwards,[31] and were concluded when the agenda of each day had been exhausted.[32] The files and documentation that went together,[33] as well as the informative evidence that had been received, were incorporated into the reading realized by the Secretary of the Court in the beginning of each session. No intervention of the affected victims was allowed as the Code of Military Justice did not permit it and because Law no 23.049 only allowed it in the event of appeals of the sentences to the Supreme Council of the Armed Forces.[34]

Between 22 April and 14 August 1985, 833 people gave their testimonies.[35] Their declarations were registered and their recordings were made available to the parties. In cases where the prosecutor considered that he already disposed of sufficient elements, he desisted from pending testimonial evidence. As a

30 The Federal Court of Appeals of Buenos Aires allowed the presence of accredited national or foreign journalists. In total, 400 licences were given. The trial was recorded by a public television station (Channel 7) which provided its recordings, images without sound, to whoever asked for them at the end of each hearing. One single photographer, who rotated, was authorized to take photos at the beginning of each declaration, and these photos were thereafter distributed to the rest who were also authorized. Bringing recorders, microphones or cameras was not allowed. The chamber where the hearings were conducted had capacity for 124 persons, except for one section that was reserved for the parties and the tribunal. The rest was distributed freely on a daily basis to those persons who requested it in the office enabled to this effect. It was prohibited to enter into the chamber with uniforms, medals or emblems. During the development of the hearing, the federal police imposed a rigid system of security and control in the Palace of Justice and its proximity.

31 In the mornings, the chamber resolved the remainder of the cases related to its competence for which there was no time extension. It is important in this context to recall that back then the existing technology of the court was limited to two electric typewriters (the rest were manual ones), two photocopy machines, and a team of 30 persons who worked in other tribunals in the morning and then worked in the trial in the evening, receiving extra wages for their work.

32 Generally, the hearing lasted between six and eight hours per day, although a few were extended until early morning of the following day.

33 The documentation consisted of 9,000 dossiers and 4,000 diplomatic claims. See *La Sentencia, dictada el 9 de diciembre de 1985 por la Cámara Nacional de Apelaciones en lo Criminal y Correccional Federal de la Capital Federal*, Buenos Aires: Imprenta del Congreso de la Nación, 1987, Nota preliminar, p IX.

34 See Law no 23.049 of 13 February 1984, Art 9. This provision foresaw the presence of the crime victim before the military tribunal only for the purpose of providing evidence or to ask for a notification of the sentence in order to appeal to a civil court. The Supreme Court affirmed this criterion in Case No F.295.XX, *Fernández Meijide, Pablo s/averiguación por privación ilegítima de la libertad*, Sentence (Decision) of 22 August 1985.

35 It is important to recognize the courage of the victims in giving their testimonies in order to clarify the facts in a period when there was no certainty about the fate of the democracy and the repressors were still active. See *La Sentencia*, fn 33 above.

result, a significant part of the 709 original cases were resolved on the basis of documentary evidence. The accusation was made between 11 and 18 September 1985, the defences pleaded between 30 September and 21 October, which was the time by which the court disposed of an intermediate quarter until the day of the delivery of the sentence. The commanders being charged were not obliged to be present at the time of the testimonies and no one was, while they did have to be present throughout the period of the accusation.[36]

4.2.2.4 *The sentence*

On 9 December 1985, 14 months after the Criminal Chamber of the Federal Court of Appeals in Buenos Aires had declared jurisdiction in the case, the sentence was delivered. With the purpose of conforming to the requirements of military law,[37] the court formulated and voted on more than 20,000 questions concerning the crimes that summarized the factual base that had been proven on the basis of the gathered evidence. Afterwards, the different exceptions invoked by the defence counsels were analyzed, among them, the amnesty exception that was recognized in the law of the military government. The chamber refuted the claim about the applicability of this exception. To this end, it based itself on precedents of other chambers of the same court which had already established the nullity and invalidity de facto of this norm,[38] taking into account its nature and conflict with a constitutional norm which, when interpreted correctly, rules out the possibility of granting amnesty for crimes having been committed while exercising the sum of public power.[39]

With regard to the orders given by the commanders, the court considered proven that those charged had ordered, within the scope of their respective competences, the suppression of terrorism using a system that can be synthesized as follows: kidnapping those who could turn out to be suspected in accordance with intelligence reports of having connections with terrorism; bringing them to secret detention centres located inside military or police units on their premises; once there, interrogating them using torture with the aim of obtaining data or information related to other persons or the terrorist organization itself; subjecting them to inhumane life conditions during detention to break down their moral resistance; giving the units full liberty to disposing of the fate of the detainees afterwards, who could be freed, placed at the disposal of the National Executive Power, be submitted to a military process or directly secretly assassinated without anyone knowing of their final destiny ("disappeared").

36 Code of Military Justice, Art 376.

37 Code of Military Justice, Art 499.

38 It is important to note that the finding that the self-amnesty law was invalid was not based on any rule of international human rights law, as is often the case today.

39 Constitution of 1 May 1853 as reformed in 1972, Art 29.

The actions had to be executed within the framework of existing legal regulations, while obviously leaving aside the compliance of those who were opposed to them, and in absolute secret, which secured the impunity of the crimes. In this manner, the state apparatus was placed at the service of this aim, negating and hiding the crimes in front of the request of the judges, families and foreign governments, carrying out campaigns in order to seek to convince the public that the denunciations were false.[40]

The orders gave rise to the commission of thousands of crimes with the characteristics mentioned: deprivations of liberty, torture, homicides and robberies.[41] Since the commanders had not realized the concrete act in person, the formal objective theory of authorship was inapplicable: the instrument in the case of mediate authorship was a subject that did not act with error and was not chargeable. Basing itself on Article 514 of the Code of Military Justice, the Court[42] established the assumption of mediate authorship,[43] which is compatible with the assumption in the military context that orders are securely followed. It thus concluded that the commanders were the mediate authors of the crimes committed by their subordinates. Hence, the determination of responsibility did not relate to the traditional dominium of will in this class of authorship since the instrument is not in this case direct authorship, which seems fungible, but instead the very system that is managed in a discretionary manner.[44]

The Court understood that each of those charged were responsible for the crimes committed by their bands, but not for the crimes committed by the members of other bands. Thus, it considered proven that the commanders' management of each band was absolutely autonomous and that mismanagement of someone else's crimes was not possible.[45] On this basis, the Court convicted each of the accused persons for crimes recognized in ordinary law having been

40 See *La Sentencia*, fn 33 above, vol I, pp 81, 127, 170, 182, 206, 216, 230, 234, 236 and 259; and vol II, pp 787 and 788.

41 As for robberies, while not typically ordered, they were seen as a necessary consequence and agreed as part of the plan.

42 See *La Sentencia*, fn 33 above, vol II, pp 787 ff.

43 Code of Military Justice, Art 514, reads: "When a crime has been committed as a result of a service order, the superior who has given the order shall be the sole responsible . . ." (unofficial translation).

44 *La Sentencia*, fn 33 above, p 804, which reads: "The dominium is therefore not over a concrete will but rather over an indeterminate will since whomever is the executor the crime occurs all the same" (unofficial translation). The chamber followed the well-known thesis of Claus Roxin concerning mediate authorship utilizing the organized power apparatus. The chamber cited his article: Roxin, C, "Sobre la autoría y participación en el derecho penal", in Bacigalupo, E et al (eds), *Problemas actuales de las ciencias penales y la filosofía del derecho. En homenaje al Profesor Luis Jiménez de Asúa*, Buenos Aires: Editorial Pannedille, 1970, pp 55 ff.

45 See *La Sentencia*, fn 33 above, pp 259 ff.

committed by subordinates under their command,[46] and acquitted them when no crime had been demonstrated in this period.[47]

Likewise, the court ordered that the Supreme Council of the Armed Forces be informed about the progress made with the objective of proceeding with the prosecution of the subordinates who had executed the orders given by the commanders.[48] On 30 December 1986, the Supreme Court substantially confirmed the sentence of the chamber.[49]

4.2.3 Other processes

During the year of 1986, other Federal Appeal Courts in the country began to request reports from the Supreme Council of the Armed Forces concerning complaints relating to crimes having occurred under their respective jurisdictions,[50] although none was removed from lower courts.

In contrast, the Federal Court of Appeals of the city of Buenos Aires declared its competence in relation to complaints involving Zone I (First Army Corps), the Army's School of Mechanics and of the Police of the Province of Buenos Aires, which was detached from the first. Between the months of August and December 1986, the court brought charges in relation to the crimes committed by the police in the province. This process evolved in a very similar way to the military junta trials and on 2 December of the same year it dictated a sentence

46 A further manifestation of the absence of international law in this period is the case of *Brigadier Agosti*, in which the chamber pronounced some 10 illegal deprivations of liberty as having passed the time limits imposed on investigation and prosecution. See Cámara Nacional de Apelaciones en lo Criminal y Correccional Federal de la Capital Federal, Case No 13/84, *Causa originariamente instruida por el Consejo Supremo de las Fuerzas Armadas en cumplimiento del decreto 158\83 del Poder Ejecutivo Nacional*, Sentencia (Decision) of 9 December 1985.

47 The criminal repression did not extend itself much further than 1979. Jorge Rafael Videla was convicted to life confinement, Emilio Eduardo Massera to life imprisonment, Orlando Ramón Agosti to four years and six months of prison, Roberto Eduardo Viola to 16 years of prison, and Armando Lambruschini to eight years of prison. The rest of the ex commanders were acquitted.

48 Cámara Nacional de Apelaciones en lo Criminal y Correccional Federal de la Capital Federal, Case No 13/84, *Causa originariamente instruida por el Consejo Supremo de las Fuerzas Armadas en cumplimiento del decreto 158\83 del Poder Ejecutivo Nacional*, Sentencia (Decision) of 9 December 1985, operational part, point 30 was intended to bring into motion the criminal prosecution "from below", a strategy that contrasted with the politics of the government, one of whose objectives was to avoid the prosecution of the officials of lower ranks in order to lower the pressure existing at the time.

49 CSJN, Case No C.895.XX, *Causa originariamente instruida por el Consejo Supremo de las Fuerzas Armadas en cumplimiento del decreto del Poder Ejecutivo Nacional*, Sentencia (Decision) of 30 December 1986.

50 During the repression, the country was divided into zones that corresponded to the different bodies of armed forces. Each of these bodies had primary responsibility in the fight against terrorism. The investigations, therefore, focused on the locations in which each of them had their seats of command (Rosario, Córdoba, Bahía Blanca and San Martín).

convicting the generals who were in charge of the First Army Corps, the Police Chief and some material authors.[51] Likewise, the court realized a traditional interpretation of due obedience as an excusing condition which only protects those persons who operated under insuperable error close to the legality of the order and does not extend to persons who followed anti-judicial orders. In a similar manner, the Court refuted the claim that in the military context obedience is "blind" on the basis that the inferiors always maintain some degree of inspection over the legitimacy of the order.

4.2.4 The interruption of the cycle

Following the "military junta trials", the government sought to hurry and delimit the number of prosecutions. Its reaction was due to the existence of a growing military dissatisfaction,[52] resulting in part from the great uncertainty as to the quantity of persons belonging to the army and the security forces that might find themselves involved in the accusations and future trials.

Thus, in April 1986, as a first measure to subdue this growing dissatisfaction, the Minister of Defense gave instructions to the General Prosecutor of the Supreme Council of the Armed Forces to extend the interpretation of due obedience as an excusing condition, so as to include the commission of atrocious and abhorrent crimes if such crimes had been ordered by superiors. However, the angry protests that emerged from different sectors of society obliged the government to leave these instructions aside.[53]

This intent having failed, Congress decided (during the Christmas period of that year) to adopt Law no 23.492, widely known as the Law of "Final Stop".[54] The Law in question exempted criminal justice action against all those who had participated in the repression of terrorism, unless he or she had been registered to give a "Declaration of Inquiry" (*Declaración indagatoria*) within 60 days counting from the day of its promulgation. While the Law had been formulated with the aim of specifying within a very short lapse of time the only persons who would still be charged for human rights violations and in this way calming the militaries, it had a paradoxical effect: the judges who until that point had acted with great sluggishness now faced the risk of being perceived by the public as responsible for impunity. As a result, within the short time frame of their disposal, they called to "inquiry" an enormous number of persons, many of them without any reason. It was a behaviour that, far from calming down military discontent, boosted it instead.

51 Ramón Camps was sentenced to 25 years' confinement, Ovidio Pablo Riccheri to 14 years' confinement, Miguel Etcheccolatz to 23 years of prison, Jorge Bergés to six years of prison and Norberto Cozzani to four years of prison.

52 It was held that the government's intention was to destroy the armed forces and that this responded to a strategy of the former guerrilla members who were gaining in politics what they had lost in the armed fight.

53 There was even the version that the judges of the Criminal Chamber would renounce if the orders were maintained. One judge actually renounced in this period.

54 Law no 23.492, *Punto Final*, of 24 December 1986, *Boletín Oficial*, 29 December 1986.

During Easter 1987, in a climate of great tension, the country experienced a first military uprising against the constitutional government,[55] motivated by, in the words of an official before a court in Córdoba, a demand for a "political solution" to the "war against subversion".[56] After several days of anxiety and uncertainty, and fearing the end of the democratic regime,[57] the rebellious required that the President of the Republic agreed personally with the quarters to solicit their surrender.[58]

Shortly thereafter, Congress adopted Law no 23.521, called "Due Obedience",[59] which established a presumption of excuse, without proof to the contrary, for those officials who had operated by virtue of superior orders, excluding chiefs-of-zones and sub-zones and others with decision capacity. Excluded from the presumption were crimes of rape, abduction of minors or the substitution of their civil status as well as the forced appropriation of real estate. A few days thereafter, on 22 June 1987, the Supreme Court, in deciding the *Camps* case, approved, by majority, the constitutionality of this Law.[60]

This development led to the termination of the criminal prosecutions of all of the personnel of the military and security forces who were not chiefs-of-zones or sub-zones or else had decision capacity. In practical terms, 30 new military chiefs were submitted to proceedings.

The impunity was established in a definitive manner when Carlos Menem became President of the government in 1989. In December that year, a series of decrees were dictated which pardoned the military officials who remained in

55 Thereafter, two more were produced, in January and December 1988, in Monte Caseros and Villa Martelli, respectively.

56 The petitioner of the revolutionary communication pronounced: "1. The hope that the current conduct of the Force put an end to the injustices and humiliations that burden the Armed Forces is considered extinguished. 2. The fearful and non-ending attack has generated the degree of indiscipline, discrediting and disgrace in which the forces find themselves. It is of such nature that it sees its existence as compromised unless its men rise and say enough. 3. We require the political solution, which corresponds to a political event, such as is the war against subversion" (unofficial translation), reproduced in Verbitsky, H, *Medio Siglo de Proclamas Militares*, Buenos Aires: Editora, 1987, p 167.

57 The government did not count on loyal forces to suppress the uprising given that the great number of the members of the armed forces understood that the claim was "just".

58 Public opinion understood that the government had negotiated with the rebels its surrender instead of an exculpatory norm of the crimes committed during the dictatorship, a perspective that was perceived as manifested through the rapid adoption of the Law on Due Obedience. Alfonsín has explained with good reasons that this was not the case, as in reality the government was already trying in this period to delimit the prosecutions. See Alfonsín, fn 17 above, pp 67 ff.

59 Law no 23.521, *Obediencia Debida*, 8 June 1987, *Boletín Oficial*, 9 June 1987.

60 The dissident vote of Dr Bacqué proclaimed the law unconstitutional, as it violated the division of powers in that the legislative branch had assumed judicial functions. International law was cited such as the Convention against Torture, which excludes as justification for torture the argument that it was ordered by a superior (Art 2.3), even if this Convention entered into force a few days following the adoption of Law no 23.521. Those voting in majority oscillated between considering the law as an objective cause for excluding penalties and, rather, as considering it directly as an amnesty.

proceedings,[61] persons who were being prosecuted for crimes of terrorism, persons who were prosecuted for the Malvinas war, and those who had risen against the previous government. In December the following year, President Menem dictated the decrees of pardon to those who had been convicted during the period of the previous government.[62]

4.2.5 *The period in balance*

This first stage of the Argentine experience demonstrates in a straightforward manner the range of difficulties encountered in seeking to conform to the principle of justice (investigation and sanction) in the direct aftermath of a dictatorship. While, by definition, the state monopolizes legitimately the use of force, in practical terms it is very difficult for democratic authorities to seek to prosecute perpetrators of grave crimes when they are found within the structures of military and security forces.[63] Also, it is essential that the principles upon which human rights are founded be deeply rooted in society, and that was not the case in Argentina during its first years of democracy.

Another element to be considered is the scarce development of the international rules and precedents and the absence of references to them in national judicial decisions in this period. The concepts that are now commonly recognized and used to tackle massive human rights violations, such as crimes against humanity, *ius cogens*, non-applicability of statutory limitations, international responsibility of states, etc had no validity in the legal knowledge of this period. Human rights conventions were ratified and entered into force only in the first years of democracy.[64] However, the incorporation of international instruments into domestic law was of great importance for future events.

The Laws of Final Stop and Due Obedience implied without any doubt a retreat in the search for justice, not least the latter law, as it left the authors of atrocious crimes without punishment. At the same time, the laws were not unconnected from the criteria of this historic period, including those of

61 The unconstitutionality of pardons to persons who were not convicted was discarded by the Supreme Court in Case No A.325.XXIII, *Aquino, Mercedes s/ denuncia (Caso Martinelli—Oliva) s/ plantea inconstitucionalidad del decreto* 1002/89, Sentencia (Decision) of 14 October 1992. The material impossibility to pardon people accused of crimes against humanity was at that time still not in question.

62 That is, in the cases of the *Junta Militares* and *Camps*. For these cases, see *La Sentencia*, fn 33 above, and CSJN, *Camps, Ramón Juan Alberto y otros*, Sentencia (Decision) of 22 June 1987.

63 Raúl Alfonsín, in an attempt to explain his policy, stated: "Several years have passed and still I ask myself the same question that I pondered then: beyond the well-intended slogans, did anybody believe, and still seriously believe that in this time, in a recently emerging democracy after years of dictatorship, that it would be possible to detain and prosecute 1500 or 2000 military officials still in function in the armed forces?" (unofficial translation). See Alfonsín, fn 17 above, p 47.

64 The Inter-American Convention on Human Rights was ratified by Argentina on 14 August 1984, the International Covenant on Civil and Political Rights on 8 November 1986, and the Convention against Torture on 26 June 1987.

monitoring international organizations,[65] which explicitly admitted the possibility of adopting amnesties.

It is important to stress several positive contributions in this initial period. With the help of domestic law, the self-amnesty of the military government was annulled; the first truth commission which produced a historic report was established; and for the first time a civil court applied rules of ordinary law to prosecute and convict the persons who were most responsible for the crimes that had been committed during the dictatorship. The judicial process may have important influences on the process of democratic consolidation in affirming certain values and principles, and constitutes an example to other countries. However, it is also important to recapture a few elements that could be replicated, such as the accusatory model that was used, the expeditiousness of the time limits, the indictment of the paradigmatic or representative cases in a universe of so many that would have been very difficult to prosecute within a short time span, and the criterion of authorship for those who ordered, from behind, the commission of aberrant crimes. These are all circumstances to consider in these kinds of processes.

4.3 The development of international law and its reception in Argentina

4.3.1 The consolidation of international rules

The 1990s were marked by an extraordinary impulse of international human rights law. In this period, the principles for which the international community had fought since Nuremberg were affirmed. Certainly, the actual incorporation of these ideas in the national legal systems and national court decisions will determine the real surroundings of the "transitional justice" process in different countries.

In the American context, the judgment of the Inter-American Court of Human Rights in the case of *Velásquez Rodríguez*[66] had great importance. In

65 The Commission literally declared: "A difficult problem that recent democracies have had to face has been the investigation of human rights violations under previous governments and the possibility of sanctions against those responsible for such violations. The Commission recognizes that this is a sensitive and extremely delicate issue where the contribution it—or any other international body for that matter—can make is minimal. The response, therefore, must come from the national sectors which are themselves affected, and the urgent need for national reconciliation and social pacification must be reconciled with the ineluctable exigencies of an understanding of the truth and of justice. Therefore, the Commission considers that the appropriate democratic institutions—usually the legislature—with the participation of all the representative sectors, are the only ones called upon to determine whether or not to decree an amnesty of the scope thereof, while amnesties decreed previously by those responsible for the violations has no juridical validity." See Inter-American Commission of Human Rights, *Annual Report 1985–1986*, OEA/Ser.L/V/II.68, Doc 8 rev 1, ch 5, available online at www.cidh.oas.org/annualrep/85.86eng/chap.5.htm.

66 IACtHR, *Velásquez Rodríguez v Honduras*, Series C No 4, Judgment of 29 July 1998.

interpreting Articles 1 and 2 of the American Convention on Human Rights, the Court established in a clear manner the obligation of states to prevent, investigate and sanction all human rights violations;[67] that impunity fails to conform to the duty of investigation;[68] and that this duty subsists while the uncertainty about the fate of the disappeared person remains.[69]

With regard to Argentina, the Inter-American Human Rights Commission approved Report no 28/92,[70] in which it considered numerous petitions from persons and organizations which had been put forth against the Laws of Final Stop, Due Obedience, and Pardon. The Commission concluded that these were incompatible with diverse regulations of the Convention since they deprived the victims of their right to obtain a judicial investigation destined to individualize and sanction those responsible, and recommended fair compensation as well as the adoption of necessary measures to clarify the crimes and individualize those who were responsible for human rights violations committed during the military dictatorship.[71]

Besides, the creation of the ad hoc International Criminal Tribunals for the Former Yugoslavia and Rwanda by the UN Security Council in 1993 and 1994 respectively also had an undeniable repercussion. Through the establishment of these tribunals, the international community indicated its commitment to prosecute and punish in an effective manner the war crimes and crimes against humanity that had been committed in these countries.[72] The establishment of the International Criminal Court culminated in the process of an old aspiration and implied an enormous step of transcendental significance in reaffirming that those behaviours, especially those considered to be grave crimes under international law, cannot be forgotten and must always be adjudicated. Even though the rules of the Rome Statute lack retroactive effects, their influence on international human rights law has been extraordinary insofar as for the first time the international community has specified in codified international law which behaviours are prohibited by international law, at least since the end of the Second World War. Finally, the UN Declaration concerning the Protection of All Persons against Enforced Disappearances (1992),[73] as well as the adoption of the Inter-American Convention concerning Enforced Disappearances of

67 IACtHR, *Velásquez Rodríguez v Honduras*, Series C No 4, Judgment of 29 July 1998, para 166.

68 IACtHR, *Velásquez Rodríguez v Honduras*, Series C No 4, Judgment of 29 July 1998, para 17.

69 IACtHR, *Velásquez Rodríguez v Honduras*, Series C No 4, Judgment of 29 July 1998, para 181.

70 Inter-American Commission on Human Rights, *Consuelo et al v Argentina*, Case Nos 10.147, 10.181, 10.240, 10.262, 10.309, 10.311, Report No 28/92, EA/Ser.L/V/II.83 Doc 14 at 41 (1993), 2 October 1992.

71 This last recommendation, which states "clarify" and "individualize", but not "sanction", was the origin of the development of the truth proceedings in Argentina.

72 Among the contributions of the statutes of these tribunals are their definitions of the concept of crimes against humanity.

73 See UN Declaration on the Protection of All Persons from Enforced Disappearances, UN Doc A/RES/47/133, adopted by the UN General Assembly on l8 December 1992. Also

Persons (1994),[74] incorporated into domestic law in Argentina with constitutional rank in 1997,[75] also contributed to the emerging context.

4.3.2 The influence in Argentina

In the 1990s, the ratification of the principal human rights conventions began to take effect both in Argentine law and in court decisions. In 1992, in the *Ekmedjian* case,[76] the Supreme Court showed that the rights established in international instruments were directly applicable, without any law having to regulate them. The constitutional reform in 1994 marked an essential advance for the human rights treaties. In particular, Article 75, section 22 came to enumerate the traditional universal and regional human rights conventions and recognized their constitutional rank. Furthermore, Congress also held that other human rights treaties could be granted a similar hierarchical place if two-thirds of their members agreed.

From this moment onwards, the Supreme Court considered that the opinions of those international organizations that apply such treaties must constitute an informative guide in the interpretation of their provisions.[77] The treaties thereby began to be increasingly used by the judges to form the base of their decisions or even to invalidate rules of domestic law.

In another important precedent,[78] the Supreme Court effected an extradition of a German ex-official, sustaining that crimes against humanity are subjected to principles of *ius cogens* and have never been prescribed, applying the Genocide Convention and that against prescription of war crimes and crimes against humanity. The crimes of appropriation of minors had been exempted from the benefits of the Law of Due Obedience. For this reason, in the case in which the commission of such crimes was being investigated, Videla and Massera were indicted as authors of orders that resulted in abductions. In December 1999, the Federal Appeals Court of the city of Buenos Aires upheld that international law prevails over domestic law and that crimes against humanity are not, by definition, prone to statutory limitations.

note the International Convention on the Protection of All Persons from Enforced Disappearances, UN Doc A/RES/61/177, adopted by the UN General Assembly on 20 December 2006. This Convention was approved in Argentina by Law no 26.298 adopted on 14 November 2007.

74 Inter-American Convention concerning Enforced Disappearances of Persons, adopted by the General Assembly to the Organization of American States on 6 September 1994.

75 Argentina ratified this Convention on 18 October 1995 (Law no 24.556) and incorporated it into its Constitution on 29 May 1997 (Law no 24.820).

76 A supposed application of the right to reply or to make a correction recognized in Art 14 of the American Convention, but not regulated in local law.

77 CSJN, Case No 32/9, *Horacio David Giroldi et al*, Sentencia (Decision) G.342.XXVI of 7 April 1995.

78 CSJN, Case No 16.063/94, *Priebke, Erich s/ solicitud de extradición*, Sentencia (Decision) of 2 November 1995. The case concerns the Italian extradition request of Erich Priebke who was charged for a massacre.

4.3.3 The right to truth without justice

It is today agreed in the international context that victims of massive human rights violations have the right to access justice (including the individualization of responsibility), to know the truth about what happened, as well as a right to integral reparation of damages, and that the first two rights are mutually complementary.[79] This means that the search for truth does not exclude the prosecution and sanction of those responsible.

This is not what happened in Argentina in the 1990s. Once the Laws of Full Stop, Due Obedience and Pardon had cancelled criminal prosecutions, the right to truth slowly began to take a foothold, disconnected from criminal sanction. In 1995, as a result of confessions from some repenting repressors,[80] which allowed the cherishing of hope to know something more about the destiny of the direct victims, families brought claims in order to open judicial proceedings that would permit them to have access to more information about the destiny suffered by their loved ones. After some hesitation about its scope of jurisdiction, the Federal Court of Appeals came to authorize the exhumations of the remains to permit their anthropological identification with the assistance of the Argentinean Anthropological Forensic Team.[81] The court finally established the obligation to uncover what had happened, as well as the right to grief and respect for the body.[82]

In adjudicating the cases of *Aguiar de Lapacó*[83] and *Urteaga*,[84] the Supreme Court affirmed the existence of the right to obtain information about what had

79 See UN Human Rights Commission, Resolution 2005/66, *Set of Principles for the Protection and Promotion of Human Rights Through Action to Combat Impunity*, E/CN.4/Sub.2/1997/20/ Rev.1 Annex II, 20 April 2005 and E/CN.4/2005/102/Add.1. See also Organization of American States, Resolution 2267/07, *Right to the Truth*, AG/RES.2267 (XXXVII-O/07), adopted by the OAS General Assembly on 5 June 2007.

80 Especially noteworthy is the public confession of the marine official Scilingo of having thrown from various airplanes living persons into the sea. His declarations provoked a natural turmoil since it was the first time that a repressor confessed such a horrendous crime.

81 The Federal Court of Appeals has worked with the identification of exhumed bodies, such as N N, with the help of the Anthropologic Forensic Team. In a work that has continued for more than 15 years and which has never faltered, the team has succeeded in identifying 70 bodies and in 51 cases the remains have been given to their families. Among the most known cases is the identification of the remains of Leonie Duquet, one of the founding mothers of the movement of the religious French, in the cemetery of Avellaneda, named *Masacre de Fátima*. See Cattani, H, "La llamada búsqueda de la verdad por los tribunales federales de la ciudad de Buenos Aires", *Lexis Nexis Revista de Derecho Penal*, vol 8, 2007, pp 1461 ff. As Cattani states: ". . . the giving of identity and the suppression of N.N. is the opposite to the monstrous anonymity of forced disappearances" (unofficial translation, p 1470).

82 See especially what was decided on 4 March and 10 July 1996 with regard to the search for the French nuns Alice Domon and Leonie Duquet. See also Corte Suprema de Justicia de la Nación, Case No 761, *ESMA Hechos que se denunciaron como ocurridos en el ámbito de la "Escuela de Mecánica de la Armada"*, Sentencia (Decision) of 29 September 1988.

83 CSJN, Case No 450, *Suárez Mason, Carlos Guillermo s/ homicidio, privación ilegal de la libertad, etc*, Sentencia (Decision) of 13 August 1998.

84 CSJN, Case No S.1085.XXXI, *Urteaga, Facundo Raúl c/ Estado Nacional—Estado*

happened through a judicial or administrative procedure unconnected from the criminal one, the object of which had been exhausted. Nevertheless, the case of *Aguiar de Lapacó* was declared admissible by the Inter-American Commission, which reached an amicable solution with Argentina in 1999.[85] According to the solution, the government must shoulder the obligation to exhaust all means to reveal the truth and to manage the adoption of legal norms that recognize the competences of the Federal Courts in the entire country, as well as the creation of an ad hoc body of prosecutors.

In the meantime, different federal courts reacted to the claims and opened "truth proceedings" in order to find out about the circumstances related to those who had disappeared and the location of the remains. These proceedings took place in La Plata, Córdoba and Bahía Blanca. During the proceedings, which were organized in an informal manner and included the organization of hearings, numerous testimonies were received and reports to public organs were delivered.

In 1998, Congress dictated Law no 24.954, which derogated the Laws of Full Stop and Due Obedience. Certainly, these Laws had already had effects. Thus, their derogation did not have retroactive effect. Nevertheless, the political and symbolic dimensions of the measure in question manifested that things were changing.

In the same period, as a result of the strong expansion of international human rights law, the universality principle to persecute crimes against humanity began to find reception in foreign legislation, or rather began to gain effective force. Human rights organizations thus effectuated denunciations outside the country and began to receive requests from foreign judges (Spain, Italy, France and Germany) who declared their courts as competent to prosecute the crimes of the dictatorship. Even the detentions of some repressors were requested for the purpose of extradition. The Government of President Fernando de la Rúa denied support for the extradition requests of the Argentineans[86] on the basis of the argument that the crimes committed on Argentine territory must be analyzed under the rules of domestic law and that this process could not be carried out in the country under foreign law. Nevertheless, it began to be more difficult to explain why Argentina did not exercise its jurisdictional competence or allowed others to do so, if there was agreement that these crimes always had to be prosecuted.

At last, on 6 March 2001, a federal judge of first instance did what had been missing,[87] by declaring unconstitutional and incurably null the Laws of Full

Mayor Conjunto de las FF.AA.—s/ amparo ley 16.986, Sentencia (Decision) of 15 October 1998.

85 Inter-American Commission on Human Rights, Report no 70/99, Case No 12.059, *Carmen Aguiar de Lapacó, Argentina*, 4 May 1999, available online at www.cidh.oas.org/annualrep/99eng/Admissible/Argentina12059.htm.

86 Decree no 1581/01 of 5 December 2001, *Boletín Oficial*, 17 December 2001.

87 See Juzgado Nacional en lo Criminal y Correccional Federal no 4 (National Court No 4 for

Stop and Due Obedience in the light of the rules of the human rights conventions and reopening the judicial investigations. The decision was confirmed shortly thereafter by the Buenos Aires Federal Appeals Court.

Eight days after this first case, the Inter-American Court of Human Rights delivered a judgment that had definitional effects in relation to the issue at hand. In the case known as *Barrios Altos*,[88] it pronounced that amnesty regulations were inadmissible, as were statutory limitations and all other laws impeding the investigation and sanction of those responsible for grave human rights violations. The laws of impunity and pardon were thus thrown away.

4.4 The reopening of all of the proceedings

4.4.1 *Another stage*

When the Government of President Kirchner came to power in 2003, several factors were favourable to the continuation of the process of justice in relation to the crimes of the dictatorship, which had been interrupted by the Laws of Full Stop, Due Obedience and Pardon. The international human rights treaties now had constitutional ranking, their rules were increasingly applied by the judges, the Supreme Court had affirmed the necessity of observing the decisions of international bodies monitoring treaty compliance, various foreign governments had requested the extradition of nationals to prosecute them abroad for crimes committed in Argentina, numerous truth proceedings were being conducted in the country and the victims, families and human rights organizations were not giving up their demands for justice.

All of these factors necessitated a final push in order to remove the legal obstacles that impeded the prosecution of the cases. The new president thus manifested a strong political commitment to initiate the reopening of the process in order to enable the prosecution and punishment of the authors of the human rights violations. In spite of not knowing of any antecedent in the field of defending human rights, in the years that he functioned as governor of a province, President Kirschner enabled the prosecution and punishment of crimes against humanity. It was one of the fundamental contributions of his governmental management.

In August 2003, Congress adopted two Laws of great importance: Law no 25.778, which accorded constitutional ranking to the International Convention on the Non-Applicability of Statutory Limitations to War Crimes and Crimes against Humanity,[89] and Law no 25.779, which annulled the Laws of Full Stop

Federal Criminal and Correctional Matters), Case No 8686/2000, *Simón, Julio, Del Cerro, Juan Antonio s/sustracción de menores de 10 anos*, Decision of 6 March 2001.

88 IACtHR, *Barrios Altos v Peru*, Series C No 75, Judgment of 14 March 2001.

89 Convention on the Non-Applicability of Statutory Limitations to War Crimes and Crimes against Humanity. UNGA Res 2391 (XXIII), 26 November 1968. As of 25 April 2011, it had 54 States Parties.

and Due Obedience.[90] Thus, in responding to petitions of victims and their families, several courts reopened the investigations in the cases they had and also initiated new ones, establishing the lack of legal validity of the Laws in question.

On 24 August 2004, the Supreme Court exhibited a new conclusion,[91] when deciding the case of *Arancibia Clavel*, which concerned a Chilean intelligence agent who had been charged for the murder of the Chilean Prats and his wife in the country. In this case, the Court considered that the crimes against humanity were not subject to statutory limitations in the light of the Convention concerning the non-statutory limitations of war crimes and crimes against humanity, and that the application of this Convention did not infringe upon the legality principle. The Court held that the crimes were already crimes against humanity according to a customary international law norm that existed prior to the commission of the crime and according to which crimes against humanity must always be prosecuted. In support of this interpretation, the Court cited as precedents the case of *Priebke*[92] and the cases *Velásquez Rodríguez*[93] and *Barrios Altos*[94] of the Inter-American Court.

Even though the case that was decided did not make any references to Argentinean law, the doctrine and arguments that were utilized were fully applicable, only waiting for a case in which the validity of the Amnesty Law would arrive to the Supreme Court. This happened on 14 June 2005, when the case of *Simón* would be settled.[95] In this case, the court pronounced the invalidity of the laws that impeded criminal prosecution. They were seen as violations of various human rights treaties ratified by Argentina, according to which no period of statutory limitations can be imposed for crimes against humanity, the crimes being unforgivable, and being in conflict with a customary international

90 Law no 25.779, *Declaranse insanablemente nulas las Leyes Nros. 23.492 y 23.52111*, 3 September 2003, *Boletín Oficial*, 3 September 2003. It is very questionable that Congress has powers to act in this manner since it gives legal effect to a norm the application of which to concrete cases is a function of the judges and not of the legislators. The adoption of this law revealed an evident political signal about the will of the government.

91 CSJN, Case No A.533.XXXVIII, *Arancibia Clavel, Enrique Lautaro s/ homicidio calificado y asociación ilícita y otros—causa no. 259*, Sentencia (Decision) of 24 August 2004. The government had initiated the dismissal of the judges who had been designated during the government of Carlos Menem, political judgment that prospered in Congress in some cases, while other judges renounced for fear of dismissal.

92 CSJN, Case No 16.063/94, *Priebke, Erich s/ solicitud de extradición*, Sentencia (Decision) of 2 November 1995.

93 IACtHR, *Velásquez Rodríguez v Honduras*, Series C No 4, Judgment of 29 July 1998.

94 IACtHR, *Barrios Altos v Peru*, Series C No 75, Judgment of 14 March 2001.

95 CSJN, Case No 17.768, *Simón, Julio Héctor y otros s/privación ilegítima de la libertad, etc*, Judgment of 15 June 2004. It concerned the case in which one had pronounced the nullity of laws in 2001. Jose Poblete and Gertrudis Hlaczik had been kidnapped together with their small daughter, Claudia, and brought to a clandestine centre known as "*El Olimpo*", where they were brutally tortured and then assassinated ("disappeared"). The case raised the paradox that the action for the parents was extinguished due to the amnesty, but in force for the daughter because it concerned a case of appropriation of minors.

law norm that requires the adjudication of such crimes without exception. To be sure, the Court was aided by the jurisprudence of the Inter-American Commission, the Inter-American Court and the UN Human Rights Committee as well as the Joinet report[96] and, finally, the Nuremberg Statute. The road towards the reopening of the proceedings was finally completed.[97]

4.4.2 *The difficulties of the present*

The new scenario brought about by the pronouncement of the Supreme Court on 14 June 2005 presented significant inconveniences with regard to the transmission of the files.

The proceedings that took place in the 1980s were transferred to the military jurisdiction and were unified in the seats of the commanders located within the different zones that had been determined for the purpose of the repression. The criterion of unification was the search for responsibility of those who had given the orders, and from there, towards direct authors. All of those files that existed throughout the country had been put into archives as a result of the legal sanction of pardons imposed to very different degrees. Thereafter, numerous "truth proceedings" were opened which, because of their peculiar nature, did not develop in an organic manner and neither were they attached to pre-determined rules. Finally, once it became clear that the Laws would be nullified, victims, families and human rights organizations presented new denunciations that were placed on top of the existing ones, or provoking the initiation of others.

The old scheme of Law no 23.049 is now incompatible with the Inter-American Convention on Forced Disappearances of Persons, as it precludes military jurisdiction for such crimes; it means that the applicable law is the domestic Code of Criminal Procedure. However, the complexity and multiplicity of crimes committed during the repression of terrorism does not find an adequate response to question the competences of the judges and the connection between the trials in Code as it has been designed to regulate proceedings concerning ordinary crimes. On the other hand, there is overwhelming agreement about the necessity of adopting a new federal system of prosecution, as

96 UN Commission on Human Rights, Sub-Commission on Prevention of Discrimination and Protection of Minorities, *The Administration of Justice and the Human Rights of Detainees. Question of the Impunity of the Perpetrators of Human Rights Violations (Civil and Political)*, Revised final report prepared by Mr Joinet pursuant to Sub-Commission decision 1996/119, E/CN.4/Sub.2/1985/16/Rev.1, 2 October 1997.

97 Evidently, the pardons of President Menem suffered the same fate as those invalidated by the Supreme Court by majority on the basis of the same foundations as in the case of *Mazzeo*. See SCJN, Case No M.2334.XLII, *Mazzeo, Julio Lilo y otros s/rec. de casación e inconstitucionalidad*, Judgment of 13 July 2007. The minority of the Supreme Court understood that the rule of unlimited prosecution must cede when in conflict with the principle of *res judicata*.

the current one, among other things, has revealed its futility in resolving, precisely, complex cases.[98]

As predicted, these circumstances led to problems and delays in the substantiation of the proceedings. In accordance with information from the organization that has worked most on this question—*Centro de Estudios Legales y Sociales*[99]—more than 200 investigations are currently underway in the country, out of which only 136 are moving at the moment or entail implicated persons. The cases involve 922 people out of which 358 have been brought to justice and 281 are conforming to preventive detention (100 of those in their homes because they are 70 years old and due to the existence of a norm authorizing this). Since the annulment of the Laws, only nine people have been convicted.[100]

In August 2007, the Office of the Public Prosecutor (*Ministerio Público Fiscal*), which created the Prosecutorial Unity for Co-ordination and Monitoring of the Cases of Violation of Human Rights during the Terrorism of the State (*Unidad Fiscal de Coordinación y Seguimiento de las Causas por violaciones a los Derechos Humanos cometidas durante el terrorismo de estado*), thus, co-ordinating and monitoring the investigations in focus,[101] presented a report outlining the factors causing delays in processing the cases.[102] The major factor is related to defects in the system of prosecution as it admits the continuous interposition of appeals, exceptions and considerations, prolonging the prospects of judgment in the cases. On 3 March 2008, the Office of the Public Prosecutor dictated Resolution 13/08 for the purpose of ensuring that the prosecutors would request the elevation of sentences in the cases with solid grounds.[103]

The absence of norms related to questions of how to group the different investigations increases the risk of atomizing them with the consequent corrosion of human and material resources. The absence of such norms also affects the victims who find themselves obliged to give declarations in multiple cases and before several instances (in the preliminary investigations and in the

98 The same government designed a commission that elaborated a draft Code of Criminal Procedure, which reflected more modern tendencies with regard to the accusatorial model, and which contemplated mechanisms to avoid, as now happens, the preliminary investigations being substituted for the actual trials.

99 More information about the Centro de Estudios Legales y Sociales (CELS) is available online at www.cels.org.ar.

100 Five of them in the same case, the rest in individual trials.

101 Ministerio Publico Fiscal, Procurador General de la Nación, Resolution PGN 14/07, 1 March 2007. Available online at www.mpf.gov.ar.

102 Ministerio Público Fiscal, Unidad Fiscal de Coordinación y Seguimiento de las Causas por violaciones a los Derechos Humanos cometidas durante el terrorismo de estado, *Informe general sobre los primeros problemas detectados para el avance de las causas*, August 2007, available online at www.mpf.gov.ar/Institucional/UnidadesFE/1-Informe-general-sobre-los-primeros-problemas-detectados-para-el-avance-de-las-causas-DDHH-Agosto-2007.pdf.

103 Ministerio Público Fiscal, Procuración General de la Nación, Resolución PGN 13/07, 3 March 2008. Available online at www.mpf.gov.ar.

trials), with the emotional burden that this implies. A possible solution to the delays and the dispersion of cases is now under consideration in the Senate. Also under consideration is the possibility of dictating a set of procedural norms for these cases that would be sensitive to their special characteristics.[104]

One issue of special importance is the protection of witnesses. On 19 September 2006, when the conviction against Miguel Etchecolatz was under way, Julio López, a survivor from a clandestine centre and one of the prosecution witnesses, disappeared. He is yet to be found. On 22 May 2007, President Kirschner created the Programme for Truth and Justice (*Programa Verdad y Justicia*).[105] The programme had to compose within a brief period of time a map outlining the risks facing the witnesses and to propose a plan for their protection, as well as co-ordinate the monitoring of the proceedings with the Office of the Public Prosecutor and judicial authorities.

On various occasions, the government has held the judges responsible for the delays in processing the cases,[106] although it does not seem to be the result of a deliberate action on their part. Rather, the delays reveal the complexities mentioned and the absence of public policies designed to resolve these difficulties.

4.5 Conclusion

Argentina is a country that has gone through all of the possible stages in the settlement of accounts with the past. It began with truth and justice, thereafter followed a stance of oblivion and impunity, then truth returned and opened a door and today there is a wish to finalize the road that began with both truth and justice. A decisive factor in this path has been the evolution of the norms of international law, the decisions of its organs and their application within the Argentinean legal system. In addition, human rights organizations have been active in defending the victims, and their families have not permitted that impunity would close the grimmest chapter in the history of the country.

104 There is a draft law in the Senate, elaborated by two of the judges who convicted the commanders, who, in response to the foundation that there is no acquired right to be tried in accordance with determined rules as long as the new ones respect the right of defence, introduces modifications to the procedure so that the causes unify according to clandestine centre, unify the representation of the indemnified, determine the defences, and the exceptions in the instructions are considered only one time, disposing of the move to trial when the procedure is fixed, etc.

105 Jefatura de Gabinete de Ministerios, Decree no 606/07, 22 May 2007, *Boletín Oficial* no 31/163, 28 May 2007, creating the Programme on Truth and Justice. For the structural organization of the Programme on Truth and Justice, see Jefatura de Gabinete de Ministerios, Decree no 851/2007 PEN, *Boletín Oficial* no 31.191, 6 July 2007.

106 Ex President Nelson Kirschner has accused in public discourse the *Cámara Nacional de Casación Penal* (National Chamber, Appellate Division) for the delays suffered in processing the cases related to human rights violations.

International human rights conventions and, especially, their interpretations put forth by the international organs assigned to apply them, have developed a kind of "canon". According to this canon, there exists an international customary rule, with the character of *ius cogens*, that is, being imperative for all states. This norm stipulates that the crimes against humanity and war crimes must always be prosecuted. There is no excusing condition in domestic law to avoid prosecuting these crimes, whether statutory limitations, amnesties or the legality principle. Certainly, this stance requires a different and flexible approach in international law to the legality principle, an issue that is a source of polemics and debate.[107] With some special features, Argentine courts have begun to apply this "canon" when reopening the cases concerning the crimes of the military dictatorship.[108]

The Argentinean experience has revealed that it is not enough to invoke the validity of the aforementioned international legal obligations. What is essential is an integrated strategy of the state in order to move the processes forward within a useful time period preserving the rights of the accused, the victims and society. For this, it is imperative to organize the human and material resources, to identify the problems and the obstacles, to establish effective programmes for the protection of witnesses, and, if necessary, also of court officials. In situations of massive human rights violations, it is indispensable to establish a database in which the victims' testimonies are registered in such a way that one can cross-reference information between the different cases.

Even if the entire criminal justice process could be said to affirm values that the norms entail and that all condemnations symbolize the repudiation of the community of behaviour that is sanctioned by law, in the case of especially grave crimes, such as crimes against humanity, the perfection of the processes and the condemnations of those responsible entail an added value since it contributes to the formation of a moral conscience in a society. This obliges us to take extreme precaution in order to ensure that the processes are unobjectionable.

107 The discussion as to whether the Nuremberg process infringed upon the principle of legality is well known. See Jimenez de Asua, L, *Tratado de Derecho Penal*, vol II, Buenos Aires: Losada, 1950, p 469. For a strict interpretation of its scope, see Gil Gil, A, *Derecho penal internacional*, Madrid: Tecnos, 1999, pp 66 ff.

108 Even if the international legal categories of crimes have not been applied directly, but rather the categories of common law, the international rules regarding prosecution have indeed been applied in a direct manner. See Malarino, E, *Persecución Penal Nacional de Crímenes Internacionales en América Latina y en España*, Montevideo: Fundación Konrad Adenauer Stiftung, 2003, pp 35 ff.

5 Chilean transitional justice and the legacy of the de facto regime

Roberto Garretón

5.1 Preliminary clarifications

A proper inquiry into the role of national courts in the Chilean process of transition cannot be done without a prior consideration of how they functioned during the dictatorship. Furthermore, such inquiry must consider the political dimension not only of the massive human rights violations that took place, but also of the processes of transition themselves. The political dimension is of special importance when assessing the Chilean case, as the national courts constituted a fundamental legitimizing element of the de facto regime. In addition, it is essential to afford special attention to the role of the Supreme Court in relation to the other components of the national judicial branch. Thus, it would be a mistake to maintain an exclusive focus on the actions of the judges in the field of criminal justice.

In Chile, the hierarchical relations that prevail between the different courts and judges have always been absolute and, given the character of the de facto regime, this reality was even more accentuated during the dictatorship. In this light, it is not of great importance to examine what a judge of lower rank does or even the courts of appeal. On the few occasions during the dictatorship in which the Chilean courts dictated a judicial settlement in favour of human rights protection, both the human rights lawyers and the lawyers of the dictatorship always interposed a variety of appeals in order to arrive finally at the highest instance, even in cases involving procedural matters of apparently minor importance. For this reason, when this chapter refers to "judges", it basically refers to those judges who belong to the highest authority in the Chilean judicial system.

The control exerted by the Chilean Supreme Court over lower courts is manifested in terms of its influence in cases before lower courts as well as the exercise of its disciplinary power granted to it by the Chilean Constitutions of 1925[1] and 1980.[2] The disciplinary power bestowed to the Supreme Court

1 Constitución Política de la República de Chile, 18 September 1925, Art 72.4.

2 Constitución Política de la República de Chile, 8 August 1980, Art 32.15.

enables it to consider complaint appeals—theoretically delimited to disciplinary matters—and authorizes it to annul and revise judicial settlements contested by the lower courts.[3] Also of relevance in this context is the existence of a system of annual assessment of judges, abusively employed by the Supreme Court during the dictatorship in order to reprimand judges who had demonstrated allegiance to President Allende's government. Later on this system was used against the judges who tried to exercise human rights protective functions and to fight against the impunity of human rights violations. The system of annual assessment of judges weakened their independence in criminal cases and the magistrates on the courts of appeal.

Besides the importance of considering the function of the courts during the dictatorship, it is equally important to bring into the limelight the characteristics of the human rights violations that were committed in the 1960s until the end of the 1990s in the Latin American region. These violations cannot be understood as isolated loathsome events, nor as the occasional manifestations of the brutality of a cruel and ambitious dictator, but rather as amounting to *systematic* attacks on human rights. The violations in question were the result of the conscientious exercise of repressive policies designed by the state and included a guarantee of impunity for their executioners. Furthermore, the violations were also *institutional* inasmuch as the entire state structure participated in the enforcement of the repressive policies designed to impose a specific political project: not only the executive power, but also the legislative and judicial branches participated, as well as public accountants, the military, the police, the prisons, the diplomatic corps, the public organs of communication, the financial power, businesses, labour unions, etc. Additionally, given the number of victims of political assassinations, enforced disappearances, torture, and other cruel, inhuman or degrading treatment, forced exiles, arbitrary detention, etc, the transgressions must also be classified as *massive*. The policies in question were also *integral* in nature as they violated absolutely all human rights: civil, cultural, economic, political and social. Finally, they must also be understood as *permanent* since they were committed from the very first until the very last day of the dictatorship. In Chile, their institutional character of the violations under consideration is reflected, above all, in the role of the judicial branch.

3 Código Orgánico de Tribunales (Organic Code on Tribunals), 9 July 1943, Art 548, s 2 in force in this period. According to this provision, the admission of an appeal (against the judges) "will include the considerations that demonstrate the faults or abuse, or the manifest and grave errors or omissions that *constitute and which exist in the resolution that motivates the appeal, will determine the measures conducive for remedying such fault or abuse* and can decide that one may give an account of the background to the tribunal in plenum for the disciplinary effects that proceeds" (emphasis added) (unofficial translation).

5.2 The judicial power during the dictatorship

The first legislative act of the de facto regime in Chile was law decree no 1 of 11 September 1973, which established the government of the military junta. Its third provision stipulated:

> The Junta, in exercising its mission, shall guarantee the full efficacy of the terms of reference of the Judicial Power and shall respect the Constitution and the laws of the Republic, to the extent that the current situation in the country permits it for the best compliance with the postulates that it advances.[4]

The initial reaction of the Supreme Court showed that it had apparently only read the first part of the clause. In a surprising declaration of its president the following day on 12 September, while the governmental palace was still burning, he stated:

> In recognition of the proposition of the new Government to respect and guarantee compliance with the decisions of the Judicial Branch without any prior review of their legality . . . it thereby manifests publicly its intimate complacency in the name of the Administration of Justice in Chile, and hopes that the Judicial Branch complies with its duty, as it has until now.[5]

On the subsequent day, all members of the Court ratified this declaration. Thereafter, its members were picked up from their homes and brought to the Palace of the Courts in a microbus of the executive branch, and carefully guarded by military personnel. The judges were not cautious enough to note that the complete text of the provision stated that the government would "respect the Constitution and the laws of the Republic, to the extent that the current situation in the country permits it and for the best compliance with the postulates that it [the military junta] advances".[6]

The text is fundamental to understand the real goals of the authors of the break with institutional democracy as it clearly established the pre-eminence of "the postulates that are advanced" by the military junta with regard to the Constitution, the laws and the terms of reference of the judicial branch.

Against this background, it becomes clear why Chile is one of the very few countries in Latin America in which the de facto authorities following a military *coup d'état*, with a clear fascist content, did not remove the sitting judges from

4 Decreto Ley no 1—Santiago de Chile, *Acta de Constitución de la Junta del Gobierno*, 11 September 1973, *Diario Oficial* no 28.563, 18 September 1973, para 3 (unofficial translation).

5 See Editorial Jurídica de Chile, *Antecedentes Histórico-Jurídicos: Años 1972–1973*, Chile: Editorial Andres Bello, 1980, p 177 (unofficial translation).

6 Decreto Ley no 1 of 11 September 1973, para 3 (unofficial translation).

the Supreme Court as has been the convention in the history of this region: since a new judge would not be more obedient, the sitting ones remained on the bench. The Court made no reference to the state of war, the state of siege or the state of emergency, which had all been declared by the de facto regime simultaneously, nor to the executions without trial that had already taken place, nor to the concentration camps that were in full operation.

From the moment of the *coup d'état* and onwards, the military regime adopted several legislative measures that went in the following directions and affected the actions of the judges:

First of all, competences were transferred from ordinary justice to military justice. Given the disavowed participation of army officers in the atrocities committed within the first minutes of political disturbances, the military tribunals always reclaimed for themselves the competence of judgment and sanction of these crimes, which has been the common cause for impunity. At the same time, from this moment on, all of the crimes classically known as political and contemplated in the *Ley de Seguridad del Estado* (Law of Security of State)[7] and *Ley de Control de Armas y Explosivos* (Law of Control of Arms and Explosives)[8] were removed from common jurisdiction.

Secondly, military justice was substituted in times of peace for military justice in times of war. The latter was set up by six army officers without any legal advisers and one military lawyer, thereby leaving all those subjected to proceedings in a situation without any possibility of defending themselves whatsoever.[9] In 1974, international pressure led to the partial re-establishment of military justice in times of peace. None of these tribunals ever brought an army officer before justice for human rights violations.

Thirdly, the sanctions for political crimes committed by opponents increased and resulted in numerous convictions sentencing them to death.

Fourthly, there was a permanent recourse to the "reinforced" and "powerful" state of exception clauses, to use the expression of the dictator. The clauses impeded the theoretical role of the judges in terms of protecting human rights and liberties, thereby permitting detentions, expulsions from the country, or the relegation of dissidents without any trial of any sort. The Supreme Court systematically rejected more than 10,000 *habeas corpus* actions submitted during the dictatorship, in Chile known as writ of *amparo*,[10] destined to obtain the

7 Ley no 12.927 de Seguridad del Estado, as updated by Decreto no 890 of 9 July 1975, *Diario Oficial* no 29.239, 26 August 1975.

8 Ley no 17.798 de Control de Armas y Explosivos, 21 October 1972, *Diario Oficial* no 28.383, 21 October 1975.

9 But note the clear wording of the Constitution of 1925, Art 86, s 1, held to be in force at the time and according to which "the Supreme Court has the directive, correctional and economic superintendence over *all courts of the Nation*, in agreement with the law that determines its organization and powers" (emphasis added) (unofficial translation). Nonetheless, the Supreme Court repeatedly declared that this norm did not govern in times of war.

10 *Amparo* is applied in several Latin American countries as well as Spain and refers to

liberty or respect for procedural guarantees of a detainee,[11] and admitted in the first instance to the Appeals Court. If the report of the detention authority stated that the person was not in detention, the *habeas corpus* action was rejected precisely for this reason without ever finding out if the petitioner actually was detained. If, in contrast, the report stated that the person was indeed detained, the action was nevertheless rejected because in states of exception, the detention authority is not required to justify the deprivations of liberty that it enforced. In this manner, *incommunicado* detentions were legitimized and authorized by laws that regulated exceptional situations. Even in the case of detaining 14-year-old children, the Supreme Court upheld the norms concerning states of exception over those related to the protection of minors. It was precisely the lack of judicial action that was the major cause for the phenomenon of enforced disappearances of persons in Chile.

Fifthly, impunity for human rights violations was guaranteed. In the initial stages of the dictatorship, it was secured de facto and as from 1978 through an amnesty law decree.[12] That year, the US Government requested the handing over of an American on the basis of collected evidence indicating that this person had presumably participated in the assassination of Orlando Letelier, former Chilean Minister of Foreign Affairs (in the period of President Allende), committed in Washington DC 17 months before. Responding to the fear among the "young officials" that they would face the same fate as the American, Pinochet dictated an amnesty law. This law, far from seeking national unity, as stated in its preamble, was intended to ensure the agents that also their future crimes would be covered by new amnesties.

A first effort of the human rights defenders to react against the deplorable situation consisted of seeking to convince the civil courts that military tribunals were not competent to prosecute crimes such as murders, torture and kidnapping, as such crimes could in no case be considered "crimes committed while in service". In this manner, the human rights defenders relied upon Article 5 of the Code of Military Justice, according to which: "It corresponds to the military jurisdiction to admit: (3) the cases involving ordinary crimes committed by army officers during the state of war,[13] when carrying out their

the ability of individuals to challenge government action in violation of constitutional rights.

11 The constitutional guarantees of detainees were recognized in the democratic Constitution of 1925 (Art 16) and in essence maintained in the Constitution imposed by Pinochet in 1980, still in force (Art 23).

12 Decreto Ley no 2191, concede amnistía a las personas que indica por los delitos que señala, 18 April 1978, *Diario Oficial* no 30.042, 19 April 1978.

13 According to law decrees nos 3, 5, 8 and 640, the "state of war" was in force between 11 September 1973 and 11 September 1974. See Decreto Ley No 1 of 11 September 1973; Decreto Ley No 3 of 11 September 1973, *Diario Oficial* no 28.653, 18 September 1973; Decreto Ley no 8 of 12 September 1973, published in the official newspaper on 12 September 1973; and Decreto Ley no 640 of 2 September 1974, *Diario Oficial* no 28.950, 10 September 1974.

missions, *when acting in military service or in connection to it*, in the barracks, camps . . . ."[14]

However, the Supreme Court never accepted this line of argumentation, deciding instead that *all* matters related to competence fell under military jurisdiction. That being said, the truth is that the behaviour of the judges of criminal justice—with the backing of the Supreme Court—did not differ much in their actions when compared with those of military justice. Neither did the former have an interest in investigating the crimes, declining instead their competences to the benefit of military tribunals and, from the time of the adoption of the amnesty law decree, suspending as well the complaints in a final and immediate manner without even finding out if the crime had been committed. On the other hand, judges of criminal justice at least seemed more likely to react positively in terms of assuming errands that military tribunals were rejecting. Thus, there was some hope of future change.

From the time of the adoption of Amnesty Law no 2.191 on 18 October 1978,[15] the Appeals Courts and the Supreme Court came to immediately and definitively close each case as a result of the Amnesty Law. Very rarely some reasoning was admitted, and the few times that it happened, the judges maintained that the crime of kidnapping had been consummated and exhausted at the time of the arrest even if the kidnapped persons never appeared again.[16] However, according to unanimous doctrine, the term "enforced disappearance" fundamentally refers to the crime of kidnapping, an arbitrary deprivation of liberty committed by state agents. As such, the crime is not limited to the time of its instant execution, but is realized on a permanent basis. In other words, the crime continues as long as the delinquent does not end his criminal activity and, so, also after the date of the adoption of the Amnesty Law.

Furthermore, the lawyers of the victims argued that since the Amnesty Law grants amnesty to "the authors, accomplices and hiders" of the kidnappings, murders, acts of torture and other crimes, it is *subjective*, which means that it can only be applied once it has been determined who the authors, accomplices and hiders are. Even so, contrary to the text of the law, the courts declared that the amnesty is *objective* in the sense that it applies to the crime—the kidnapping—and not in relation to the authors, accomplices and hiders. Another

14 Código de Justicia Militar, S. 2. 3336, Santiago, 19 December 1944. The code was most recently reformed by Law 20.084 of 7 December 2005.

15 The text grants amnesty "to all persons who, in quality of authors, accomplices, or co-participants, have incurred in delinquent activities, while the State of War was in force, between 11 September 1973 and 10 March 1978, as long as they do not already currently find themselves subjected to processes or condemned" (unofficial translation).

16 The most well-reasoned and well-known judgment pronounced by the Supreme Court in the recently recuperated democracy was delivered on 24 August 1990. It entails all of its own lines of argument as well as those of inferior judges or courts, many times contradictory. See Corte Suprema de Justicia de Chile, case of *recurso de inaplicabilidad por inconstitucionalidad deducido por Alfonso Insunza Bascuñán, en causa rol 553-78 de la Segunda Fiscalía del Juzgado Militar de Santiago*, Judgment of 24 August 1990.

kind of argument invoked by the defenders of the affected families was that, if the dictatorship maintained that there was a "war" in Chile, the laws of war must be fully applicable, especially the four Geneva Conventions of 1949, which had been in force in Chile since 1952. These Conventions govern not only armed conflicts between two or more contracting parties, but also those without international character, occurring in one of their contracting parties. However, once more, the Court dodged all of the reasoning and upheld that the amnesty must be applied either on the basis of the sheer conviction that it must be so,[17] or because the acts in question being covered by the amnesty: "it becomes unnecessary [for the Court] to examine further the legal regulations and the treaties that were denounced as having been violated". Finally, the Court concluded that the Geneva Conventions did not govern because in Chile there was no war, but only a "state of war".[18]

The alleged incompatibility between the Chilean Amnesty Law and international human rights law, principally the International Covenant on Civil and Political Rights[19] whose instruments of ratification had been deposited by the overthrown constitutional government back in 1972 was rejected by the courts, upholding that the Covenant was not in force in Chile since it had not been published, a requirement invented by the regime precisely to ensure that it would not be applied. This formal requirement did not exist at the time of signing the Covenant, nor when Congress approved it or at the time of depositing the instrument of ratification.

In this light, one may ponder the lapidary judgment of the National Commission of Truth and Reconciliation (NCTR),[20] according to which "the

17 In 1978, the remains of 15 peasants who had been detained in October 1973 and buried alive in some abandoned lime mine ovens in the rural town of Lonquén were found. The investigation of a brave civil judge (Judge of the Court of Santiago, who also years later condemned the assassination of Orlando Letelier) individualized and processed the authors, accomplices and co-participants, but declined the competence of his court in favour of the military tribunals in the case; the latter obviously only applied the amnesty law, and their rulings were confirmed by the Supreme Court. See Corte Suprema de Justicia, decision of 24 August 1990.

18 Corte Suprema de Justicia, decision of 24 August 1990.

19 International Covenant on Civil and Political Rights, UNGA Res 2200A (XXI), adopted on 16 December 1996.

20 One of the first actions of President Aylwin was to create the Chilean National Commission on Truth and Reconciliation (NCTR), destined to investigate and release a report on the gravest human rights violations covering "the situations of the detainees, the disappeared, the tortured with death as result, which generate the moral responsibility of the State for acts of its agents or persons in its service, as well as the kidnappers, and the attacks against the life of persons committed by private individuals with political pretext", Supreme Decree no 355 of 25 April 1990, *Diario Oficial* no 33665, 5 September 1990, Art 1. The excellent work culminated in a report presented by the Commission to the President of the Republic on 8 February 1991 and circulated one month later, which was known as the "Rettig report" because of the name of its President, Raúl Rettig. See NCTR, *Report*, vol 1, pt 1, handed over by the Commission to the former President Aylwin on 8 February, p 107. The re-edition published in Santiago by *Corporación Nacional de Reparación*

judicial branch did not respond vigorously enough to human rights violations",[21] and adding that "the country was surprised to see the courts take such a stance, for it was accustomed to regard the judiciary as a staunch defender of the rule of law".[22] Thus, the Commission censored the political legitimization of the regime exercised by the President of the Supreme Court when he stated in his inaugural speech of the judicial year in March 1975 that:

> Chile, which is not a land of barbarians, as it has come to be perceived abroad, by bad Chileans or foreign individuals who align with a politics of interest, has conscientiously conformed to these rights. When it comes to torture and other atrocities, I can affirm that here there are no thick walls or iron curtains and whatever affirmation to the contrary is due to a proselytizing press of ideas that could not or will not prosper in our country.[23]

5.3 The judicial power and the transition to democracy

The Chilean transition can be divided into two periods: "before" and "after" 16 October 1998. The latter is the day when the former dictator was arrested in London.

5.3.1 From 11 March 1990 until 15 October 1998

During the first years of transition, absolutely nothing changed. In general terms, in spite of the democratic restoration, the courts continued to consecrate impunity. Reflecting this fact was the harsh response of the Supreme Court to the NCTR report. In a document infested by excuses, ambiguities, errors and falsities, the court qualified the report as "a flagrant attack on the norms that regulate the principal institutions of the State and on the sound equilibrium that the constituent carefully has established between them".[24] The court also

y Reconciliación, 1996 is available online at www.ddhh.gov.cl/ddhh_rettig.html. The report has been translated into English by the US Institute for Peace (USIP). See USIP, *Report of the Chilean National Commission on Truth and Reconciliation*, Notre Dame, Indiana: University of Notre Dame Press, 1993, available online at www.usip.org/files/resources/collections/truth_commissions/Chile90-Report/Chile90-Report.pdf.

21 See NCTR Report (Spanish Version), vol 1, pt 1, p 85; and USIP, NCTR Report (English version), p 140.

22 See NCTR Report (Spanish version), p 86; and NCTR Report (English version), p 141.

23 President of the Supreme Court, Inaugural speech of the judicial year on 1 March 1975, when tribunals and courts of the entire country, including the Supreme Court, had ruled in relation to nearly 1,000 *habeas corpus* appeals as well as denunciations of assassinations and disappearances. See NCTR Report (Spanish version), p 86; and NCTR Report (English version), p 141.

24 See Corte Suprema de Justicia, "Respuesta de la Corte Suprema al Informe de la Comisión Nacional de Verdad y Reconciliación", 13 May 1991, *Estudios Públicos*, vol 42, 1991 (unofficial translation), p 244.

added that the criticisms set forth in the report were "tainted with political passion that is principally based on subjective perceptions that go to the extreme in terms of attributing intentions and imagining a tacit consensus between the judges and administrative authorities, a kind of deceitful complicity directed to protect abuses of the liberty and integrity of persons".[25]

Not even the incorporation into Chilean law—at a constitutional level—of the international and Inter-American human rights instruments changed the nationalist convictions of the judges. The courts systematically refused to apply the formally incorporated norms in spite of the constitutional mandate recognized in the constitutional reform that explicitly made them governing instruments in Chile.[26]

Furthermore, the military justice system continued to reclaim for itself all of the cases in process and involving human rights violations; the Supreme Court continued to resolve questions of competence irremediably in its favour, in whose seat, also in an irremediable manner, the cases ended with the argument that nothing is proved, or by the declaration of suspension by virtue of the Amnesty Law, which in turn was confirmed by the Martial Court (*Corte Marcial*) and finally by the Supreme Court.

A remarkable example of the Supreme Court's open rejection of the laws emanating from the new democratic authorities[27] was its acceptance of what is best understood as an authentic act of rebellion of the military justice system in reaction to a legal modification that formally removed from the sphere of military jurisdiction the investigation and prosecution of the crime of insult committed by civilians against the armed forces. The judges with military jurisdiction continued to initiate proceedings against political leaders, journalists and human rights lawyers for having made declarations or expressed opinions that were not favourable to the armed forces or which questioned the atrocities of the dictatorship. However, since the legal modification hindered them from classifying such acts as crimes of insult against the armed forces, in the examination of such cases, they held that such declarations or opinions did not amount to crimes of insult, but rather of sedition,[28] to which a penalty

25 Corte Suprema de Justicia, fn 24 above, p 239.

26 The Constitution of 1980 (original text) only declared that: "The exercise of sovereignty recognizes as a limitation the respect for the essential rights that emanate from human nature" (Art 5). The constitutional reform agreed upon by democratic parties following the referendum that ended the perpetuity of Pinochet's aspirations, incorporated in an explicit manner the international human rights treaties into the Constitution. The new second part of Art 5 reaffirms that: "The exercise of sovereignty recognizes as limitation the respect for the essential rights that emanate from human nature", and adds that: "It is the duty of the organs of the State to respect and promote such rights, as guaranteed by this Constitution as well as international treaties ratified by Chile and which are in force."

27 During the dictatorship, the Supreme Court experienced an intergenerational change of its members so that at the moment of transition Pinochet had appointed all of them.

28 Until 2005, Art 276 of the Code of Military Justice of 19 December 1944 defined the crime of sedition as inducing "whatever riot or disorder, by word, by writing, or making

consisting of 61 days' to five years' imprisonment was attached. The Supreme Court legitimized this abuse by recognizing that the military tribunals indeed had the competence to rule in the latter cases.

Neither did the civil courts receive the democratic message from the citizens, but preferred instead to associate themselves with the more ambiguous President Aylwin, who maintained that what mattered was to establish the truth of what had happened during the dictatorship, but that justice could only be done "to the extent possible". His thesis thus realigned itself with the idea that the courts could apply the Amnesty Law decree provided that the crimes and their authors had been identified. As a result, the outcome in the cases under consideration and in the hands of the civil courts was in general the same as for those subjected to military court proceedings, save some relevant exceptions.

Toward the mid-1990s, there are some first positive decisions isolated from a few old civil judges who were now accompanied by new colleagues who had entered the judicial system as a result of intergenerational changes. Because of the controversial constitutional modification, it became possible partly to clean up the Supreme Court, although it had a price: giving to "Pinochetismo" an unprecedented right of veto upon the nomination of its judges. This "right" has actually been exercised. It was in this way that those responsible for the crimes in the cases of the *degollados*[29]—committed after the adoption of the Amnesty Law[30]—and of *Orlando Letelier*,[31] were convicted and thereafter ended up being exempted from criminal responsibility once snatched by military justice. There are a few more honouring settlements, although within a few days of a positive sentence, the Supreme Court would deliver a contrary ruling.

On 9 September 1998, the Supreme Court declared that the disappearance of Pedro Poblete Córdoba in July 1974 happened at a time when the state of war exception was in force, which meant that the four Geneva Conventions of 1949 were applicable, and these Conventions do not admit amnesties in case of grave infringements of their rules.[32]

The author of this chapter prepared a report (an *affidavit*) and sent it to the House of Lords in the United Kingdom in January 1999 holding that Pinochet

use of whatever other means, or making known to the troop groups destined to cause them displeasure or tepidness in service or gossiping . . ." (unofficial translation). The provision was derogated by Law 2008 of 7 December 2005. The thesis of the military and the Supreme Court was that objectionable opinions were destined to cause displeasure or tepidness in service.

29 Three opponents, one of whom was a sociologist of the *Vicaría de la Solidaridad* and work colleague of the author of this chapter, were detained and assassinated (beheaded) by the police of the regime in 1985. In 1994, 16 officials of the civil guard, including two colonels, were convicted for this crime, some to life imprisonment.

30 Corte Suprema de Justicia, case of *Degollado*, fallo definitivo (27-10-95), Judgment of 27 October 1995.

31 Corte Suprema de Justicia, case of *Orlando Letelier*, Judgment of 24 August 1990.

32 Corte Suprema de Justicia, case of *Pedro Poblete Córdoba*, Judgment of 9 September 1998.

could not, as a matter of fact, be prosecuted in Chile.[33] While there were no formal legal obstacles that would bar action by the Chilean territorial courts, the affidavit stressed the reality of the political dimension of the courts; since the time of the "intimate complacency with the propositions" of the Government of the Junta, very little had changed. According to the affidavit, the Supreme Court's judgment in the case of *Poblete Córdoba*[34] was an exception given that it had constantly applied the amnesty to close investigations in previous cases. From this perspective, the judgment did not indicate a significant change in terms of the application of the self-amnesty law. Also, in accordance with Chilean legislation, the judgment of the Supreme Court is valid only in relation to the case in question, and does not constitute a mandatory precedent. The appalling tendencies of the Chilean courts have been to apply the Amnesty Law decree without making any references to international law, although there are different opinions about the value of international norms in the judiciary. Furthermore, since the settlement in the case of *Poblete Córdoba*,[35] the Supreme Court has confirmed the suspension (closure) of four cases of disappearances and in conformity with the amnesty as decided by the Martial Court. These cases are *Ziede Gómez*;[36] *López Stewart, Enríquez Espinosa, Eltit Contreras, Acuña Reyes*;[37] *Martínez Hernández*;[38] and *Quiñones Lembach*.[39] The judgments in each of these cases indicate a return to the traditional previous interpretative doctrine as proposed by President Aylwin and, thus, evince a clear contradiction with the reasoning adopted in the case of *Poblete Córdoba*. The Court affirmed in these four cases that it is unnecessary to complete a criminal investigation before applying the amnesty. It also denied the applicability of the Geneva Conventions and the International Covenant on Civil and Political Rights.

33 Human Rights Watch, an international NGO, integrated into a group of organizations—led by Amnesty International—admitted as party in the appeal against the judgment of the Superior Court of London which admitted a *habeas corpus* action before the House of Lords. It requested a legal report concerning the juridical impossibility that the former dictator and at that time lifetime senator in Chile, Augusto Pinochet, would be tried in Chile. The undersigned refuted the task in the proposed terms because in reality there was no *legal* obstacle that hindered Chilean courts to bring him to justice, although political ones did exist. This is how the report was understood.

34 Corte Suprema de Justicia, case of *Pedro Poblete Córdoba*, no 469-98, Judgment of 9 September 1998.

35 Corte Suprema de Justicia, case of *Pedro Poblete Córdoba*, no 469-98, Judgment of 9 September 1998.

36 Corte Suprema de Justicia, case of *Ziede Gómez*, no 293-97, Judgment of 16 September 1998.

37 Corte Suprema de Justicia, case of *López Stewart, Enríquez Espinosa, Eltit Contreras, Acuña Reyes*, no 564-95, Judgment of 13 October 1998.

38 Corte Suprema de Justicia, case of *Martínez Hernández*, no 477-97, Judgment of 11 November 1998.

39 Corte Suprema de Justicia, case of *Quiñones Lembach* (file number and date unknown).

5.3.2 From 16 October 1998 onwards

Chile changed on 16 October 1998, the day on which the former dictator was detained in London as a result of having been accused by the Spanish criminal justice for crimes against humanity, genocide, torture and terrorism. Until that moment, the official discourse of the political elite had been that the country had already reconciled; that the transition had been successful; and that Chileans lived in a democracy (which, of course, could be perfected as can all democracies); that the militaries were subordinated to civil authority; that the law had once again become democratic; that the human rights issue was of interest to no one; and that it had in any case been settled through the uncovering of the truth—in an important but partial manner—as published in the report of the NCTR in 1991.

The detention of Pinochet manifested that all of that discourse was fictive. The reconciliation was limited to the political elite as a result of the failure of the democratic sectors actually to democratize the country; the transition was not about to end, but in truth had not even begun; the alleged democratic right did not appear anywhere; the militaries sympathized with their old boss; and the passage of time had not led to the vanishing of the memory of the horrors. At once, the question about human rights violations committed by the dictatorship came to occupy a centre stage in the political debate.

The stimulus that the judges needed to do justice did not come from the political elite in the country, but from outside. The Chilean judges had been impacted by the "Garzón effect" and wishful of recuperating the lost credit for its submission to the dictatorship, they began to bring to trial army officers who had been involved in the perpetration of crimes against humanity. In the course of this process, arguments for not applying the self-amnesty of 1978 were set forth. And, when the United Kingdom returned the former dictator to Chile, its national courts lifted the parliamentary immunity from which he had benefited as a senator on the basis that he had flaunted—formally—his position as President of the Republic, a right that had been given to him by the Constitution.

Neither the political leaders nor the Chilean Government in particular managed to understand what had happened. Instead, they ended up defending the dictator by virtue of the discredited argument of the "reason of state" together with old-fashioned concepts of patriotism and sovereignty that they sought to impose over justice and human rights. According to statistics, however, the great majority of the Chileans wanted Pinochet to be brought to justice.

Disorder and political failure in resolving the problem led the government to organize a roundtable dialogue on human rights (*Mesa de Diálogo sobre derechos humanos*)[40] in 1999 for the purpose of at least finding the remains of the

40 The roundtable was convened by the Central Government of Chile. The Agreement on the Roundtable of Human Rights (*Acuerdo de la mesa de derechos humanos*), in session from

disappeared, and inviting victims and the highest army officers in service together with church representatives and cultural and academic leaders. Even though some organizations of family relatives to direct victims refused to take part in the dialogue, lawyers with a long history of defending human rights stepped in to perform a role, including the author of this chapter. The mere existence of this roundtable was a direct and positive message to the judges and turned out to have remarkable effects: during the time in which the roundtable sat in session, the number of army officers faced with charges for crimes against humanity almost doubled (from 45 in the beginning of the session to 79, including seven generals, 10 months later).

The roundtable's official recognition of the atrocities that had been carried out by the generals and explicitly authorized by the commanders-in-chief of each branch of the armed forces, on the one hand,[41] and its call upon the designation of "visiting judges" to investigate cases of human rights violations, on the other, reinforced its message.[42] By 21 April 2008—only days before our roundtable in Madrid[43]—345 processes had been opened or ended with convictions whereby *investigations* into the situation of 1,135 victims of execution or disappearance have been carried out. Charges had been brought against 629 army officers and policemen, among them, 40 generals and admirals. Eighty-four of these men have been condemned to most severe sentences, and some of them in different cases.[44] Nevertheless, only 38 were deprived of liberty as some had already completed their sentences or received beneficial prison treatment in terms of reduced sentences. In addition, there are 28 proceedings—

21 August 1999–13 June 2000, is available online at www.derechoschile.com/prensa/espanol/temas/ddhhhoy/index.html.

41 See Declaration of the Roundtable Dialogue on Human Rights (*Declaración de la Mesa de Diálogo sobre Derechos Humanos. Reflexiones Fundamentales*). Available online at www.ddhh.gov.cl/filesapp/Declaracion_Acuerdo_Final.pdf. As also stated in the declaration: "There are other activities that do not allow any other legitimate attitude than the rejection and condemnation, as well as the firm decision of their non-repetition. We refer to the grave human rights violations incurred by the agents of organizations of the State during the military government. We also refer to the political violence committed by some opponents to the military regime" (unofficial translation).

42 The Organic Code of Courts authorizes the Supreme Court and the Appeals Courts to elect Ministers of the respective court to act as judge of first instance, as visitors to the regular courts, in cases that can affect international relations or produce public alarm. The Supreme Court only appointed two visiting ministers, but designated numerous judges with exclusive commitment, and others with privileged dedication to investigate the crimes committed in the period of 1973–1990.

43 For information about the roundtable in Madrid, see the acknowledgements section of this book.

44 e.g. the ex-Director of the National Intelligence Agency (DINA), General Manuel Contreras, has already accumulated convictions in numerous cases for a period of 219 years, and is awaiting confirmation in another 15 in which he has been convicted, in first and second instances, to a total of 197 years' imprisonment. This without consideration of the seven years' conviction already completed for the assassination of Orlando Letelier in Washington.

all of them initiated in the last six years—concerning crimes of torture, and an immense proceeding for crimes that took place in the famous *Colonia Dignidad*.

5.4 The current situation—advancements

Today, judges of first instance, Courts of Appeal and the Supreme Court all accept what human rights defenders had been saying since 11 September 1973:

1. The courts with competence to rule in cases of human rights violations are the civil ones. It is not reasonable that such violations can be committed as part of a military order.
2. The detainees who disappeared existed: it was not a combination of names supposedly invented by the extremists to discredit the "military government"; they did not die in battles; they did not escape, nor did they commit suicide, as the judges were saying until 1998, and also the ambassadors, the spokespersons and ministers of the dictator.
3. To the contrary, all who disappeared were detained alive, as the human rights defenders had said in thousands of *amparo* cases and complaints that the courts had pretended not to believe.
4. The detentions were not only effective, but also, as was said all along, illegal. What was still worse: they were criminal. As a result, all of the *habeas corpus* actions had to be accepted.
5. The amnesty is not "objective" and can therefore not be applied until the authors, accomplices and hiders have been identified. This conclusion was reached in the judgment of first instance on 3 May 2004 in the case of *Rio Negro*,[45] thereafter confirmed by the Supreme Court,[46] and reiterated in practically all of the condemnatory sentences.
6. In the cases related to kidnapping, the amnesty cannot be applied, nor can the statutory limitations as it is a permanent crime. As long as it is not proven that the kidnapped person was liberated or died, it must be assumed that the kidnapping continues and the authors of the crime can therefore not benefit from legal pardon. This is the conclusion now upheld in many judgments, among them, the final unanimous Supreme Court judgment delivered on 17 November 2004 in which it rejected the appeal for annulment (*casación*) by the convicted for the disappearance of Miguel Ángel Sandoval Rodríguez.[47] This sentence has been reaffirmed on numerous occasions, although not always unanimously.
7. If in Chile a state of war had been formally declared, it had to be governed by the laws that regulate armed conflict of non-international character, and

45 Ministro de Fuero ("civil Judie") Alejandro Solís, case of *Río Negro*, no 2.182 98, Decision of 3 May 2004.

46 Corte Suprema de Justicia, case of *Río Negro*, no 3925-05, Judgment of 27 December 2005.

47 Corte Suprema, case of *Miguel Ángel Sandoval Rodríguez*, no 517-04, Judgment of 17 November 2004.

which prohibit the reliance upon extinction of criminal responsibility—such as amnesty and statutory limitations—for crimes considered as grave infringements (according to the four Geneva Conventions of 1949). This position was upheld in the decision of the Santiago Appeals Court in the proceedings concerning the disappearance of *Miguel Ángel Sandoval*, the case of *Río Negro* as well as in the case of *Diana Frida Arón*.[48]

8. The precepts of the International Covenant on Civil and Political Rights and the Inter-American Convention on Human Rights are applicable in the cases of violations of the right to life, and this is what the judges and the courts have maintained since the time of the judgments of the Supreme Court in the cases of *Río Negro* and *Miguel Ángel Sandoval*. It is a criterion that has continued to be imposed in the immense majority of judicial decisions that have been dictated, although frequently on the basis of a slight majority of three judges over two.

However, the "subjectivity" of the amnesty, the principles of non-statutory limitations and the non-amnestiability of the crimes against international law, the applicability of the human rights treaties and international humanitarian law, are not accepted by a minority of judges. The arguments of these judges were pronounced in the recent judgment delivered in the case concerning the double assassination of General Carlos Prats and his wife on 8 July 2010.[49] According to this minority:

> The institution of time limits is not affected by the international legislation frequently invoked, especially if the facts that are the motive for the present case do not have the character of crimes against humanity and it is important to concretize the arguments that this dissident has sustained in cases regarding crimes committed during the military government and which the agents of that administration have been made responsible for.[50]

Furthermore, also held by the same judges is that in 1973:

> . . . actions were carried out against the physical integrity of the Armed Forces, the *Carabineros*, and the population in general, and that grave crimes specified in the *Law of Arms Control* were often committed. However, the occurrence of such acts whose veracity is not in doubt is not a sufficient

48 Corte Suprema de Justicia, case of *Diana Frida Arón Svigilsky*, no 3215-05, Judgment of 30 May 2006.

49 On 30 November 1974, the vehicle in which General Carlos Prats, Augusto Pinochet's predecessor as commander-in-chief of the Chilean army, and his wife were going home in exploded in Buenos Aires (Argentina). The murder was carried out by DINA. See Corte Suprema de Justicia (Supreme Court of Justice), case of *Carlos Prats*, no 2.182-98, Judgment of 8 July 2010. The dissenting opinion starts on p 63.

50 Supreme Court of Justice, case of *Carlos Prats*, no 2.182-98, Judgment of 8 July 2010, p 64.

> reason for, in the period of perpetrating the acts investigated, taking as a given that in Chile there was a "non-international armed conflict" in the terms of common article 3 of the Geneva Conventions of 1949.[51]

Nevertheless, the argumentation of these judges is false, as none of the two victims had committed "grave crimes contemplated in the Law of Arms Control and Explosives".[52] It is furthermore inconsistent, as it speaks of the "occurrence of such acts whose veracity is not in doubt", although the historical facts are politically and legally disputed. Finally, it is contradictory. If the argument had been true, there would at least have been a situation of internal disturbances and probably an internal armed conflict. In addition, the dissenting judges maintain that the International Covenant on Civil and Political Rights was not in force in the period in which the crimes that are the object of these criminal proceedings were committed.

Regrettably, when some judge belonging to the majority opinion of the Supreme Court is supplanted the outcome in these cases is reverted. This has happened in 14 cases, with the result that the occasional majority has come to affirm the amnesty exception. This is how impunity has been granted to numerous crimes of kidnappings with the disappearances of the victims and murders, which are normally punished.

The new developments over the last two years have had as an effect that on 30 June 2010, 432 criminal proceedings concerning crimes against humanity are open, a number that reflects the new admissions as well as the closing of cases that have ended in convictions and, occasionally, in acquittals, as well as in some dismissals due to the death of the accused. The number of prosecuted and convicted has risen to 782 (that is, by 23 per cent in two years), 64 of whom have been deprived of their liberty (which is 68 per cent more than in 2008). To this number may be added another three people who were recently convicted by the highest instance to effective deprivation of liberty. The 551 sentences have affected 291 repressors, although it must be noted that the courts of first and second instances have delivered many of these sentences.[53] Some have been convicted in more than one proceeding and there are individuals who have been condemned for more than 20 crimes, such as General Manuel Contreras.[54]

As indicated in the Informative Bulletin no 8 of the Universidad de Diego Portales, the number of repressors convicted for such crimes is the highest in Latin America.[55]

51 Supreme Court of Justice, case of *Carlos Prats*, no 2.182-98, Judgment of 8 July 2010, p 69.

52 Ley no 17.798 de Control de Armas y Explosivos, fn 8 above.

53 Centro de Derechos Humanos de la Universidad de Diegos Portales, "Juicios por Derechos Humanos en Chile y la región", *Boletín Informativo* no 8, July 2010, p 3.

54 At the moment, General Manuel Contreras is facing 219 years and eight days in 24 final and executed sentences. But to this should be added 18 definitive sentences of first and second instances with punishments that together total 178 years and 545 days, without prejudice of what will be decided in 26 cases in process in first instance.

55 Centro de Derechos Humanos, fn 53 above.

All of these advancements are the result of two factors with an (delayed) impact on domestic courts and political leaders. The first is the defence of human rights, initiated in Chile by the churches within a few days after the military *coup d'état*.[56] Civil society and especially the persecuted and the family relatives of victims found within the organizations defending human rights a formidable space for assistance and protection. Against this background, it might be maintained that, in spite of the behaviour of the judges, the Chilean people never lost faith in justice and law.

The second factor is international human rights law as well as the existence of an international community—intergovernmental and non-governmental—that has established a new legal culture: the human right to justice for grave human rights violations. This right is a specific facet of the human right to justice as recognized, among others, in Articles 8, 9 and 25 of the Inter-American Convention of Human Rights, 2.3 and 14 of the International Covenant on Civil and Political Rights; and Articles 5, 6 and 7 of the European Convention for the Protection of Fundamental Rights and Freedoms. The human right to justice is the right for any person who has been the victim of massive human rights violations to obtain truth, justice and reparation. It is a right that in its criminal dimension can be exercised before national, international, foreign or mixed courts and tribunals and, in its human rights dimension, before regional human rights commissions and courts, international treaty-based human rights committees as well as UN special rapporteurs and working groups.[57]

The achievements of the Chilean courts since 16 October 1998 have motivated an increasing number of judicial actions for crimes that had never been revealed; indeed, as a result of 16 October, even the Chilean Government came to see itself as forced to create a new commission to investigate crimes of the dictatorship: the *Comisión Nacional de Prisión Política y Tortura* (National Commission on Political Imprisonment and Torture),[58] known more commonly

56 On 4 October 1973, before even a month had passed since the military *coup d'état* on 11 September 1973, which brought 140 years of republican life to an end, a diversity of religious congregations (Catholic Church, Lutheran Evangelists, Methodist Evangelist, Baptists, some Pentecost churches, the Orthodox and the Great Rabbis of Chile) founded the *Comité de Cooperación de la Paz* (Committee on Co-operation for Peace) in Chile to bestow legal and humanitarian assistance to the victims of the repression. The organ had to be dissolved in 1975 as a result of pressures exerted by the dictatorship. Instead it established itself as the *Vicaría de la Solidaridad del Arzobispado de Santiago*, which continued performing the same functions from 1 January 1976 until its voluntary dissolution in 1992. Thereafter the laic organizations appeared.

57 Until a few years ago dictators felt disdain for the international community. Pinochet manifested his objection to absurdity when he called for a national consultation against the United Nations for the aggression implied by its decision taken on 4 January 1978 to establish a working group to investigate his violations.

58 Minister of Interior (Chile), Decreto no 1040, crea Comisión Nacional sobre prisión política y tortura, para el esclaracimiento de la verdad acerca de las violaciones de derechos humanos en Chile, 11 September 2003.

as the "Valech Commission",[59] the report of which was released in 2004.[60] At the beginning of 2010—when the two parties opposing the dictatorship were still in government—a new law was adopted that recognized cases of summary executions, enforced disappearances, deaths caused by torture and political imprisonment which had not been accounted for in the reports of Rettig (1990/1991) and Valech (2003/2004).

In 2008, it was observed that in spite of the evident progress made, a grey area in the military justice system still subsisted. Even if the competence of the military justice system to prosecute civilians had been delimited, the law permits military tribunals to prosecute civilians *rationæ materiæ* (that is, as crimes against the external and internal sovereignty of the state as defined in the Code of Military Justice[61] and the Law of the Security of the State,[62] as well as under the heading of other crimes contemplated in the Code of Military Justice, such as that of improper sedition).[63] In addition, civilians can be prosecuted by military tribunals *rationæ personæ* if the victim is an army officer or a civil guard (*carabinero*), or if civilians and army officers have acted together in committing a crime. Indeed, military tribunals are competent to prosecute not only the author of a crime that falls within military jurisdiction, but also all of the other persons responsible for that crime even if they are not subjects according to custom.[64] In 2007, the number of cases against civilians brought to military justice was still about 20 per cent, although it is in any case a number that is clearly inferior to what happened in Chile until the mid-1990s.

In recent years, another grey area appeared: the infringement of the international legal principle stipulating that war crimes or crimes against humanity must be sanctioned with penalties that are adequate and proportionate to the gravity of the crimes. The principle in question is upheld, for example, in Article 6 of the Slavery Convention[65] ("severe penalties"); Article 4 of the Convention against Torture and Other Cruel, Inhuman or Degrading Treatment or Punishment[66] ("appropriate penalties which take into account their grave nature"); Article V of the Convention of the Prevention and Punishment of the Crime of Genocide[67] ("effective penalties"); principle 1 of the Principles on

59 The name is taken from Bishop Sergio Valech, who presided over this Commission.

60 La Comisión Nacional de Prisión Política y Tortura, Report, published on the internet (first part) in November 2004 and (second part) in June 2005. Available online (in Spanish) at www.comisionvalech.gov.cl/InformeValech.html.

61 For a consideration of crimes against the internal and external sovereignty of the state, see Código de Justicia Militar (Code of Military Justice), 19 December 1944 as reformed in 1995, Heading 2, Arts 254–258.

62 See Ley sobre Seguridad del Estado, no 890, 3 July 1975, Heading 1, Arts 1–3.

63 Code of Military Justice, fn 61 above, Art 276.

64 Code of Military Justice, fn 61 above, Art 11.

65 Slavery Convention, signed in Geneva on 25 September 1926.

66 Convention against Torture, Cruel and Inhuman or Degrading Treatment or Punishment, UNGA Res 39/46, adopted on 10 December 1984.

67 Convention on the Prevention and Punishment of the Crime of Genocide, UNGA Res 260 (III) A, adopted on 9 December 1948.

the Effective Prevention and Investigation of Extra-legal, Arbitrary and Summary Executions[68] ("appropriate penalties which take into account the seriousness of such offences"); Article 6 of the Convention on the Elimination of All Forms of Discrimination against Women[69] ("appropriate measures to combat all forms of traffic of women and the exploitation of the prostitution of women, which implies appropriate penalties"); Article 3 of the Inter-American Convention on Forced Disappearances of Persons[70] ("appropriate punishment commensurate with its extreme gravity"); and Article 4 of the Declaration on the Protection of all Persons from Enforced Disappearance,[71] as well as Article 7.1 of the International Convention for the Protection of all Persons from Enforced Disappearance[72] ("appropriate penalties which shall take into account their extreme seriousness"). We also find similar formulations in the area of international humanitarian law. All four Geneva Conventions include a provision according to which the States Parties are obliged to impose "effective penal sanctions for persons committing, or ordering to be committed, any of the grave breaches of the present Convention".[73]

The judges on the Supreme Court—usually revising the judgments of first and second instances, the latter being generally harsher and more adjusted to law—apply a criterion when determining the sentence which is widely known to be incompatible with the norms and principles of international law. To this end, they have recourse to two subterfuges. First of all, the judges apply the extenuating circumstance contemplated in the Penal Code related to the previously irreproachable conduct of the delinquent to subjects who have committed tens of crimes.[74] For example, in the case of General Carlos Prats and to the benefit of those who have been convicted to hundreds of years in prison, the judges held that:

> Even though the defences of the accused Juan Manuel Contreras Sepúlveda, Pedro Espinoza Bravo and Cristoph Willeke Flöel did not request the application of the referred extenuating circumstance in the event of

68 Principles on the Effective Prevention and Investigation of Extra-legal, Arbitrary and Summary Executions, recommended by ECOSOC Res 1989/65, 24 May 1989.

69 Convention on the Elimination of All Forms of Discrimination against Women, UNGA Res 34/180, adopted on 18 December 1979.

70 Inter-American Convention on Forced Disappearances of Persons, OASGA Res A-60, adopted on 6 September 1994.

71 Declaration on the Protection of all Persons from Enforced Disappearance, UNGA Res 147/183, adopted on 18 December 1992.

72 International Convention for the Protection of all Persons from Enforced Disappearance, UNGA Res 61/177, adopted on 12 January 2007.

73 The Four Geneva Conventions, adopted on 12 August 1949: Geneva Convention I, Art 49; Geneva Convention II, Art 50; Geneva Convention III, Art 129; and Geneva Convention IV, Art 149.

74 Penal Code no 18472 of 12 November 1874, Art 11.6 recognizes as an extenuating circumstance "if the previous conduct of the delinquent has been irreproachable".

> conviction, it can be inferred from their criminal records . . . given that there is no registration in these instruments of previous convictions for the perpetration of the crimes under consideration in these cases and, hence, one takes as agreed the modifying circumstance in question.[75]

The second subterfuge to reduce the sentences is the extenuating circumstance known as "partial statutory limitations" (in Chile defined as *media prescripción*) affirmed in Article 103 of the Penal Code.[76] This circumstance makes it possible for those who have been convicted for human rights violations to obtain a reduced sentence in consideration of the time elapsed since the criminal act. According to the majority of the Supreme Court, the time limits placed on the legal action that extinguishes criminal responsibility is clearly distinguishable from the qualified extenuating circumstance affirmed in Article 103. The fact that the time lapse since the commission of the crime is understood as a qualified extenuating circumstance authorizes the judges to lower, to a significant extent, the sentences given to those who are convicted for human rights violations.

5.5 Future challenges for transitional justice

Notwithstanding the celebrated advances made in recent years, it is essential to address some critical issues that still remain to be tackled (in addition to the final and absolute suppression of military justice and its prosecution of civilians as well as of army officers for crimes against civilians). The first is that many judges are still confronting difficulties when seeking to invoke international human rights law in the domestic judicial context. More than affecting the cases related to the violations that took place during the dictatorship, the challenge is present in the adjudication of new cases, particularly in the context of economic, social and cultural rights, and in the fight against all forms of discrimination. The second issue is the absence of real and effective measures to eradicate torture as well as all forms of cruel, inhuman or degrading treatment or punishment, which—although having lost their systematic character—continue to be committed against ordinary crime suspects.

However, in this context, it must also be noted that in the last two years Chile ratified three principal international instruments that have been mentioned in this chapter: the Rome Statute of the International Criminal Court (1998),[77] the Inter-American Convention on Forced Disappearances of Persons (1994)[78] and the International Convention for the Protection of all

75 Supreme Court of Justice, case of *Carlos Prats*, no 2.182-98, Judgment of 8 July 2010, legal considerations, para 28 (unofficial translation).

76 Penal Code, fn 74 above, Art 103.

77 Chile ratified the Rome Statute, adopted on 17 July 1998, on 29 June 2009. The statute entered into force for Chile on 1 September 2009.

78 Chile ratified the Inter-American Convention on Forced Disappearances, adopted on 9 June 1994, on 13 January 2010.

Persons from Enforced Disappearance (2006),[79] although in the case of the latter two instruments, laws to improve their implementation remain to be adopted.

At the same time, as I have stated repeatedly, criminal justice is only one of the forms—even if perhaps the most important one—to tackle impunity. In my judgment, impunity has four dimensions: *legal* impunity (that is, the absence of sanction for crimes that evidently fall within all the definitions of crimes against humanity); *political* impunity (that is, the absence of measures to disable those who exercised authority in despotic regimes, independently of their eventual criminal responsibility); *moral* impunity (that is, the absence of measures to remedy the fact that the criminals who proclaimed themselves to be "saviours of the fatherland" today declare they have nothing to repent); and *historical* impunity (that is, the absence of measures aimed at ensuring that the registered events will forever remain intact in their original version always with the lie with which they were presented).

In comparison with the eradication of criminal impunity, the fight against political, moral and historical impunity is fraught with delays. Nevertheless, there is also some progress. One example is the democratic Constitution of Guatemala of 1985 and its prohibition against the election of leaders and chiefs of the military *coup d'état*, as well as persons who, as a consequence of these events, assumed leadership of the government that was installed (Article 186).[80] A controversial interpretation of this provision permitted a former dictator (José Efraín Ríos Montt) to present himself for elections in 2003, but the popular wisdom relegated him to a third place following a humiliating vote. Furthermore, in its Final Observations on the third report presented by Argentina, the UN Human Rights Committee held that:

> Despite positive measures taken recently to overcome past injustices, including the repeal in 1998 of the Law of Due Obedience and the *Punto Final* Law, the Committee is concerned that many persons whose actions were covered by these laws continue to serve in the military or in public office, with some having enjoyed promotions in the ensuing years. It therefore reiterates its concern at the atmosphere of impunity for those responsible for gross human rights violations under military rule.[81]

And, with regard to El Salvador, the same committee urged "continuing vigorous action to ensure that persons closely associated with human rights abuses do not re-enter the police, army or security forces".[82]

79 Chile ratified the International Convention on Enforced Disappearances, adopted on 20 December 2006, Doc Ref UN Doc A/RES/61/177, on 8 December 2009.

80 Constitución Política de la República de Guatemala, adopted on 30 May 1985.

81 UN Human Rights Committee, "Concluding Observations of Argentina", UN Doc CCPR/CO/70/ARG), 3 November 2000, para 9.

82 UN Human Rights Committee, "Concluding Observations of El Salvador", UN Doc CCPR/C/79/add.34, 18 April 1994, para 14.

In none of these cases, criminal responsibility for human rights violations must generate a disinterest to fight against the other manifestations of impunity. The reconciliation and consolidation of democracy are goals possible to realize only if all four dimensions of impunity are eliminated.

6 Spain as an example of total oblivion with partial rehabilitation

*Alicia Gil Gil**

6.1 The Spanish Civil War and the Francoist dictatorship

The Spanish Civil War began on 17 July 1936 following a *coup d'état* led by the military against the lawful government of the Spanish Second Republic and ended on 1 April 1939 with the victory of the rebels and the establishment of the dictatorial regime of General Francisco Franco, who was announced as the "Spanish leader for the Grace of God" (*Caudillo de España por la Gracia de Dios*).[1] The Civil War, which lasted for three years, was extremely bloody, characterized as it was, by the systematic non-compliance with international humanitarian law that is now in force.[2] According to the General Report of the Inter-ministerial Commission for the Study of the Situation of the Victims of the Civil War and of Francoism (2006),[3] which reflects the majority opinion among Spanish historians, atrocities were committed by both bands in the conflict, including extrajudicial executions and the violent repression of political adversaries.[4]

* This chapter has its origins in a broader research project organized by the Latin American Group of the Study of International Criminal Law and sponsored by the Rule of Law Programme for South America of the Konrad Adenauer Foundation. The reports of the group have been published in Ambos, K et al, *Justicia de Transición*, Montevideo: Georg August Universität Göttingen/Konrad Adenauer Stiftung, 2009, available online at www.kas.de/wf/doc/kas_15990-1522-4-30.pdf?090629220310. See also Gil Gil, A, *La justicia de transición en España. De la amnistía a la memoria histórica*, Barcelona: Atelier, 2009.

1 Muñoz Conde, F, "La transformación jurídica de la dictadura franquista en un Estado de Derecho", paper presented in Congreso de Historiadores de Derecho de Alemania (September 2006), pp 6 ff. Available online at http://portal.uclm.es/descargas/idp_docs/doctrinas/munoz%20conde-franquismo.pdf.

2 Juliá, S et al (eds), *Víctimas de la guerra civil*, Madrid: Temas de Hoy, 1999 (reprinted in 2006), pp 175 ff.

3 *Informe General de la Comisión Interministerial para el Estudio de la Situación de las Víctimas de la Guerra Civil y del Franquismo*, 28 July 2006, p 22 (*General Report of the Inter-ministerial Commission for the Study of the Situation of the Victims of the Civil War and of Francoism*) (unofficial translation). Available online at www1.mpr.es/uploads/media/pdf/6/informe general2_1232475655.pdf.

4 Concerning the extremely violent acts committed by both bands, see Juliá, fn 2 above, pp 25 ff, 183–185 and 248–250; González Calleja, E, "El Estado ante la violencia", in

With the end of the Civil War, the regime tried the persons responsible for the "crimes" that had been committed by the Republican band as part of what was defined as the "General Cause". The purpose was to collect the evidence of the delinquent acts committed in the entire national territory during the "Red domination".[5] It also promulgated a series of laws destined to protect, compensate and praise the killed, wounded and families of victims in the Civil War, and envisaged the search for and exhumation of bodies.[6] However, all of these measures evidently only benefited the victims who had fought on the side of the victors.[7]

The systematic commission of serious human rights violations distinguished the first period of the Francoist regime. Between 1936 and 1950, acts of illegal detentions ending with extrajudicial executions and the concealment of the bodies in graves were committed on a massive scale.[8] Also common in this period was the organization of summary trials before so-called Tribunals of Exception that gravely violated the rights of the accused and often resulted in death sentences.[9] To this should be added that hundreds of thousands of Spaniards were obliged to go into exile and came to suffer the painful conditions of life in refugee and internment camps that some of them were locked into upon arrival in their countries of destination.[10] Also frequent were prison camps, detention camps and labour camps for political prisoners. Thousands of people died in these camps, the majority because of hunger or tuberculosis, but also as a result of executions and maltreatment.[11] In addition, a strategy of massive and

Juliá, S (ed), *Violencia política en la España del siglo XX*, Madrid: Taurus, 2000, pp 387–391; and De La Cueva Merino, J, "Si los curas y frailes supieran . . . La violencia anticlerical", in Juliá, S (ed), *Violencia política en la España del siglo XX*, Madrid: Taurus, 2000, pp 221 ff.

5 Decreto de 26 de abril de 1940, *Boletín Oficial del Estado*, 4 May 1940. These crimes have been documented in the *General Report of the Inter-ministerial Commission*, fn 3 above, p 23 (although in an exaggerated version) (see Juliá, fn 2 above, p 133), among them, the acts of torture committed in the "checas", i.e. improvized prisons in the Republican zones, the executions realized during the "sacas", i.e. taking out for a stroll, etc.

6 Orden de 1 de mayo de 1940, *Boletín Oficial del Estado*, 9 May 1940 (concerning the exhumations and burials of the "bodies of those murdered by the Reds").

7 *General Report of the Inter-ministerial Commission*, fn 3 above, p 24.

8 Capellà, M, "Las 'desapariciones forzadas' en España durante la guerra civil y el franquismo: violaciones y crímenes de derecho internacional sin reparación ni castigo", in Soroeta Liceras, J (ed), *Conflictos y protección de derechos humanos en el orden internacional. Cursos de Derechos Humanos de Donostia-San Sebastián*, vol VI, 2006, pp 265–301; and Juliá, *Víctimas de la Guerra Civil*, fn 2 above, pp 29 and 132 ff.

9 Jiménez Villarejo, C, "La destrucción del orden republicano (apuntes jurídicos)", *Hispania Nova Revista de Historia Contemporánea*, no 7, 2007, p 15. Available online at http://hispanianova.rediris.es/6/index.htm.

10 *General Report of the Inter-ministerial Commission*, fn 3 above. See also Moreno Gómez, F, "La represión en la posguerra", in Juliá, fn 2 above, pp 282 ff.

11 *General Report of the Inter-ministerial Commission*, fn 3 above, p 74. See also Rodrigo, J, Cautivos. *Campos de concentración en la España franquista, 1936–1947*, Madrid: Ed Crítica, 2005; Gómez Bravo, G, "El desarrollo penitenciario en el primer franquismo (1939–1945)", *Hispania Nova Revista de Historia Contemporánea*, no 6, 2006, p 9. Available online

generalized torture in the form of beating prisoners was installed. The deaths caused by the strategy were officially explained as the result of "intent to escape".[12] Furthermore, more than 5,000 Spaniards died in Nazi camps, the majority of whom had been brought there by the French and with the knowledge and passivity of the Spanish government.

The Francoist dictatorship eliminated public rights and liberties and exerted harsh repression of all political and ideological dissent.[13] From the outset, it articulated a complex set of rules that were meant to dismantle its republican predecessor, banning political parties and labour unions as well as repressing all manifestations of political, religious and moral dissent.[14] It also rapidly proceeded with a "depuration" of all state institutions as well as publicly owned enterprises with private management,[15] which meant that many public officials were suspended from their jobs, in particular, teachers and professors.[16] The measures in question were systematized in the Law of Political Responsibilities (*Ley de Responsabilidades Políticas*) of 9 February 1939[17] and the Law of Depuration of Publicly Employed (*Ley de Depuración de Empleados Públicos*) of 10 February 1939.[18] Furthermore, the administration of justice machinery was

at http://hispanianova.rediris.es/6/dossier/6d017.pdf; González Calleja, fn 4 above, p 396; Moreno Gómez, F, "La represión en la posguerra", in Juliá, fn 2 above, pp 288 ff; and Ortiz Heras, M, "Instrumentos legales del terror franquista", *Historia del Presente*, no 3, 2004, p 22.

12 Moreno Gómez, fn 11 above, p 301.

13 Ortiz Heras, M, "Instrumentos *legales* del terror franquista", *Historia del Presente*, no 3, 2004, pp 203–220; Aragoneses, A, "El Derecho bajo el franquismo. Transformaciones del sistema jurídico español (1936–1978)", in Capellà, M and Ginard, D (eds), *Represión política, justicia y preparación. La memoria histórica en perspectiva jurídica*, Palma de Mallorca: Plural, 2009, pp 123–159.

14 *General Report of the Inter-ministerial Commission*, fn 3 above, p 23; and Jiménez Villarejo, fn 9 above, pp 15 ff.

15 Cabrera, M and Del Rey Reguillo, F, "La patronal y la brutalización de la política", in Juliá, fn 4 above, pp 284 ff.

16 Moreno Gómez, F, "La represión en la posguerra", in Juliá, fn 2 above, p 330; and Reig Tapia, A, "La depuración 'intelectual' del nuevo estado franquista", *Revista de estudios políticos*, no 88, 1995, pp 175–198.

17 See Ley de Responsabilidades Políticas de 9 de febrero de 1939 (Jefatura del Estado), *Boletín del Estado*, no 81, 22 March 1939. For a comment on this law, see Jiménez Villarejo, fn 9 above, p 5 (recalling that the legal provisions were complemented by the Law of 23 September 1939 related to "property of the former Marxist and anarchist labour unions", p 8). See also Alcaraz Abellán, J, "La Ley de Responsabilidades políticas y su aplicación en Fuerteventura (1939–1942)", *Anuario del Archivo Histórico Insular de Fuerteventura*, no 3, 1990, pp 147 ff; Aguilar Fernández, P, "Justicia, política y memoria: los legados del franquismo la transición española", in Barahona de Brito, A, Aguilar Fernández, P and González Enríquez, C (eds), *Las políticas hacia el pasado. Juicios, depuraciones, perdón y olvido en las nuevas democracias*, Logroño, La Rioja: Ediciones Istmo, 2002, p 154; and González Calleja, fn 4 above, p 394.

18 Ley de Depuración de Empleados Públicos de 10 de febrero de 1939 (Jefatura del Estado), *Boletín del Estado*, no 45, 14 February 1939. See also *General Report of the Inter-ministerial Commission*, fn 3 above, p 23; and Jiménez Villarejo, fn 9 above, p 13.

reorganized to suit the interests of the new regime. Indeed, already in 1938 a new law concerning the organization of the Supreme Court was passed according to which new judges and prosecutors were to be nominated by government.[19]

The political repression was also manifested in the Law on Repression of Freemasonry and Communism (*Ley de Represión de la masonería y el comunismo*) of 1 March 1940[20] and the Law on the Security of the State (*Ley de Seguridad del Estado*) of 29 March 1941.[21] The latter criminalized a long list of acts for the purpose of protecting the "legal good of prestige, security and unity of the nation" and imposed the death sentence for those acts that were considered as especially grave.[22] The Law of 2 March 1943 classified a series of acts as amounting to the crime of military rebellion.[23] Law Decree of 18 April 1947 concerning Banditry and Terrorism (*Decreto-Ley sobre bandidaje y terrorismo*) entered into force during the harshest period of the post-war repression which implied three years of terror, including the ruthless pursuit of fugitives who had fled to the mountains and the persecution of all kinds of clandestine political activity.[24] The Law on Public Order (*Ley de Orden Público*) of 30 July 1959 outlawed collective strikes, demonstrations and political meetings.[25] Thereafter, a law adopted on 2 December 1963 created the so-called Tribunal of Public Order, with competence to prosecute political crimes and crimes of labour unions.[26]

In addition, the regime criminalized activities of other minority groups who, similar to political dissenters, were said to threaten its foundational principles.[27] Notably, the Law on Vagabonds and Villains (*Ley de Vagos y Maleantes*) of 4 August 1933 was extended to cover "new threats" such as homosexual acts that were punished with imprisonment.[28] In 1970, that law was replaced by the Law on Peril and Social Rehabilitation (*Ley de Peligrosidad y Rehabilitación*

19 See Jiménez Villarejo, fn 9 above, pp 12 ff.

20 Ley de Represión de la Masonería y Comunismo de 1 de marzo de 1940, *Boletín del Estado*, no 12.667, 2 March 1939. For an account of the application of this law, see Portilla, G, *La consagración del Derecho penal de autor durante el franquismo. El Tribual Especial para la Represión de la Masonería y el Comunismo*, Granada: Editorial Comares, 2009.

21 Ley de Seguridad del Estado de 29 de marzo de 1941, *Gazeta* (Ref 1940/2123).

22 *General Report of the Inter-ministerial Commission*, fn 3 above, p 24.

23 Ley de 2 de marzo de 1943 de reforma del Código de Justicia Militar, *Gazeta* (Ref 1943/2677). See also Cerezo Mir, J, *Curso de Derecho penal español, T. I. Introducción*, 6th edn, Madrid: Tecnos, 2004, p 143.

24 Decreto-Ley de 18 de abril de 1947 sobre bandidaje y terrorismo, *Gazeta* (Ref 1947/4518). See also González Calleja, fn 4 above, pp 396–397.

25 Ley de Orden Público de 30 de julio 1959, *Boletín Oficial del Estado*, no 182, 31 July 1959.

26 Ley de 2 de diciembre 1963, sobre creación del Juzgado y Tribunales de Orden Público, *Boletín Oficial del Estado*, no 291, 5 December 1963. See also González Calleja, fn 4 above, p 397, and *General Report of the Inter-ministerial Commission*, fn 3 above, p 24.

27 *General Report of the Inter-ministerial Commission*, fn 3 above, p 24.

28 Ley de Vagos y Maleantes, de 4 de agosto de 1933, *Gazeta Histórica* (Ref 1933/06761). Modificación de 15 de julio de 1954, *Boletín Oficial del Estado*, no 198, 17 July 1954. See also Cerezo Mir, fn 23 above, p 147.

Social);[29] similar to its predecessor, it affirmed that "those who commit acts of homosexuality" constituted a "threat" and punished such acts by the internment of homosexuals in re-educational establishments. Also the persecution of the Roma was legitimized and their language was classified as "slang of criminals" and prohibited.[30]

In a lead to legitimize itself, the dictatorship invented an official discourse about the war and according to which its victory was seen as the successful crusade against evil. The spirit of this discourse was manifested in monuments, parades, street names, festivities, textbooks, news bulletins, documentaries, etc. These culture-specific measures meant that the Spanish population came to live in a context of indoctrination and imposed memory and that, as a result, the defeated side of the war never spoke of the war or the repressive period that followed.[31]

The human rights violations that were committed in the second period of Francoism cannot be compared with those in the 1940s, although the violations became more frequent towards the end of this period, especially in the Basque Country.[32] Numerous states of exception were issued during the last years of the dictatorship and torture was frequently practised.[33]

Finally, although the Spanish transition is always referred to as an example of peaceful transition *par excellence*, the truth is that, between 1975 and 1982, 644 people faced violent deaths because of the political situation.[34] While the majority of these people were killed by terrorist groups, 140 deaths are attributable to the state as they were caused by police repression of street demonstrations, etc.[35]

29 Ley 16/1979, de 4 de agosto, sobre peligrosidad y rehabilitación social, *Boletín Oficial del Estado*, no 187, 6 August 1970.

30 See Declaration of recognition of the persecution and the genocide of the Roma people, Parliament of Cataluña. Read in Plenary Session of the Parliament of Cataluña, 29 March 2007 (unofficial translation).

31 Juliá, fn 2 above, p 37. See also Aróstegui, J and Godicheau, F (eds), *Guerra civil, Mito y Memoria*, Madrid: Marcial Pons, 2006.

32 Aguilar Fernández, fn 17 above, p 162.

33 Aguilar Fernández, fn 17 above, p 162, fn 61.

34 Concerning the earlier contacts that had already begun in the mid-1940s between small opposition groups from both bands of the Civil War with the aim of agreeing upon a transition to democracy, see Juliá, fn 2 above, pp 38 ff.

35 The statistics have been extrapolated from Sánchez-Cuenca, I and Aguilar Fernández, P, "Database on Political Violence" (not yet published). The database forms part of the research project "Explaining Terrorist Target Selection", financed by the Spanish Ministry of Education, available online at www.march.es/ceacs/proyectos/dtv/index.asp. See also Aguilar Fernández, fn 17 above, p 168. Concerning the attacks committed during this period, see also Juliá, S, "La estrategia de la tensión", in *Memoria de la transición*, Madrid: El País, 1996, pp 125 ff. In this context, one must also consider the subsequent dirty war against terrorism. See Ruiz De Azúa, V, "Las manos sucias", in *Memoria de la Transición*, Madrid: El País, 1996, at 393ff; and Gil Calvo, E, "Aprendices de brujo y avestruces", in *Memoria de la Transición*, Madrid: El País, 1996, pp 401 ff.

6.2 Overcoming the conflictive past

With the dictator dead, a referendum on the Law on Political Reform was held in 1976 opening the door for a call for the holding of general democratic elections; a reform of the Penal Code in 1976 which eliminated the classification of all political parties as illegal associations; the legalization of the Communist Party in April 1977; the celebration of general elections in June that same year; and the approval by way of a popular referendum of the new Constitution in 1978.[36]

At the time of the transition, no political, labour or social forces demanded the adoption of measures of political justice.[37] There were no purges of the principal civil and military institutions that had been inherited from the dictatorship,[38] including the army, the police and the judiciary.[39] No effort was made to eliminate the symbols of Franco; rather, the street names that honoured persons who had taken part in the dictatorship and the monuments dedicated to Franco were maintained.[40] No truth commission was established to investigate the human rights violations of the previous regime,[41] and no trials were held.

6.2.1 The Amnesty Law

The democratically adopted Amnesty Law,[42] approved in October 1977, gained the support of 93.3 per cent of parliamentary members[43] and has been celebrated as "the most significant milestone in the whole process of reparation and restitution of the personal liberty of those who had been deprived of it for

36 Muñoz Conde, fn 1 above, pp 5 ff.
37 Aguilar Fernández, fn 17 above, p 166.
38 For the counterproductive effect that this decision may have had for the proper functioning of our democracy, see Aguilar Fernández, fn 17 above, p 149.
39 See Aguilar Fernández, fn 17 above, p 171, fn 81.
40 Aguilar Fernández, fn 17 above, pp 179 and 184 ff.
41 Aguilar Fernández, fn 17 above, pp 136 ff.
42 Ley 46/1977, de 15 de octubre, de Amnistia, *Boletín Oficial del Estado*, no 248, 17 October 1977. This law completed Real Decreto-Ley 19/1977, de 14 de marzo, *Boletín Oficial del Estado*, no 65, 17 March 1977. Also note Decreto 2940/1975, de 25 de noviembre, por el que se concede indulto general con motivo de la proclamación de Su Majestad don Juan Carlos de Borbón como Rey de España, *Boletín Oficial del Estado*, no 284, 26 November 1975. The latter grants a general pardon and was proclaimed by His Majesty Juan Carlos of Borbón as King of Spain. It does not contemplate in an explicit manner the possibility of applying the measure of pardon for crimes with a political character.
43 The law was approved with 296 votes in favour, 2 against, 18 abstentions and 1 vote annulled. See *General Report of the Inter-ministerial Commission*, fn 3 above, pp 29 ff. See also Chinchón Álvarez, J, "El viaje a ninguna parte: Memoria, leyes, historia y olvido sobre la guerra civil y el pasado autoritario en España. Un examen desde el derecho internacional", *Revista del Instituto Interamericano de Derechos Humanos*, vol 45, 2007, p 126, fn 23; Aguilar Fernández, fn 17 above, p 162; and Aguilar Fernández, P, *Memoria y olvido de la Guerra Civil española*, Madrid: Alianza Editorial, pp 266–271.

political reasons related to the war and the dictatorship".[44] In reality, this statement conceals the fact that it granted protection from prosecution not only to the democratic opposition, including terrorist groups that had fought against the dictatorship and committed politically motivated crimes, but also to public authorities and officials who had committed crimes to defend the Francoist regime.[45]

In general, the Amnesty Law covered all acts that had been committed with political intent regardless of their results; criminal acts and omissions realized prior to 15 December 1976; and acts of the same character realized between 15 December 1976 and 15 June 1977. Furthermore, to the extent that the law also amnestied acts of the same nature and intentionality realized until 16 October 1977, provided that they had not resulted in grave violence against the life and integrity of persons, its adoption was perceived as inducing the re-establishment of public liberties and as revindicating the autonomy of the peoples of Spain. In particular, the law in question amnestied the crimes of rebellion and sedition, conscientious objection to military service, contempt of court for not having denounced political crimes as well as acts of expression and opinion (Article 1). However, also amnestied were those criminal acts and omissions that had been committed by authorities and public officials when conducting investigations or prosecutions of acts with political intent as well as the crimes committed by the public officials and agents against the exercise of the rights of persons (Article 2).

6.2.2 *Outside the criminal justice context*

With the arrival of democracy, a series of laws were adopted for the purpose of affording economic benefits to victims who had fought in the war on the side of the Republicans and victims of Francoist repression. In the light of these measures, it may be argued that transitional politics moved away from a model of absolute oblivion to one that aspired to rehabilitate victims whose fate until that point had been totally neglected.[46]

Indeed, already in 1975, the newly elected democratic government enacted laws to rehabilitate public officials who had lost their positions during the Civil War or because of the depuration measures that followed.[47] The Law Decree

44 *General Report of the Inter-ministerial Commission*, fn 3 above, p 27.

45 For a detailed account of the general pardons granted between 1936 and 1975, see Linde Paniagua, E, *Amnistía e indulto en España*, Madrid: Tucar, 1976, pp 117 ff. In 1969, Franco published the Decreto-Ley 10/1969, *Boletín Oficial del Estado*, no 78, 1 April 1969, statute-barring all crimes committed prior to 1 April 1939.

46 Chinchón Álvarez, fn 43 above, p 137.

47 See, e.g. Decreto 3357/1975, de 5 de diciembre, por el que se declaran revisadas de oficio y anuladas las sanciones administrativas acordadas de conformidad con lo establecido en la Ley de 10 de febrero de 1939, de responsabilidad politica, *Boletín Oficial del Estado*, no 308, 24 December 1975 (declaring the administrative sanctions adopted within the framework

10/1976 of 30 July related to amnesty[48] as well as the definitive Amnesty Law of 1977 envisaged the full restitution of active and passive rights of civil servants. These legislative acts were then complemented with others that rehabilitated local public officials, assistant personnel in courts and tribunals, teaching staff as well as military personnel who had been separated from service during the dictatorship.[49] The Republican army officers who had not been able to reintegrate into the armed forces in 1977 and had instead retired were also given some benefits.[50]

In fact, at the time of the transition, significant efforts were made to ensure that economic benefits (mainly in the form of pensions) were given to persons who had been injured during the Civil War and the dictatorship.[51] Many of those who had opposed the previous regime and been prosecuted for criminal acts and omissions with political intent (or their surviving family members) were thus granted pensions. As from 1975 onwards, an extravagant body of

of Law on Political Responsibility of 10 February 1939 revised and annulled *ex oficio*); and Orden de 5 de diciembre de 1975 por la que se extienden los beneficios del decreto de indulto al ámbito académico, *Boletín Oficial del Estado*, no 298, 12 December 1975 (extending the benefits of the decree granting general pardon to the academic realm). See also Orden por la que se hace extensivo a las Entidades Locales la aplicación del indulto concedido por el Decreto 2940/1975, de 25 de noviembre, *Boletín Oficial del Estado*, no 308, 24 December 1975 (extending the effects of the decree granting pardons to public officials of corporations and business franchise holders of public services); Real Decreto 1135/1977, de 27 de mayo, sobre indulto a personal de las Fuerzas Armadas, *Boletín Oficial del Estado*, no 127, 28 May 1977 (concerning pardons to personnel of the armed forces); and Real Decreto 1554/1977, de 2 de junio, sobre integración en el Cuerpo de Profesores Agregados de Institutos de Enseñanza Media de los Profesores procedentes de los Cursillos de Selección y Perfeccionamiento de 1933 y 1936, *Boletín Oficial del Estado*, no 158, 4 July 1977 (related to professional integration of teachers). I am grateful to Paloma Aguilar for sharing all of this information with me. For a chronological list with all of the measures (related to rehabilitation, compensation and personal recognition), see Aguilar Fernández, P, *Políticas de la memoria y memorias de la política en la dictadura y en la democracia*, Madrid: Alianza Editorial, 2008, pp 506–520.

48 Real Decreto-ley 10/1976, de 10 de julio, sobre amnistia, *Boletín Oficial del Estado*, no 186, 4 August 1976.

49 For a more comprehensive account of this field of legislation, see Gil Gil, fn * at the start of this chapter, pp 47 ff.

50 Real Decreto-ley 6/1978, de 6 de marzo, sobre situación de los militares que tomaron parte en la guerra civil, *Boletín Oficial del Estado*, no 56, 7 March 1978; Ley 10/1980, de 14 de marzo, sobre modificación del Real Decreto-ley 6/1978, de 6 de marzo, por el que se regula la situación de los militares que intervinieron en la guerra civil, *Boletín Oficial del Estado*, no 76, 28 March 1980; and Ley 37/1984, de 22 de octubre, de reconocimiento de derechos y servicios prestados a quienes durante la guerra civil formaron parte de las Fuerzas Armadas, Fuerzas de Orden Público y Cuerpo de Carabineros de la República, *Boletín Oficial del Estado*, no 262, 1 November 1984. For a more detailed analysis, see Chinchón Álvarez, fn 43 above, pp 138 ff.

51 See also *General Report of the Inter-ministerial Commission*, fn 3 above, p 38. For an account of how difficult it was to equate the pensions of the mutilated, public officials and widows of republicans, and the years of discriminations suffered, see pp 180–183.

legislation devoted to pensions, benefits and economic assistance emerged.[52] The Autonomous Communities complemented the system of state pensions to cover other persons whose liberty had been deprived on political grounds;[53] they also adopted laws related to the restitution of property that had been confiscated from political parties and labour unions.[54] A few Autonomous Communities even initiated a process of searching and recuperating the bodies of persons who had suffered extrajudicial executions and disappeared.[55]

Renewed public attention to these and similar questions was manifested in November 2002 when the Spanish Parliament adopted a Declaration concerning the Recognition of the Rights of the Victims of the Civil War and the Francoist regime.[56] The declaration called for the recuperation of documents related to the Civil War; the establishment of a General Archive to collect these documents,[57] and for public assistance in the localization and exhumation of mass graves as well as the identification of the human remains in these graves.[58] Thereafter, in September 2004, the government created an Inter-ministerial Commission for the Study of the Situation of Victims of the Civil War and

52 Gil Gil, fn * at the start of this chapter, pp 62 ff.

53 See also Chinchón Álvarez, fn 43 above, p 143.

54 Law 4/1986 of 8 January concerning concession of accumulated goods of labour unionist patrimony (elaborated by Royal Decree 1671/1986 of 1 August); Law 43/1998 of 15 December concerning restitution and compensation to political parties of goods and rights confiscated in the application of Law on Political Responsibility in the period between 1936 and 1939 (elaborated by Royal Decree 610/1999 of 16 April and modified recently by Law 26/12/2007). For the outcome of the restitution process, see *General Report of the Inter-ministerial Commission*, fn 3 above, pp 62 ff. But note, however, that, with the exception of the Basque Country, no similar measures have been adopted for the purpose of restitution of property that had been confiscated from private persons and associations other than the labour unions.

55 *General Report of the Inter-ministerial Commission*, fn 3 above, pp 80 ff. Prior to the adoption of the Historic Memory Law in 2007, the Autonomous Communities treated this issue differently; while some showed great sensibility and interest, others did not. By the end of 2008, 284 mass graves from the Civil War and the Francoist regime had been identified. Over six years, the Association for the Recuperation of Historic Memory had exhumed 900 bodies in about 80 graves. Among the most recent studies worthy of citation is a report and a map of mass graves published in December 2010 by the government of Andalusia, which registers more than 600 mass graves only in Andalucía containing about 47,000 victims. One calculates that there may be some 2,000 mass graves in Spain. See Consejería de Justicia de Andalucía, *Mapa de fosas communes de la Guerra Civil y la repression franquista*, 29 December 2010. Available online at http://memoriahistorica.org.es/joomla/index.php/component/content/article/108-andalucia-desvela-pueblo-a-pueblo-el-terror-franquista.

56 The declaration was approved by unanimity while the conservative party governed. For other measures of recognition or reparation with symbolic character adopted since 1978, see Table 11 in Aguilar, fn 47 above, pp 513 ff.

57 See Chinchón Álvarez, fn 43 above, p 144.

58 Aguilar, P, "Presencia y ausencia de la guerra civil en la democracia española. Reflexiones en torno a la articulación y ruptura del 'pacto de silencio'", in Aróstegui, J and Godicheau, F (eds), *Guerra civil, Mito y Memoria*, Madrid: Marcial Pons, 2006, p 272.

Francoism,[59] with the task of studying all of the legislative actions that had been adopted until that point with the objective of enforcing the right to reparation for victims of the Civil War and Francoism and to examine the need for additional measures. In its concluding recommendations, the Commission set forth a number of proposals that came to be incorporated into the Law 52/2007 of 26 December which recognizes and amplifies rights and establishes measures in favour of those who suffered persecution or violence during the Civil War and the dictatorship (in popular parlance, referred to as the "Historic Memory Law").[60]

In the process of drafting the Historic Memory Law, a sour and undeserved polemic emerged between the government and the main opposition party: the Popular Party (*Partido Popular*). In the end, the law gained the support of all the parliamentary groups except for that party and the Catalonian Left Republican Party (*Esquerra Republicana de Catalunya*). Both opposed the law, but on very different grounds. While the former perceived the law as unnecessary and even harmful to society as it would "reopen wounds", the latter, in contrast, maintained that it was insufficient as it failed to annul the unjust or wrongful sentences that had been dictated during the Francoist regime.

What follows is a summary of the principal actions called for in the Historic Memory Law.

6.2.2.1 *Condemning the laws, tribunals and convictions of the past*

To begin with, the law publicly declares the *radically unjust character* of all convictions, sanctions and other forms of violent acts produced for political, ideological or religious reasons, or against conduct manifesting a person's choice of culture, language or sexual orientation during the Civil War and the dictatorship. It also entails an official declaration about the injustice implied by the exiles of many Spaniards during these periods (Article 2).[61]

Furthermore, the law in question publicly proclaims as *illegitimate* those tribunals, juries and any other penal or administrative organs which had been constituted during the Civil War for the purpose of imposing sanctions of a personal character to suppress and punish political, ideological motives or religious convictions. In a similar manner, it affirms as illegitimate a series of

59 Chinchón Álvarez, fn 43 above, pp 144 ff.

60 Ley 52/2007, de 26 de diciembre, por la que se reconocen y amplían derechos y se establecen medidas en favor de quienes padecieron persecución o violencia durante la guerra civil y la dictadura, *Boletín Oficial del Estado*, no 310, 27 December 2007.

61 The provision gives a right to the victims or his or her relatives to obtain from the Ministry of Justice a Declaration of reparation and personal recognition which is compatible with any other form of reparation envisaged in the legal order, but which shall not constitute an entitlement to recognition of patrimonial responsibility of the State neither of any Public Administration, nor shall it give effect to reparation or indemnity of economic or professional character (Art 4) (unofficial translation).

sentences and decisions, in particular, those that had been handed down by the Tribunal for the Repression of Freemasonry and Communism, the Tribunal for Public Order, as well as the Tribunals for Political Responsibilities and the War Councils that had been created to punish crimes committed with political and ideological motives or on the basis of religious convictions. Also asserted as illegitimate are the convictions and sanctions dictated by tribunals or penal or administrative organs operating during the dictatorship to target those who defended the legality of the Second Republic and sought to re-establish a democratic regime or to exercise rights and liberties that are now recognized by the Constitution (Article 3).[62]

The law also proclaims the derogation of the following laws: the War Faction of 28 July 1936, the National Defence Junta approved by Decree no 79, the Faction of 31 August 1936, and especially Decree no 55 of General Franco, adopted on 1 November 1936; the Laws of State Security of 12 July 1940 and 29 March 1941 concerning reform of the Penal Code to include a list of crimes against the state; the Law of 2 March 1943 modifying the crime of military rebellion; Law Decree of 18 April 1947 concerning banditry and terrorism, as well as Laws 42/1971 and 44/1971 reforming the Military Justice Code; the Laws of 9 February 1939 and 19 February 1942 on Political Responsibilities, and the Law of 1 March 1940 concerning repression of freemasonry and communism, the Law of 30 July 1959 on public order and Law 15/1963 creating the Tribunal on Public Order.[63]

6.2.2.2 *Benefits, indemnities and pensions*

Besides these public declarations, the law seeks to improve the scheme of benefits recognized in Law 5/1979 of 18 September. In particular, it affords pensions, medical-pharmaceutical assistance and social assistance to widows, children and other relatives of Spaniards who died as a consequence or as a result of the Civil War (Article 5). It also extends the scheme in question to persons who can demonstrate that they have suffered deprivation of liberty in penitentiary establishments or in disciplinary confinements (*Batallones Disciplinarios*)[64] and to families of those convicted to death and executed before having completed three years in prison (Article 7) and had reached the age of 60 years in 31 December 1990.[65] In addition, it also proclaims that the pensions

62 The aforementioned affords a right to the victim and his or her relatives to obtain from the Ministry of Justice a Declaration of Reparation and Personal Recognition with the effects envisaged in the preceding paragraph (Art 4) (unofficial translation).

63 In reality, this provision is superfluous because all of these laws have already been expressly derogated, if not during the dictatorship, then by the Spanish Constitution of 1978.

64 This extension has its origin in the decision of the Tribunal Constitucional de España (Spanish Constitutional Court), Segunda Sala, STC 180/2005, 4 July 2005. Available online at www.tribunalconstitucional.es/es/jurisprudencia/Paginas/Sentencia.aspx?cod=8634.

65 These indemnities are exempted from taxation (Art 8). Also envisaged is the restitution in the form of assistance to those who in previous years have been subject to taxation of these indemnities (Art 9) (unofficial translation).

granted by Law 37/1984 of 22 October will extend to personnel of the *Marina Mercante* who had been incorporated into the Republican Army as from 18 July 1936. Also affirmed is the granting of indemnities in the case of death resulting from the defence and revindication of liberties and democratic rights during the period between 1 January 1968 and 6 October 1977 (Article 10).

6.2.2.3 The mass graves

The Historic Memory Law creates an obligation for the public administration to assist family relatives of those who disappeared during the Civil War and the dictatorship in their search and identification of their loved ones. It furthermore upholds a commitment of the central government to elaborate work plans and to provide subsidies to carry out these tasks. In particular, it mandates the government to develop a protocol of co-ordinated action and to preserve the areas in which the mass graves may be localized as well as to allow the temporal occupation of these areas (Articles 11 to 14).

6.2.2.4 Symbols, public monuments and archives

The law in focus also stipulates the withdrawal of coats of arms, insignias and other objects as well as other commemorative acknowledgements (personal and collective) appraising the military uprising in 1936, the Civil War and the repression exerted by the dictatorship (Article 15).[66] It also affirms that the monument *Valle de los Caídos* where Franco is buried is to be strictly governed by general laws applicable to places of worship and public cemeteries as well as prohibit the performance of political or passionate acts meant to acclaim the Civil War, its leaders or the Francoist regime on its premises (Article 16). Moreover, the law envisages the creation of a Historical Memory Documentary Centre and a General Archive in Salamanca to collect the documents related to the Civil War for the purpose of facilitating research about the Civil War and dictatorship (Article 20). In this context, it also recognizes the right of private persons to access the documents deposited in public or private archives and sustained by public funds, as well as to obtain copies of requested documents (Article 22).

6.3 Revisiting the possibility of criminal justice and the limited competences of the *Audiencia Nacional*

Until recently, few private persons had denounced the crimes of the past before Spanish courts because the Amnesty Law of 1977 was perceived as ruling out any such action. One exception is the *Ruano* case, in which the accusing lawyer

66 The withdrawal of subsidies and public assistance may be included among the measures. Exempted are the acknowledgements that are of strict private memory, without exalting the confronted, or those who are motivated by artistic, architectural or artistic-religious reasons protected by law.

had requested the confession of the accused in order to admit the application of the Amnesty Law in relation to two policemen who stood accused for having killed a young student. From the standpoint of the accusing lawyer, the application of the Amnesty Law was not disputed; what he argued was that, in order for the application to proceed, the accused had to confess that their act had been based on political motives and that this fact legitimated the application of the Amnesty Law. Nevertheless, since the policemen denied both the charge of having killed Ruano and the charge that they had acted with political intent, the amnesty was not considered by the court.[67] While the accusation strategy in this case seems to have been an attempt to use the Amnesty Law as a mechanism of inquiry into the truth of what happened to Ruano and not as a way of imposing absolute oblivion of the event, the strategy has nevertheless not been followed in any other case.

A second attempt to resort to criminal justice occurred in 1998 when a complaint was brought to the *Audiencia Nacional* by a "victims' association" for the murder of *Paracuellos del Jarama* during the Civil War.[68] However, in a decision on 8 March 2000, the investigating judge in the case, Judge Baltasar Garzón, rejected the complaint by upholding the prosecutorial objections that the crimes in question had been prescribed and amnestied and that the crime of genocide had not been codified in international law at the time of the facts. Instead, he decided that the documents related to the case were to be shelved.[69]

However, the panorama changed on 16 October 2008 when Judge Garzón decided to open a criminal investigation into the allegations concerning the detentions, murders and concealment of bodies of thousands of Spaniards which had been realized during the Civil War and the post-war period (between 17 July 1936 and 31 December 1951).[70] According to Garzón, the acts amounted to illegal detentions without giving any account of the final destination of the victims, enforced disappearances and crimes against humanity. No less than 50 people—all of them already dead—were accused by the judge of being responsible for these acts. On 20 October 2008, Javier Zaragoza, Chief-Prosecutor of the *Audencia Nacional*, interposed a motion of appeal against Garzón's decision.[71] While admitting that he personally understood the purpose behind the order, that is, to speed up the implementation of the Historic Memory Law related to the recuperation of bodies of persons who had disappeared and been buried in the fields and gutters as well as to rectify some of that law's deficiencies, in

67 Audiencia Provincial de Madrid, Sección II, Sumario 6/69, "Caso Enrique Ruano", Auto (Decision), 19 December 1995. In the end, the two accused were set free as a result of lack of evidence. For a more detailed account of this case, see Gil Gil, fn * at the start of this chapter, pp 85 ff.

68 I am grateful to Manuel Ollé, who has provided me with all of this information.

69 For a more detailed account, see Gil Gil, fn * at the start of this chapter, p 90.

70 *Audiencia Nacional*, Juzgado Central de Instrucción no 5, Diligencias Previas-Procedimiento Abreviado 399/2006 V, Auto (Decision) of 16 October 2008.

71 Recurso de Apelación del Fiscal Jefe de la Audiencia Nacional, 20 October 2008 (on file with the author).

particular, the absence of any official investigation into the events and the passivity of the public administration in general, the prosecutor affirmed that the criminal justice process was simply not the adequate means to pursue these ends.[72]

From a legal technical standpoint, the order of Judge Garzón is replete with controversial legal reasoning. In what follows is a critical examination of four strategies that he developed to overcome what in my view constitute fundamental limits imposed by domestic law and which impede the *Audiencia Nacional* from investigating and prosecuting the crimes of the past today: the limited competence of the *Audencia* itself; the constitutional (and international) prohibition against retroactive law to the detriment of the accused; the rules regarding the time limitations of the crimes in focus; and the legal validity of the Amnesty Law.

According to the decision of 16 October 2008, the alleged facts in the case amount to crimes against humanity. However, the *Audiencia Nacional* would only be competent to open proceedings in relation to these types of crimes if committed abroad (on the basis of its universal jurisdiction competence according to Article 23.4 of the Organic Law of the Judicial Branch (*Ley Orgánica del Poder Judicial*—LOPJ)).[73] If the crimes were committed in Spain the courts of first instance would be competent to consider the allegations. In order to circumvent this problem, the judge classifies the facts in the case as constituting a series of crimes connected with another crime that the *Audiencia Nacional* indeed has competence to try (including "connected crimes" connected to it), namely, "the crime against the High Organs of the Nation and Form of Government" (that is, a *coup d'état* against the legitimate government of the Republic).[74]

Nevertheless, the prosecutor in the case opposed this strategy. As he noted, "the crime against the High Organs of the Nation and Form of Government" is no longer included in the Penal Code. On the other hand, the crime of rebellion which now would be applicable to these kinds of facts and which is recognized in the current Spanish Penal Code (Title XXI) was not considered as a "crime against the High Organs of the Nation and Form of Government" in the Penal Code of 1932. Furthermore, according to the prosecutor, it is important not to abuse the provision related to connected crimes (Article 17 of the Law of Criminal Procedure)[75] so as to set in motion a general framework trial

72 For an argument against "truth proceedings", i.e. to use criminal justice as a mechanism only to find out what happened and to oblige the state to engage itself in an active manner in the search for the disappeared and not to impose a criminal sanction, which is a mechanism imported from Argentina, see Pastor, D, "Procesos penales sólo para conocer la verdad?" *Jueces para la Democracia*, no 59, July 2007, pp 95 ff and 101 ff.

73 Ley Orgánica 6/1985 de 1 de Julio, de Poder Judicial, *Boletín Oficial del Estado*, no 157, 2 July 1985.

74 LOPJ, Art 65.1.a.

75 Ley de Enjuiciamiento Criminal (Spanish law on criminal procedure). Gaceta no 260, 17 September 1882—Gaceta no 283, 10 October 1882, available online at http://noticias.juridicas.com/base_datos/Penal/lecr.html.

which would not facilitate but rather would frustrate the task of investigation. Furthermore, in my opinion, it is a procedural fraud to consider only "connecting crimes" as an object of procedure, leaving aside the principal crime.

6.3.1 The principle of non-retroactive law

Although Judge Garzón admits that Article 607*bis* of the Penal Code (regarding crimes against humanity) was included only in 2003 and entered into force in 2004 and that, out of respect for the constitutional provision prohibiting non-retroactive application of unfavourable law, cannot be applied to facts that took place prior to this incorporation, he nevertheless qualifies the facts as amounting to crimes against humanity.

However, in order to consider the facts as punishable under Spanish criminal law, he defines the same facts as amounting to ordinary crimes under the domestic Penal Code (that is, as illegal detentions with aggravated circumstances). In my view, this kind of double qualification is unacceptable. Even if this way of proceeding is certainly not an invention of the investigating judge of the *Audiencia Nacional*, but has been practised extensively in Latin America for the purpose of bringing under the heading of crimes against humanity a series of alleged consequences which at the time of their commission had not yet been crystallized into law,[76] this strategy is especially problematic to apply in the Spanish case considering that the facts in the case are prior to any national or international regulation of crimes against humanity and their alleged consequences.

The atrocities committed during the Civil War cannot be classified as crimes against humanity as defined in international law since it developed only later on.[77] From the standpoint of international law, at the time of the events, only the Martens Clause (included in the Preamble of the Hague Convention of 1899) was in force; still, as we know, that clause is formulated in very broad terms and does not include a definition of a crime.[78] To this should be added that the Laws of War in force at the time of the Civil War were limited to international armed conflicts and did not cover internal ones. For this reason, the law of the war of that time would not be applicable to the Spanish case.[79]

76 For a critical account of this body of case law, see Malarino, E, *Jurisprudencia latinoamericana sobre derecho penal internacional*, Montevideo: Konrad-Adenauer Stiftung, 2008, pp 420 ff and 442 ff. According to Malarino, this way of proceeding implies the creation of differentiated and exceptional criminal law for certain crimes or delinquents which infringes upon the principle of legality and the rights of the accused.

77 For a more detailed account, see Gil Gil, fn * at the start of this chapter, pp 114 ff.

78 This opinion is also expressed by the Chief Prosecutor of the *Audiencia Nacional*, Javier Zaragoza, in his motion of appeal on 20 October 2008. The same opinion is shared by Ambos, K, Prologue, in Gil Gil, fn * at the start of this chapter, p 14.

79 It is not true that the Geneva Convention of 12 October 1949 refers to the Nuremberg Principles (neither in Art 85 nor in any other part) as the judge affirms in his decision. The judge also alludes to Law no 10 of the Allied Control Council of 1945 to support the

The situation is different when it comes to the crimes committed after 1954[80] because of the international legal developments that took place as a result of the Nuremberg Principles. Nevertheless, two problems emerge for the Spanish courts when seeking to apply the category of crimes against humanity as recognized in these principles to the criminal activities that were committed by the Francoist regime after 1954. The first problem is that the Spanish Penal Code incorporated the notion of crimes against humanity only in 2003[81] given that the Spanish Constitution prohibits the retroactive application of criminal law to the detriment of the accused and also upholds the principle of legality. In particular, according to the Spanish Supreme Court, the investigation and prosecution of acts committed prior to 2003 on the basis that such acts amount to crimes against humanity under customary international law would violate these constitutionally entrenched rights.[82]

argument about the independence of crimes against humanity from the war situation. However, it is doubtful whether Law no 10 reflected customary international law in force at the time of its adoption. First of all, because it was part of a law of occupation, i.e. domestic law emanating from occupying authorities and, secondly, because both the Statute of the Nuremberg Tribunal on which this law was based as well as the Nuremberg Principles which were approved later on reaffirmed the connection with an international conflict. The debate in the International Law Commission lasted until agreement was finally reached on an independent concept of crime against humanity in 1954. For an account of the development of the crime against humanity and the reasons for which Law no 10 abstained from requiring a connection with war, see Gil Gil, A, *Derecho penal internacional*, Madrid: Tecnos, 1999, pp 106 ff, in particular, fn 39.

80 Date in which for the first time the crime against humanity is independent from the connection of international armed conflict. This position requires that we interpret the final version of the First Draft Articles of the Code of Crimes against Peace and Security of Humanity as representing the codification of what was already international custom, which is doubtful given that the Draft Articles were not endorsed until 1998 and that the drafting of the crimes against humanity had changed in a considerable manner since 1954 until today. For example, the 1954 version required that the actions had been realized on the basis of a given set of motives (a requirement that thereafter disappeared) while not imposing the requirement of a generalized or systematic character (a requirement that is introduced in 1996). See Gil Gil, fn 79 above, pp 139–143. For a detailed account of the development of the contents of the crime in each of the UN Draft Articles, see Liñán Lafuente, A, *El desarrollo del crimen de persecución en el ámbito del crimen contra la humanidad y su reformulación en el art. 607. bis, del Cp español: Una propuesta alternativa*, Doctoral thesis, University of Complutense in Madrid, 2007 (unpublished manuscript), pp 161 ff.

81 Ley Orgánica 15/2003, de 25 de noviembre, por la que se modifica la Ley Orgánica 10/1995, de 23 de noviembre, del Código Penal, *Boletín Oficial del Estado*, no 283, 26 November 2003, concerning Art 607*bis*. The new provision entered into force in 2004.

82 *Audiencia Nacional*, Sala de lo Penal, Sección Tercera, "Caso de Scilingo", Sumario 19/1997, Sentencia (Sentence) 16/2005, 16 April 2005. Available online at www.apdhe.org/InformacionDestacada/documentos/SentenciaAN19abril05ScilingoArgentina.pdf. The Spanish doctrine defended the principle of legality and the prohibition against unfavourable criminal law. See Lamarca Pérez, C, "Jurisprudencia aplicada a la práctica. Internacionalización del Derecho Penal y principio de legalidad: el Caso Scilingo", *La ley penal: revista de derecho penal, procesal y penitenciario*, no 34, 2007, pp 69–77; Bueno Arús, F, "Jurisprudencia

A similar problem emerges when seeking to resort to domestic law in the qualification of the facts. Indeed, the investigating judge determines that the acts in focus amount to ordinary crimes under Spanish law, namely, that of illegal detention aggravated by not giving any account of the fate or final destiny of the detainee (which according to contemporary international criminal law constitute "enforced disappearances"). Still, it must be noted that such acts had not yet been criminalized in the Spanish Penal Code of 1932. And, even if it is true that from 1944 onwards the Penal Code did include the crime of illegal detention with the aggravated circumstance resulting from withholding information of the whereabouts of the detained,[83] according to the law this aggravated crime of illegal detention could only be committed by private persons and not by officials. It must be recalled that, at the time, the common illegal detentions realized by public officials and authorities were seen as privileged actions and punished by ridiculous sanctions.[84]

6.3.2 The statutory limitations on legal action

The investigating judge in the case advances the claim that the alleged crimes have not been statute barred due to a time limitation and sets forth several legal arguments in support. First, he argues that crimes against humanity are not subject to any rules of time limitation. However, besides the fact that the classification of the acts in focus as amounting to crimes against humanity is in any case incorrect (see previous section), there was no international legal provision in force at the time of the criminal activities that prohibited the application of statutory limitations for crimes against humanity. In fact, it would be very problematic to argue that events that took place prior to the

aplicada a la práctica. Fuentes y principios del Derecho Penal Internacional de nuestro tiempo: reflexiones sobre la sentencia de la Audiencia Nacional en el Caso Scilingo", *La ley penal: revista de derecho penal, procesal y penitenciario*, no 34, 2007, pp 78–96; and Gil Gil, A, "La sentencia de la Audiencia Nacional en el caso Scilingo", *Jueces para la Democracia*, July 2005, pp 7 ff. Carlos Castresana, in contrast, defended the judicial decision. See Castresana, C, "De Nüremberg a Madrid: la sentencia del caso Scilingo", *Jueces para la Democracia*, November 2005, pp 3–11. However, the Supreme Court rejected that argument in a judgment on 1 October 2007. See Tribunal Supremo, Sala de lo Penal, STS 798/2007, 1 October 2007. Available online at www.derechos.org/nizkor/espana/juicioral/doc/sentenciats.html#Tribunal. For an analysis of the Supreme Court judgment on 1 October 2007, see Gil Gil, A, "Principio de legalidad y crímenes internacionales. Luces y sombras en la sentencia del Tribunal Supremo en el caso Scilingo", in Cuerda Riezu, A and Jiménez García, F, *Nuevos Desafíos del Derecho penal internacional*, Madrid: Tecnos, 2009, pp 391 ff.

83 See Art 483, which was reintroduced in 1944; it did not exist in the Penal Code of 1932.

84 See Arts 184 ff and the previous Penal Code as already in 1944 the crimes in question existed and imposed only sanctions of suspension for illegal detentions during less than three days or suspension and fine if the detention lasted for 15 days, forestalling prison only if the detention lasted for more than a month. According to the Penal Code now in force, the fact that the perpetrator was a public official or authority is seen as an aggravating circumstance and not a privilege (Art 167).

adoption of the Rome Statute in July 1998 could be subject to the international rule of non-statutory limitations for crimes against humanity as it can hardly be said that that rule was part of customary international law prior to its adoption. In any case, it would be even more doubtful if such a rule existed prior to its international codification in 1968.[85] To this should be added that the international rule concerning non-statutory limitations for crimes against humanity was incorporated into Spanish law for the first time in 2003. On several occasions, the Supreme Court has manifested its opposition against the retroactive application of any changes of the law regarding statutory limitations as it could prejudice the accused.[86]

Probably conscious of this range of difficulties, Judge Baltasar Garzón argues, in the second place, that the crime of illegal detention with aggravated circumstance has not been prescribed given that it is a permanent crime that lasts until the bodies of the detainees who disappeared have been found. However, according to the prosecutor in the case, such interpretation would be incompatible with the constitutional interpretation of that crime and he insists that the facts amounted to murders and not illegal detentions.[87] In general, the argument that the crimes are still lasting seems problematic to sustain as the anti-legal situation must be seen as having been brought to an end when the detainees were set free or died. In any case, the crime of aggravated illegal detention is only applicable if committed from 1944 onwards and by private subjects. And, if only the common crime of illegal detention is applicable—and not the aggravated one—the calculation of the time period for prescription must necessarily begin when the deprivation of liberty ended whether by death or because the person was freed.

85 Spain is not party to the Convention on the Non-Applicability of Statutory Limitations to War Crimes and Crimes against Humanity, UNGA Res 2391 (XXIII), annex, 23, UN Doc A/7218, 26 November 1968 (entering into force for its States Parties on 11 November 1970). For an argument against the idea that the Convention of 1968 represents international custom in the light of its modest number of States Parties, see Remiro Brotons, A, "Los crímenes de Derecho Internacional y su persecución judicial", *El Derecho penal Internacional—Cuadernos de Derecho Judicial*, no 7, 2001, p 120.

86 For a more detailed account, see Gil Gil, fn * at the start of this chapter, pp 117 ff.

87 According to the Chief-Prosecutor: "One has avoided the application of time-limits rules to delinquent acts perpetrated in the best of cases almost 60 years ago, and one used as a norm to cover-up the criminal law category of the crime of detention without giving any information about the whereabouts of the victim, to arrive at a particular interpretation of the rules of prescription for this crime, when it is public and notorious that the victims were thereafter executed and that, as a consequence, we find ourselves clearly before the crime of murder, a circumstance that brought the illicit situation consisting of liberty deprivation to an end (requisite contemplated in article 132 to initiate the calculation of the prescription) . . . In consequence, the critical moment for calculating the time-limits in the case of illegal detention begins, as for each and every one of the crimes recognized in articles 163 to 166, is that in which the situation of liberty deprivation ended, whether it was because the subject was freed or because the subject evidently died as happened in all these cases" (unofficial translation).

Furthermore, the argument about the permanence of the crime appears somewhat surrealistic in the case in focus given that those who are accused of the crime are already dead. In order to sustain this discourse, the judge mixes wrongfully the alleged international responsibility of the state to search for those who disappeared with the alleged criminal responsibility of the accused.[88] To this end, he argues that as long as the Spanish state does not find the bodies, the crime has not been consumed. Nevertheless, it is clear that criminal liability is personal and does not depend on the passivity of the state. Still, a person who is dead neither acts nor omits and can therefore not continue committing a crime.

Finally, the judge in the case also argues that the time period for calculating prescription must be seen as having been suspended during the dictatorship given that it was not possible to investigate or prosecute the crimes in question during this period. Nevertheless, the truth is that the Penal Code does not establish a possibility of suspending the time period for prescription for this reason, although perhaps it should. Even so, as the prosecutor in the case rightly affirms, even if we were to admit this kind of interruption, it would in any case only last until 1978 when the new Constitution entered into force (something which the judge also admits). But since 1978 and until now sufficient time has passed to consider the crimes in question as statute barred (a maximum of 20 years).

6.3.3 The Amnesty Law

The judge in the case also sets aside the Amnesty Law of 1977. In support, he cites jurisprudence related to the inadmissibility of amnesties in the case of grave human rights violations.[89] Certainly, recent criticism has been mounted against the validity of the Spanish Amnesty Law in light of contemporary international law.[90] Indeed, the question as to whether there is an international legal obligation to prosecute grave crimes is now settled; above all, it has been affirmed in the Rome Statute as well as the Convention against Genocide, the

88 The term "supposed" is used because it is not clear if the obligations that were assumed by the Spanish state later on extend to events that took place prior to the signing of the international conventions. However, in any case, there is at least a moral obligation of the state to involve itself in a more active manner in the localization, recuperation and identification of the bodies.

89 See below my criticism of this argument.

90 Chinchón Álvarez, fn 43 above, pp 123 ff and 201. The same opinion has been expressed by Amnesty International (Spanish section), "Víctimas de la guerra civil y el franquismo: no hay derecho. Preocupaciones sobre el Proyecto de Ley de Derechos de las Víctimas de la Guerra Civil y del Franquismo", Report, 16 November 2006, pp 19 ff, according to which amnesty laws even when approved by democratic parliaments are illegal under international law. Available online at https://doc.es.amnesty.org/cgi-bin/ai/BRSCGI?CMD=VERDOC&BASE=SIAI&SORT=&DOCR=1&RNG=10&SEPARADOR=&&INAI=EUR4100406.

Convention against Torture and the Four Geneva Conventions. Still, these Conventions oblige only those states that have ratified them and are applicable only with regard to certain crimes.[91] And, in any case, none of these conventions challenges the Spanish Amnesty Law either because they were adopted after the Amnesty Law came into force or because the crimes committed in Spain do not correspond to the crimes specified in these Conventions.

Some international human rights experts understand the UN International Covenant on Civil and Political Rights (ICCPR) and in particular its Article 2(3) in which the right to an effective remedy is affirmed as entailing an international legal obligation to investigate and prosecute human rights violations.[92] This understanding echoes the interpretation set forth by the Inter-American Commission and Court of Human Rights of similar provisions in the Inter-American Convention on Human Rights.[93] But it must be noted that the UN Human Rights Committee has limited the application of Article 2(3) to human rights violations committed following its entry into force in relation to the affected state with the argument that if the human rights violations in question are prior to the entry into force of the Covenant, the right to remedy under Article 2(3) does not come into play given that there has been no violation of the Covenant.[94] According to the Committee, this means that an amnesty law concerning such abuses is outside the reach of the Covenant. Basing itself on a literal reading of the relevant provision, the Committee holds that the right to an effective remedy can be effectively upheld only when these temporal limits are respected.[95] Thus, from the standpoint of the Committee, the Spanish

91 Ambos, K, *El marco jurídico de la justicia de transición*, Bogotá: Editorial Temis, 2008, pp 30–31.

92 Chinchón, J, "Transición española y justicia transicional: ¿qué papel juega el ordenamiento jurídico internacional en un proceso de transición? A propósito de la coherencia, buena fe y otros principios de derecho internacional postergados en la transición política de España", in *La memoria como conflicto. Memoria e Historia de la Guerra Civil y el Franquismo*, Entelequia, Dossier monográfico, *Revista Interdisciplinar*, no 7, 2008, p 23. Available online at www.nodo50.org/pozosdecaude/noticias_breves/La%20memoria%20como%20conflicto_Alesandre%20Froidevaux.pdf.

93 For a more detailed account of this argument and my response, see Gil Gil, fn * at the start of this chapter, pp 100 ff.

94 The case concerned the validity of the Argentinean Final Stop Law in the light of Art 2.3 of the International Covenant on Civil and Political Rights in relation to murders and disappearances. The UN Human Rights Committee declared the non-retroactive character of the Covenant, including in relation to cases involving disappearances where the victim was still missing. See the decisions of the UN Human Rights Committee in response to the following communications: *S.E. v Argentina*, Communication no 275/1988, UN Doc CCPR/C/38/D/275/1988 (1990), 4 April 1990; *RAVN et al v Argentina*, Communication nos 343, 344 and 345/1988, UN Doc CCPR/C/38/D/344/1988, 5 April 1990. For a similar communication, see also *Acuña Inostroza et al (represented by Fundación de Ayuda Social de las Iglesias Cristianas) v Chile*, Communication No 717/1996, UN Doc CCPR/C/66/D/717/1996, 16 September 1999.

95 Ambos, K, *Impunidad y Derecho penal internacional*, 2nd edn, Buenos Aires: Editorial Ad Hoc, 1999, p 136.

Amnesty Law does not amount to a violation of Article 2(3) since the human rights violations took place before the Covenant entered into force in relation to Spain (that is, 27 July 1977). In 1977, there were no other international treaties in force that prohibited an Amnesty Law.

Another possibility may be to affirm that the obligation to investigate and prosecute human rights violations (such as acts of torture and extrajudicial executions) was part of customary international law and even constituted *ius cogens* norms prior to 1977.[96] However, the problem faced by those who entertain this claim is that there is no state practice and not even an *opinio iuris* that demonstrate the actual existence of such an obligation before 1977.[97] It is in the 1990s when a radical change of attitude first occurred in favour of an understanding of international law as comprising an international legal obligation to investigate and prosecute serious human rights violations and perhaps also a prohibition of blank amnesty laws.[98]

The judge also adds that the Spanish Amnesty Law does not apply to the facts that he is analyzing, first of all, because they do not constitute political crimes and, secondly, because the crimes continue to be committed after the period envisaged in that law and after the entry into force of the Constitution. Nevertheless, the first ground is difficult to uphold given that the Amnesty

96 *Audiencia Nacional*, Sala de lo Penal, Sección Tercera, Recurso de Apelación no 84/1998 (ARP1998\5943), Auto (Decision) of 4 November 1998, eighth legal reasoning. In relation to the Argentinean Final Stop and Due Obedience laws the *Audiencia Nacional* admitted the possibility that these laws were contrary to *ius cogens* and the treaties ratified by Argentina. However, this was not the decisive argument for not applying them, but rather that this interpretation did not amount to a kind of pardon that prevented the Spanish courts from acting on the basis of their universal jurisdiction competence under Art 23.4 of the LOPJ: "With independence of the fact that the said laws may be contrary to international *ius cogens* and international treaties that Argentina have ratified, the indicated laws become depenalizing norms . . . it would not be possible to fit in the case of acquittal or pardon of an accused in foreign territory (LOPJ, art. 23.2.c), but rather in the case of non-punishable conduct—because of the posterior depenalizing norm—in the country where the crime was committed (LOJP, art. 23.2.a.) for which there is no possibility in the case of extraterritorial jurisdiction or universal persecution by Spanish courts, given what is stated in paragraph 5 of the above-mentioned article 23 . . .". Thus, the *Audiencia Nacional* recognized the possible existence of a general norm that prohibited blanket amnesties, but only by the end of the 1980s, while the Spanish Amnesty Law had been adopted 10 years earlier.

97 It would not even have occurred to Spanish scholars in this period that the amnesty could be legally invalid in the light of international law. Linde Paniagua, who defended his doctoral thesis in the University of Bologna in 1975, refers to amnesty as an instrument to facilitate legal changes that are required as a result of political and social changes and proposes a parliamentary approval as a condition for its acceptability, that its scope relates to its basis and that it respects the principle of equality. However, there is no consideration whatsoever of the idea about limits imposed by human rights. See Paniagua, L, *Amnistía e indulto en España*, Guadalajara: Tucar Ediciones, 1976.

98 Chinchón, J, *Derecho Internacional y transiciones a la democracia y la paz: Hacia un modelo para el castigo de los crímenes pasados a través de la experiencia iberoamericana*, Madrid: Ediciones Parthenon, 2007, p 445.

Law is not limited to political crimes. As the prosecutor in the case reminds us, Article 1(1) of the Amnesty Law refers to crimes with political intent and not political crimes as such, which is not the same thing considering that crimes against humanity, while not amounting to political crimes, can be committed for political motives.[99] On the other hand, quite surprisingly, the judge refrains from mentioning Article 2 of the Amnesty Law, which refers to the crimes of public authorities, agents and officials even if this provision does not require any specific motive or intention.[100] According to this provision, the Amnesty Law covers:

> In any case the criminal acts and omissions committed by authorities, public officials, and the agents of the public order for motives or on the occasion of the investigation and prosecution of the acts entailed in their ambit as well as the crimes committed by the public officials and agents of the public order against the exercise of rights of persons.

From this standpoint, the crimes committed by public authorities would be amnestied even if not amounting to political crimes. To this should be added that, as the prosecutor in the case argues, it is incorrect to equate a self-amnesty law—such as the Chilean or Argentinean ones—with an amnesty law that was adopted by a democratically elected parliament. Evidently, while from the standpoint of contemporary international law this argument could not be sustained, it was not a controversial one in the light of the international law that was in force in 1977.[101]

The second ground that the judge invokes is problematic because it fails to distinguish between the "permanent consummation of a crime" and the "continued commission of a crime". The truth is that the Amnesty Law covers crimes that are initiated within the envisaged time period even if consumed later on. In principle, the permanent character of the crime of enforced disappearance is not incompatible with an amnesty law, but depends upon how that law has been formulated.[102] According to the Spanish Amnesty Law, all acts committed prior to certain dates are amnestied. In addition, Article 1(II) adds that the law

99 For an account of distinct concepts of political crimes, see Cerezo Mir, fn 23 above, p 143. For Cerezo Mir, what is a crime with a political intention and a political crime can only be defined in a subjective sense. However, this understanding does not in any case reflect the interpretation of the 1977 Amnesty Law as it also was applied to terrorists who had committed blood crimes. Hence, given that the equation of the two concepts must be false, it cannot be deduced, as the judge suggests, that everything that is not political crime was excluded from the ambit of the amnesty.

100 This finality was only required with regard to the crimes of the repressors in the *Ruano* case.

101 Spanish scholars active in this period conditioned the legality of an amnesty to its democratic origins, but did not see possible limits imposed for reasons related to the crime itself. See Gil Gil, fn * at the start of this chapter, p 109.

102 See Capellà, fn 8 above (maintaining that enforced disappearances of persons are incapable of being amnestied). See also Rodríguez Arias, M A, "Las fosas de Franco y la diligencia

"understands by the moment of the realization of the act that in which the criminal activity was *initiated*".[103] In general, the argument that the crime continues to be committed is unacceptable since, although the judge focuses only on the second part of the crime, that is, the omission to inform, this part cannot be separated from the act of detention. And, in any case, there are no longer any persons who can be said to continue to commit the crime in question given that the ones listed in the court order are all dead. In addition, as already mentioned, the crime of aggravated illegal detention for withholding information about the whereabouts of the detainee, which the judge utilizes to set forth the argument about the continued commission of the crime, is inapplicable as this crime was not in force at the time of the commission of the acts from the standpoint of the accused.

To conclude, at the time of the Spanish transition, there was no rule of international law in force prohibiting the amnesty. At the same time, it must be noted that the law in question does not impede a foreign court from investigating and prosecuting the crimes committed in Spain; if the selected crimes can be classified as international crimes at the time of their commission and have not been prescribed according to the national laws of that court. And, in the same way, when the *Audiencia* disregarded the Argentinean Final Stop and Due Obedience Laws in the *Scilingo* case, it acted in a correct manner, legally speaking'.[104] The procedural obstacles imposed on national jurisdictions where the crimes were committed do not extend to foreign national courts.[105]

debida del estado ante el crimen de desaparición forzada a la luz de la jurisprudencia de la Corte Interamericana de Derechos Humanos", *Jueces para la democracia*, no 60, November 2007, p 73, basing his argument in Art 18 of the UN Declaration concerning the Protection of All Persons against Enforced Disappearances (1992). However, it is evident that this declaration is not legally binding and that, in case it was, it would not have retroactive effect.

103 Tribunal Supremo de España, Sala de lo Penal, case of *Francisco Soto Nieto*, STS 12637/1986, Judgment of 20 January 1986. In this case, the Supreme Court apparently sidestepped this precept in a case in which it qualified as permanent crime, but in reality it referred to continued criminal activity after the time limits established in the law and not to a merely permanent crime. The case referred to two accused of collaborating with ETA who had maintained a bank account open with money from the organization, realizing transfers following order by ETA after the dates covered by the Amnesty Law. The actions do not amount to permanent crimes, like illegal detention, but crimes with continued character.

104 *Audiencia Nacional*, Sala de lo Penal, Sección Tercera, Recurso de Apelación no 84/1998 (ARP 1998/5943), Auto (Decision) of 4 November 1998, para 8. See also Gil Gil, A, "Spain", in Ambos, K and Malarino, E (eds), *Persecución Penal Nacional de Crímenes Internacionales en América Latina y España*, Montevideo: Konrad-Adenauer-Stiftung, 2003, p 357; and Sancinetti, M and Ferrante, M, *El Derecho penal en la protección de los derechos humanos*, Buenos Aires: Editorial Hammurabi, 1999, p 15.

105 Ambos, fn 91 above, pp 103 ff.

6.4 Outstanding issues

In my view, the Spanish transition is an example of absolute oblivion with partial rehabilitation of the victims. It was the fruit of necessity and the particular political and social juncture in which it was developed. Among the circumstances especially relevant in the Spanish case are the distance between the most bloody crimes and the transition; the fear of the outbreak of a new civil war;[106] as well as the sentiment of culpability among those who participated in the war because of the atrocities that were committed on both sides, and among those who did not fight in the war because of the non-opposition to Francoism of a great part of the population.[107] The primordial desire for peace among the Spaniards made it possible to arrive at an agreement to "stay the hand of vengeance" and not to call for trials.

Several experts continue to insist that the decision to leave the past behind was correct and reflects a degree of political maturity among the Spaniards.[108] Indeed, the Spanish transition is a source of pride for the great majority of the Spanish population. According to an opinion poll in 2000, 86.1 per cent of the Spanish population feels extremely satisfied with the transition.[109] Paloma Aguilar, when reflecting on the outcome of this poll, notes that: "The elevated pride that the transition to democracy provokes allows us to think that a process of reconciliation of the Spanish citizenry has taken place."[110] Quite surprisingly, according to an opinion poll carried out in 2000, Spanish citizens perceive Francoism as a period in Spanish history with both good and bad things.[111] To this sentiment of ambivalence about the past should be added a significant degree of apathy and political estrangement as well as a sentiment of culpability for the brutality of the war and for the complicity of a great part of the population with the dictatorship. Taken together, these factors have contributed to a generalized preference to dodge all that is linked with these crimes.

At the same time, an opinion poll of 2005 indicates that the majority of the Spanish population believes that reparation is owed to the victims of the Civil War.[112] Especially significant about this poll is the different opinions that prevail between those who live in small villages compared to cities, as well as between different age groups and especially between those who led the transition and the younger generations.[113] In the view of Aguilar, it is surprising

106 In this context, it is important to consider that even though Franco died, the power remained in the hands of his supporters at the time of the transition and the democratic opposition found itself in a vulnerable situation in the negotiations.

107 Aguilar Fernández, fn 17 above.

108 Aguilar Fernández, fn 17 above, p 190.

109 Aguilar Fernández, fn 58 above, p 264.

110 Aguilar Fernández, fn 58 above, p 265.

111 For an analysis of the different polls and their results, see Aguilar Fernández, fn 58 above, pp 264 ff and 268–269.

112 See Aguilar Fernández, fn 47 above, pp 402 ff, criticizing the poll because most of the questions were badly formulated and could distort the responses.

113 Aguilar Fernández, fn 47 above, pp 404 ff. According to Aguilar Fernández, resistance

how little disagreement there is in the generation who took the lead in the transition about these measures (those who in 2005 were between 55 and 64 years old). This cohort seems to be more convinced that the best Spanish society can continue to do is to leave the past behind. According to Aguilar, the most likely explanation of this attitude is that this older generation understands the success of the Spanish transition as owed in great part to the decision to leave old quarrels behind. In contrast, several associations that promote the recuperation of historic memory are led by persons who are between 30 and 40 years old, that is, by the grandchildren of those who fought in the Civil War.

However, even if my conclusion is that Spain is an example of reconciliation without justice, it is important to consider the negative consequences of the way in which the transition was undertaken on the Spanish political system. While it was a "peaceful" transition without ruptures, it was plagued by incoherence and imperfection. While for some historians the transition was exemplary, for others the absence of political justice has had negative effects upon Spanish democracy as it has induced the oligarchic behaviour of our political parties, corruption, episodes such as that of GAL,[114] and democratic cultural deficits.[115] As Josep Maria Colomer explains: "The virtues of the transition have been transformed into democratic vices."[116] His reflection reveals that even if one did the only thing that could be done at the time of the transition to pass on in a peaceful manner to democracy, what was done was imperfect and had negative effects on the political system, which continue to be felt until this day.

The contemporary claim about the need to revisit the past creates polemics.[117] However, even if the majority of academics, politicians and civil society actors believe that this is not the time to pursue criminal justice, but that we must honour and give adequate indemnity to the victims, there is still no agreement on the best way of going about this task. The truth is that, until now, neither the children nor the grandchildren who reclaim recognition of their loved ones have demanded that the ones responsible for the crimes should be punished; rather, they only insist on moral reparation[118] and in particular the active involvement of the state in the search for the truth and in the localization of the

against prying into the past is most strongly felt in the towns and small cities where responsibility for the past could be more clearly attributed.

114 For a summary of the different opinions, see Aguilar Fernández, fn 17 above, p 186.

115 Navarro, V, "Consecuencias de la transición inmodélica", *El País*, 8 January 2003. For an argument about the "incomplete transition", see Muñoz Conde, fn 1 above, p 3.

116 Cited by Aguilar Fernández, fn 17 above, p 191.

117 The political turmoil is manifested in the discourses of the parliamentary representatives of the Conservative Party when defending their proposed amendments of the law. For example, in its amendment no 91 the Popular Group defines the law as one more step in a "strategy to destroy the pact of coexistence that the Spaniards formulated through the Constitution of 1978". See *Boletín Oficial de las Cortes Generales*, Congreso de los Diputados, VIII Legislatura, Proyectos de ley, Serie A, no 99-20, 14 March 2007.

118 Muñoz Conde, fn 1 above, p 15.

remains of their families. While the Historic Memory Law seeks to respond to these claims, it still leaves much to be desired in order to be able to "close the books", so to speak. Of particular concern are the failure to annul the unjust convictions; the scheme of indemnities; and the passivity of the government in relation to the localization and exhumations of the remains of the victims.

6.4.1 The unjust convictions

Reparation is still owed to the victims of the violations of the past. Especially problematic is the fact that the Historic Memory Law fails to annul the historical sentences that were handed down for political crimes and/or without any procedural guarantees. The declaration of reparation and personal recognition (granted by the law) seeks in part to remedy the absence of personal recognition. Nevertheless, this measure is also fraught with defects, not least as it falls upon the victim to prove his or her condition as victim who must also take the initiative in order to be recognized. Another concern relates to the limited effect of this measure; indeed, the fact that the Historic Memory Law refrains from annulling the Francoist sentences related to political crimes and those dictated without judicial guarantees has been one of the most criticized aspects of the new law.[119] By resorting to the extraordinary legal institution of relief, the Supreme Court has annulled only one sentence so far,[120] while refraining from doing so when the relief seekers have not succeeded in bringing new evidence or have failed to bring sufficient evidence in support of their claims that the convicted persons were, in fact, innocent.[121]

The institution of relief as formulated in Spain does not permit the judges to annul sentences on the basis that the laws applied to a given case were unjust or because the principle of legality was not respected.[122] In my opinion, only

119 See, e.g. the criticism put forth by Carrillo, M, "El Tribunal Constitucional y la memoria histórica", *El País*, 27 August 2004. Also in favour of the annulment of the condemnatory sentences is Supreme Court Judge Martin Pallín, "Nacido en el 36", *El País*, 12 November 2004. See also Escudero, R, "La declaración de ilegitimidad de los tribunales franquistas: una vía para la nulidad de sus sentencias", in Pallín, M and Escudero, R (eds), *Derecho y memoria histórica*, Madrid: Trotta, 2008, pp 209–234 (basing his argument on the Radbuch thesis). According to Escudero, the declaration obtained by virtue of the Historic Memory Law may prompt appeal for review or reconsideration of the case. He also upholds that the declaration of reparation and personal recognition should be recognized as a new valid fact. See also Sáez Valcárcel, R, "Anular las sentencias de la represión franquista. Una tarea de higiene pública", *Jueces para la democracia*, no 64, 2009, pp 61–78.

120 Ley Orgánica 2/1989, de 13 de abril, Procesal Militar, Art 328 (recognizing the possibility of reopening or reconsidering a case).

121 See Tribunal Supremo de España (Supreme Court of Spain), Sala de lo Militar, case of *Augustin Corrales Elizondoroj*, ATS 9725/2007, 5 July 2007; and Tribunal Supremo, Sala de lo Militar, case of *Javier Juliani Hernan*, ATS 18720/2006, 18 December 2006.

122 See Tribunal Supremo de España, Sala de lo Militar, case of *Augustin Corrales Elizondo*, ATS 15770/2006, 21 September 2006 (providing a summary of relevant Spanish case law).

the Parliament has the competence to modify the scope of the institution of relief so as to allow the judges to annul sentences on grounds of injustice, especially those that amount to convictions of acts defined by the Spanish Constitution of 1978 as the legitimate exercise of fundamental rights, or which emanate from processes that failed to respect even the most basic judicial guarantees. In Germany, the issue was resolved through the promulgation of the Law concerning the Rehabilitation and Indemnity to Victims of Criminal Sentences contrary to the Rule of Law in 1992,[123] and the Law to Annul Unjust Sentences Imposed during the National Socialist Administration of Criminal Justice in 1998.[124] However, until now, the Spanish Parliament has not followed this path.

6.4.2 The scheme of indemnities

Even though the economic measures that have been adopted by the legislator have been generally welcomed by NGOs, they have also been criticized for their partial character—the limits imposed on age and dates with the consequence that some victims are still excluded as a result.[125] According to the Constitutional Court, none of the economic measures adopted amount to indemnities, but are best understood as benefits distributed by the legislature as a matter of grace.[126] And this is precisely their most troublesome aspect.[127] Furthermore, the Historic Memory Law envisages a distribution of indemnities as a matter of grace and not on the basis of a prior determination of the condition of victim. To this should be added that those who seek to benefit from the scheme of indemnities that has been set up bear the burden of proving their condition. Also criticized is the casuistic character of the mechanisms and that the right to obtain a declaration of reparation and personal recognition is a way of evading the patrimonial responsibility of the state.[128]

123 See Gesetz über die Rehabilitierung und Entschädigung von Opfern rechtsstaatswidriger Strafverfolgungsmaßnahmen im Beitrittsgebiet, 29 October 1992. The law in question is available at www.gesetze-im-internet.de/strrehag/index.html.

124 See Gesetz zur Aufhebung nationalsozialistischer Unrechtsurteile in der Strafrechtspflege, 25 August 1998. The law is available online at www.gesetze-im-internet.de/ns-aufhg/BJNR250110998.html. The law has been translated into Spanish by Joan Queralt and is available online at www.juristasporlamemoriademocratica.org/documentos/Alem_LcST injusta_20_27b3.pdf.

125 For a more comprehensive analysis of this problem, see Aguilar Fernández, fn 47 above, pp 455 ff and 478; Gil Gil, fn * at the start of this chapter, pp 9 ff; and Escudero, R, "La sombra del franquismo es alargada: el fracaso de la llamada ley de memoria histórica", in Fernández-Crehuet, F and García López, D J (eds), *Derecho, Memoria histórica y Dictaduras*, Granada: Comares, 2009.

126 Chinchón Álvarez, fn 43 above, p 143.

127 Chinchón Álvarez, fn 43 above, p 181.

128 Amnesty International (Spanish Section), fn 90 above, pp 31 ff.

6.4.3 The localization and exhumation of the remains of the victims

Also subject to criticism is the passivity shown by the Spanish Government until now in relation to the implementation of the provisions of the Historic Memory Law related to the exhumation of mass graves. Having disapproved the court order of Judge Garzón from the standpoint of criminal law, it may well be the case that his true intention was not criminal prosecution, but rather to redress the failure of the legislative branch in its implementation of the Historic Memory Law. However, while we may acknowledge the political success of other similar initiatives that have been undertaken by Judge Garzón, I continue to believe that the criminal process must not be utilized for ends that are alien to it, that is, for ends other than the criminal conviction of a crime that has been committed. Out of respect for the division of power that prevails in a constitutional and democratic state, it is preferable that other sectors of society, such as NGOs, labour unions, associations and academics, seek to push the legislator to improve the laws and to shoulder the task of implementing them.

6.5 Conclusion

The Spanish transition is an example of absolute oblivion with partial rehabilitation of the victims. It was the fruit of necessity and the particular political and social juncture in which it was developed. While it was a "peaceful" transition without ruptures, it was plagued by incoherence and imperfection. Nevertheless, as has been suggested in this chapter, the Spanish Amnesty Law is not contrary to the body of international law that was in force at the time it was adopted. Thus, in spite of the absence of criminal justice, the transition was produced in accordance with international law. Even so, the Spanish courts have been criticized for acting in a politically incoherent manner: while upholding the Amnesty Law and thus not insisting on the need for criminal justice for serious human rights violations committed on Spanish territory, they have opened criminal proceedings in relation to such violations when committed abroad.[129] Still, respect for the principles of separation of powers and judicial independence does not necessarily mean that judicial decisions will be *politically* coherent or correct. In my opinion, the decisions of the *Audiencia* with regard to the Argentinean Final Stop and Due Obedience Laws (on the one hand) and the Spanish Amnesty Law (on the other) are both legally sound.

That being said, even if the Spanish transition was successful in terms of achieving national reconciliation, reparation is still owed to the victims of the crimes committed in the Spanish Civil War and the Francoist period. Especially problematic is the fact that the Historic Memory Law refrains from annulling the historical sentences that were handed down for political crimes or in the

129 Sancinetti, M and Ferrante, M, *El Derecho penal en la protección de los derechos humanos*, Buenos Aires: Hammurabi, 1999, p 15.

absence of any procedural guarantees. Also troublesome is the fact that it envisages a distribution of indemnities as a matter of grace and not on the basis of the recognition of the status of victim. Furthermore, the persons who seek to benefit from the scheme of indemnities must themselves provide the evidence in support of their condition, which in the majority of cases is a very difficult task, or when seeking to obtain a subsidy to search for and identify their family relatives who disappeared.

7 The challenges posed to the recent investigation of crimes committed during the Spanish Civil War and Francoism

Javier Chinchón Álvarez

7.1 Introduction

In response to the complaint presented to the Argentinean Federal Court on criminal and correctional matters on 14 April 2010, María Servini de Cubría, judge of this court, sent a rogatory letter to the Spanish authorities asking for information:

> . . . as to whether there is an investigation about the existence of a systematic, generalized, deliberate, and organized plan to terrorize Spaniards who supported the representative form of government through their physical elimination, and a plan which favoured the "legalized" disappearance of minors with the loss of their identity, realized in the period between 17 July 1936 and 15 June 1977.[1]

This document puts a judicial heading to a reality that has been accurately characterized in a recent study of Professor Sánchez Legido as follows:

> Although it is common to situate the *Nacht und Nebel* Decree of 1941 as the origin of enforced disappearances, numerous historical facts occurred a few years before in the Iberian peninsula which mark the initiation of the execution of systematic and generalized plans similar to the ones that were extended until the beginning of the 50s of last century and which left all the national geography plagued by ignominious graves of Francoism. In spite of everything, with the pretext of national reconciliation, the amnesty law of 1977 has supported until this date the most absolute impunity; the recent events, both at the legislative and judicial levels, do not let us foresee

1 Juzgado Nacional en lo Criminal y Correccional Federal, case of *N.N. s/ genocidio,* No 4.591/2.010 (A-12.447), decision of 14 October 2010 (unofficial translation). Available online at https://docs.google.com/fileview?id=1HLOsLcWY4s3-rmJtw1qTyN6DhORPr6-NDya7rnfSMsj3McLmm9kLa_PhddpT&hl=es.

> substantial changes to this panorama. It is not strange, in this context, that the then chancellor Insulza, on the occasion of Pinochet's detention, questioned the legitimacy of our country to do, with respect to what happens abroad, what we have not been capable of doing here . . . The objection is, without any doubt, irrefutable . . .[2]

Nevertheless, the official position of Spanish authorities on this matter can be found in their response to a recommendation that was set forth by Mexico during the UN-based Universal Periodical Exam of Spain in 2010, urging Spain to "investigate, punish and redress crimes of enforced disappearance, regardless of the time of their occurrence, in the light of the continuous nature of the crime and in accordance with its international obligations".[3] Spain replied that:

> In the Spanish legal order, the judges and courts instruct and prosecute all complaints concerning enforced disappearances that come before them and settle them in accordance with the principles that govern the judicial function in Spain: independence, irremovability, responsibility, and the submission to law and laws only.[4]

Furthermore:

> The current Spanish legal order obliges, in a clear and sufficient manner, the persecution of crimes against humanity and of genocide, in the terms of, and within the scope recognized, among others, in the International Covenant on Civil and Political Rights, the Convention for the Sanction of Genocide, the Convention for the Protection of All Persons against Enforced Disappearances as well as in the rest of the national and international legislation which our Constitution recognizes and protects.[5]

Against this background, the objective of this chapter is to give a general account of what the Spanish courts have done so far in terms of investigating and prosecuting the past violations of human rights. This general account elaborates on the grave crimes that were committed: (i) in the Spanish Civil War (1936–1939); (ii) in the immediate post-war period—years that have been

2 Sánchez Legido, A, "Diez años de Derecho internacional penal", in Soroeta Liceras, J (ed), *Conflictos y protección de derechos humanos en el orden internacional.* Cursos de Derechos Humanos de Donostia-San Sebastián, vol VI, Bilbao: Universidad Del País Vasco, 2009, pp 318–319 (unofficial translation).

3 UN Human Rights Council, *Report of the Working Group on the Universal Periodic Review: Spain* (A/HRC/15/6), 16 June 2010, para 86.26.

4 UN Human Rights Council, fn 3 above, Addendum (A/HRC/15/6/Add.1), 13 September 2010, para 20.

5 UN Human Rights Council, fn 3 above, Addendum (A/HRC/15/6/Add.1), 13 September 2010, para 21.

designated as "the great repression" (1939–1948);[6] (iii) in the years that followed and were labelled by the Council of Europe as the "deeply disturbing human rights record" of Francoism;[7] and, finally, (iv) the crimes committed in the initial stages of the transition to democracy.[8] These crimes include cases of enforced disappearances which have been explicitly recognized by the UN Working Group on Enforced and Involuntary Disappearance.[9]

7.2 From the Amnesty Law of 1977 to the Historic Memory Law of 2007

The initial stage of the most recent Spanish transition to democracy (1975–1978) was characterized by the election of what has come to be known as the "model of absolute oblivion of the past",[10] that is, a posture towards the past—the crimes of the past—founded on the renouncement of all kinds of punishing and reparatory measures as well as all forms of investigation and searches for the truth. This choice was made without any consideration, at least not in the public arena, about the viability and conformity of such decision with international law.[11] From this point of view, a crucial element of the

6 See Núñez Días-Balart, M, (ed), *La gran represión. Los años de plomo de la posguerra (1939–1948)*, Barcelona: Flor de Viento Ediciones, 2009.

7 Council of Europe, *Need for International Condemnation of the Franco Regime*, report of the Political Affairs Committee, Doc 10078, 4 October 2005, para 51.

8 For an account of this period, see, e.g. Soler, M, *La transición sangrienta. Una historia violenta del proceso democrático en España (1975–1983)*, Barcelona: Península, 2010.

9 *Report of the UN Working Group on Enforced or Involuntary Disappearances*, UN Doc E/CN.4/2004/58, 21 January 2004, paras 259–267; *Report of the UN Working Group on Enforced or Involuntary Disappearances*, UN Doc A/HRC/4/41, 25 January 2007, para 380; and *Report of the UN Working Group on Enforced and Involuntary Disappearances*, UN Doc A/HRC/13/31, 21 December 2009, paras 478–495.

10 This is the terminology employed by the Max-Planck Institute for Foreign and International Criminal Law in its study devoted to different transnational experiences. See Arnold, J, "Cambio de sistema político y criminalidad de Estado desde una visión del derecho penal"; "Esbozo del Proyecto: Elaboración jurídico-penal del pasado tras un cambio de sistema político en diversos países", in Sancinetti, M A and Ferrante, M, *El derecho penal en la protección de los derechos humanos. La protección de los derechos humanos mediante el derecho penal en las transiciones democráticas*, Argentina: Ed Hammurabi, 1999.

11 For a consideration of this perspective, see, e.g. Chinchón Álvarez, J, "Transición española y Justicia Transicional: ¿Qué papel juega el ordenamiento jurídico internacional en un proceso de transición? A propósito de la coherencia, buena fe y otros principios de derecho internacional postergados en la transición política española", in Gálvez Biesca, S (ed), *La memoria como conflicto. Memoria e historia de la Guerra Civil y el Franquismo, Entelequia, Revista Interdisciplinar*, no 7, 2008, pp 331–354. For a more general account of the problem in focus, see, e.g. Chinchón Álvarez, J, "Derecho internacional y 'transformaciones del Estado': Del desuso, uso y abuso del ordenamiento jurídico internacional cuando de ciertas transformaciones que afectan a la forma de gobierno", in Soroeta Liceras, J (ed), *Cursos de Derechos Humanos de Donostia-San Sebastián. Volumen XI*, Bilbao: Servicio Editorial de la Universidad del País Vasco, 2010.

inaugural design of the Spanish model was the adoption of the Amnesty Law in October 1977,[12] Article 2, paragraphs (e) and (f)[13] of which give amnesty to *all crimes committed by public officials and agents of the public order against the exercise of the rights of persons*. The contents of this provision is notably similar to subsequent laws that have come to be commonly defined as "impunity laws", such as the Chilean Law Decree of 19 April 1978,[14] the Argentinean Amnesty Law related to terrorism or subversive crimes between 25 May 1973 and 17 June 1982 (1983),[15] thc woefully celebrated Uruguayan Caducity Law (1986),[16] the Argentinean Laws of Final Stop and Due Obedience (1986–1987),[17] the Honduran Decree (1990),[18] the El Salvadorian General Amnesty Law for the Consolidation of Peace (1993),[19] and Peruvian Law no 26479 (1995),[20] grotesquely complemented a few months later by Law no 26492 (1995).[21]

Following the adoption of the Amnesty Law in 1977, a slow and confused process developed in which a wide range of measures purportedly reparatory in character were adopted, but never affecting the validity of the Amnesty Law,[22] which until this day continues to receive official support through "omission"[23]

12 Ley 46/1977, de 15 de octubre, de Amnistia, *Boletín Oficial del Estado*, no 248, 17 October 1977.

13 See, e.g. Chinchón Álvarez, J, "El viaje a ninguna parte: Memoria, leyes, historia y olvido sobre la Guerra Civil y el pasado autoritario en España. Un examen desde el derecho internacional", *Revista del Instituto Interamericano de Derechos Humanos*, no 45, 2007, pp 12–129.

14 Decreto Ley no. 2191, 19 April 1978 (Chile).

15 Ley no 22924, 23 March 1983 (Argentina).

16 Law 15848 of 22 December 1986 (Uruguay).

17 Ley no 23492 ("Punto Final"), 23 December 1986 and Ley no 23521 ("Obediencia Debida"), 5 June 1987 (Argentina).

18 Decreto no 30-90 of 14 December 1990 (Honduras).

19 Ley General de Amnistía para la Consolidación de la Paz, no 486, 20 March 1993 (El Salvador).

20 Ley no 26479, 14 June 1995 (Peru).

21 Ley no 26492, 30 June 1995 (Peru). For an account of the legislative measures under consideration, see Chinchón Álvarez, J, "Modelos de persecución penal y Justicia Transicional en Iberoamérica. Algunas enseñanzas jurídico-internacionales tras los procesos de transición iberoamericanos: Impunidad fáctica, amnistías e indultos", in Capellà I Roig, M and Ginard I Ferón, D (eds), *Represión política, justicia y reparación. La memoria histórica en perspectiva jurídica (1936–2008)*, Palma de Mallorca: Ediciones Documenta Balear, 2009, pp 255–339.

22 Aguilar, P, *Políticas de la memoria y memorias de la política*, Madrid: Alianza Editorial, 2008, pp 233 ff, including the tables on pp 506–520. See also Gil Gil, A, *La justicia de transición en España. De la amnistía a la memoria histórica*, Barcelona: Atelier, 2009, pp 47–92.

23 *Informe General de la Comisión Interministerial para el Estudio de la Situación de las Víctimas de la Guerra Civil y del Franquismo*, 28 July 2006, p 30 (General Report of the Interministerial Commission for the Study of the Situation of the Victims of the Civil War and of Francoism) (unofficial translation). Available online at www1.mpr.es/uploads/media/pdf/6/informegeneral2_1232475655.pdf. According to the Commission, the Amnesty Law of 1977 reflects the political decision to renounce the judicial persecution of the servants of the Francoist regime who had participated in the repression.

and "action".[24] For many, this process was finalized 30 years later with the adoption in December 2007 of what has come to be popularly known as the Historic Memory Law.[25] In fact, according to its preamble, the law in question represents a complete and final response to the demands voiced by Spanish society in relation to the past and will thus contribute to the closing of wounds that are still open in the Spaniards and to the full satisfaction for those who suffered, directly or in the name of their family relatives, the consequences of the Civil War and the Francoist repression.[26]

Both the Historic Memory Law and the great majority of measures that had been adopted earlier on are based on a common logic the unravelling of which will help to understand the background and motives behind the complaints that have come to be presented by different persons and associations of victims[27] to Spanish courts and especially the *Audiencia Nacional* (AN) from the end of 2006 onwards.[28] Already at the beginning of the 1990s, the Spanish Constitutional

24 See, e.g. UN Human Rights Committee, Comentarios del Gobierno de España sobre las observaciones finales del Comité de Derechos Humanos, UN Doc CCPR/C/ESP/CO/5/Add.1, 13 January 2009, p 3.

25 Ley 52/2007, de 26 de diciembre, por la que se reconocen y amplían derechos y se establecen medidas en favor de quienes padecieron persecución o violencia durante la Guerra Civil y la dictadura, *Boletín del Estado*, no 310, 27 December 2007.

26 Ley 52/2007, paras 3 and 18.

27 According to Art 24.1 of the UN Convention on the Protection of All Persons from Enforced Disappearances, "victim" means the disappeared person and any individual who has suffered harm as the direct result of an enforced disappearance. Considering the jurisprudence derived from the European Court of Human Rights, family relatives of a direct victim of enforced disappearance are also considered to be victims of torture and inhuman, cruel or degrading treatment. See the ECtHR, case of *Kurt v Turkey*, Application 24276/94, Judgment of 25 May 1998, paras 130–134; ECtHR, case of *Çakici v Turkey*, Application 23657/94, Judgment of 8 July 1999, paras 88–99, esp 98; ECtHR, case of *Orhan v Turkey*, Application 25656/94, Judgment of 18 June 2002, para 358; ECtHR, case of *İpek v Turkey*, Application 25760/94, Judgment of 17 February 2004; paras 178–183, esp 181–183; and ECtHR, case of *Osmanoğlu v Turkey*, Application 48804/99, Judgment of 24 January 2008, paras 96–97.

28 See *Audiencia Nacional*, Juzgado Central de Instrucción no 5, Diligencias Previas-Procedimiento Abreviado 399/2006 V, Auto (Decision) of 16 October 2008, referring to previous complaints: complaint presented on 14 December 2006 by Mr Marcial Muñoz Sánchez in his name and on behalf of the association Nuestra Memoria, Sierra de Gredos y Toledo; complaint presented on 14 December 2006 by the Associació per a la recuperació de la Memòria Històrica de Catalunya; complaint presented on 14 December 2006 by the Asociación por la Recuperación de la Memoria Histórica en Aragón; complaint presented on 14 December 2006 by the Comisión po la Memoria Histórica do 36 en Ponteareas; complaint presented on 14 December 2006 by the Asociación por la Recuperación de la Memoria Histórica de Arúcas; complaint presented on 15 December 2006 by the Associació per a la recuperació de la Memòria Històrica de Mallorca; complaint presented on 15 December 2006 by Ms Carmen Dorado Ortiz; complaint presented on 4 June 2007 by Teófilo Goldaracena Rodríguez; complaint presented on 18 July 2007 by the Asociación Andaluza Memoria Histórica y Justicia; complaint presented on 14 September 2007 by Politeia, asociación para la defensa y

Court held that while some of the measures adopted in relation to the past had been officially defined as "indemnities", the measures were in reality "benefits" that had been established by the legislator as a matter of grace on the basis of a political decision which, in the case before it, must be brought into relation with the amnesty-related legislation.[29]

From my point of view, this is the key to understanding the background of the Spanish experience. In spite of what has been said in multiple forums and although many of the measures that have been implemented in recent years deserve to be celebrated, all of them, including the Historic Memory Law, are based on the idea that such measures are afforded as a matter of grace and not obligation. Indeed, the Historic Memory Law never speaks of "obligations" or "rights", but only of "legitimate claims or demands" of some citizens[30] as though the questions of justice, truth and reparations for past crimes concerned the relations among persons or private subjects and the function of the state would be limited to that of a facilitator or subject that is capable of "establishing subsidies".[31] In fact, the Supreme Court has admitted that the Historic Memory Law implies nothing more than "the mere collaboration with private persons (and) the contribution of public powers in the desired reparation of the victims

progreso de los intereses ciudadanos; complaint presented on 24 December 2007 by the Asociación para la Recuperación de la Memoria Histórica de Valladolid; complaint presented on 19 May 2008 by Mr Francisco Javier Jiménez Corcho, Mr Juan Pérez Silva and Mrs Francisca Maqueda Fernández; complaint presented on 28 July 2008 by the association Fòrum per la Memòria del País Valencià; complaint presented on 31 July 2008 by the Confederación General del Trabajo; complaint presented on 12 September 2008 by the Asociación para la Recuperación de la Memoria Histórica de Granada and by Mrs Nieves García Catalán; complaint presented on 12 September 2008 by Mr José Luis Cerdeira Villegas; complaint presented on 12 September 2008 by Mr Críspulo Nieto Cicuéndez; complaint presented on 22 September 2008 by the Asociación de Familiares de Fusilados y Desaparecidos de Navarra, Asociación de Héroes de la República y la Libertad, Asociación para la Recuperación de la Memoria Histórica en El Bierzo, León, Burgos y Zamora, Asociación para la Recuperación de la Memoria Histórica de Soria; complaint presented on 26 September by the Asociación Todos los Nombres de Asturias; complaint presented on 3 October by Mrs María Nieves Galindo Arroyo; complaint presented on 6 October by Grup per la Recerca de la Memòria Històrica de Castelló, Izquierda Republicana de Castilla y León, by Mrs Julia Maroto Velasco and by Mr Julián de la Morena López.

29 See Tribunal Constitucional de España (Spanish Constitutional Court), *las cuestiones de inconstitucionalidad acumuladas 2.645, 2.646, 2.647 y 2.648/92 y 12 y 420/93, promovidas, las cuatro primeras, por la Sala de lo Contencioso-Administrativo del Tribunal Superior de Justicia de Asturias, y la quinta y la sexta por las Salas del mismo orden jurisdiccional de los Tribunales Superiores de Justicia de Castilla-La Mancha y de Madrid, respectivamente, en las que se plantea la posible inconstitucionalidad de la Disposición adicional decimoctava de la Ley 4/1990, de 29 de junio, de Presupuestos Generales del Estado para 1990*, STC 361/1993, Judgment of 3 December 1993, legal reasonings, para 2.

30 See Exposición de los Motivos de la Ley 52/2007, de 26 de diciembre (Exposition of the motives for the Historic Memory Law).

31 See, e.g. Historic Memory Law, Art 11.2.

of the Civil War and the dictatorship that followed".[32] The reality is such that, as says Alicia Gil Gil, "the Law renounces an official investigation of human rights violations . . . maintaining the rule of impunity and no-investigation".[33] In this light, the response by the Spanish authorities to the allegation set forth by the UN Working Group on Enforced and Involuntary Disappearances and cited in its December 2009 Report must be seen as clearly unjustified, when it maintains that:

> Regarding the allegation that there have been no investigations into disappearances that took place during the Spanish civil war and General Franco's regime, the Government quoted a number of measures that have been taken since 2004, including the creation of the Historical Memory Documentation Centre, and the passing of a law in 2007, which recognizes and expands rights and establishes measures for persons who suffered persecution or violence during the civil war and dictatorship.[34]

That the adoption of the Historic Memory Law is based on the same logic as previous measures becomes evident when attention is turned to the formulation of Articles 11 to 14 related to the victims of enforced disappearances during the Civil War and the Francoist period.[35] The wording, spirit and design of these

32 Tribunal Supremo de España (Spanish Supreme Court), Causa Especial No 20048/2009, Judgment of 3 February 2010, p 52.

33 See Gil Gil, A, *La justicia de transición en España. De la amnistía a la memoria histórica*, Barcelona: Atelier, 2009, p 76.

34 Report of the UN Working Group on Enforced or Involuntary Disappearances, UN Doc A/HRC/13/31, 21 December 2009, para 486.

35 Historic Memory Law, Art 11: Collaboration of public administrations with individuals to locate and identify victims. 1. The public administrations, in the framework of their competences, will *facilitate*, for the direct descendants of victims who so request, the activities of investigation, location and identification of persons who disappeared in violent circumstances during the Civil War or the subsequent political repression and whose whereabouts are unknown . . . 2. The General State Administration will prepare work plans and establish subsidies to assist with the costs of the activities foreseen in this article. Article 12: Measures for the identification and location of victims. 1. The Government, together with the public administrations, will prepare a protocol of scientific and interdisciplinary activities to ensure institutional collaborations and an adequate control of the exhumations. *Similarly, it will prepare appropriate collaboration agreements to subsidize the social bodies which take part in the work*. . . . Article 13. Administrative authorizations for location and identification activities. 1. The competent public administrations *will authorize* search activities to locate the remains of victims referred to in article 11, paragraph 1 . . . The findings will immediately be communicated to the competent administrative and judicial authorities. 2. The public administrations will exercise their powers to establish the procedure and conditions in which the direct descendants of the victims referred to in article 11, paragraph 1, or the bodies acting in their name, *may recover* the remains buried in common graves, to be identified and eventually removed elsewhere. . . . Article 14. Access to locations affected by identification and localization activity. 1. The activities of localization and eventual identification or removal of the remains of

provisions reveal that the Spanish official understanding of these measures is that they are the result of the will of the Spanish state to exercise its discretional powers and not efforts to fulfil any obligation. Nevertheless, such understanding is difficult to reconcile with any recognition about the existence of (international) state responsibility to investigate and repair to the persons whose rights have been violated, in conformity with the detailed international rules regulating this realm. And this understanding also includes the victims of enforced disappearance, in spite of the permanent and continued character of said crime,[36] unquestioned in the international legal context, as recently recalled by the European Court of Human Rights (ECtHR).[37]

When it became evident that such recognition would be withheld in the final version of the Historic Memory Law, the victims of enforced disappearances lost their patience and ended up convincing themselves that the only avenue that remained to vindicate their rights—hushed and ignored for decades[38]—was to turn to the *Audiencia Nacional.*

Before analyzing the complaints set forth by the victims to the *Audiencia* in December 2006 onwards, it must be noted that these were by no means the first or only complaints related to the crimes of enforced disappearance to be brought before judicial organs. However, the different actions prior to the end of 2006

persons referred to in article 13, paragraph 1, are considered to be of public utility and social interest, with a view to permitting, where necessary and in accordance with articles 108 to 199 of the Compulsory Expropriation Law, the temporary occupation of the land where they are to be carried out. For the activities described in the previous paragraph, the appropriate authorities will *authorize* the temporary occupation of publicly owned lands except where justified by the public interest. 3. In the case of privately owned lands, the descendants, or the organizations authorized in accordance with the preceding paragraph, *should seek* the consent of the holders of the affected rights over the lands where the remains are. If such consent is not forthcoming, the public administrations may *authorize* temporary occupation, though only after hearing the holders of the affected rights, considering their arguments, and *determining the compensation to be paid by the occupiers*. (Unofficial translation, emphasis added).

36 In contrast with domestic law, both qualifications are common and accepted under international law. See, e.g. UN Report of the Intersessional Open-ended Working Group to elaborate a draft legally binding normative instrument for the protection of all persons from enforced disappearance, UN Doc 4/2006/57, 2 February 2006, para 113: "At the proposal of one delegation, and to take into account the varying terms used in the legislation of Latin American countries, the Working Group agreed that the expression 'continuous nature' in paragraph 1(b) should be translated in the Spanish version of the instrument as 'carácter continuo o permanente'."

37 See European Court of Human Rights, case of *Vardana and Others v Turkey* (GC), Application nos 16064/90, 16065/90, 16066/90, 16068/90, 16069/90, 16070/90, 16071/90, 16072/90 and 16073/90, Judgment of 18 September 2009.

38 See Davis, M, "Spain Recovering its Memory? Breaking the Pacto del Olvido", *Human Rights Quarterly*, vol 27, no 3, 2005, pp 858–880. See also Capellà I Roig, M, "Las 'desapariciones forzadas' en España durante la guerra civil y el franquismo: violaciones y crímenes de derecho internacional sin reparación ni castigo", in Soroeta Liceras, vol VI, fn 2 above.

did not find any other response but the impossibility to advance any investigation; as the decision on 15 December 1999 by the Court of Instruction no 1 in the case of *Arenas de San Pedro* well illustrates.[39] Furthermore, even if by now there seems to be a widely shared conviction that the recent judicial developments in relation to the crimes of the past is the result of a personal initiative by Judge Baltasar Garzón, which will end with his removal, in reality, they are the result of years of struggle by the pro-memory movement. As the historian Espinosa Maestre observes:

> Although it is not said, this generalized recognition to honour the victims of fascism is fully the fruit of the pro-memory movement, which since the 90s and more concretely since the year of 2000 has succeeded to demonstrate to society a reality that was hidden and prohibited during Francoism and also from the time of the transition and onwards (the exhumations at the time were done at the margins of the system when not against).[40]

Thus, in an important sense, the *Audiencia* presented itself as the only and last effective way to advance the demands of family relatives of those who had suffered as direct victims of enforced disappearances during the Civil War and Francoism, following years of difficult and unproductive efforts of turning to political and judicial authorities with their demands.

7.3 Judicial actions and responses: the decision on 18 October 2008

The first judicial actions by the *Audiencia Nacional* were the result of a process initiated by a series of complaints as from mid-December 2006 onwards by different associations and individuals about the alleged commission of crimes against humanity (enforced disappearances) during the Civil War and Francoism. The core of these actions was especially complex as the petitioners' representatives on several occasions manifested that it was not their intention to seek the establishment of criminal responsibility for the crimes that had been committed. Rather, as one of the first petitioners, *Associació per a la Recuperació de la Memoria Històrica de Mallorca*, put it, and which reflects the basic demand of the great majority of petitioners: "On the basis of all this told, we ask for the assistance by justice to localize the whereabouts or final destiny of the listed persons."[41]

A first general question to be asked then was (and is) in which manner an organ with the character of a court/criminal chamber of the *Audiencia Nacional*

39 Juzgado de Instrucción no 1 de Arenas de San Pedro, Diligencias Previas, Procedimiento Abreviado 1557/1999, Auto (Decision), 15 December 1999.

40 For a more detailed analysis, see Espinosa Maestre, F, "De saturaciones y olvidos. Reflexiones en torno a un pasado que no puede pasar", *Hispania Nova-Revista de Historia Contemporánea*, no 7, 2007, pp 427–428. See also Espinosa Maestre, F, "Cuando el presente excluye el pasado", *Todos los nombres*, August 2010, available online at www.todoslosnombres.org.

41 Complaint by Associació per a la Recuperació de la Memoria Històrica de Mallorca addressed to Juzgado de Instrucción Central de Guardia, 14 December 2006, p 31.

may attend to this fundamental demand. The question was present, directly or indirectly, in the entire jurisdictional vicissitude, although it competes with an aspect that became the object of most polemics, that is, the more than likely death of the majority of the persons most responsible for the crimes.

The complaints received a judicial response in the decision of 16 October 2008.[42] The judge behind that decision, Baltasar Garzón, who was probably aware of the enormous consequences and possible opposition that his decision would have on several levels, initiated his decision by stressing that it had been produced with the utmost respect for all of the victims who suffered violent hideous acts, massacres and very grave violations of their rights during the Civil War and the post-war period. No distinction whatsoever was made among the victims on the basis of their differing political, ideological, religious, or other attributes.[43] Judge Garzón furthermore indicated that the current proceeding did not pretend to undertake a revision of the Spanish Civil War in a judicial setting, since that would imply the formulation of a "General Cause".[44] The judge also noted that, unlike other crimes from the Civil War period, the ones in focus in the case in question had never been subjected to criminal investigations by the Spanish judiciary; they also exhibited a number of magnifying facts that rendered it appropriate to characterize them as amounting to crimes against humanity.[45]

Following these preliminary clarifications, the magistrate elaborates on the alleged facts in the case and, to this end, differentiates among three periods: the massive repression realized by the bands in the Civil War (from 17 July 1936 to February 1937), the period of the emergency War Councils (from March 1937 to the first months of 1945), and, finally, the repression exerted by the dictatorship to eliminate the guerrillas and those who assisted them (from 1945 to 1952).[46] Also noted in this context is that these temporal limits are not fixed in a final manner, but may be extended if other cases were to appear later on provided that it can be proved that they formed part of a systematic plan of enforced disappearances, the fundamental object of the investigation.[47] According to the first provisional estimates, approximately 114,266 people were victims of enforced disappearances in these periods.[48] However, more recent estimates raise this number to 136,062 and even up to 152,237 victims.[49]

42 *Audiencia Nacional*, Juzgado Central de Instrucción no 5, Diligencias Previas-Procedimiento Abreviado 399/2006 V, Auto (Decision) of 16 October 2008.
43 Auto (Decision) of 16 October 2008, fn 42 above, Legal Reason I, para 2.
44 Auto (Decision) of 16 October 2008, fn 42 above, para 3.
45 Auto (Decision) of 16 October 2008, fn 42 above, Legal Reason I, para 1, and Legal Reason XIV.
46 Auto (Decision) of 16 October 2008, fn 42 above, Legal Reason I, para 6.
47 Auto (Decision) of 16 October 2008, fn 42 above, Legal Reason VI.
48 Auto (Decision) of 16 October 2008, fn 42 above, Legal Reason VI.
49 *Audiencia Nacional*, Juzgado Central de Instrucción no 5, Sumario (Procedimiento Ordinario) 0000053/2008 E, Auto (Decision) of 26 December 2008, para 7.

The magistrate thereafter engages in a detailed analysis of what, as we quoted before, Leo Brincat has defined as Franco's "deeply disturbing human rights record".[50] From the standpoint of many of the victims, this part of the decision is of great significance in that it approximates their demands in terms of affording public recognition of the crimes that were committed during the Francoist dictatorship.[51] The following lines stand out:

> . . . of the facts that happened following 18 July 1936, one can confirm that the armed uprising or insurrection which was materialized that date, was a decision perfectly planned and directed to end with the form of government in Spain, in that moment, attacking and ordering the detention and including the physical elimination of persons who had responsibilities in the high organs of the Nation and this, as a means or at least as an indispensable step to develop and execute the decisions that had been previously adopted concerning detention, torture, enforced disappearance and the physical elimination of thousands of persons for political and ideological reasons, procuring, in this manner, the displacement and exile of thousands of persons inside and outside national territory, a situation that continued, to a greater or lesser extent, during subsequent years, once the Civil War had been brought to an end.[52]

Thereafter, the magistrate outlines seven critical legal questions that must be addressed in the case and to which he refers as "obstacles" (*escollos*). One refers to the prohibition against retroactive criminal law and the rules of international (customary) law. A second question is related to the permanence (or non-permanence) of the crimes, essentially illegal detentions without any information about the whereabouts or final destiny of the detainees ("enforced disappearances") and its effects on statutory limitations. Also under consideration are matters such as the possible application of the Amnesty Law in relation to the alleged crimes in the present case, the competence of the Court of Instruction no 5 and the Criminal Chamber of the *Audiencia Nacional* to investigate the crimes, the identification of the persons possibly responsible for having committed them, as well as the protection of the victims of these acts.[53] It would be impossible to analyze, within the space of this chapter, all of these important legal questions in great detail; however, as I have argued elsewhere, several of them probably emerge as a result of the deficient Spanish legislation related to the investigation and prosecution of grave crime committed in Spain,

50 Council of Europe, fn 7 above.

51 Auto (Decision) of 16 October 2008, fn 42 above, Legal Reason XIV.

52 Auto (Decision) of 16 October 2008, fn 42 above, Legal Reason XIII (unofficial translation).

53 Auto (Decision) of 16 October 2008, fn 42 above, Legal Reason V.

especially in comparison with the legislation related to grave crime committed abroad.[54] Perhaps it never occurred to the Spanish legislator's narrow or biased mind that these types of crimes could be or had been committed in Spain.

Furthermore, the essential question here is to note that the magistrate's decision on 18 December 2008 in which he affirms the competence of the *Audencia Nacional* to open a criminal investigation related to crimes that occurred during the Civil War and Francoist dictatorship was based on a sophisticated and complex legal construction, partially sustained by international law as well as the Spanish Supreme Court judgment in the *Scilingo* case.[55] The decision ends by affirming the competence of the *Audiencia* to investigate the crimes, committed during the Civil War and Francoism, amounting to illegal detention without giving information about the whereabouts, or to forced disappearance, in the context of crimes against humanity, in connection with crimes against the Constitution and the High Organs of the Nation. The conclusions, evidently, lead to the non-acceptance of the intended effects of the Amnesty Law.[56]

Although the operative clauses of the decision begin only on page 66, already in the 16th and 18th Legal Foundations, important concrete decisions are taken, which are then reaffirmed in the final part of the decision.[57] Following a recognition of the factual difficulties to which the investigation of the denounced crimes would give rise, the magistrate opted for the creation of an "Expert Group" and a Judicial Police Group for the purpose of advancing the search for and localization of the disappeared persons so as to be able to respond to the petitions by the victims within a reasonable period.[58] The Judicial Police Group was given the task of localizing and systematizing the victims, clarifying the circumstances for their disappearances and deaths, and those who intervened in the disappearances. Its investigations would be carried out under the direction of the competent judicial authority until sufficient evidence related to the commission of the crimes had been established. The much more significant Expert Group, in contrast, would be established on the basis of a request from

54 See, e.g. Chinchón Álvarez, J, "Examen del Auto del Juzgado de Instrucción No 5 de la Audiencia Nacional por el que se acepta la competencia para investigar los crímenes contra la humanidad cometidos en la Guerra Civil y el franquismo", *La Ley: Revista Jurídica Española de Doctrina, Jurisprudencia y Bibliografía*, vol 5, 2008, pp 1388–1397.

55 Tribunal Supremo, Sala de lo Penal, STS 798/2007, Judgment of 1 October 2007. Available online at www.derechos.org/nizkor/espana/juicioral/doc/sentenciats.html#Tribunal. See also Ollé Sesé, M, *Justicia universal para crímenes internacionales*, Madrid: La Ley, 2008, pp 64–67 and 161–183, whose views I fully share. For a somewhat contrasting perspective, see Gil Gil, A, "Principio de legalidad y crímenes internacionales. Luces y sombras en la Sentencia del Tribunal Supremo en el caso Scilingo", in Cuerda Riezu, A and Jiménez García, F, *Nuevos Desafíos del Derecho penal internacional: Terrorismo, crímenes internacionales y derechos fundamentales*, Madrid: Tecnos, 2009.

56 Auto (Decision) of 16 October 2008, fn 42 above, Legal Reason XI.

57 Auto (Decision) of 16 October 2008, fn 42 above, operative paras 4 and 5.

58 Auto (Decision) of 16 October 2008, fn 42 above, Legal Reason XVI.

the parties of the judicial procedure. While these parties would designate the names of five people to form part of this group, the Investigating Chamber no 5 would nominate two other people. The task of the Expert Group would be to publish a report in which it would present its study, analysis, evaluation and conclusions about the location, situation and identification of the victims. The report would include the total number of victims in the period under examination (17 July 1936 to 31 December 1951) and it would make a threefold distinction among the victims following an examination of all the collected evidence: (i) detained and disappeared persons, accompanied by a proposal on how to localize, recuperate and identify their remains; (ii) detained and disappeared persons whose bodies had already been recuperated but were still unidentified, followed by their identification; and (iii) detained and disappeared persons who had already been identified.[59]

In spite of the overtly "technical" character of the Expert Group, it is evident that for those familiar with the concept of transitional justice the functions of this group resemble a truth commission.[60] Formally speaking, the Expert Group certainly does not amount to such a mechanism, although in effect its functions do point in that direction. Had it been the case, it would have been possible finally to fill a shameful vacuum in the Spanish history of "transitional justice" insofar as no truth-seeking activities have ever been undertaken. Furthermore, leaving to the side the question about potential conflicts between what should have been the future task of the Expert Group and what is stipulated in provisions such as Article 12 of the Historic Memory Law,[61] and the normative developments of the International Covenant for the Protection of All Persons against Enforced Disappearance,[62] it is evident that its eventual accomplishment would depend on its definitive composition, and the mode in which its members would focus and advance its mandate.

The decision also addresses various petitions for exhumations deduced from the case and establishes a set of basic criteria both for current as well as future exhumations with views to authorizing their initiation, development and continuation.[63] Furthermore, the magistrate undertakes to send inquiries to the corresponding Civil Registries asking them to provide death certificates of the persons who *a priori* have been identified as the most responsible ones for

59 Auto (Decision) of 16 October 2008, fn 42 above, Legal Reason XVI.

60 Hayner, P, *Unspeakable Truths. Confronting Terror and Atrocity*, New York: Routledge, 2001.

61 See fn 35 above.

62 UN International Convention for the Protection of All Persons against Enforced Disappearances, UN Doc A/RES/61/177, adopted by the UN General Assembly on 20 December 2006. For more details, see Chinchón Álvarez, J, "La Convención Internacional para la Protección de Todas las Personas contra las Desapariciones Forzadas: Nunca es tarde si la dicha es ¿buena? Examen general y perspectivas en España tras la aprobación de la Ley de Memoria Histórica", *Revista de Ciencias Jurídicas y Sociales, Foro, Nueva Época*, no 7/2008, pp 11–55.

63 Auto (Decision) of 16 October 2008, fn 42 above, Legal Reason XVII.

the crimes under consideration with a view to thereafter declaring the criminal responsibility of these persons as extinguished for reasons related to their death.[64] Additionally, he undertakes to send a request to the Ministry of Interior soliciting information as to who were the highest leaders of the Spanish fascist group *Falange Española* during the period between 17 July 1936 and 31 December 1951. Once identified and in case of death, the magistrate would proceed to resolve the matters related to the imputation of the crimes and extinction of criminal responsibility.[65] However, even if the decision lists a considerable number of possible perpetrators without prejudicing the possibility that there might be others who are still alive but who have still not been identified,[66] this leaves unanswered a question of critical importance for the subsequent judicial development: what will happen once it has been clarified that the persons identified are dead?

7.4 Subsequent judicial developments: from the decision on 16 October 2008 to the decision of the Criminal Chamber on 2 December 2008

While the victims had to wait for about two years before their first complaints received a judicial response on 8 October 2008, from that moment onwards, the process unfolded with astonishing speed. A period of six weeks, which is the time it took for the Criminal Chamber of the *Audiencia Nacional* to deliver its decision on 2 December 2008, is extremely fast, considering the enormous difficulties that were expected to be encountered in a criminal investigation into the sorts of crimes in focus,[67] and which the Spanish judiciary had never carried out before, and in relation to which up to this point impunity had been

64 The decision mentions the following names: Francisco Franco Bahamonde, Miguel Cabanellas Ferrer, Andrés Saliquet Zumeta, Miguel Ponte Manso de Zúñiga, Emilio Mola Vidal, Fidel Dávila Arrondo, Federico Montaner Canet, Fernando Moreno Calderón, Francisco Moreno Fernández, Germán Gil y Yuste, Luis Orgaz Yoldi, Gonzalo Queipo de Llano y Sierra, Francisco Gómez-Jordana y Souza, Francisco Fermoso Blanco, Luis Valdés Cabanilla, Nicolás Franco Bahamonde, Francisco de Asís Serrat i Bonastre, José Cortés López, Ramón Serrano Súñer, Severiano Martínez Anido, Tomás Domínguez Arévalo, Raimundo Fernández Cuesta y Merelo, Valentín Galarza Morante, Esteban Bilbao y Eguía, Jose Luis Arrese y Magra, Juan Yagüe Blanco, Salvador Moreno Fernández, Agustín Muñoz Grandes, José Enrique Varela Iglesias, Juan Vigón Suerodíaz, Blas Pérez González, Carlos Asensio Cabanillas, Eduardo Aunós Pérez, Eduardo González Gallarza, and Francisco Regalado Rodríguez. See Auto (Decision) of 16 October 2008, fn 42 above, operative para 3.

65 Auto (Decision) of 16 October 2008, fn 42 above, operative para 3.

66 Auto (Decision) of 16 October 2008, fn 42 above, Legal Reason VI.

67 Auto (Decision) of 16 October 2008, fn 42 above, Legal Reason I: "The investigation is very complex, agreed; it presents several difficulties related to evidence, because of the time that has passed, agreed; it is improbable that the authors are still alive, possibly but not impossibly since there are victims [who are still] alive; it will be a different question that related to prosecution in function of age . . ." (unofficial translation). *Audiencia Nacional*, Juzgado Central de Instrucción no 5, Sumario (Procedimiento Ordinario) 53/2008 E, Auto (Decision) of 18 November 2008, p 132.

the rule.[68] To use the words of three magistrates of the *Audiencia Nacional*: de Prada Solaesa, Bayarrui García and Sáez Valcárcel, the case presupposed the examination of a lawsuit of singular "historical importance"[69] since the intensity and magnitude of the alleged crimes meant that they were the most serious ones that had ever been investigated by Spanish courts.[70] Nevertheless, in contrast with this prognostic, the decision on 8 October came to be followed by a frenetic and not very uplifting succession of judicial actions and reactions, which started with the decision on 17 October, the day on which Judge Garzón transformed *Diligencias Preliminarias* 399/2006 into *Sumario* 53/2006[71] (a fact that would have repercussions in terms of the eventual appeals), and culminated in the decision by the Criminal Chamber in Plenary Session on 2 December 2008.[72]

Following this event, the Chief Prosecutor of the *Audiencia Nacional* interposed an extraordinarily severe appeal[73] on 20 October.[74] Having refuted each and every point by Judge Garzón, the prosecutor requested that in the light of the nature and significance of the case the decision should be taken by the plenary of the Criminal Chamber of the *Audiencia Nacional*.[75] This action coincided with Garzón's appointment of the ex-Prosecutor of Anticorruption, Carlos Jiménez Villarejo, and the ex-President of Barcelona's *Audiencia Provincial*, Antonio Doñate Martín, as members of the "Expert Group", created by the decision on 16 October. The appeal was declared inadmissible by Judge Garzón in a decision on 23 October 2008,[76] in which he also fixed a time period

68 Auto (Decision) of 16 October 2008, fn 42 above, Legal Reason I, para 1 and Legal Reason XIV.

69 Audiencia Nacional, Pleno de la Sala de lo Penal, Procedimiento ordinario número 53/08 del Juzgado Central de Instrucción No 5, Expediente número 34/08, Cuestión de competencia del artículo 23 LECR, Auto (Decision) of 2 December 2008, para I.1. Dissenting Vote (*voto particular discrepante*) by Magistrates de Prada Solaesa, Bayarrui García and Sáez Valcárcel.

70 Ibid.

71 *Audiencia Nacional*, Juzgado Central de Instrucción no 5, Diligencias Previas-Procedimiento Abreviado 0000399/2006 E, Auto (Decision) of 17 October 2008.

72 Auto (Decision) of 2 December 2008, fn 69 above.

73 For a perspective of the position of the Prosecutor's Office in relation to these proceedings, see Amnesty International (Spanish Section), "ESPAÑA: La obligación de investigar los crímenes del pasado y garantizar los derechos de las victimas de desaparición forzada durante la guerra civil y el franquismo", November 2008, esp pp 9–10. Available online at https://doc.es.amnesty.org/cgi-bin/ai/BRSCGI?CMD=VERDOC&BASE=SIAI&SORT=&DOCR=1&RNG=10&FMT=SIAIWEB3.fmt&SEPARADOR=&&INAI=EUR410008. See also Plataforma por las Víctimas de las Desaparaciones Forzadas del Franquismo, "Nota de Prensa", 18 October 2008; and Plataforma por las Víctimas de las Desaparaciones Forzadas del Franquismo, "Comunicado Público tras la Jornada de Trabajo de Asociaciones de la Memoria en Barcelona", 15 November 2008 (on file with author).

74 *Audiencia Nacional*, Recurso de Apelación del Fiscal Jefe (Motion of Appeal by the Chief Prosecutor of the *Audiencia Nacional*), 20 October 2008 (original on file with author).

75 *Audiencia Nacional*, Recurso de Apelación del Fiscal Jefe.

76 *Audiencia Nacional*, Juzgado Central de Instrucción no 5, Sumario (Procedimiento Ordinario) 0000053/2008 E, Auto (Decision) of 23 October 2008.

of three days to interpose a request for revision.[77] Garzón's response came to coincide with the appointment by the parties of the five remaining members of the Expert Group: the four historians Julián Casanova, Queralt Solé, Maribel Brenes and Francisco Espinosa Maestre, and the forensic expert, Francisco Etxeberria.

Even so, and perhaps after having read the decision on 17 October together with the internalization of its possible procedural consequences, the Chief Prosecutor, on 21 October, filed the almost unprecedented,[78] ambiguous[79] and extraordinary[80] incident contemplated in Article 23 of the Law on Criminal Procedure,[81] with the result that if the Criminal Chamber of the *Audiencia Nacional* responded that Central Court of Instruction no 5 lacked competence, it also meant that all of its previous actions would be annulled[82] (in accordance with Article 238.1 of the Organic Law on Judicial Power).[83] And that without the Chief Prosecutor having indicated which judicial organ would then, in his view, be competent to rule in the case. Indeed, before this moment, the majority of his arguments had not been designed to challenge the competence of the *Audiencia Nacional* as such, but rather to defend the extinction of possible criminal responsibility.[84]

However, almost two days after the UN Human Rights Committee had communicated its position on the legality of the Amnesty Law of 1977, recommending a few concrete measures to be adopted by Spain in response to the human rights violations that had been committed during the Spanish Civil War,[85] the Central Court of Instruction no 5—of which Judge Pedraz was now

77 Auto (Decision) of 23 October 2008, operative para 2.

78 Auto (Decision) of 2 December 2008, fn 69 above, para III.1.1 (Dissenting opinion by Magistrates de Prada Solaesa, Bayarrui García and Sáez Valcárcel).

79 See De la Oliva Santos, A et al, *Derecho Procesal Penal*, Madrid: Centro de Estudios Ramón Areces, 2007, pp 138 ff. See also Auto (Decision) of 2 December 2008, fn 69 above, p 2 (Concurring Opinion by Magistrate Javier Martín Lázaro).

80 Auto (Decision) of 2 December 2008, fn 69 above, pp 5–7. For a harsher interpretation, see dissenting opinion (de Prada Solaesa, Bayarrui García and Sáez Valcárcel) in this case (para III).

81 *Audiencia Nacional*, "Escrito del Fiscal Jefe de la Audiencia Nacional del 21 de octubre de 2008 por el que se promueve el incidente previsto en el artículo 23 de la Ley de Enjuiciamiento Criminal" (original on file with author). According to it: "If during the summary procedure or in whatever phase of instruction of a criminal procedure the Office of the Prosecutor or whomever of the parties understand that the examining judge does not have competence to act in the case can file a claim to the higher court to whom it concerns, which, prior to the reports that it considers necessary, resolves entirely and without ultimate recourse" (unofficial translation). See Ley de Enjuiciamiento Criminal (Spanish Law on Criminal Procedure), Art 23, Gaceta no 260, 17 September 1882—Gaceta no 283, 10 October 1882. Available online at http://noticias.juridicas.com/base_datos/Penal/lecr.html.

82 Auto (Decision) of 2 December 2008, fn 69 above, Legal reasoning.

83 Ley Orgánica 6/1985 de 1 de Julio, de Poder Judicial (Organic Law on the Judicial Branch), *Boletín Oficial del Estado*, no 157, 2 July 1985.

84 Auto (Decision) of 2 December 2008, fn 69 above (Dissenting opinion by Magistrates de Prada Solaesa, Bayarrui García and Sáez Valcárcel), para III.1.2.

85 UN Human Rights Committee, *Considerations of Reports Submitted by States Parties under*

in charge as Garzón was on medical leave—dictated a new decision in which it ordered some new petitions related to exhumations.[86] The National Prosecutor did not react to this latter decision with evident opposition. Indeed, he had not reacted against any of the previous decisions related to exhumations that had been taken prior to the one on 16 October.[87] And, perhaps along the same lines, he wished to affirm in his motion of appeal on 20 October on the basis of a very particular and generous interpretation of the Historic Memory Law that, in the localization, identification and exhumation of the remains of those who had been assassinated and executed during this bleak period of Spanish recent history, the victims could count on the unconditional collaboration of the National Prosecutor.[88]

Only a day after the authorization of the exhumation of the remains of eight persons who had been buried in the Valle de los Caídos without the knowledge or consent of their families,[89] the Chief Prosecutor presented (on 7 November) an unexpected document requesting the Criminal Chamber of the *Audiencia Nacional*[90] to order the judge in the Central Court of Instruction no 5 to limit himself to basic formalities without causing irreversible damages to third persons which would be very difficult to repair.[91]

At this point, it must be noted that even if there is no doubt that the decision on 16 October 2008 addresses a range of complex questions and the diversity of opinions seems fully legitimate, it is surprising that the Chief Prosecutor discussed and objected to each and every argument that had been set forth by Judge Garzón, even resorting to startling arguments—that is, about the Amnesty Law—relying on a partially contradictory and hitherto unprecedented

Article 40 of the Covenant. Concluding Observations: Spain, CCPR/C/ESP/CO/5, 27 October 2008, para 9.

86 Among them, in Cáceres, Granada, Valencia (the public cemetery), and in cemeteries in Mallorca (Porreres and Calviá), cemetery of Aguilar de la Frontera in Córdoba, and in the Valle de los Caídos.

87 This fact is mentioned by the Chief Prosecutor in his appeal transmitted on 20 October 2008: "These measures of localization, identification, exhumation and removal of remains of disappeared can also be agreed in the criminal procedure by the examining judge on the basis of articles 13, 326ff and 334ff of the Law on Criminal Procedure and one must leave on explicit record that the Office of the Prosecutor has never opposed its adoption in a jurisdictional setting, reason for which it did not consider it appropriate the interposition and formalization of any appeal against the providences of 28 August and 25 September" (unofficial translation). See *Audiencia Nacional*, Recurso de Apelación del Fiscal Jefe, fn 74 above, p 7.

88 *Audiencia Nacional*, Recurso de Apelación del Fiscal Jefe, fn 74 above.

89 Valerico Canales, Celestino Puebla, Emilio Caro, Flora Labajos, Pedro Ángel Sanz, Román González and Víctor Blázquez, members of Casa del Pueblo de Pajares de Adaja (Ávila), and Fidel Canales, who was buried in the cemetary of Griñón (Madrid) until 30 December 1968 when his remains were brought to Valle de los Caídos.

90 *Audiencia Nacional*, Fiscal Jefe, Escrito de ampliación de 7 de noviembre de 2008 al escrito de 21 de octubre 2008 (Extension transmitted on 7 November 2008 of the brief transmitted on 21 October 2008) (unofficial translation).

91 *Audiencia Nacional*, Fiscal Jefe, fn 90 above, para 4.

procedural mechanism with regard to form and substance. In fact, some judges of the *Audiencia Nacional* (de Prada Solaesa, Bayarrui García and Sáez Valcárcel) stated that the resort to this procedural mechanism amounts to an abuse of the law that has no legal support.[92] Furthermore, in the view of the same judges, some fundamental points of the decision of the prosecutor on 2 December were taken without the knowledge of the parties to the procedure which represented the victims; a fact that may well mean that he had the intention to simply put an end to the process.[93]

That being said, on the same 7 November, the Criminal Chamber of the *Audiencia Nacional* held a surprising "emergency meeting" and adopted a decision affirming the request of the prosecutor.[94] In particular, the chamber stressed that the activities related to exhumations had to be suspended until the question about the incompetence of the Central Court of Instruction no 5 had been resolved.[95] The five judges of the Criminal Chamber who voted against this decision (Magistrates Palacios Criado, Fernández Prado, Barreiro Avellaneda, Martínez Lázaro and Sáez Valcárcel) stressed that it had been taken without any prior hearing of the parties and in the absence of any appeal.[96] The decision on 7 November generated several new actions, among them, one on 10 November by the legal representatives of Carmen Negrín Fetter, Juan Negrín's grandchild, which was declared inadmissible by the Criminal Chamber in Plenary Session on 1 December,[97] and one on 17 November, which amounted to a lawsuit to the Supreme Court for breach of official duty against the 10 judges of the Criminal Chamber of the *Audiencia* who had voted in favour of the decision on 7 November.[98]

However, the intensity of judicial activity did not end at this point. Instead, on 18 November, Judge Garzón published a new and extensive decision,[99] affirming the extinction of criminal responsibility because of the death of the persons who had been listed in the decision of 16 October as possibly responsible for the crimes against the High Organs of the Nation and the Form of Government as well as the crimes of illegal detention/enforced disappearances, amounting to crimes against humanity. In this manner, the

92 Auto (Decision) of 2 December 2008, fn 69 above, Dissenting Opinion, para III.1.1.

93 Auto (Decision) of 2 December 2008, fn 69 above, Dissenting Opinion, paras III, III.3 and V.2.

94 *Audiencia Nacional*, Pleno de la Sala de lo Penal, Procedimiento Ordinario 53/08 del Juzgado Central de Instrucción no 5, Cuestión de incompetencia expediente no 34/08, Auto (Decision) of 7 November 2008.

95 Auto (Decision) of 7 November 2008, operative para 2.

96 Auto (Decision) of 7 November 2008, para 4 (Dissenting Opinion by Magistrates Palacios Criado, Fernández Prado, Barreiro Avellaneda, Martínez Lázaro and Sáez Valcárcel).

97 *Audiencia Nacional*, Pleno de la Sala de lo Penal, Expediente no 34/2008, Cuestión de competencia del artículo 23 LECR, Auto (Decision) of 1 December 2008.

98 This complaint is extended on 27 November.

99 *Audiencia Nacional*, Juzgado Central de Instrucción no 5, Sumario (Procedimiento Ordinario) 53/2008 E, Auto (Decision) of 18 November 2008.

case was inhibited in favour of the courts in the localities where the graves had been identified[100] (these localities were enumerated in a decision on 24 November),[101] and where such graves would be identified in the future.[102] In reality, however, far from simply inhibiting the case and sending it to these courts, the magistrate reaffirmed his basic position providing more solid foundations and responded to each and every argument that had been set forth by the prosecutor in his appeals,[103] extending them so as to include new sinister facts, in particular, those related to the "Children lost by Francoism". Indeed, the magistrate affirmed that documents and studies revealed that, in Spain, "a system of disappearances of underage children of republican mothers", who were dead, imprisoned, executed or simply disappeared, took place under the cover of apparent legality during various years between 1937 and 1950. For the magistrate, the Judicial Power has the obligation to investigate the criminal scope of these facts, "because of their permanent character and contextualization as crimes against humanity", which "are neither affected by statutory limitations nor amnestied".[104]

100 That is, in Coruña, Asturias, Badajoz, Burgos, Castellón, Córdoba, Granada, Huelva Huesca, León, Lugo, Madrid, Navarra, Palencia, Pontevedra, Salamanca, Soria, Toledo, Zamora and Zaragoza. In favour of the *Juzgados de Instrucción Decanos* in Barcelona, Burgos, Valencia, Vizcaya, Madrid, Málaga and Zaragoza. Auto (Decision) of 7 November 2008, operative para 2.

101 *Audiencia Nacional*, Juzgado Central de Instrucción no 5, Sumario (Procedimiento Ordinario) 0000053/2008 E, Auto (Decision) of 24 November 2008. According to this decision, at this time there are petitions of exhumations of bodies in the following locations, where common graves have been found, or knowledge about the existence of remains of persons referred to in this investigation: Aranga (A Coruña); San Martin del Rey Aurelio (Asturias); Finca "La Crespa" and Santa Amalia (Badajoz); Montes Rasineros (Castellón); Cordoba; Las Gabias, Viznar and Alfacar (Granada); La Palma del Condado, Niebla y Bonares and Calañas (Helva); Artieda (Huesca); Portomarin and Mondoñedo (Lugo); Parrillas (Toledo); Adrada de Haza, Milagros, San Juan del Monte and Valdenoceda (Burgos); La Robla, Ponferrada, Balboa, Dehesas, Camponaraya, Magaz de Abajo, Tejedo del Sil, Lago de Carucedo, Brañuelas, Friera, Rodanillo, San Juan de la Mata, Ocero, Sobrado, Algadefes, Fuentes Nuevas, Vilasumil, Toreno, Santa Lucia de Gordón, Busdongo, La Collada de Carmenes, Villaceid, Quintanilla de Combarros, Pombriego, Santalla, Fresnedo, San Pedro Mallo and Toral de Merayo (León); La Serena (Madrid); Valle de los Caídos (San Lorenzo del Escorial); Fuerte San Cristóbal (Navarra); Ventosa de Pisuerga y Villamedina (Palencia); Baiona-O Rosal, Porriño y San Andrés de Xeve (Pontevedra); Robleda (Salamanca); Berlanga de Duero (Soria); Maire de Castroponce and Santa Marta de Tera (Zamora); Calatayud (Zaragoza); Porreres and Calvià (Mallorca). In favour of the trial courts in the locations to which these places pertain and where the identified graves have been found: Coruña, Alicante, Asturias, Badajoz, Burgos, Castellón, Córdoba, Granada, Huelva Huesca, León, Lugo, Madrid, Navarra, Palencia, Pontevedra, Salamanca, Soria, Toledo, Valencia, Zamora and Zaragoza; as well as in favour of the superior trial courts in Barcelona, Burgos, Valencia, Vizcaya, Madrid, Málaga, Manacor, Palma and Zaragoza (operative part, para 2).

102 Auto (Decision) of 24 November 2008, fn 101 above, operative part, s III.

103 Auto (Decision) of 24 November 2008, fn 101 above, pp 18, 36–39, 44, 74, 78, 79, 81–83, 85, 91, 92, 95–97, and esp pp 118–139.

104 Auto (Decision) of 24 November 2008, fn 101 above, pp 6–10, 50–75 and 73–74.

It is important to point out that the impressive degree of social and media interest given to the new fact related to the Lost Children must be contrasted with the absolute silence of the Criminal Chamber of the *Audiencia Nacional*.[105]

Finally, in the same decision, the Central Court of Instruction no 5 resolved to end the function of the Expert Group, the members of which had only had the time to meet on a few occasions, and to inform the Ministry of Justice about its existence and that it was creating a database, including all information and documents which might be made compatible with the activities of this ministry related to the implementation of the Historic Memory Law.[106]

Despite the decision on 18 November, on 2 December 2008 the Criminal Chamber in plenary session came to consider the appeal of the prosecutor related to Article 23 of the Law on Criminal Procedure and decided that the Investigating Chamber no 5 lacked objective competence to investigate the alleged crimes in the case and, thus, left without effect all of the judicial decisions that had been adopted by that court since 18 October. The Criminal Chamber upheld that other judicial organs may be competent in the case, but without making clear which organs those would be.[107] But it should be noted that not all of the judges in the Criminal Chamber agreed with this judgment. Three judges presented an extensive dissenting opinion in which they expressed their conviction that closing the process "without indicating the scope of competence of another judicial organ" affected "the right to access justice and the right to an effective judicial remedy or the rights of those who are the victims and their associations, among them, the right to an adequate investigation". The dissenting judges also spoke of denial of justice, the eventual international responsibility of the Spanish state, and the obligations of the Spanish judiciary to respect international human rights law.[108]

Similarly, on 16 December 2009, various associations that assisted in the case presented a motion of appeal, which was united with diverse motions of complaint, expedients to annul actions, as well as recusals. Petitions have also been presented to the Supreme Court and the Constitutional Court. Finally, on 2 July 2010, a petition was transmitted to the European Court of Human Rights.[109]

To conclude, the 12 pages of the decision on 2 December, in which the Criminal Chamber of the *Audiencia* declares all of the positive judicial actions that had been taken up until that point to be without effect, lead us to a relatively simple conclusion. Indeed, after more than 70 years since the Civil War began, more than 30 years since the formal initiation of the Spanish political transition, and after 90 days of frenetic judicial activity that has been

105 See below.
106 Auto (Decision) of 24 November 2008, fn 101 above, operative para VI.
107 Auto (Decision) of 24 November 2008, fn 101 above, pp 11–12.
108 Auto (Decision) of 2 December 2008, fn 69 above, Dissenting Opinion, pp 16–17.
109 European Court of Human Rights, App no 37853/10, 2 July 2010.

under consideration in this chapter, the only thing that has been finally clarified by Spanish judicial organs is that the *coup d'état* in July 1936 was a crime of rebellion, but that the *Audiencia Nacional* is not competent to investigate the (connecting) international crimes that were (or may have been) committed during the Civil War and the dictatorship that followed. Who is thus the competent organ? Nowhere has this question been clarified or indicated.

7.5 The most recent developments: from the legal debate to the accusation of Judge Garzón for breach of duty

From what has been said, it is clear that the jurisdictional situation in Spain seemed to be condemned to a panorama in which the final response to the immense majority of the questions related to the merits, which arose between Judge Garzón and the Chief Prosecutor of the *Audiencia*, would be postponed for a long time. And all of this, in a scenario in which, considering the judicial decisions commented upon, it was difficult to conclude, already from the outset, what were the competent jurisdictional organs in Spain to investigate the crimes committed during the Civil War and Francoism; evidently, not a reassuring situation. Nevertheless, especially since May 2009, the issue took a new turn, which has placed us in a radically different territory. This new event was nothing less than the accusation of Judge Garzón of having breached official duties. This accusation had originated from the complaints that had been set forth by the so-called labour union *Manos Limpias* on 26 January 2009, the Organization of Liberty and Identity on 9 March and the ultra-right-wing party *Falange Española de las JONS* on 20 July of the same year.[110] All of these organizations had accused Judge Garzón of having committed the crime of breach of official duty as a result of his decision to investigate in the case in focus.

Nevertheless, before entering into the analysis of this question, it is pertinent to at least point out that in the last days of 2008, I wrote that even if one had followed the path of resorting to the different territorial courts (which had been done prior to turning to the *Audiencia Nacional*), there was no guarantee that these courts would have given a uniform interpretation of the norms at stake, an argument in line with what Judge Garzón had indicated in his decision and consistent with the position defended by the Chief Prosecutor of the *Audiencia*.[111] Indeed, we did not have to wait for long until it became evident that these courts would interpret the norms at stake in vastly different ways. Thus, while courts declared the case inadmissible and invoked the Amnesty Law, statutory limitations or the Historic Memory Law, and sometimes all three

110 The complete text of the three complaints is available at www.crimenesinternacionales-franquismo-casogarzon.es/p/documentos-legales.html (accessed on 25 March 2011).

111 Chinchón Álvarez, J, "Del Auto de 16 de octubre a la decisión del Pleno de la Sala de lo Penal de 2 de diciembre de 2008", *La Ley: Revista Jurídica Española de Doctrina, Jurisprudencia y Bibliografía*, vol 1, 2009, p 1421.

at once,[112] others supported the points made by Judge Garzón, and simply sent back the complaints to the *Audiencia* in the light of their consideration that it was still the competent organ, in spite of everything.[113] It is a regrettable development and reveals the way in which the complaints concerning the crimes of the past had given rise to "a total chaos of responses from whatever instances in the Spanish judicial system".[114]

In the end, it seemed to be the Supreme Court that would have to clarify the question as to which judicial organ was competent to investigate the crimes under consideration and this is what was put forward in the case of *Cuestión de Competencia*.[115] However, the High Tribunal decided something rather different. Having admitted the complaints presented against Judge Garzón, the Supreme Court did not reject his suspension,[116] and agreed to suspend the question about competence until the pending case against Garzón for breach of official duty had been settled.[117] It thus subjected, in the end and surprisingly, a decision concerning competence to what was a criminal case.

Then, what had started out as an initiative to request the *Audiencia Nacional* to investigate the crimes during the Civil War and Francoism had converted itself into a surprising debate as to whether or not the actions of Judge Garzón had been criminal. The words of Luciano Varela Castro, instructing judge of the Supreme Court, are especially telling. He concludes in his decision on 3 February 2010 that the actions of Garzón indicated:

> . . . as probable fact, that the accused magistrate acted with the objective to evade the decision of the legislator concerning the regime to localize and exhume the victims of the horrendous crimes of Francoism, constructed as an apparent object of the proceeding, knowing that these had been the object of amnesty by the democratic Parliament in Spain, whose will he deliberately decided to ignore or pass around. Such fact can constitute the crime of breach of official duty in article 446.3 of the Penal Code.[118]

112 Juzgado de Instrucción no 2 de Aranda de Duero, Diligencias Previas no 304/09, Auto (Decision) of 8 February 2010.

113 Juzgado de Instrucción no 3 de Granada, Diligencias Previas no 3209/2009, Auto (Decision) of 28 May 2009; and Juzgado de Primera Instancia e Instrucción no 2 de San Lorenzo de El Escorial, Diligencias Previas no 427/2009, Auto (Decision) of 2 July 2009.

114 See the manifesto signed by different associations: "Contra el ataque a la independencia de un juez, a favor del proceso contra el Franquismo, y a favor de la investigación de todos los crímenes de lesa humanidad", 10 September 2009. Available online at http://dimemarchena.blogspot.com/2009/09/manifiesto-contra-el-ataque-al-juez.html.

115 Tribunal Supremo, Cuestión de Competencia 6/20380/2009 (acumulada 6/20431/2009), Auto de Providencia, 26 March 2010.

116 Tribunal Supremo, Causa Especial no 20048/2009, Supreme Court, Auto (Decision) of 3 February 2010.

117 Tribunal Supremo, Auto de Providencia, 26 March 2010, fn 115 above.

118 Tribunal Supremo, Causa Especial no 20048/2009, Auto (Decision) of 3 February 2010, p 54.

The characterization of the actions of Garzón as constituting a breach of official duty has been highly criticized[119] as amounting to procedural operations that should not be allowed.[120] The arguments set forth by the Supreme Court in defence of this move are notably deficient.[121] Especially remarkable are the lines of attack invoked by the instructing judge with regard to Garzón's reliance upon international law.[122] In fact, as I wrote elsewhere, the proceedings before the Supreme Court seem to attest the maxim: "Everything for the law, but without international law."[123]

All of these developments leave the big questions concerning the viability of investigating the crimes of the Civil War and Francoism in a regrettable limbo. Moreover, it must be emphasized that the position of the Supreme Court (and that of the Chief Prosecutor of the *Audiencia*) has influenced, directly or indirectly, some decisions by other courts.[124] Indeed, all of them have united in the claim which has been restated by the Central Court of Instruction no 2 of Talavera de la Reina: "that there is no legal obligation to open a criminal investigation",[125] with the effect that the crimes in question "will end up unpunished as a result of applying the Law of Amnesty of 46/1977 of 15 October".[126]

In my view, quite regardless of the Historic Memory Law, it is not correct that the decision to open a criminal investigation in relation to the crimes under

119 See, e.g. Manjón-Cabeza, A, "Prevaricación e interpretación judicial. (A propósito del Auto del Tribunal Supremo, de 3 de febrero de 2010, por el que se deniega el sobreseimiento pedido por el Juez Baltasar Garzón en la causa de la 'Guerra Civil')", *Diario la Ley*, año XXXI, no 7367, 2010.

120 See, e.g. Gimeno Sendra, V, "Posibilidad de subsanación de determinados requisitos del escrito de acusación. Comentario al ATS de 28 de julio de 2010", *Diario la Ley*, año XXXI, no 7497, 2010.

121 Chinchón Álvarez, J and Vicente Márquez, L, "La investigación de los crímenes cometidos en la Guerra Civil y el franquismo como delito de prevaricación. Análisis crítico del Auto del Tribunal Supremo de 3 de febrero de 2010 desde la perspectiva del Derecho internacional", *Revista Electrónica de Estudios Internacionales*, no 19, 2010.

122 To be sure, it does not give rise to such extremes as shown by this statement by the Provincial Court of Palma de Mallorca when, in the view of relevant Spanish legislation, it affirmed that "there is no room to consider the incorporation of other rules with an international character, as the existence of a criminal law of this nature cannot at the moment be a desideratum" (unofficial translation). See *Audiencia Provinicial*, Sección Segunda, Palma de Mallorca, Auto (Decision) of 25 February 2010, p 2.

123 See Chinchón Álvarez, J and Vicente Márquez, L, "A propósito de los argumentos esgrimidos en la causa contra Baltasar Garzón. Todo por el Derecho, pero sin el Derecho internacional", *Diario Rebelión*, 23 April 2010. Available online at www.rebelion.org/noticia.php?id=104580.

124 For an explicit reception of this stance, see, e.g. *Audiencia Provincial*, Sección Decimoquinta, de Madrid, Auto (Decision) of 8 February 2010, p 4.

125 Juzgado de Instrucción no 2, Talavera de la Reina, Diligencias Indeterminadas 22/05, Auto (Decision) of 8 February 2007, pp 1–2.

126 Audiencia Provincial de Burgos, Auto (Decision) on 18 July 2010, p 3, reaffirming the position laid down in the decision of Juzgado de Instrucción no 2 de Aranda de Duero, Diligencias Previas no 304/09, Auto (Decision) of 8 February 2010.

consideration would have as "objective to evade the decision of the legislator"; quite the contrary.[127] Moreover, it is well known that there is a wealth of international jurisprudence in support of the claim that the effective remedy to be made available in the event of grave human rights violations must be essentially judicial in character.[128] And at this point, it is important to recall that with regard to enforced disappearances, as the Inter-American Court of Human Rights upholds:

> The duty to investigate facts of this type continues as long as there is uncertainty about the fate of the person who has disappeared. Even in the hypothetical case that those individually responsible for crimes of this type cannot be legally punished under certain circumstances, the state is obligated to use the means at its disposal to inform the relatives of the fate of the victims and, if they have been killed, the location of their remains.[129]

From an international legal perspective, the arguments set forth by the Supreme Court in relation to the Amnesty Law of 1977 are questionable and, at times, even unsustainable. In any case, these arguments are insufficient if one wishes to take them as evidence of a behaviour classified as a breach of judicial duty. The argument that can be considered crucial—set also by the Chief Prosecutor of the *Audiencia*[130]—relates to the democratic character of this law. This is in spite of the fact that there is no support in international law for the claim that the international legality of a measure in response to grave crime depends on

127 See Historic Memory Law, Art 4.1 and additional provision 2.

128 See, i.e. UN Human Rights Committee, case of *Nydia Erika Bautista* (Colombia), UN Doc CCPR/C/55/D/563/1993, decision of 13 November 1995, para 8.2. See also European Court of Human Rights, case of *Aksoy v Turkey*, Judgment of 18 December 1996 (clarifying the notion of effective recourse as including the availability of relevant and effective investigations towards the identification and punishment of those responsible).

129 IACtHR, case of *Godínez Cruz v Honduras*, Series C No 5, Judgment of 20 January 1989.

130 "It must not be forgotten, finally, by those who question the validity of the Amnesty Law by equating it with the laws of 'Final Stop' and 'Due Obedience', promulgated in the Republic of Argentina in 1986 and 1987 during the Government of 'Alfonsín', or with other norms of similar nature adopted in other countries, such as Chile or Peru, clearly illegal in the judgment of the Inter-American Court of Human Rights—which while the latter can be qualified openly as 'laws of impunity', as they were dictated—and to a significant extent imposed with the threat of a military coup—with the end of avoiding the criminal prosecution for the very grave crimes perpetrated by the State apparatus, during the military dictatorship in the period 1976–1983, and demand responsibility from its participants, the law of Amnesty was, during the entire process of its coming into being and approval, an act of democratic political forces, widely supported by Spanish society, and approved by the Parliament that was created by the first democratic elections held on 15 June 1977, the same parliamentary chambers that drafted and approved the Constitution in 1978. It would therefore be an absolute judicial mistake to question the legitimacy of the origin of this norm and, what is worse, attribute it with the stigma of being a 'law of impunity'." *Audiencia Nacional*, Recurso de Apelación del Fiscal Jefe, fn 74 above, p 34.

whether or not it has been adopted by a democratic parliament. Rather, what ultimately matters is whether the content of that measure is contradictory with international legal obligations. A different conclusion would imply the denial of the existence of international law and contradict relevant jurisprudence that denies in absolute terms such line of reasoning. To quote only one example, one may refer to the recent judgment of the Inter-American Court of Human Rights in the case of *Gomes Lund and Others*, which also provides a complete summary of the international and national practice attesting to the illegality of such laws.[131]

Another line of argumentation relates to Article 6.5 of the Second Protocol to the Geneva Conventions and is construed on the basis of a very questionable literal interpretation of that provision as it is directly opposed to the common understanding interpretation given to this provision, that is, by the International Committee of the Red Cross.[132] Namely, that it is not possible to extract from it that it is lawful that some war criminals—or other persons responsible for crimes against humanity—would evade criminal sanction.

Finally, even though the decisions of the Supreme Court do not deny that Articles 2(e) and (f) of the Amnesty Law of 1977 could be or are with difficulty compatible with Article 2.3(a) of the International Covenant on Civil and Political Rights,[133] it maintains that this Covenant is inapplicable in spite of the fact that it was binding for Spain prior to the adoption of the Amnesty Law. In doing so, one equates in an automatic manner the lack of competence of the UN Human Rights Committee to admit an individual petition with the question concerning the compatibility between a law that favours impunity (the amnesty) and international law. However, this bold conclusion is debatable and does not even reflect the unanimous position of the Human Rights Committee itself or the position of international human rights courts for that matter, such as the Inter-American Court of Human Rights,[134] and partly the European Court of Human Rights.[135]

Furthermore, it must be noted that the Supreme Court does not fully address the deeply controversial and debatable question as to when the crimes against humanity gained their full relevance in the ambit of criminal responsibility and at what point the international rule of non-statutory limitations was recognized. Nor did it address the possible relevance of its judgment in the

131 IACtHR, case of *Gomes-Lund ("Guerrilha do Araguai") et al v Brasil*, Series C No 219, Judgment of 24 November 2010, paras 148–169.

132 See Henckaerts, J M, Dowald-Beck, L et al, *Customary International Humanitarian Law*, New York: Cambridge University Press, 2005.

133 UN Covenant on Civil and Political Rights (adopted on 16 December 1966), published in *Boletín Oficial del Estado* on 30 April 1977. The Covenant entered into force in Spain on 27 July 1977.

134 IACtHR, case of *Gomes-Lund ("Guerrilha do Araguai") et al v Brasil*, Series C No 219, Judgment of 24 November 2010.

135 ECtHR, case of *Vardana and Others v Turkey* (GC), Application nos 16064/90, 16065/90, 16066/90, 16068/90, 16069/90, 16070/90, 16071/90, 16072/90 and 16073/90, Judgment of 18 September 2009.

Scilingo case.[136] This disregard did not impede it from extensively considering the claim that the crimes under consideration have passed the temporal limits imposed on criminal investigation and prosecution. An even more significant element of the judgment is the way in which it brings to the surface the resistance against any consideration of the continuous character of the crime of enforced disappearances, even though this character has been universally recognized, also in the most recent jurisprudence of the European Court of Human Rights.[137]

7.6 Concluding remarks

In the light of what has been related in this chapter, it may be concluded that the position of the majority of Spanish judicial organs has been to defend, among the many possible legal interpretations, that "there exists no legal obligation to open a criminal investigation"[138] in relation to the crimes that took place during the Civil War and Francoism. Indeed, the majority of the Spanish courts have discarded all possibilities to search for a path that would have made such an investigation viable, as was proposed and demanded, that is, by Judge Amaya Olivas in 2008,[139] and, more recently, by Magistrate Martín Pallín[140] and Professor Paredes Castañon.[141]

Given this, we may return to our starting point and quote again Professor Sánchez Legido, not only to remind ourselves of the main idea, but also to add another important line:

> It is not strange, in this context, that the then chancellor Insulza, on the occasion of Pinochet's detention, questioned the legitimacy of our country to do, with respect to what happens abroad, what we have not been capable of doing here . . . The objection is, without any doubt, irrefutable . . . The question, however, is whether the necessary resolution of the contradiction

136 See Tribunal Supremo, Sala de lo Penal, STS 798/2007, 1 October 2007. Available online at www.derechos.org/nizkor/espana/juicioral/doc/sentenciats.html#Tribunal.

137 ECtHR, case of *Vardana and Others v Turkey* (GC), Application nos 16064/90, 16065/90, 16066/90, 16068/90, 16069/90, 16070/90, 16071/90, 16072/90 and 16073/90, Judgment of 18 September 2009.

138 Juzgado de Instrucción no 2, Talavera de la Reina, Diligencias indeterminadas 22/05, Auto (Decision) of 9 February 2007, pp 1–2.

139 Olivas Díaz, A, "La intervención del juez de instrucción en las diligencias de investigación seguidas por desapariciones forzadas en la dictadura franquista", *Jueces para la Democracia*, no 63, 2008, pp 86–102.

140 Martín Pallín, J A, "¿Es posible iniciar un proceso penal contra una persona fallecida?", *Diario La Ley* (in printing) (document on file with the author).

141 Paredes Castañón, J M, "Soluciones, haberlas, haylas: Acerca de garantismos falsos y de desconsideraciones verdaderas hacia el Derecho internacional de los derechos humanos", 12 May 2010, available online at www.crimenesinternacionales-franquismo-casogarzon.es/2010/05/colaboraciones-jose-manuel-paredes.html.

> must not, instead of fostering measures that in the end favour the survival of impunity abroad, aim at the removal of the obstacles upon which that impunity is sustained at home.[142]

It must not be forgotten that the families of the direct victims of enforced disappearances and crimes against humanity who presented the complaints to the *Audiencia Nacional* about four years ago are still waiting for a reply to their legitimate demands. They have not had "their moment" yet.[143] All of them seem to be eternally subjected to that ancient military Japanese precept, *ikasazu, korasazu*: "You do not let them live, you do not let them die."

142 Sánchez Legido, fn 2 above, p 319.

143 Capellà I Roig, M, "Las 'desapariciones forzadas' en España durante la guerra civil y el franquismo: violaciones y crímenes de derecho internacional sin reparación ni castigo", in Soroeta Liceras, J (ed), *Conflictos y protección de derechos humanos en el orden internacional*. Curos de Derechos Humanos de Donostia-San Sebastián, vol VI, 2006, p 302.

8 Responding to human rights violations committed during the internal armed conflict in Peru

The limits and advances of Peruvian criminal justice

Yván Montoya Vivanco

8.1 Introduction: the internal armed conflict

This chapter examines the role of Peruvian criminal justice and the problems its institutions have had to face in the investigation, prosecution and sanctioning of grave human rights violations that were committed in Peru during the 1980s and 1990s. In order to understand the character of these problems, it is necessary to consider the nature and evolution of the internal armed conflict in Peru, which began in 1980 and started to decline in 1992, and the 10 years of authoritarian government under President Fujimori (1990 to 2000).[1]

8.1.1 Peru before the internal armed conflict

Since the independence from the Spanish monarchy on July 1821 until the start of the internal armed conflict, Peru has been characterized by military dictatorships alternating in brief periods of formal democracy.[2] It is also a country that is institutionally centralized and considerably poor, affected by continuous economic crises.[3] Four of its poorest provinces (Ayacucho, Huancavelica, Huánuco and Junín) were most affected by the political violence.[4]

1 This summary is based on the description and analysis of the Peruvian Truth and Reconciliation Commission (TRC) as presented in its Final Report on 28 August 2003. See Comisión de la Verdad y Reconciliación, *Informe Final*, available online at www.cverdad.org.pe/ifinal/index.php. The TRC was created during the government of President Alejandro Toledo by Supreme Decree no 065- 2001 PCM of 4 July 2001. Its function was to clarify the process, crimes and responsibilities for the terrorist violence and the human rights violations committed between May 1980 and November 2000, as well as to propose initiatives towards peace and agreement among Peruvians (Art 2.b of the aforementioned decree).

2 Comisión Especial del Senado sobre las Causas de la Violencia y Alternativas de Pacificación en el Perú, *Violencia y Pacificación*, Lima: DESCO-Comisión Andina de Juristas, 1989, p 125.

3 TRC Final Report, fn 1 above, pp 124–125.

4 Comisión de la Verdad y Reconciliación (Hatun Willakuy), *Versión abreviada del Informe Final de la Comisión de la Verdad y Reconciliación*, Lima: Pontificia Universidad Católica del

Directly before the armed conflict began, Peru had been ruled by a military dictatorship of a reformist character (1968 to 1979). The failure of the military project, augmented by the economic crisis and popular demonstrations against the military regime,[5] especially by Leftist groups, pressured the military government to call for the establishment of a Constituent Assembly to draft a new constitution and thereafter for general elections of a democratic government. The results of the general elections celebrated on 17 May 1980 meant that the architect Fernando Belaunde Terry from the Popular Action Party (*Acción Popular*) came into power. However, simultaneously, the Peruvian Communist Party *Sendero Luminoso* (PCP-SL), a Maoist group that had emerged in the wake of the multiple divisions of the Communist Party in 1970, decided to create the first military school on the premises of which the actions that initiated the Popular War (*Guerra Popular*) were decided.[6] Its first documented action was realized on the day of the general elections in May 1980, when an armed group attacked the site of the national elections juries in the town of Chuschi (Ayacucho) and burned the voting urns.

8.1.2 The internal armed conflict

The Peruvian Truth and Reconciliation Commission (TRC) divided the internal armed conflict into four different periods.[7] The first period spans from 17 May 1980 and ends on 29 December 1982. It is initiated by the first acts of violence committed by the PCP-SL in Ayacucho and ends on the day of the presidential order to engage the armed forces in the counter-subversive fight in Ayacucho. As the TRC explains, in this period the PCP-SL carried out sporadic terrorist attacks, at first mainly against public and private property, but then in a progressive manner also came to perpetrate systematic attacks against members of the police, essentially in the regions of Ayacucho and Huancavelica. The appearance of the Maoist group, which had a cell-like and clandestine structure, confused the police force, as it expected that it was a guerrilla movement similar to those that had emerged in Peru in the 1970s. There are documented cases of human rights violations stemming already from this period, although these

Perú, 2004. According to the TRC, a characteristic of the conflict in focus is social exclusion and discrimination of the Peruvian peasants who lived in the rural parts of the Andean zones.

5 The popular discontent manifested as from 1975 onwards among middle-class and poor sectors was a response to economic and social measures that affected them. Following the demonstrations in 1976 of the labour unionists from the mining and fishing sectors, national strikes were realized (22 and 23 May 1977; 14 July 1977 and 22 and 23 February 1978) which forced the military government to hold general elections in 1980. See Portocarrero Grados, R, "El Perú contemporáneo", in *Historia del Perú*, Barcelona: Lexus Editores, 2000, p 1112.

6 Portocarrero Grados, fn 5 above, pp 1064 ff.

7 Comisión de la Verdad y Reconciliación (Hatun Willakuy), Abbreviated version of the Report of the Commission, Lima, 2004, pp 60 ff.

violations were forgotten in the national context as a result of the importance given to the democratic transition process.

In the second period, the conflict becomes militarized. This period begins on 1 January 1983 with the instalment of the first political military commander in Ayacucho, General EP Roberto Clemente Noel Moral, and concludes with the death of prisoners in various prisons in Lima on 18 and 19 June 1986.[8] It is characterized not only by the increase of terrorist actions by the PCP-SL, but also by the massive escalation of human rights violations by the police forces, which also from this moment onwards assumed the political-military leadership of the internal war. One may mention the massacres in Soccos attributed to members of the national police, in Pucayacu attributed to the infantry of war marine, and in Putis and Accomarca attributed to members of the infantry of the armed forces. Multiple massacres can also be attributed to the members of the PCP-SL, such as the collective assassinations in Lucanamarca and Huancasancos. The majority of these events took place in the province of Ayacucho. Subversive terrorist actions by the Castro-inspired Revolutionary Movement Tupac Amaru (MRTA) were also initiated in this period (1984).

The third period is characterized by demonstrations of violence at the national level. It is initiated with the killings in prisons in June 1986 and lasts until 27 March 1989, when *Sendero Luminoso*, helped by drug traffickers, attacked the police office in Uchiza in the province of San Martín. In this period, the internal armed conflict, which until then had been limited to the provinces of Ayacucho and Huancavelica, acquires a national dimension (extending to Puno, Junín, Valley of Huallaga, among others). The attack against the police base in Uchiza amounted to one of the most serious armed actions that had been carried out by *Sendero Luminoso* until this point.

The fourth period, which spans from March 1989 to September 1992, is dominated by extreme crises, subversive offences and contra-offences by the state. The armed conflict is intensified. While *Sendero Luminoso* defined a new goal of achieving a strategic equilibrium, the armed forces started to pursue a new integral strategy that amounted to the systematic (although not indiscriminate) violation of human rights. Simultaneously, in March 1990, the Special Intelligence Group (GEIN) was formed within the national police, more specifically, within the Direction against Terrorism. Its exclusive dedication was to develop secret intelligence operations to capture the principal leaders of the subversive organizations. As a result, after various important detentions and searches and seizures, on 12 September 1992, the national police managed to localize and detain the highest leader of the PCP-SL, Abimael Guzmán Reynoso, together with several of the principal leaders of the terrorist group.

8 In June 1986, during the government of President Alan García, interns belonging to *Sendero Luminoso* rebelled in three prisons of Lima. The rebellion was met by harsh repression that caused about 200 deaths as a consequence of the disproportionate use of force.

Furthermore, in July 1990 the engineer Alberto Fujimori came into power as President of the Republic following democratically held elections in which he had been presented as an independent candidate. Following a series of tensions between the executive and legislative branches of government, on 5 April 1992, President Alberto Fujimori decided, together with the armed forces, to conduct a self-made *coup d'état*, ordering the closing of the principal democratic institutions of the country: the legislative branch, the Court of Constitutional Guarantees, the National Council of the Magistracy and the regional governments. He also decided to reorganize the Peruvian judiciary.

Between September 1992 and November 2000, there is a decline of terrorist actions and the corrupt authoritarianism of the government. The absence of a leader of *Sendero Luminoso* to fill the gap brought about by the capture of Abimael Guzmán and others led to a substantive decrease of terrorist actions. In October 1999, acting from his prison in the naval base of Callao, Guzmán proposed a peace agreement to the state and a ceasefire. Even if that proposal was not accepted by the state, it gave origin to a division among the members of the organization: on the one hand, the followers of Guzmán and, on the other, those who wanted to carry on with the armed fight. Meanwhile, the government, following the *coup d'état* and the detention of Guzmán, continued to project its popular image as a pacifier of the country and a victor over the subversion without concessions. The package of anti-subversive laws following the self-made *coup d'état* manifests this projection.

Furthermore, the power of the Adviser to President Fujimori, Vladimiro Montesinos Torres, was consolidated. As a consequence of his influence, administrative, functional and personal changes of intelligence organs of the armed forces and the police were realized. The changes determined that the President of the Republic acquired more direct power over the operational intelligence apparatus, in particular, over those organs that had been created within the armed forces. In consequence, an extermination group named *Colina* was formed within the Executive Branch of Government with a direct relation with the Adviser and the President of the Republic. The *Colina* group initiated its actions in November 1991 by killing 15 persons and injuring four others, all of them neighbours in the enclosure of Lima in the Barrios Altos district.[9] Another tragic event (among many others) which is also attributed to the *Colina* group is the disappearance and subsequent execution of nine students and one professor of the University of La Cantuta on 18 July 1992.[10]

In the same period, numerous new complaints concerning human rights violations were filed not least because of the discovery of the graves containing the remains of the students and the professor from the University of La Cantuta.

Having the National Intelligence Service (SIN) as its principal political apparatus, the government enacted a series of legislative changes to eliminate

9 IACtHR, case of *Barrios Altos v Peru*, Series C No 75, Judgment of 14 March 2001.

10 IACtHR, case of *La Cantuta v Peru*, Series C No 162, Judgment of 29 November 2006.

the independence of the judiciary and the parliament and in this manner securing impunity to state agents implicated in human rights violations. In July 1995, the government promulgated Law no 26749, which amnestied all of the members of the military and the police who were being investigated or prosecuted or had been convicted for crimes committed during the counter-subversive fight. Nevertheless, Judge Antonia Saquicuray, who was investigating the *La Cantuta* case, decided to exercise her constitutional competences of "diffuse control" (*control difuso*) of the law in question, leaving the amnesty law without application. In response, Parliament decided to issue Law no 26492 upholding that Law no 26749 could not be subjected to constitutional review. Thereafter and until 2011, it was practically impossible to investigate and judicialize the cases related to human rights violations perpetrated by state agents.

Meanwhile, although the number of grave human rights violations diminished following the fall of Guzmán, the arbitrary detentions, which were the product of unconstitutional anti-subversive legislation that had been adopted after the *coup d'état*, continued.

In the years that followed, the government benefited from the scarcity of subversive actions to legitimize politically its policies; in particular, it utilized its contra-subversive fight, such as the capture of Feliciano, to weaken its political opponents. As a consequence of the unconstitutional ambitions of Fujimori to be re-elected a second time together with the growing suspicions of corruption of the highest levels of government, the tension between the government and the opposition intensified profoundly.[11] Fujimori won the elections in the midst of grave complaints about electoral fraud. On 14 September 2000, shortly after Fujimori had assumed office in a situation marked by political instability, a video was spread with images of the President's Adviser, Vladimiro Montesinos Torres, handing over a considerable sum of money to a congressman who had been elected by the opposition so that he would change to the party of the government. This event was decisive to Montesinos's exit, the calling for new presidential elections, and Fujimori's escape to Japan in November 2000.

In its Final Report, the TRC established the following among its most important conclusions:

- The internal armed conflict in Peru (from May 1980 to September 1992) represents the most intense and extended period of prolonged violence in the entire history of the republic, disclosing the most profound disagreements and ruptures in Peruvian society.

11 The most acute expression of the conflict between the government and the opposition was the demonstration known as the "*Marcha de los 4 suyos*", headed by the then leader of the opposition Alejandro Toledo. Around 100,000 persons from different places in Peru joined the march, which took place on 26, 27 and 28 July 2000, protesting against what they considered to be an electoral fraud.

- 23,969 Peruvians had been identified as dead or disappeared. According to statistical estimates, however, the total number of fatal victims in this period may amount to about 69,000 persons.
- The principal victims of the violence were peasants. Out of the totality of reported victims, 79 per cent had lived in rural areas and 56 per cent had worked in the agricultural sector.
- The immediate and fundamental cause for the outbreak of the conflict was the decision by the PCP-SL to initiate an armed fight against the Peruvian state. The terrorist organization is the greatest perpetrator of crimes and human rights violations, as it is responsible for 54 per cent of the fatal victims (murdered and disappeared).
- The members of the armed forces and the police are responsible for about 45 per cent of the extrajudicial executions and disappearances that occurred in Peru during the armed conflict. Of special significance are the periods between 1983 and 1984 (with the highest number of reported victims) and 1989 and 1991.

The present chapter will focus on the human rights violations perpetrated by state agents, especially members of the armed forces and police. The limitation depends not only on the lack of space, but also on the particularities to which these violations have given rise from the standpoint of transitional justice in Peru.[12]

8.2 The mechanism of impunity

8.2.1 The criminal justice system during the internal armed conflict

There is evidence that repressive acts by state agents (that is, the armed forces and police) were committed during the early stages of the conflict and were the first subversive actions. These acts generated the first denunciations by victims or their family relatives to the Peruvian criminal justice system. Nevertheless, the efforts to investigate and prosecute the reported human rights violations encountered several obstacles. As the TRC affirms, already prior to the conflict the judicial system suffered from a lack of autonomy and independence. To this must be added the absence of security suffered by the judges and the Public Prosecutor.[13] These factors explain the difficulties faced by the courts in investigating cases involving state institutions of power and more so as the latter often

12 I fully share the understanding of the concept of transitional justice as developed by Ambos, K, *Justicia de Transición. Informes de América Latina, Alemania, España e Italia*, Lima: Konrad Adenauer, 2009. According to Ambos, transitional justice "comprises the entire realm of the processes and mechanisms associated with the efforts of a society to affront a legacy of past abuse on a large scale, to secure responsibility, render justice and achieve reconciliation".

13 TRC, *Final Report*, vol III, ch 2, p 256.

resorted to intimidation and threats. An emblematic example is the criminal investigation into the Cayara massacre. As the TRC explains:

> In this case, Dr. Manuel Catacora Gonzáles, in charge of the National Office of the Prosecutor, delegated to Dr. Carlos Escobar Pineda, Chief Prosecutor commissioned in Ayacucho, the investigation of the complaints with respect to the death and disappearance of the joint owners of land in the district of Cayara, on 14 May 1988, concluding that there existed sufficient elements to denounce the facts, presuming the responsibility of the Chief of the Political-Military Command in the Central National Security Zone no. 05 of Ayacucho, General of the Armed Forces, José Valdivia Dueñas.

Nevertheless, during the investigation conducted by this authority, several activities of grave kind took place, such as the death of witnesses and the repeated threats to the Prosecutor, to the point of having to change the title-holder of the investigation. As a consequence, in the ambit of the Ministry for Public Affairs, there were up to three rulings or pronouncements about the investigation of what had happened in Cayara, culminating in what was reported by Dr. Jesús Granda Olaecha, Provincial Prosecutor, concluding that there existed no elements to denounce any person and ordering that the investigation be provisionally filed, leaving it, in fact, with impunity . . .[14]

A different obstacle was the inefficient structure and weakening of the criminal justice system.[15] The inefficient structure was manifested, above all, in the absence of economic resources and infrastructure that could have facilitated the collection of evidentiary material and the Institute of Legal Medicine's lack of forensic anthropology teams. The inability of the criminal justice system to investigate the human rights violations led to the creation of specialized organs, but without the necessary competences to investigate highly complex cases. For example, the General Human Rights Office, created in 1985 (Resolution no 614-85-MP-FN), became entrusted with the task of assisting the Public Prosecutor in processing information and following up the complaints about human rights violations. Furthermore, through the adoption of Resolution no 192-89-MP-FN on 27 April 1989, the Public Prosecutor decided to create a Special Office of the Prosecutor for the Defence of the People and Human Rights, but without including any type of regulation to govern its functions. The lack of competences to formalize complaints once the investigations were concluded meant that the investigations into cases involving human rights violations duplicated from a bureaucratic standpoint between the Special Office of the Prosecutor and the common prosecutors with competences to charge persons. The bureaucratization of the complaints

14 TRC, *Final Report*, vol III, ch 2.6, p 8.
15 TRC, *Final Report*, vol III, pp 41 ff.

paralyzed the different prosecutors' offices and meant that the cases were put into the archives already in the preliminary stages of investigation.[16]

A third obstacle is the incapacity of prosecutors and judges to tackle systemic crime. In particular, there is no prior training of judges in how to utilize constitutional law or international human rights law when dealing with cases of arbitrary detention and disappearances. As Professor Eguiguren Praeli notes,[17] the declining number of *habeas corpus* claims from 1986 onwards was the result of repeated judicial dismissals based on prolonged states of emergencies in diverse parts of the country. According to him, what was missing in these cases was the judicial respect for the requisites of legal reasoning when examining the motives for the detentions.[18] There was no judicial attempt to invoke the Constitution in its status as the supreme law. The problems related to the application of constitutional law as well as international human rights and criminal law intensified in 2001 onwards due to passage of time since the criminal activities had been perpetrated. The temporal dimension led to the imposition of statutory limitations.

A fourth obstacle is the lack of co-operation by military and police institutions with the judiciary. The authorities have not responded or repeatedly refused to answer requests for information from the Public Prosecutor. For example, in the *Cayara Massacre* case, neither the Public Prosecutor nor the Parliamentary Commission for Investigation was given access to the place of the crime during 15 days. The military used this time to hide the traces of the massacre. The sexual abuses in the Manta and Vilca communities are identical inasmuch as the military agents accused of these abuses were transferred to other military zones to avoid identification.

A fifth obstacle relates to the frequently employed transferral of competences from common criminal jurisdictions to military tribunals. Evidently, the military tribunals have simply put the majority of the complaints into archives and in this manner imposed impunity in response to the gravest human rights violations. The TRC questioned such transferrals in the harshest terms:

> The abdication of jurisdiction by the judicial system in favour of the military justice system was also an alleged omission of duties as it rendered

16 For a brief study of the cases related to the insufficient action of the first prosecutor specialized in Defender of the People and Human Rights, see Defensoría del Pueblo, *Ejecuciones extrajudiciales*, *Informe Defensorial*, no 77, Lima, 2003, pp 52 ff. The first reports on Peru produced by Amnesty International (AI) affirm this fact. AI indicates that it has not received information that Peru has initiated independent investigations in response to the numerous reports on torture produced by AI, the Catholic Church and the Parliamentary Commission on Human Rights. See AI Report, *Tortura*, Madrid, 1984, p 154.

17 See Eguiguren Praeli, F, *Los retos de una democracia insuficiente. Diez años de régimen constitucional en el Perú 1980–1990*, Lima: Comisión Andina de Juristas, 1990, pp 52–53.

18 The *habeas corpus* claims related to the enforced disappearances of persons were systematically declared as unfounded to the extent that the judges absurdly required the presence of the detained in order to pronounce themselves. See Montoya Vivanco, Y, *Poder Judicial y Estado democrático*, Lima: Instituto de Defensa Legal, 1997.

the judicial system into an agent violating fundamental rights. In fact, during the period that lasted until 1992, the judges of the common jurisdiction inhibited themselves in favour of military jurisdiction or were ordered to do so by higher instances, whenever a question of competence emerged.

> . . . notorious cases such as the ones related to the behaviour of the infantry of the Marine in Huanta as the Pucayacu case and the Callqui case in 1984 were resolved by military jurisdiction . . . This pattern of renunciation was thereafter deepened with the Accomarca case and the Parcco-Pomatambo and Cayara cases, which were left with impunity once handed over to military justice.[19]

8.2.2 The post-conflict situation: the institutionalization of impunity

That the internal armed conflict was coming to an end was manifested by the fall of the leader of *Sendero Luminoso*[20] and the disintegration of the Revolutionary Movement Tupac Amaru (MRTA). Nevertheless, instead of creating a possibility for truth-seeking and justice, impunity was institutionalized. This development was largely due to Fujimori's political exploitation of the defeat of the subversive movement and the alliance that its government had established with the military project since the time of the *coup d'état* in April 1992. The impunity mechanisms were no longer limited to the lack of co-operation by the police and acts of intimidation against the judicial system, but included governmental and legislative actions with a general and permanent reach (profiting from the parliamentary majority fraudulently gained by Fujimori).

A qualitative difference between the impunity mechanisms of the conflict period as opposed to the post-conflict one was a notable public discouragement of any attempt to take judicial action. One example is the unusual lining up of tanks on 21 and 22 April 1993 in the streets of Lima. The act had been ordered by the Commander-in-Chief of the Joined Armed Forces, Nicolás de Bari Hermosa, as a protest against the investigations that had been initiated in relation to the murders in Barrios Altos and La Cantuta and attributed to agents of the army. No governmental authority declared this manifestation of threat as illegal.

That being said, the acts that most clearly manifest the way in which impunity was institutionalized are the self-amnesty laws adopted by the Fujimori Government in 1995 with the help of his parliamentary majority. As mentioned earlier in this chapter, Law no 26479 is a general amnesty that

19 TRC, *Final Report*, vol III, ch 2.6, p 14.

20 Abimael Guzmán Reynoso, leader of *Sendero Luminoso*, was captured on 11 September 1992 together with various leaders of the organization following an elaborated work of the intelligence service of the national police.

benefited not only persons who had already been convicted of human rights violations, but also the accused, investigated and any other person susceptible of being investigated on these grounds. However, Judge Saquicuray, who was investigating the *La Cantuta* case, considered the law to be incompatible with the Constitution. In response to this legitimate judicial action, Parliament decided to intervene in the process, thus, approving Law no 26492 according to which the judiciary did not have the competence to revise the amnesty law.

The effect of the two amnesty laws was that multiple judicial proceedings and investigations were filed away.[21] Those who had been convicted for human rights violations were released from prison, among them, members of the Colina group. The situation of absolute impunity lasted until around the end of 2000 when the authoritarian and corrupt government of Fujimori was overturned and President Valentín Panigua, with clearly democratic ambitions, took office.

Another method to ensure impunity, which is employed in Peru, is to submit the courts to governmental control and severely suppress their condition as independent and autonomous institutions of state. In fact, a stated "reason" for the *coup d'état* on 5 April 1992 was the inefficacy and corruption of the judiciary. It was for this reason that the de facto government maintained a negative position towards the judiciary and decided arbitrarily to remove 133 judges, among them, 12 members of the Supreme Court and 33 members of the Higher Court in Lima, and eight members of the judicial district of Callao.[22] These were substituted by provisional judges who were subjected to governmental organs controlled by the executive branch. Notably, the authoritarian government promulgated Law no 26546 creating the Executive Commission of Judicial Power, substituting all of the regular organs of the judicial power. This new structure assured that no case involving human rights violations attributed to state agents would be investigated or judicialized and that the judges on the bench would not dare to question the constitutional legality of the government.

A fourth mechanism of impunity was the separation from the Inter-American system of human rights protection. Even if the government maintained control over questions related to impunity in the domestic ambit, the international ambit had not been taken into account. A series of pronouncements of the Inter-American Court of Human Rights against the Peruvian state (especially in the *Castillo Petruzzi* case,[23] which concerned the arbitrary termination of employment for three magistrates of the Constitutional Court, and the *Loayza Tamayo*

21 The Public Defender has found that out of the 32 judicial proceedings that were reactivated in 2001, 17 had been filed away by virtue of the Amnesty Law. See Defensoria del Pueblo, *Un año de la Comisión de la Verdad y Reconciliación*. Informe Defensorial no 86, Lima, 2004.

22 Comisión Especial para la Reforma Integral de la Administración de Justicia, *Los problemas de la Justicia en el Perú: hacia un enfoque sistémico*, Lima: Comisión Andina de juristas, 2004, p 35.

23 IACtHR, case of *Castillo Petruzzi*, Series C No 52, Judgment of 30 May 1999. In this case, the court ordered the annulment of the process pursued by the Peruvian state against members of the terrorist organization MRTA as well as the opening of a new proceeding.

case,[24] among other more recent cases, such as the killing of 15 people in Barrios Altos by the Colina group) gave rise to the governmental consideration that the proximity of various judgments of the Inter-American Court was harmful to Peru as it was possibly contrary to its interests.[25] Thus, during the first months in 1999, the government initiated a campaign to discredit the Inter-American Court, depicting it as an obstacle to its counter-terrorist policies. Thereafter, on 14 July 1999, the Peruvian state remitted a communication to the Secretary of the Organization of American States (OAS) announcing in a unilateral manner and without respecting the internal procedures that had been established in the San José Covenant its withdrawal from the provisions related to the contentious competence of the Inter-American Court.[26]

8.3 The mechanisms of resistance and the end of impunity

8.3.1 Identifying the mechanisms of resistance

The process toward the end of impunity in Peru would have been impossible without the continued resistance of national and international civil society organizations present since the early stages of the armed conflict.[27]

Since the commencement of the conflict, different institutions and persons decided to act in defence of human rights, protecting the citizens from possible abuses of the state. In 1985, these institutions came to organize themselves into a significant movement united around the National Co-ordinator of Human Rights (CNDH). The co-ordinator was converted into an efficient instrument for victims of violence to find protection and legal advice. Moreover, the rigour and seriousness of the co-ordinator transformed it into an essential ethical reference within the national political scenario and was clearly differentiated from any political project of the Left, in spite of the ascendance of some of its members. One of its fundamental principles was the denial of violence whether deriving from the state agents or terrorist groups.

Already from the outset of the conflict, human rights organizations united around the co-ordinator started to denounce human rights violations committed by state agents and violations of international humanitarian law committed by subversive organizations. At the domestic level, the actions against the state perpetrators materialized into complaints to the Public Prosecutor for crimes defined in domestic law (among them, murders, kidnappings and injuries). However, the co-ordinator also formulated communications to international human rights institutions, including the UN Human Rights Committee, UN

24 IACtHR, case of *Loayza Tamayo*, Series C No 52, Order of 27 November 1998.

25 TRC, *Final Report*, vol III, pp 125 ff, paras 2–3.

26 On 7 July 1999, the Peruvian Congress approved by simple majority a draft law remitted by the President of the Republic by virtue of which it decided that Peru withdraws from the contentious competence of the court with immediate effect.

27 TRC, *Final Report*, vol III, ch 3, pp 293 ff.

Thematic Groups and especially the Inter-American system. These actions, particularly the complaints before the Inter-American Human Rights Commission and the first judgments by the Inter-American Court, brought into permanent question the legitimacy of the exercise of power by the different Peruvian governments, and even conditioned economic co-operation with the United States.[28] Between 1990 and 2000, the Inter-American Commission on Human Rights dealt with 159 Peruvian cases involving human rights violations, recommending the investigation, prosecution and sanctioning of the perpetrators. The fact that the Peruvian state did not respond to the requirements of the Inter-American Commission or gave insufficient replies led to the progressive accumulation of international decisions against it.

The Catholic Church, especially the constituent church, has also been a voice of complaint regarding the crimes and human rights violations, proclaiming and defending the value of life and dignity of persons. In fact, not only did the Catholic Church formulate complaints to the criminal justice system, but it also repeatedly promoted mobilizations for peace and against the violence. The complaints set forth by the majority of bishops as well as by national institutions of the church (Episcopal Conference for Social Action) irritated the authorities. The Evangelical Church, in turn, spoke out in different denominations and para-ecclesiastical entities, constituting what was named CONEP. The evangelical community reported not only acts of terror of subversive groups, but also of other members of the armed forces. During the violent period, it defended cases in which its members had been victims of violations of their civil and political rights, as well as cases related to evangelical leaders and citizens who had been unjustly accused and imprisoned mainly in Lima, Chiclayo, Cajamarca, Huancayo, Huancavelica, Puno and Cuzco for crimes of terrorism in prisons.

The TRC also highlights the role of investigating journalism, differentiating between three phases. The first is marked by the confusion resulting from the lack of knowledge of the terrorist phenomenon *Sendero Luminoso*. The second phase is marked by a sensationalist diffusion of this phenomenon. In the third phase, investigating journalism becomes professionalized; it examines sources, maintaining a critical distance to the events, and provides information in an independent manner. The TRC stressed especially the investigations undertaken by journalists to unveil crimes perpetrated by paramilitary groups and death squads. One emblematic example is the investigation carried out by journalist Ricardo Uceda of those responsible for the disappearance and subsequent execution of nine students and a professor from the University of La Cantuta. The journalistic work has served as important documentary evidence in human rights trials, including against Fujimori.

28 TRC, *Final Report*, vol III, ch 3.1, p 14.

8.3.2 Factors contributing to ending impunity

In spite of the efforts undertaken by the range of organizations and institutions mentioned in the previous section, the panorama that emerged in 1995 onwards when the Amnesty Law entered into force was that of absolute impunity. The process of overcoming this situation must be explained in the light of a series of factors that converged in a favourable manner.

All studies of the Peruvian case coincide in their affirmation that one of the most important factors was the fall of Fujimori's regime. The unconstitutional ambitions of the second presidential re-election, the complaints about the relationship of the president—through his adviser Vladimiro Montesinos—with the Colina group and the grave situations of corruption which implicated the president and the highest officials, led to Fujimori's exit from government, the instalment of a transitional government and the anticipated call for presidential elections. An important fact is the grave situation of corruption that involved high officials from the armed forces and the police, which meant that they moved away from a situation of certain prestige for the military defeat of terrorism to a loss of prestige and legitimacy.

The transitional government led by President Valentín Paniagua initiated a process of reconstitution of the democratic institutions that had been severely weakened by the previous government. To begin with, two members of the Constitutional Court who had been arbitrarily expelled were rehabilitated, and two members elected by qualified majority by Congress were added. Since then, the Constitutional Court has been able to intervene in a decisive manner in the process to end impunity and delivered important judgments that have aided the development of a constitutional doctrine related to the protection of fundamental rights.[29] Furthermore, Congress was reconstituted. From having been absolutely dependent upon the executive branch of government, it was transformed into an independent and autonomous institution. The work of its Commission on Constitutional Accusations is worthy of special mention, as it accused before Congress in plenary session the former President of the Republic and Ministers of the Government for human rights violations during the armed conflict. It also commended the Public Prosecutor to investigate these cases based on political pre-judgment (*antejuicio politico*).

29 STC (Constitutional Court), *Villegas Namuche* case 2488-2002-PHC/TC, Judgment of 8 March 2004, related to the permanent nature of the crime of enforced disappearance and its immediate and non-retroactive application in relation to acts initiated prior to the entry into force of the crime in national law and there is still no certainty as to the whereabouts of the victim. It also recognizes the right to the truth for the victims and society in the case of human rights violations. STC, *Martín Rivas* case 679-2005-PA/TC, Judgment of 2 March 2007, related to the invalidity of the amnesty law and *res judicata* as mechanisms to extinguish penal action. See also STC, Código de Justicia Militar (Exp 0012-2006 PI/TC), Judgment of 15 December 2006 concerning the delimitation of crimes of function and the competence of military tribunals. In this case, military tribunals have no competence to admit common crimes that amount to human rights violations.

Reference must also be made to the Office of the Ombudsman. This public institution did not suffer any intervention by the Fujimori Government, but has managed to maintain its independence and autonomy since the first ombudsman took office until now. Since 2002, it elaborates reports[30] related to the discovery of graves containing the remains of persons presumably murdered by state agents. Also, it repeatedly recommended the creation of a truth and reconciliation commission with competence to clarify the period of political violence experienced in Peru. In November 2000, it adopted Resolution no 57 DP–2000, recommending the creation of such a commission that would clarify the circumstances in which grave human rights violations had been perpetrated, to assign personal and institutional responsibilities and to grant reparations.[31] Furthermore, the Office of the Ombudsman has contributed to the process of ending impunity. In its Report no 77, it recommends the investigation of 11 cases of extrajudicial executions and the unveiling of the problems facing criminal justice in seeking to investigate, prosecute and sanction the human rights violations in focus. Finally, the ombudsman is the depositor of the archives of the TRC and supervises the compliance with its recommendations. In performing this function, the Office has elaborated annual reports on the state of affairs with regard to the complaints on human rights violations which itself and the TRC have presented to the Public Prosecutor. These reports reveal diversity of obstacles that impede the judicialization of these cases ranging from organizational shortcomings in the judiciary to difficulties of applying criminal law in specific cases; it also stresses the need to adjust the law related to reparations and exhumations.

A third factor that has promoted the process toward the overcoming of impunity is the TRC, which was created by virtue of a Supreme Decree (no 065-2001 PCM) that was approved by the transitional government of Valentín Paniagua on 4 June 2001. The Commission had the competence to clarify the truth, and determine the causes and consequences of the internal armed conflict as well as how to realize justice. Once it had ended its work, it communicated its conclusions concerning the crimes and human rights violations in focus, including the identification of the victims and possible perpetrators, to the institutions of criminal justice. Thereafter, on the basis of the Supreme Decree no 101-2001 PCM, passed in August 2001, the government of Alejandro Toledo modified the name of the Truth Commission to the Truth and Reconciliation Commission, extending the number of its members from eight to 12 persons. The former dean of the Catholic University of Peru, Salomón

30 See Informe Defensorial no 002-2002-DP/ADDHH, *Investigación defensorial sobre la existencia de presuntas fosas comunes con restos humanos en el paraje de Sancaypata del Distrito de Totos, provincia de Cangallo, Ayacucho*. See also Informe Defensorial no 03-2002 DP/ADDHH, *Investigación defensorial sobre la existencia de presuntas fosas comunes con restos humanos en el paraje de Ccarpacase del distrito de Totos, provincia de Cangallo, Ayacucho*.

31 The recommendation was reiterated in Resolution nº15 DP-2001, adopted on 24 May 2001.

Lerner Febres, chaired the commission, the work of which lasted for two years. Its Final Report was presented on 28 August 2003.

The commission investigated not only general patterns of human rights violating practices, but also came to analyze 73 concrete cases of crimes committed both by the terrorist organizations and the members of the armed forces and police. Also of significance is that, once its mandate ended, the TRC remitted 43 reports about concrete cases of human rights violations to the Public Prosecutor,[32] adding these ones to four others that had already been forwarded. The reports entail different recommendations related to investigations and proceedings. To this end, in some cases, it has recommended the formalization of complaints against possible perpetrators, while in others, the initiation of a prior investigation, and in others again, extending the investigation or continuing an already ongoing one. Out of the 47 cases, 40 were already the object of the prosecutor's investigations or judicial proceedings when the commission's reports were presented. In the majority of cases, the reactivation of the judicial system was the result of the respect given to the recommendations of the Inter-American Human Rights Commission.[33]

Furthermore, while the Inter-American system and the TRC's Final Report were critical to the activation of the criminal justice system in relation to the cases in focus, in order to ensure continuity to this process, completing it in an efficient manner, it was necessary to redress the absence of judicial independence and the lack of sufficient skills to tackle the complexities presented in doctrine and criminal procedural law. Thus, the transitional government initiated a process of ending the provisional nature of the magistracy and also reconstructing the independent structure of criminal justice. While so far inconclusive, the process has brought some significant results.[34] A somewhat different process of equal relevance is that of creating a criminal justice system specializing in crimes that amount to grave human rights violations.[35] Nevertheless, so far not enough has been done to redress the insufficient capacity of our prosecutors and judges and the considerable dominance of a legal positivistic culture among a majority of them.[36]

32 For a comprehensive account of these cases, see Defensoría del Pueblo, *A un año de la Comisión de la Verdad y Reconciliación, Informe Defensorial*, no 86, Lima, 2004, pp 22–23.

33 Note the Peruvian commitment to the Inter-American system following the fall of the Fujimori regime, and the legitimate arrival of President Valentín Paniagua. For a more detailed account of the procedural situation of the cases presented to the National Prosecutor by the TRC, see Defensoría del Pueblo, fn 32 above.

34 From June 2001 onwards, various processes related to the selection and appointment of magistrates to the National Council of the Magistracy were initiated. See Villavicencio Ríos, A, *La reestructuración silenciosa. La labor del Consejo Nacional de la Magistratura en la selección y nombramiento de magistrados noviembre del 2000—marzo del 2004*, Lima: Justicia Viva, 2004.

35 See Defensoria del Pueblo, *El Estado frente a las víctimas de la violencia ¿hacia dónde vamos en políticas de reparación y justicia?* Informe Defensorial, no 128, Lima, 2007.

36 For an account of the formalistic conception of law as a product of the traditional legal education in Peru, see Gonzáles Mantilla, G, "Enseñanza del Derecho, cultura legal y

Attention must also be paid to the judgments of the Inter-American Court and their impact in terms of removing diverse criminal and procedural barriers that impeded the continued investigation and prosecution of the cases in focus, not least by virtue of their binding and directly enforceable character. Especially important to the Peruvian case are the judgments recognizing the international duty of states to punish grave human rights violations, the invalidity of amnesty laws, the inapplicability of statutory limitations, as well as the lack of competence of the military tribunals to investigate and prosecute the cases related to grave human rights violations.[37] The Inter-American Court has in several judgments reiterated its interpretation of Articles 1.1 and 1.2 of the San José Covenant as imposing a legal obligation on the Peruvian state to investigate and sanction those responsible for human rights violations and that such investigations are to be carried out in a serious manner by independent magistrates and not as a matter of formality which are bound to lead to unproductive results.[38] Furthermore, the court had indicated already in the initial stages that the amnesty laws that had been passed by the former president Fujimori amounted to unacceptable obstacles to the investigation, processing and sanctioning of the perpetrators of the crimes in focus, and could not be invoked.[39] In a judgment in the *Barrios Altos* case, the court sets forth a conclusive ruling about the invalidity of these kinds of provisions. The latter decision had a major impact when, in the judgment related to the interpretation of that case, the court affirmed the *erga omnes* character of the judgment on the merits in all equivalent cases.[40]

The Inter-American Court has also tackled the issue of statutory-based limitations as a mechanism relied upon by the accused to evade criminal responsibility. Especially important in this regard are the judgment on the merits in the *Barrios Altos* case and the judgment concerning the interpretation

Reforma Judicial", in Peirano Torriani, G and Pease García, H, *Reforma del Estado peruano. Seminario en los 90 años de la Pontificia Universidad Católica del Perú*, Lima: Fondo Editorial PUCP, 2008, pp 400 ff.

37 The jurisprudence of the Inter-American Court of Human Rights, even when not directly related to Peru (cases of *Velásquez Rodríguez* and *Godínez Cruz* among others), has been important for Peru to the extent that it has been considered as binding on all of the organs of the judicial power. See STC, *Vera Navarrete* case (Exp 2798-04 HC/TC), Judgment of 9 December 2004, eighth legal reasoning.

38 See, e.g. IACtHR, case of *Neyra Alegría and Others v Peru*, Series C No 20, Judgment of 19 January 1995, para 65; IACtHR, case of *Durand and Ugarte v Peru*, Series C No 68, Judgment of 16 August 2000, para 125; IACtHR, case of *Cantoral-Benavides v Peru*, Series C No 69, Judgment of 18 August 2000, operative para 12; and IACtHR, case of *Barrios Altos v Peru*, Series C No 75, Judgment of 14 March 2001.

39 See IACtHR, case of *Castillo Paez v Peru*, Series C No 43, Judgment of 27 November 1998, para 104; and IACtHR, case of *Loayza Tamayo v Peru*, Series C No 42, Judgment of 27 November 1998, para 168.

40 IACtHR, case of *Barrios Altos v Peru*, Series C No 83, Judgment of 3 September 2001 (interpretation of the judgment on the merits).

of the *Cantoral Benavides* case.[41] The jurisprudence that the court has produced in relation to time limits has been extremely valuable for Peruvian justice in the face of the recent ambition of the government of President García to incorporate a new legal ground for filing away cases related to human rights violations, namely that the formal deadline for judicial investigation has expired (Legislative Decree no 107). In particular, in the *La Cantuta* case, the Special Criminal Chamber of the Higher Court of Lima exercised judicial review (*control difuso*) over the mentioned decree, deciding on its non-applicability for incompatibility of the decree with the Constitution and the American Convention on Human Rights.[42]

Another contributing factor is the lack of competence for military tribunals to prosecute crimes that amount to human rights violations. As noted earlier in this chapter, a traditional mechanism of impunity has been the continuous transfer of competences in the cases in focus from ordinary justice to military tribunals. However, in the *Durand Ugarte* case,[43] the Inter-American Court established that military tribunals are not competent to rule in cases related to common crimes such as the disproportionate use of force and the subsequent death of a considerable number of rioting prisoners in the prison of Frontón. The court considered that, in these cases, the prosecution of military personnel for common crime in military tribunals constituted a violation of the right to an independent and impartial judge.[44]

8.4 Substantive and procedural problems in the judicialization process

The process of judicial reactivation in relation to the cases at hand has relied upon the new Penal Code of 1991, which to a considerable extent maintained the common crimes that were included in the Penal Code of 1924 (murders, injuries and kidnapping), although with somewhat more benign penalties. However, the 1991 Code includes some new crimes, such as that of genocide and the crime of enforced disappearance of persons. In the procedural ambit, Peru has relied on a Code of Criminal Procedure in force since 1940, which builds upon an inquisitorial and formal procedural model in contrast with the

41 IACtHR, case of *Cantoral-Benavides v Peru,* Series C No 88, Judgment of 3 December 2001 (reparations and costs). See also IACtHR, case of *Maritza Urrutia v Guatemala*, Series C No 103, Judgment of 27 November 2003 (reparations and costs).

42 Primera Sala Penal Especial de la Corte Superior de Lima, case of *Barrios Altos*, Judgment of 15 September 2010.

43 IACtHR, case of *Durand Ugarte v Peru*, Series C No 68, Judgment of 16 August 2000.

44 The Inter-American Court of Human Rights has pronounced the military tribunals' lack of competence to judge civilians. See, e.g. case of *Loayza Tamayo v Peru*, Series C No 47, Order of 17 September 1997; case of *Castillo Petruzzi v Peru*, Series C No 52, Judgment of 30 May 1999; and case of *Cantoral Benavides v Peru*, Series C No 69, Judgment of 18 August 2000.

recent Code of Criminal Procedure of 2004, setting forth an accusatorial adversarial model. Until now, the old model has been used in most of the cases in focus.

In the process of reactivating criminal justice in relation to the cases in focus, the Peruvian courts had to seek to render the requirements derived from international human rights law, international criminal law and constitutional law compatible with the principles and categories that inspire our criminal law and criminal procedural law, especially the legality principle. While international human rights and international criminal law proscribe what must be done (for example, that amnesty or statutory time limits cannot be invoked; that grave human rights violations, such as torture, enforced disappearance and extrajudicial executions must be sanctioned; and that all those responsible—directly or indirectly—for these crimes must be punished), it does not indicate how these obligations must be concretized in the context of domestic criminal justice (for example, how not to apply time limits when the national law applies to all crimes or how to sanction an act of torture when the crime had not been included in the national penal code in force at the time when the act was committed). In what follows is an account of the concrete problems created by the criminalization of human rights violations in the context of substantive and procedural criminal law.

8.4.1 The legality principle and its relationship with international human rights and criminal law

The legality principle,[45] to use the words of the Peruvian Constitutional Court, constitutes a principle and also a fundamental right,[46] which operates principally as a limit on the punitive authority of the state. The principle integrates a series of guarantees that constitute the essential core of this principle and right. The guarantee, known as *Reserva de Ley* (*nullum crimen sine lege- lex scripta*), postulates that the creation or extension of crimes or aggravating circumstances must be effected by virtue of a law understood in a formal sense and only exceptionally, in a material sense.[47] According to our Constitution, the guarantee covers not

45 For an account of the problems that the legality principle gives rise to in the judicialization of cases involving grave human rights violations in Peru, see Montoya Vivanco, Y, "El Derecho internacional y los delitos", in Instituto de Democracia y Derechos Humanos de la Pontificia Universidad Católica del Perú (ed), *Los caminos de la Justicia Penal y los Derechos Humanos*, Lima: IDEHPUCP, 2007.

46 STC, case of *Bedoya de Vivanco* (Exp 2758- 2004 HC TC), Judgment of 23 November 2004, third legal reasoning.

47 See IACtHR, Advisory Opinion 6/86 of 9 May 1986. The court defines law as a "general legal norm tied to the general welfare, passed by democratically elected legislative bodies established by the Constitution, and formulated according to the procedures set forth by the constitutions of the States Parties for that purpose" (para 35). However, "the above does not necessarily negate the possibility of delegations of authority in this area, provided that such delegations are authorized by the Constitution, are exercised within the limits

only the alleged crime but also the legal consequence, that is, the penalty (*nullum pena sine legum*). The guarantee related to the prohibition against retroactive application of unfavourable criminal law (*lex praevia*) upholds that criminal law provisions cannot be applied to acts that occurred prior to their entry into force, except for in cases in which the provisions turn out to be favourable to the accused or convicted. In pursuance to the guarantee of taxitivity (*lex certa*), the legislator is obliged to redact the prohibited conduct and the anticipated consequence (sanction) with a sufficient degree of precision so that the ordinary citizen can find out the object of the prohibition and its sanction. These are all guarantees protected in the Peruvian Constitution,[48] which have become obstacles to the prosecution and sanctioning of the cases in focus.

A first problem that the Peruvian courts had to address in the process of judicial reactivation was how to classify the acts in focus. In Peru, there are four possible classifications of the same act. First, one may qualify an act as a "common crime", which means that the act can be subsumed under traditional penal concepts, such as homicide, kidnapping, injuries, sexual abuse, abuse of authority, etc. Such crimes are included in both the Penal Code of 1924 and that of 1991. Secondly, an act could be classified as genocide (Article 319) or enforced disappearance (Article 320), both incorporated into the Penal Code of 1991, and torture (Article 321), which was included in February 1998.

According to one strand of legal interpretation, the legality principle would impede the opening of national judicial proceedings in which categories such as extrajudicial execution, enforced disappearance and torture are applied (considered in an isolated manner or as crimes against humanity) to acts such as the Cayara massacre,[49] or the detention and the subsequent disappearance of the student Ernesto Castillo Paez or the physical abuse of the leader Saúl Cantoral Benavides. This interpretation is based on the contention that these criminal categories were incorporated into domestic law and entered into force following the realization of the acts. Principally furthered by criminal law specialists, the interpretation is based on the understanding that the legality principle entails an obligation to classify the acts and sanction them as ordinary crimes.[50] Until now, the majority of the magistrates of the Peruvian criminal

imposed by the Constitution and the delegating law, and that the exercise of the power delegated is subject to effective controls, so that it does not impair nor can it be used to impair the fundamental nature of the rights and freedoms protected by the Convention" (para 36).

48 See STC, case of *Legislación Antiterrorista* (Exp 0010- 2002 AI/TC), Judgment of 3 January 2003. See also STC, case of *Bedoya de Vivanco* (Exp 2758- 2004 HC/TC), Judgment of 23 November 2004, para 2. The latter expressly recognizes the guarantees related to *lex previa* and *lex scripta*.

49 Murder of about 20 joint landowners in Cayara in Ayacucho in May 1988 by members of the Peruvian military.

50 For an opposite position of an internationalist, see Andreu Guzman, F, "Imprescriptibilidad de los crímenes de lesa humanidad versus irretroactividad de la ley penal: un falso dilema", in Coordinadora Nacional de Derechos Humanos (ed), *Retos de la judicialización. En el proceso de verdad, justicia, reparación y reconciliación*, Lima: CNDH, 2005, p 155.

justice system have supported this interpretation.[51] However, some Peruvian judges have made a basic characterization of the criminal acts involved in the light of common criminal law categories (murders, kidnapping, etc),[52] and thereafter continued with a complementary classification of the criminal acts (torture, extrajudicial execution or crimes against humanity) that permits the application of further consequences, such as non-applicability of statutory limitations and the invalidity of amnesties.[53] From this perspective, one and the same act, such as the killings in Barrios Altos, can be characterized in the first instance as murders (Article 108 of the Penal Code) and in a complementary manner as crimes against humanity (considering that the acts were produced in the context of a systematic and generalized attack) or as common crimes that amount to grave human rights violations (given that the acts were committed by state agents while exercising public power). In this manner, the perpetrators were prosecuted and convicted for crimes of murder and injuries, but as the same acts were also classified as crimes against humanity, time limits or amnesties or any other measure that would impede the investigation, prosecution or sanctioning of those responsible were inapplicable.

This proposal derived from Peruvian case law seems reasonable, as it respects the fundamental requirements that flow from the legality principle. According to this principle, the perpetrators of human rights violations must be prosecuted and sanctioned for crimes in force in the domestic legal order at the time of their commission. At the same time, it also respects the international obligation to investigate and sanction those responsible for these acts without any impediment of domestic legislative measures or procedural mechanisms.[54]

A second challenge to the legality principle is the international legal prohibition against the application of statutory limitations, amnesties or other similar procedural mechanisms (Article 78 of the Penal Code of 1991). Indeed, once the judicial proceedings had been reactivated, the accused invoked

51 Exceptionally, in some cases, such as the one concerning human rights violations in the military barrack los Cabitos no 51, the Second Court of Huamanga decided on 21 January 2005 to initiate a criminal investigation for the crime of torture (Art 321 of the Penal Code) against the perpetrators.

52 The crime of enforced disappearance of persons has been treated in a special manner. The Constitutional Court (in STC, case of *Villegas Namuche*, Judgment of 18 March 2004) and the National Criminal Chamber (case of *Castillo Páez*, Judgment of 20 March 2006) consider that this crime can be applied to acts that were initiated prior to its inclusion in the Penal Code of 1991, given its permanent nature the commission of which lasts until information has been given about the whereabouts of the victim.

53 See Defensoria del Pueblo, *A dos años de la Comisión de la Verdad y Reconciliación*, Informe Defensorial, no 97, Lima, 2005, p 114; and Special Criminal Chamber of the Supreme Court (AV 19-2011), Judgment of 7 April 2009, convicting the former President Fujimori for the murders in Barrios Altos and La Cantuta.

54 For another view, see Gil Gil, A, *Derecho penal internacional. Especial Consideración del delito de genocidio*, Madrid: Tecnos, 1989, p 103, who also questions the compatibility between the crimes against humanity and the taxativity principle.

systematically various procedural defences.[55] As for *res judicata*, the accused argued that they had already been judged and acquitted as a result of final decisions by military tribunals.[56] However, the ordinary criminal courts followed the judgment by the Inter-American Court of Human Rights in the *Barrios Altos* case, pointing out that the decisions of the military tribunals in cases concerning human rights violations violated fundamental principles of due process and thus lacked validity. Considering that the decisions were null, they did not constitute final judicial decisions and, thus, *res judicata* did not apply. As for amnesties,[57] the accused invoked Amnesty Law no 26479, but the common courts declared all of these requests as unfounded by virtue of the judgment of the Inter-American Court on Human Rights in the *Barrios Altos* case. In that case, the court declared that self-imposed amnesties were incompatible with the Inter-American Convention on Human Rights and, thus, lacked legal effect.[58]

As for time limits,[59] the accused have argued that as a consequence of the passage of time the penal action had been extinguished. Indeed, a great number of violent incidents had occurred in the 1980s, which meant that 20 years or more had passed since the acts had been committed.[60] Following some resistance by the courts of first instance, Peruvian justice has declared this mechanism as unfounded, appealing in some cases to the obligations derived from the Inter-American system of human rights and in others to the obligations derived from international criminal law. In some cases, Peruvian courts have upheld the case law of the Inter-American Court in the *Barrios Altos* case, maintaining that "the provisions related to amnesty, the provisions related to time-limits and the establishment of exceptions of responsibility for grave human rights violations are inadmissible".[61] In other cases, the courts have relied upon the principle of international criminal law that proscribes the non-applicability of statutory limitations in the case of crimes against humanity.[62] However, the courts have

55 See Defensoria del Pueblo, fn 53 above, pp 115 ff.

56 See Defensoria del Pueblo, fn 53 above, pp 122–125. Among the cases in which the accused invoked the exceptions and cited in this report are the cases of *Destacamento Colina*, *Los sucesos de los penales en junio de 1986*; and *Desaparición de candidatos en Huancapi*.

57 See Defensoria del Pueblo, fn 53 above, p 125.

58 IACtHR, case of *Barrios Altos v Perú*, Series C No 75, Judgment of 14 March 2001, paras 41, 43 and 44.

59 See Defensoria del Pueblo, fn 53 above, pp 126 and 128.

60 A detailed account of the treatment of the exceptions related to time limits can be found in Informes Defensoriales nos 97 and 112. *El difícil camino de la reconciliación, justicia y reparación para las víctimas*, December 2006, available online at www.defensoria.gob.pe/inform-defensoriales.php.

61 STC, case of *Destacamento de Colina* (Exp no 028-01), Judgment of 9 May 2005.

62 Defensoria del Pueblo, Informe Defensorial no 97, fn 60 above, p 114. In the case of *Operativo Chavin de Huantar y ejecución extrajudicial de miembros del MRTA*, the Third Special Trial Court on Criminal Justice upheld on 11 June 2002 that the subordination of acts of torture to the crime of injury does not in any way eliminate the character of crimes against humanity of the conducts.

not explained if it is a rule of customary international law[63] or a *jus cogens* norm and, in the latter case, why this is so and at which point the rule regarding non-applicability of statutory limitations became a *jus cogens* norm.

When the judiciary has based its findings related to this rule in the jurisprudence of the Inter-American Court, it has not clearly determined if it is a retroactive application of that jurisprudence or a reinterpretation of Articles 1.1 and 1.2 of the American Convention, in force in Peru since 1984. That being said, some judicial resolutions reveal a valid effort to address this theme from the perspective of the methods of reasoning about principles. Thus, in the case of the Colina Group, the Chamber for Anti-corruption of the Higher Court of Justice in Lima maintained that:

> Even though the institution of time-limits is founded in the value of legal security in the face of the value of justice, in the case of the crimes such as those informed (because of their special gravity and nature), such primacy is inverted in favour of justice and hence the state finds itself obliged to exercise the mechanisms and legal procedures destined to the investigation and sanction of those who are found to be responsible for such crimes.[64]

8.4.2 Attribution of criminal responsibility

The crimes in focus are generally considered as macro-crimes, that is, the crimes have macro-social structural repercussions in the sense that organized power is used in committing them.[65] The criminal incidents at hand involve persons who are responsible directly (materially) and indirectly (intellectually) for their commission. The latter are clearly those with higher or superior ranks who issued the orders. Most emblematic cases are those in which not only the operative group Colina, but also higher military officials, the Adviser to the President, and the President of the Republic himself, were found responsible.

The attribution of criminal responsibility to higher chiefs has turned out to be a problem for the Public Prosecutor and the judiciary. Recent discussions focus on the insufficiency or inadequacy of depicting superiors or leaders who in fact controlled the situation by virtue of their powers of segments of the

63 The Convention on the Non-Applicability of Statutory Limitations to War Crimes and Crimes against Humanity (adopted in 1968) was ratified by the Peruvian Government in September 2003. It has been understood that this Convention does not have retroactive effects and can thus not be applied to the crimes committed during the internal armed conflict. Hence, the sole foundation of the rule regarding non-applicability of time limits is that it is a *jus cogens* norm.

64 See Defensoria del Pueblo, fn 53 above, pp 127–128.

65 Jager, H, *Makrokriminalität. Studien zur Kriminologie Kollektiver Gewalt*, Frankfurt am Main: Suhrkamp, 1989, cited by Alpaca Perez, J A, *Acerca de la Teoría de la Mepresa Criminal Conjunta como mecanismo de imputación a superiores jerárquicos en escenarios macrocriminales según la jurisprudencia del Tribunal Penal para la antigua Yugoslavia*. Thesis to obtain the title of lawyer, Lima, 2010 (on file with the author), p 20.

military as mere "accomplices" or "instigators".[66] Peruvian courts have progressively adopted the dominion of the organization thesis introduced by Claus Roxin to the detriment of the co-authorship approach.[67] In my view, this position is the consequence of the positive reception of the former by the majority of Peruvian legal scholars.[68] Importantly, the dominion thesis was applied in the case decided on 7 April 2009, in which the former President Fujimori was convicted for the murders in Barrios Altos and La Cantuta. However, it has also been applied in other judicial decisions, such as that of 13 October 2006, when the National Criminal Chamber convicted the leader of *Sendero Luminoso* for murders carried out by militants of this organization during the internal armed conflict, and the decision of 8 April 2008 in which the First Special Criminal Chamber of the Higher Court in Lima held General Salazar Monroe and other officials responsible for the enforced disappearances of the students and the professor in La Cantuta.

8.4.3 Evidentiary problems and the adequacy of the standard of proof

Out of the range of difficulties facing the Peruvian courts, those related to evidence are the most pressing ones at present. Of special importance are the passage of time and the persistent reluctance of the armed institutions to provide information about the identity of the military personnel who were performing functions in the conflict zones.

The passage of time has given rise to serious difficulties in terms of precaution and use of evidence, such as testimonies of persons who have died or who are not localizable, the impossibility of medical-forensic exams of living tissue, insufficient memory of the incidents under investigation, etc. This situation is complicated by the formalist and traditional culture received by Peruvian magistrates and which restrain them from accepting any other evidence than of a traditional type.[69] From this perspective, the sentence on 7 April 2009 by

66 Peru has still not implemented the Rome Statute. For this reason, its domestic legislation does not contemplate the responsibility of commanders and other superiors (Art 28 of the Rome Statute). For a discussion on the doctrinal nature of the responsibility of superiors (pure omission v proper omission), see Ambos, K, *La Parte General del Derecho Penal Internacional*, Lima: Konrad Adenauer, 2005, pp 295 ff.

67 For an account of the evolution of the mediate authorship theory and its reception in our legislation and jurisprudence, see Montoya Vivanco, Y, "La autoría mediata por dominio de organización en el Código Penal de 1991", in Pozo, H (ed), *Anuario de Derecho Penal*, 2009.

68 For accounts that accept the mediate authorship theory as a mechanism to impute systemic crimes, see Meini Mendez, I, *El dominio de la organización en Derecho Penal*, Lima: Palestra, 2008; Pariona, R, "La autoría mediata en el Delito de usurpación de funciones", *Revista Jus Jurisprudencia*, February 2008; and Montoya Vivanco, Y, "La autoría mediata por dominio de organización. Replanteamiento factico normativo y requerimientos probatorios", *Revista Jurídica del Perú*, vol 84, February 2008.

69 The same document (*Instituto Defensa Legal*, October 2009) cautions that the National Criminal Chamber requires direct proof in the prosecution of these crimes leading to acquittals.

the Special Criminal Chamber of the Supreme Court, which convicted the former President Fujimori to 35 years' imprisonment, represents a milestone, since it extends the type of evidence susceptible for consideration in hearings and adapts the rules for their proper evaluation. The Special Chamber focuses on the diverse aspects of the criminal evidence that will be considered in the sentence, including all elements of proof that have been legally obtained, which goes beyond the means of proof that have been taxatively recognized in the Code of Criminal Procedure. Likewise, the Chamber considers, citing the jurisprudence of the *Audiencia Nacional* in Madrid,[70] that in the case of systemic crimes, the indirect evidence is of transcendental significance for establishing an eventual criminal responsibility of the accused.[71] On these grounds, it accepted and valued correctly, as elements of evidence, reportages and news, texts or books published by journalists or social researchers, the judgments of the Inter-American Court and the Peruvian Constitutional Court when these courts have pronounced themselves in relation to certain events, witnesses' declarations (including by the police and experts), manuals and guidelines not necessarily recognized by military institutions but referred to by some of the witnesses, as well as audios and videos retrieved from the public realm and with the authorization of at least one of the intervening parties. Also, the Chamber points out that the TRC report is a public document of significant value, above all, when proving contextual incidents, that is, those that reveal a pattern of governmental criminal conduct or political contra-subversive conduct. Finally, the Chamber has considered contradictory testimonies offered by one and the same person in a proceeding without annulling both declarations. With regard to the testimony given by General Nicolás de Bari Hermoza in the *Fujimori* case, the Chamber held that in the light of the pile of collected evidence, it was possible to afford evidentiary incriminating value to one of the two testimonies.

8.4.4 International judicial co-operation: the extradition

International judicial co-operation has been crucial to advance some cases, such as that of the former President Fujimori who had sought his refuge in Japan since he fled the country in November 2000 until his trip to Chile in November 2005. Once in Chile, Peru formulated various extradition requests. In the end, these requests were favourably considered and Chile provisionally detained the former president as a precautionary measure. In a decision of a Chilean court of first instance related to the extradition process, the judgment of the Inter-American Court in the *La Cantuta* case on 27 November 2006 turned out to be

70 See Criminal Chamber of the Supreme Court (Exp 1362-2004), Judgment of 15 November 2004, ch I, pt 2.

71 The indicative or indirect evidence has been broadly recognized and used by the Peruvian judiciary. In the conviction of the former president for the murders in Barrios Altos and La Cantuta, the Criminal Chamber of the Supreme Court cited in the previous footnote resorted to broad chains of inferences to prove a hypothesis of what happened.

relevant.[72] In that judgment, on the basis of the right to access justice, the Inter-American Court called upon Chilean justice to co-operate with Peru in order to submit the former president to criminal proceedings.[73] Finally, on 21 September 2007, the Chilean Supreme Court authorized the extradition request in two cases of human rights violations and seven cases of corruption.

8.5 Concluding remarks

Peru has started a difficult process to overcome impunity. These advances have been made possible, first of all, thanks to different civil society actors who persistently denounced the crimes in focus before domestic and international institutions and, secondly, thanks to the confluence of a series of relevant factors, such as the political will to clarify the criminal acts, the strengthening of judicial independence, and the repeated pronouncements by the Inter-American Commission and Court of Human Rights in relation to Peru. The pronouncements of the Inter American Court and later also the Peruvian Constitutional Court have contributed in a critical manner to the removal of the most significant obstacles facing the courts left behind by the former regime. Especially important are their rulings concerning the prohibition against the invocation of amnesties and time limits, as well as their insistence on a general competence of the common courts to admit the cases in focus.

Nevertheless, there is still a need to improve the capacity of criminal justice to use adequately the proper legal concepts and instruments as well as the available international human rights procedures. A specialized training of Peruvian judges and prosecutors would advance their understanding of the relation between the international obligations of Peru to criminalize the conducts in focus and the traditional principles of criminal law, especially the legality principle, and to use modern categories that would allow them to attribute criminal conduct to hierarchical superiors and to adjust the standard of proof for systemic crimes.

Various proceedings are still pending and so is the need to give a solution to other aspects of the effects of the political violence as well as the implementation of a policy of individual reparations and massive exhumations that would permit a clarification of thousands who have disappeared and are still not identified. Nevertheless, the current decline of political will together with the fatigue of the institutions of criminal justice to continue the judicialization of these cases may undermine the prospects of a successful finalization of the process of overcoming the past through criminal justice.

72 One of the most serious difficulties faced in the extradition process of Fujimori from Chile has been the active extradition model followed in this country. In contrast to the French model in which only formal aspects of the petition are verified, the Chilean model entails the examination of circumstantial evidence of the commission of the crime, thus, evaluating evidence and in this manner confusing an extradition process with a criminal proceeding.

73 IACtHR, case of *La Cantuta v Peru*, Series C No 162, Judgment of 29 November 2006, paras 159 and 160.

9 Many roads to justice

Transnational prosecutions and international support for criminal investigations in post-conflict Guatemala

Naomi Roht-Arriaza and Almudena Bernabeu

9.1 Introduction

In November 2006, a local trial court in Guatemala's capital ordered the arrest of the country's ex-President, Oscar Mejía Víctores, along with ex-Defence Minister Aníbal Guevara, ex-Police Chief Germán Chupina, and ex-head of the Secret Police Pedro Arredondo on charges of genocide, torture, enforced disappearances, arbitrary detention and terrorism.[1] The defendants, together with two others whose arrest warrants were not executed, were deeply implicated in the conceptualization and execution of a repressive state strategy that resulted in the deaths of 200,000 Guatemalans and the destruction of over 400 villages. Although the arrest order was carried out through a Guatemalan court, it was issued by a Spanish judge,[2] Santiago Pedraz. Judge Pedraz of Spain's *Audiencia Nacional*[3] issued the warrants in July 2006, followed by formal extradition requests. He based Spanish jurisdiction over crimes committed by Guatemalans in Guatemala on a Spanish law that allows universal jurisdiction over certain international crimes.

Mejía holed himself up in his house and the secret police chief fled, while the ex-defence minister and the ex-police chief were held in a military hospital under guard. This case represents the first time members of the military high command were affected by any legal action against them, and one of a handful of cases where any Guatemalan military officer has been subject to judicial

1 Elías, J, "Tres Militares y un Civil Guatemaltecos, en el Banquillo", *El País* (Spain), 14 November 2006. Available online at www.elpais.com/articulo/internacional/militares/civil/guatemaltecos/banquillo/elpporint/20061114elpepuint_4/Tes/.

2 Ministerio de Justicia, Juzgado Central de Instrucción No 1, Audiencia Nacional, Diligencias Previas 331/1999-10, 7 July 2005 (Spain). Available online at www.cja.org/downloads/Guatemala_Judge_Pedraz_Request_for_Extradition.pdf.

3 The *Audiencia Nacional* hears cases involving drug smuggling, terrorism, state corruption and international crimes that cannot adequately be dealt with at the level of provinces and autonomous communities. Although divided into chambers, it is roughly equivalent to a US district court.

proceedings.[4] After over a year in detention, the defendants were freed when Guatemala's Constitutional Court (GCC) decided on 12 December 2007 that it would not honour Spanish arrest warrants or extradition requests.[5] The court held that Spanish courts did not constitute a "competent authority" because Spain did not have jurisdiction over events that took place in Guatemala; the effort to exercise universal jurisdiction was unacceptable and an affront to Guatemala's sovereignty. The court added that the charges were related to political crimes and thus not extraditable, and that Spain's participation in the 1980s Central American peace process meant that it was bound by the commitments made by the government and the insurgents that an official truth commission would have no judicial effects. Given that commitment, the GCC concluded, it would be inconsistent for Spain to now seek to prosecute crimes arising out of the region's civil conflicts.

The problem of near-complete impunity for crimes committed during periods of repression and internal armed conflict is not unique to Guatemala. The powerful military and civilian figures who order such crimes usually retain a large amount of power—de jure or de facto—even after the conflict ends or the government changes and are singularly uninterested in criminal investigations into the past. In contrast, the post-conflict state tends to be weak, with limited resources and a culture of corruption and self-dealing among state authorities. Moreover, in Guatemala as elsewhere, post-conflict military and paramilitary networks have mutated into criminal networks, engaged in drug running, human trafficking and similar violent enterprises, with a degree of impunity similar to that enjoyed by former military officials in human-rights-related cases.[6]

4 There have been high-profile trials of military officers in the killings of Bishop Juan Gerardi and anthropologist Myrna Mack. The *Mack* case, after over a dozen years, resulted in the convictions of three officers, one of whom promptly went into hiding. The sentence is at Corte Suprema de Justicia, Recurso de Casación Conexados 109-2003 y 110-2003, 15 January 2004. Available online at www.derechos.org/nizkor/guatemala/myrna/myrnacs.html. In the *Gerardi* case, the Supreme Court upheld the convictions of two officers in January 2006. See Conie Reynoso, "Confirman Sentencia: Continúa Pena de 20 Años de Cárcel para Sindicados", *Prensa Libre*, 14 January 2006. Available online at http://prensalibre.com/noticias/Confirman-sentencia_0_126588023.html (accessed on 15 March 2011). For an excellent description of the *Gerardi* case, see Goldman, F, *The Art of Political Murder: Who Killed the Bishop?* New York: Grove Press, 2007. A handful of civil patrollers, members of paramilitary groups created and controlled by the army, have also been convicted of murder in Guatemalan courts, as has one colonel for a disappearance case. But as detailed in this chapter, by and large the prosecutors' office has not pursued cases arising out of the armed conflict, and judges have been intimidated, threatened or bought off.

5 Sentencia del 12 de Diciembre de 2007, Corte de Constitucionalidad (Guatemala), Expediente 3380-2007, Audiencia Nacional de Espana. Available online at www.cc.gob.gt/siged2009/mdlWeb/frmConsultaWebVerAnexo.aspx?St_DocumentoId=813917.3380-2007.pdf&St_VersionDocumentoId=551055&St_Anexos=1.

6 See Calderon, E, "Capturan a Ex Militares", *La Prensa*, 9 November 2006. Available online at www-ni.laprensa.com.ni/archivo/2006/noviembre/09/noticias/internacionales/155170.shtml.

Much of the international institution-building over the last two decades in the field of human rights and international humanitarian law has been aimed at overcoming the impunity of powerful, untouchable actors. An emerging international norm[7] holds that when large-scale humanitarian violations have been committed, action must be taken to deal with the past, including measures to allow victims to find out what happened to their loved ones, to sanction those responsible and to provide redress. The International Criminal Tribunal for the Former Yugoslavia (ICTY) and the International Criminal Tribunal for Rwanda (ICTR) were built on the idea that only an international prosecution and trial would have the ability and legitimacy to try high-ranking perpetrators, including heads of state. Similarly, the International Criminal Court (ICC) was founded out of concern that states would be unwilling or unable to prosecute powerful actors domestically, and that therefore a complementary forum was needed. However, the experience of the ICTY and ICTR, while positive in many ways, soon gave rise to criticism that the tribunals were enormously expensive, remote from the societies where the crimes took place, and did not help to restore or create viable national justice systems.[8]

Hybrid tribunals, combining national and international law, procedure and personnel, seemed the appropriate response, and variants on such hybrid courts were created in Sierra Leone, Cambodia, East Timor and Kosovo. In particular, hybrid courts are theorized to be better at creating legitimacy and relevance for local audiences, embedding international legal norms in national legal systems, and training local lawyers and judges to use these norms and to carry out complex criminal investigations, all at a lower cost than international tribunals.[9] Initial evaluations of these courts showed varied results. While the Sierra Leone Special Court was relatively successful in its outreach to the local society, on a per case basis it was still quite expensive and the results vis-à-vis local legacy are still unclear.[10] The other hybrids were seen, by and large, as less successful, although in the Cambodia and Bosnia cases it is still too early for definitive assessments.[11] Still, even assuming unequivocal success, setting up hybrids is an expensive and time-consuming proposition, and one unlikely to be used in

7 See, e.g. UN Security Council, Report of the Secretary-General, *The Rule of Law and Transitional Justice in Conflict and Post-Conflict Societies*, S/2004/616, 23 August 2004. See generally Mallinder, L, "Can Amnesties and International Justice be Reconciled?", *International Journal of Transitional Justice*, vol 1, 2007, pp 208 ff.

8 Stover, E and Weinstein, H M, *My Neighbor, My Enemy: Justice and Community in the Aftermath of Mass Atrocity*, Cambridge: Cambridge University Press, 2004 (providing a detailed look at this problem).

9 See generally Dickinson, L, Note, "The Promise of Hybrid Courts", *American Journal of International Law*, vol 97, 2003, pp 295 ff; and Higonnet, E, "Restructuring Hybrid Courts: Local Empowerment and National Criminal Justice Reform", *Arizona Journal of International & Comparative Law*, vol 23, 2006, pp 347 ff.

10 See Dickinson, L, Remarks, "Justice Should be Done, But Where? The Relationship between National and International Courts", *ASIL Proceedings*, vol 101, 2007, pp 297–299.

11 Dickinson, fn 10 above.

many situations where the government is unwilling to support it or the international community does not provide adequate resources.

The Guatemalan case suggests another way to "hybridize" prosecutions in the face of dysfunctional national justice systems and rampant impunity. With regard to the security forces' high command, cases for genocide, torture, massacres (extrajudicial killing) and enforced disappearance have been brought simultaneously in national courts in Guatemala, Spain and Belgium.[12] Victims' groups have pursued a combined inside and outside legal strategy, pushing for domestic prosecutions for genocide, while also focusing on transnational prosecution based on universal jurisdiction in other states' national courts. The effort to obtain witness testimony and extradition of the defendants in the transnational cases has led to considerable litigation in Guatemalan courts on international law issues. At the same time, an agreement between the Guatemalan Government and the United Nations in 2006 created the International Commission against Impunity in Guatemala, or *Comisión Internacional Contra la Impunidad en Guatemala* (CICIG), which looks into the workings of current clandestine groups and pushes for their investigation and prosecution by local prosecutors in the local courts. A third mechanism, prosecutions for visa fraud of rights violators found in the United States, has also played a significant role in efforts to obtain justice for the crimes of the early 1980s in Guatemala. Among them, these efforts aim to impel the local prosecutors and courts into action against impunity, with international support and oversight.[13]

This chapter will first briefly describe the background of the Guatemalan conflict and the evolution of the transnational cases against the military high command. It will then focus on some of the legal strategy issues involved and on the gains and losses of this transnational networking approach to combating impunity. In particular, it will look at how the multinational legal team, working simultaneously in the Spanish and Guatemalan courts on different aspects of the case, has allowed for learning and training opportunities for the lawyers involved, has forced local courts to engage with international law, and has tried to use the power of foreign courts to leverage domestic processes. It

12 The Belgian cases involve the deaths of two Belgian priests—Serge Berten and Walter Voordeckers—during the early 1980s, presumably at the hands of security forces. Family members of the victims brought a case in Belgian courts in January 2001 under Belgium's then-expansive universal jurisdiction law. The case remained open after the law was amended in 2003. See Roht-Arriaza, N, *The Pinochet Effect: Transnational Justice in the Age of Human Rights*, Philadelphia: University of Pennsylvania Press, 2005, ch 7.

13 A fourth strategy, also important in the Guatemalan context, involves the role of the Inter-American Commission and Court of Human Rights in pushing for an end to impunity and awarding redress to some victims. However, a full discussion of the role of the Inter-American system is beyond the scope of this chapter. For more information, see Due Process of Law Foundation, *Victims Unsilenced: The Inter-American Human Rights System and Transitional Justice in Latin America*, Washington DC: Due Process of Law Foundation, 2007. Available online at www.dplf.org/uploads/1190403828.pdf.

will consider the content and impact of the Guatemalan and Spanish jurisprudence generated by the case and its current prospects. It will then describe the mandate and goals of CICIG and the fraud cases in the United States, to conclude with some initial thoughts on how these initiatives might complement each other and serve as an example elsewhere.

9.2 The context and the Spanish proceedings

Guatemala's internal armed conflict began in 1960 and ended officially in 1996. Over that period, according to the UN-sponsored Commission on Historical Clarification (CEH), some 200,000 people were killed, over 90 per cent of them by the military. Some 40,000 were the victims of enforced disappearance.[14] The bulk of the atrocities were committed in the late 1970s and early 1980s; the vast majority of the victims were Mayan indigenous people who were considered to be the support base for a guerrilla movement. The CEH found that in at least four specific areas of the country, the army had committed "acts of genocide". The CEH's rationale, adopted by complainants in the genocide cases, was that:

> It is very important to distinguish between "the intent to destroy a group in whole or in part", that is, the positive determination to do so, and the motives of such an intent. In order to determine genocide, it is only necessary to demonstrate that there exists an intent to destroy the group, regardless of motive. For example, if the motive of the intent to destroy an ethnic group is not a racist orientation but only a military objective, the crime may nevertheless be understood to be genocide.[15]

However, despite the fact that a 1996 amnesty law specifically excludes genocide, forced disappearance, torture and other international crimes from its ambit,[16] no charges were ever filed against the organizers and planners of the campaigns. To this day, less than a handful of cases arising out of the internal armed conflict have ever been prosecuted, and most of those involve leaders of the paramilitary militias (civil patrols) instituted by the army.

14 Comisión para el Esclarecimiento Histórico (CEH), *Guatemala: Memoria del Silencio*, vol 3 (1999), § 1252. Available online in Spanish at http://shr.aaas.org/guatemala/ceh/mds/spanish/. The summary and recommendations, as well as a discussion of the genocide, are available in English at pp 108–123. Available online at http://shr.aaas.org/guatemala/ceh/report/english/conc2.html.

15 CEH, *Guatemala: Memoria del Silencio*, vol 3, fn 14 above, § 855 (quoting the Convention on the Prevention and Punishment of the Crime of Genocide (1948), Art II, 78 UN Treaty Series 277 (1951), which defines genocide as a series of acts, including killing and creating conditions of life aimed at the physical destruction of victims, when committed with the "intent to destroy, in whole or in part, a racial, religious, national or ethnical group as such").

16 El Congreso de la República de Guatemala, Ley de Reconciliación Nacional, Decreto no 145-1996, 27 December 1996, Art 8. Available online at www.acnur.org/biblioteca/pdf/0148.pdf.

Given this panorama, in December 1999, Nobel Peace Prize winner Rigoberta Menchú and others brought a complaint in the Spanish *Audiencia Nacional*[17] alleging genocide, torture, terrorism, summary execution and unlawful detention perpetrated against Guatemala's Mayan indigenous people and their supporters during the 1970s and 1980s. The complainants' rationale for the genocide charges included the targeting of Mayans as an ethnic group. It was also based, following a gloss on the definition of genocide accepted by the *Audiencia* in earlier cases involving Chilean and Argentine defendants, on the intended elimination of a part of the Guatemalan "national" group due to its perceived ideology.[18] Among the events underlying the complaint was the massacre of Menchú's father and 35 other people in the 1980 firebombing of the Spanish embassy, the killing or disappearance of four Spanish priests, and a large number of rural massacres, rapes, cases of torture and enforced disappearance. The complainants grounded Spanish jurisdiction on Article 23.4 of the Organic Law of the Judicial Branch (LOPJ).[19] That provision allows for prosecution of certain crimes committed by non-Spaniards outside Spain, including genocide, terrorism and other crimes recognized in international treaties ratified by Spain. On 27 March 2000, Investigating Judge Guillermo Ruíz Polanco of the *Audiencia Nacional* accepted the Guatemalan complaint and agreed to open an investigation.[20] In reaching that decision, the judge noted that several of the victims were Spanish and that the Guatemalan courts had failed to investigate the crimes.[21]

The Spanish Public Prosecutors' Office, at the time in the hands of the conservative Popular Party, appealed the judge's jurisdiction.[22] An appeals panel

17 See explanation in fn 3 above.

18 See *Auto de la Sala de lo Penal de la Audiencia Nacional confirmando la jurisdicción de España para Conocer de los Crímenes de Genocidio y Terrorismo Cometido Durante la Dictadura Argentina (Decision (Auto) of the Full Penal Chamber Confirming Spanish Jurisdiction Over the Crimes of Genocide and Terrorism Committed During the Argentine Dictatorship)*, Appeal No 84-98, 3rd Section, File 19/97 from Judicial Chamber 5, Autos (Audiencia Nacional, 5 November 1998) (Spain). Available online at www.derechos.org/nizkor/arg/espana/audi.html (authors' translation); *Auto de la Sala de lo Penal de la Audiencia Nacional Confirmando la Jurisdicción de España para Conocer de los Crímenes de Genocidio y Terrorismo Cometido Durante la Dictadura Chilena (Decision (Auto) of the Full Penal Chamber Confirming Spanish Jurisdiction to Investigate Genocide in Chile)*, Appeal No 173/98, 1st Section, File 1/98 from Judicial Chamber 6 (Audiencia Nacional, 5 November 1998) (Spain). Available online at www.derechos.org/nizkor/chile/juicio/audi.html (authors' translation). See also the English translation of the decision regarding Chile in Brody, R and Ratner, M (eds), *The Pinochet Papers: The Case of Augusto Pinochet in Spain and Britain*, The Hague: Kluwer Law International, 2000.

19 Ley Orgánica 6/1985 de 1 de Julio, del Poder Judicial, *Boletín Oficial del Estado*, 1985, p 157. Available online at http://noticias.juridicas.com/base_datos/Admin/lo6-1985.l1t1.html.

20 *Juzgado Central de Instrucción No 1, Audiencia Nacional, Madrid, Diligencias Previas 331/99*, Auto (Decision) on 27 March 2000 (on file with authors).

21 Auto (Decision) on 27 March 2000.

22 See Roht-Arriaza, fn 12 above, ch 1. The Public Prosecutors' Office dropped its opposition to this and other universal jurisdiction cases when the Socialist Party assumed office. See

of the *Audiencia Nacional*, and then the Spanish Supreme Court, found that the Spanish courts had no jurisdiction. The Supreme Court held, by a vote of eight to seven, that customary international law required a link to the forum state when universal jurisdiction was not grounded in specific treaty provisions or authorized by the United Nations.[23] Thus, only those cases involving Spanish citizens could proceed. In September 2005, Spain's highest tribunal, the Constitutional Tribunal, reversed.[24] The Tribunal began with the plain language and legislative intent of Article 23.4 of the LOPJ. As the Constitutional Tribunal pointed out, the law itself establishes only a single limitation: the suspect cannot have been convicted, found innocent or pardoned abroad. It contains no implicit or explicit hierarchy of potential jurisdictions and focuses only on the nature of the crime, not on any ties to the forum; it establishes concurrent jurisdiction. Given the absence of textual support for a restrictive interpretation of the law, such a construction would be overly strict and unwarranted given the grave nature of the crimes. The tribunal re-opened the case for all complainants, including large numbers of Guatemalans who were survivors or family members of massacre victims.[25] The full case, focusing on genocide, could then go forward.

The next step in the reopened case, which was assigned to Judge Santiago Pedraz, was to take the statements of the suspects, a procedure designed to allow defendants to tell their side of the story before any arrest warrants were issued. Judge Pedraz, following long-established rules for taking statements in another state through a rogatory commission, worked through a Guatemalan judge to set up the dates, and the judge, along with the Spanish prosecutor, travelled to Guatemala. The defendants apparently did not see much advantage to telling their side of the story; they filed extraordinary writs of *amparo* before the local courts claiming their appearance would violate their constitutional rights. In most Latin American countries, the ability to challenge government action in violation of constitutional rights, known as *amparo*, is a cornerstone of individual rights, and the defendants made constant use of the procedure from this point on.[26] At this time as well, the Center for Justice and

Amnistia Internacional, "La Audiencia Nacional condena a el ex militar argentino Adolfo Scilingo por Crímenes de Lesa Humanidad", 19 April 2005. Available online at www.es.amnesty.org/noticias/noticias/articulo/la-audiencia-nacional-condena-a-el-ex-militar-argentino-adolfo-scilingo-por-crimenes-de-lesa-humanid/.

23 *Sentencia del Tribunal Supremo sobre el caso Guatemala por Genocidio*, Sentencia No 327/2003, Appeal Roll 115/2000, Case 331/99, File 162/2000 (Tribunal Supremo, Second Penal Chamber, 25 February 2003) (Spain). Available online at www.derechos.org/nizkor/guatemala/doc/gtmsent.html.

24 Roht-Arriaza, N, "Guatemala Genocide Case", *American Journal of International Law*, vol 100, 2006, p 207.

25 Roht-Arriaza, fn 24 above, p 211.

26 See Brewer-Carías, A R, "Some Aspects of the 'Amparo' Proceeding in Latin America as a Constitutional Judicial Mean Specifically Established for the Protection of Human Rights", Paper presented at Colloquium in International and Comparative Law, University

Accountability (CJA), a US-based NGO that had experience in litigating transnational cases through its work using the US Alien Tort Statute,[27] came into the case representing several families of victims. CJA and its international attorney Almudena Bernabeu would soon put together and lead an international legal team for this new phase of the case.

Fortunately, despite the inability to take formal statements, Judge Pedraz did not leave Guatemala entirely empty-handed. He met informally with several representatives of victims organizations who told their stories and detailed the lack of justice in the local courts. In particular, they told the judge that an association of survivors, the Association for Justice and Reconciliation (AJR), had been trying to get the local prosecutors' office to investigate the same set of defendants since 2000, but that aside from a few early depositions of other retired military officers, nothing had been done.[28] Guatemala, like most countries in Latin America, changed its criminal procedure during the 1990s to make it more prosecutor-driven; only the prosecutors' office (*Ministerio Público*) rather than victims or judges could press forward with an investigation. And despite millions in international aid, training and support,[29] the prosecutors' office remained ineffective, disrespectful to victims and vulnerable to threats and corruption, and was reportedly infiltrated by military intelligence and criminal networks of various sorts.[30]

In any event, Judge Pedraz returned to Spain, and a month later, on 7 July 2006, issued charges and international arrest warrants for the defendants on charges of genocide, state terrorism, torture and related crimes.[31] In early

of Maryland School of Law (October 2007). Available online at http://digitalcommons.law.umaryland.edu/cgi/viewcontent.cgi?article=1001&context=iclc_papers.

27 28 USC § 1350 (2006). The statute allows for civil suits in US federal courts by aliens for torts in violation of the law of nations or a US treaty.

28 The AJR case was brought by a Guatemalan human rights group, the Center for Legal Action for Human Rights, in two phases: in 2000 against officials of the Lucas Garcia regime and in 2001 against those of the subsequent Rios Montt regime. Case No 3920-2000, *Ministerio Público*, Guatemala (on file with authors). Although the complaints are unpublished, information (in Spanish) on them is available online at www.caldh.org.

29 See, e.g. World Bank Group, *Guatemala Judicial Reform Project*. Available online at http://go.worldbank.org/INV9FVR420.

30 Peacock, S and Beltrán, A, *Hidden Powers in Post-Conflict Guatemala: Illegal Armed Groups and the Forces behind Them*, Washington DC: Washington Office on Latin America, September 2003, pp 43–44. Available online at http://cgrs.uchastings.edu/pdfs/HiddenPowersFull.pdf. According to the US State Department Country Report for 2006: "While the constitution and the law provide for an independent judiciary, the judicial system often failed to provide fair or timely trials due to inefficiency, corruption, insufficient personnel and funds, and intimidation of judges, prosecutors, and witnesses. The majority of serious crimes were not investigated or punished. Many high-profile criminal cases remained pending in the courts for long periods as defense attorneys employed successive appeals and motions." US Department of State, *Country Reports on Human Rights Practices: Guatemala 2006*, 6 March 2007, Section 1.e. Available online at www.state.gov/g/drl/rls/hrrpt/2006/78893.htm.

31 See fn 2 above.

November, Guatemala's Fifth Tribunal for Crime, Drug Trafficking and Environmental Offences (the local trial court) executed four of the six arrest warrants. Two others were rejected for technical reasons.[32] Although the technical problems were cleared up soon after, those warrants have never been executed.[33] One of them was for General Ríos Montt, the former head of state from 1982 to 1983, who by that time was running for Congress, and the other for General Benedicto Lucas, former army chief of staff from 1978 to 1980. The four defendants reacted differently: one fled, one holed himself up in his house, one was in a military hospital and was put under guard, and the other turned himself in and also ended up in a military hospital. They all, however, hired lawyers in Guatemala to contest the extraditions.

On 22 November, Judge Pedraz followed up with formal extradition requests.[34] He cited an 1895 Extradition Treaty between Guatemala and Spain and explained in detail why each article of the treaty applied in this case. He also discussed the crime of genocide and attached a copy of the 2005 Spanish Constitutional Court decision to show that he had jurisdiction under Spanish law.[35]

9.3 The parallel advantages of hybrid tribunals and transnational prosecutions

The effort to use Spanish courts to bring high-ranking Guatemalan security force officers to justice, especially from 2006 onwards, exemplifies how, in many ways, transnational litigation shares some of the advantages of litigation in hybrid tribunals. In particular, both emphasize creating new movement within domestic legal systems and lowering costs. In other aspects, however, especially the ability to execute arrest warrants, the litigation has shared the disadvantages of other forms of international criminal prosecution.

9.4 Training local lawyers in international law and complex criminal investigation

One of the often-mentioned benefits of hybrid tribunals is their ability to impact local jurisprudence and train local staff, both lawyers and judges. By creating

32 Guatemala does not typically publish lower court pre-trial decisions, hence no published record of these rejections is available. (Reference documents on file with authors.)

33 The warrants were initially rejected because of a clerical error; the ones that reached Guatemala included only the allegations surrounding the 1980 Spanish Embassy massacre, not the genocide charges stemming from the entire 1979–1985 period. New, corrected arrest orders were sent immediately, but by that time the case was suspended due to the first of many *amparos*. The lower court judges then left them pending until the legal issues around the executed warrants could be settled, which is why they were never executed. See Calderon, fn 6 above.

34 Juzgado Central de Instrucción No 1, *Diligencias Previas* 331/99, Auto (Decision), 22 November 2006 (on file with authors).

35 Auto (Decision), 22 November 2006.

mixed national-international judicial panels and mixed professional staffs, hybrid courts combine the expertise and legitimacy of international judges and staff with the knowledge of local law and legal culture and the long-term commitment to the country of national personnel. International investigations and prosecutions provide on-the-job training for national lawyers in international law and complex criminal cases.[36] They also, at least in theory, help to imbue newly reformed or (re)created justice systems with the ethics and spirit of the rule of law. In practice, that theoretical promise has not always materialized. Critics have pointed out that most of the substantive legal jobs may well, under time constraints, go to outsiders, that the judges are not necessarily qualified in international law nor willing or able to impart whatever expertise they have to local counterparts, and that links to the local bar may be tenuous at best.[37]

Compared to the creation of hybrid institutions, transnational prosecutions can also provide advantages, including some of the same training and norm diffusion benefits. Early transnational prosecutions involving international crimes like genocide, torture and other crimes against humanity often incorporated exiled lawyers from the state where the atrocities took place. National human rights and legal groups served more as information sources, witness-seekers and media channels, while the litigation team was based largely abroad. This distinction was true, for instance, of the earlier cases in the Spanish courts against the high command of the Argentine and Chilean militaries for their crimes during the 1970s.[38] Subsequent cases, including the ongoing effort to prosecute former Chadian dictator Hissene Habré in Senegal and Belgium[39] and the attempt to prosecute high-ranking US officials in German courts,[40] involved the creation of complex multinational legal teams. The Guatemalan case followed and elaborated on this approach.

In the Guatemalan case, Rigoberta Menchú had been initially represented in Spain by labour and criminal lawyers who focused on the validity of Spain's jurisdiction. Once the genocide case was reopened, and after the judge's visit to Guatemala in June 2006, a new legal team led by the CJA began working with lawyers in Menchú's local foundation offices in Guatemala to develop the evidence for the Spanish case. At the same time, the team began dealing with the extradition and rogatory commission cases in the Guatemalan courts.

36 See, e.g. Dickinson, fn 9 above, p 307.

37 See, e.g. Higonnet, fn 9 above, pp 368–369.

38 For a narrative of those cases, see generally Roht-Arriaza, fn 12 above.

39 The International Committee for the Trial of Hissene Habré included Human Rights Watch Special Counsel Reed Brody and human rights groups and lawyers from Chad, Senegal, the United Kingdom and France. See Brody, R, "The Prosecution of Hissene Habré: An 'African Pinochet'", *New England Law Review*, vol 35, 2001, p 324.

40 See Center for Constitutional Rights, *German War Crimes Complaint Against Donald Rumsfeld, et al*. Available online at http://ccrjustice.org/ourcases/current-cases/german-war-crimes-complaint-against-donald-rumsfeld%2C-et-al. (describing the case brought against Donald Rumsfeld and others for torture in Abu Ghraib).

Eventually, the legal team grew to include local counsel in Spain with experience litigating universal jurisdiction cases, lawyers in The Hague and San Francisco with knowledge of both international and national criminal law, law students at the University of California-Hastings and Harvard human rights legal clinics, and the Menchú Foundation lawyers in Guatemala (who were co-ordinating with other legal human rights groups there).

These international and national lawyers have strategized and worked together on pleadings before both the Spanish and Guatemalan courts and, most recently, before international human rights bodies. There have been advantages to this approach: rather than a (potentially paternalistic) one-way transmission of knowledge from the international lawyers to the local ones, there has been a partnership wherein both sides learn. The international lawyers have had to grapple with how to present international law arguments in the (rather byzantine, at least by US standards) Guatemalan legal system, while the national lawyers get the experience and access to non-Spanish language research materials of the internationals. Interestingly, prior experience with civil Alien Tort cases in the United States has proven particularly useful in thinking about how to protect witnesses from retraumatization and give complainants an active protagonistic role in the proceedings and in witness preparation, selection and presentation. When it came time to present witnesses before the Spanish judge, for example, the judge accepted that witnesses be asked specific questions by their lawyers, a style of deposition more familiar to US trial lawyers than to the traditionally less oral, less structured style of Spanish pre-trial procedure.

Working with witnesses has also opened the way for incorporating new, young Guatemalan lawyers into complex criminal cases. Once the case began moving forward in Spain, the legal team laid out a strategy for proving genocide. Building on the findings of the CEH, they put together witness lists involving people from the hardest-hit areas and people who could testify about different aspects of genocide: massacres, bombings, forced displacement, destruction of community structures, and targeting of local religious and secular authorities. The team also added new complainants who were survivors and eyewitnesses to massacres. Most of the attorneys working with these witnesses to accompany them to give testimony before the Spanish court have been young Mayan women who can communicate with the witnesses in the witnesses' own language (which is generally not Spanish). These young lawyers returned to Guatemala with exposure to methods of investigation, witness preparation and criminal procedure that will inform their work at home. Through this joint work, these cases begin to build up a cohort of international human rights lawyers equally at home in their national systems and with international law and with enough knowledge of foreign legal systems to be able to conceive of multi-layered strategies that move from the national to the international and back.

9.5 Making local courts engage with international law

A related advantage of hybrid courts is their ability to foster local ownership of justice processes. By combining national and international law and personnel, such courts may foster the (re)construction of a viable domestic legal system which may act as a source of justice rather than of oppression or corruption. Hybrid courts may be able to reflect local culture, language and law while remaining anchored to the core values of international human rights and humanitarian law.[41] Because proceedings take place locally, the affected population and the press can observe them. On the other hand, hybrids, like national courts generally, are for these same reasons no doubt more vulnerable to threats, political influence and corruption than their purely international counterparts.[42]

Transnational investigation and prosecution can in theory penetrate national legal systems in ways similar to those posited for hybrid courts, but they are also subject to limitations. A case in point is the intense judicial activity surrounding Judge Pedraz's 2006 arrest orders and extradition requests. These orders and requests set off a furious battle in the Guatemalan courts. The local courts had to decide whether to execute the arrest warrants, whether to grant extradition[43] and how to deal with requests for judicial co-operation involving witnesses, defendants, documents and assets. Along the way, the local courts had to grapple with complex arguments about the propriety of universal jurisdiction, the nature of international crimes and the role of international law in Guatemala's constitutional order. Each of these involved a combination of local and international law.

In general, the rules on extradition are designed to deal with common crimes, not international crimes like genocide. Most extradition treaties, including the Spain–Guatemala Treaty,[44] have a similar set of rules. The alleged acts must be criminalized in both legal systems, and the requested state must only satisfy

41 See, e.g. Higonnet, fn 9 above, p 411.

42 See, e.g. Justice Initiative, "Security Council Must Address Costs of Moving Taylor Trial to The Hague", 4 April 2006. Available online at www.soros.org/initiatives/justice/focus/international_justice/news/taylor_20060404 (reviewing the debates around removing the Charles Taylor trial in the Sierra Leone Special Court to The Hague due to security concerns in West Africa); Justice Initiative, "Corruption Allegations at Khmer Rouge Court Must Be Investigated Thoroughly", 14 February 2007. Available online at www.soros.org/initiatives/justice/focus/international_justice/news/cambodia_20070214 (accessed on 5 April 2008) (for an example of concerns about the lack of independence of the Cambodian Extraordinary Chambers).

43 Even if the courts allowed the extraditions to proceed, the Executive Branch would still have a chance to stop them at a later point. Ministerio de Relaciones Exteriores de Guatemala, *El Procedimiento de Extradición en Guatemala*, DAJUT/SUAJ, pp 6–7. Available online at www.oas.org/juridico/MLA/sp/gtm/sp_gtm-ext-gen-procedure.pdf.

44 Tratado de Extradición entre España y Guatemala, signed on 7 November 1895, *Gaceta de Madrid*, no 161, 10 June 1895; and Protocolo Adicional aclarando su articulo VII (23 February 1897).

itself that the requesting state has jurisdiction under its own laws and has made out the rough equivalent of probable cause; a full evidentiary showing is not required. Political crimes, and common crimes connected to them, are not subject to extradition; however, the treaty does not define what constitutes a political crime. Also like many extradition treaties, the Spain–Guatemala Treaty does not require (but does allow) the extradition of nationals.[45] Guatemala's Constitution also contains a prohibition on the extradition of nationals, but its Article 27 has an exception that seems tailor-made for this case: it excludes alleged crimes contained in "treaties and conventions with respect to crimes against humanity or against international law".[46]

Even though the arrest orders came from a Spanish court, they would have to be enforced through Guatemalan courts ordering the police to execute the warrants. Extradition proceedings had the immense advantage of bypassing the public prosecutors' office, which had long held up domestic proceedings and was not considered particularly eager to move any of the armed conflict or genocide cases along given their political sensitivity and complexity. If the courts moved towards extradition, at the very least, that might embarrass the prosecutors' office into action. Indeed, in July 2007 the prosecutors' office began threatening to call witnesses in the Spanish Embassy massacre case of 1980, in what seemed to be a feeble attempt to pre-empt the Spanish proceedings by showing they were prosecuting the case at home. This response vindicated the complainants' legal strategy: by pushing for prosecution abroad, they could prod the courts into acting at home, even if the prosecutor's actual motivation was to undermine the foreign proceedings.[47]

The defendants immediately filed writs of *amparo* complaining that their constitutional rights had been violated by the local court's execution of the arrest warrants.[48] The defendants argued, among other things, that the Spanish courts were not a "competent authority" to issue an arrest warrant and could not exercise extraterritorial jurisdiction because Guatemalan sovereignty forbade it. They further argued that the language of the extradition treaty referred to those who had "taken refuge" in Guatemala, and that as Guatemalan citizens therefore they were not covered by the treaty, that the alleged crimes were not covered by the treaty, and that the treaty was too old and outdated to be effective. The trial court rejected these arguments and found that Spanish jurisdiction was proper.[49] That decision was appealed, but the appeals court

45 Tratado de Extradición entre España y Guatemala, Art IV.

46 Guatemala Constitution (Constitución Política reformada por Acuerdo Legislativo No 18-93 del 17 de Noviembre de 1993), Art 27. Available online at http://pdba.georgetown.edu/constitutions/guate/guate93.html (authors' translation).

47 For a fuller explanation of how this insider/outsider theory has worked in the case of Spanish investigations into military dictatorships in the Southern Cone, see Roht-Arriaza, fn 12 above, chs 7 and 8.

48 For a description of *amparo*, see text accompanying fn 26 of this chapter.

49 Resolución, Tribunal Quinto, No 2-2006, 28 March 2007 (on file with authors).

sent the case back to the lower court.[50] The trial court again found jurisdiction, and the appeals court, in October 2007, agreed.[51] The court recognized that the extradition treaty was binding, that Spanish jurisdiction was proper, and that the crimes at issue were of "grave importance" under international law and thus subject to extradition even though they were not—and could not have been in 1897—listed as extraditable crimes in the treaty. The trial court also fined the defendants' lawyers for filing frivolous appeals.[52]

The defendants, throughout the process, filed challenge after challenge, some of them almost exact repetitions of earlier ones. The defendants' repeated challenges suspended the proceedings over and over again, to the immense frustration of the complainants. No one begrudged the defendants a legitimate right to defence, but as their lawyers refiled arguments that had already been rejected over and over, it became clear that here, as in other criminal cases involving powerful defendants,[53] the writ of *amparo* had become a mechanism for delay and abuse.

As soon as the arrest warrants were announced, three complainants in the Spanish case—Rigoberta Menchú, Jesús Tecú and Juan Manuel Gerónimo—asked for and were admitted to the case as intervenors (*terceros interesados*). Yet despite their intervenor status, they were continually denied access to the file, notification of hearings and copies of relevant documents. By August 2007, they were frustrated and decided to file their own *amparo* alleging violations of their rights as victims of human rights violations. Advised by the international legal team, they cited the jurisprudence of the Inter-American Commission and Court on the right to the truth, the right to information, the right to prompt and effective justice without excessive delay and the right to an independent tribunal.[54] Shortly thereafter, the trial court agreed with them and

50 Resolución, Sala Primera de Apelaciones, No 2-2006, 1 June 2007 (on file with authors).

51 The trial court found jurisdiction for a second time on 31 July 2007, and the appeals court agreed on 26 October 2007. Sala Primera de la Corte de Apelaciones, Amparo 87-2006/543-2006, Sentencia, 26 October 2007 (on file with authors).

52 Amparo 87-2006/543-2006, Sentencia, 26 October 2007.

53 The use of abusive *amparos* was documented, e.g. in the *Myrna Mack* case, one of the few cases in which the Guatemalan courts convicted military officers of killing. See Fundación Myrna Mack, *Caso Myrna Mack, Resumen de las Audiencias ante el Tribunal Tercero de Sentencia del 3 de Septiembre al 3 de Octubre de 2002*. Available online at www.myrnamack.org.gt/index.php/casomyrnamack/procesonacional/sentencias19932004. Guatemala does not typically publish lower court pre-trial decisions, hence there is no public record of these *amparos*. A bill has been pending in the Guatemalan Congress to reform the *amparo* procedure.

54 See, e.g. IACtHR, Judicial Guarantees in States of Emergency, Art 27(2), 25 and 8, Advisory Opinion OC 9-87, Series A No 9, 6 October 1987, para 24. See also case of *Blake v Guatemala*, Series C No 48, Judgment of 22 January 1999 (reparations), paras 61 and 63. The complainants also cited, as persuasive authority, cases of the Colombian Supreme Court that balanced defendants' due process rights against victims' rights to truth and access to justice. Corte Constitucional de Colombia, Sentencia C-004/03, Demanda de Inconstitucionalidad, 20 January 2003. Available online at www.corteconstitucional.gov.co/relatoria/2003/C-004-03.htm.

ordered the case file to be released. The release was suspended when the defendants filed—yet another—writ of *amparo*. Nonetheless, the offensive (rather than defensive) use of the *amparo* proceeding to claim rights as victims under international law to limit the abusive use of dilatory motions is an innovation in Guatemala. While the use of dilatory writs will, in the end, be curbed only by either legislation or a change in attitude of the higher courts, at least it established a precedent that victims do indeed have internationally recognized rights that must be given effect in local courts.

Through this complicated set of domestic proceedings, triggered by an international warrant, trial-level Guatemalan courts had to grapple with international law and compare their procedures and ways of thinking with the jurisprudence generated by international courts as well as other Latin American courts facing similar issues. Through the offensive use of the *amparo* writ, international law—in this instance concerning the rights of victims—was brought into an area of domestic law where international law had not previously been applied. In this way, transnational prosecutions allow local courts to become familiar with international law and to modernize and innovate, while remaining grounded in local legal culture and practice.

9.6 Limits to effectiveness: the Constitutional Court decision of December 2007 and the Spanish judge's response

On 12 December 2007, the GCC ruled that the Spanish arrest warrants were invalid and that defendants could not be extradited.[55] The 60-plus page ruling responded to yet another *amparo*, lodged by Guevara and Arredondo, against the constitutionality of the arrest warrants issued in November 2006. The *amparo* questions only the validity of the arrest warrants, yet the GCC looked beyond that question to consider the validity of the entire extradition proceeding. The ruling began by accepting that the 1895 extradition treaty between Spain and Guatemala is still valid, but found that it must be interpreted in light of the drafters' intentions. Nothing in the treaty explicitly refers to extraterritorial jurisdiction, they noted, and the fact that the treaty speaks of those seeking asylum or refuge in another state indicates that the drafters were thinking about nationals of another state hiding in the requested state.[56] The treaty, they argued, must be read in light of the territorial principle of the criminal law. Therefore, they concluded, the treaty does not apply to crimes committed within Guatemala.

The GCC added that it can look into Spanish law because it needed to convince itself that the courts of the requesting country are a "competent

55 Sentencia del 12 de Diciembre de 2007, fn 5 above.

56 Sentencia del 12 de Diciembre de 2007, paras 15–17. This method of interpreting the treaty is at odds with the method of treaty interpretation set out in the Vienna Convention on the Law of Treaties (1980), 1155 UNTS 331, Art 31.

authority" under the Extradition Treaty.[57] Although from 2005 onwards, Spain clearly had jurisdiction under Spanish law, the GCC asks whether the 2005 Spanish Constitutional Court decision that allowed reopening of the full investigation comports with international law.

It concludes that universal jurisdiction cannot be maintained because it affronts Guatemalan sovereignty. While Guatemala might recognize an international tribunal, the GCC stated, it will not recognize the extraterritorial jurisdiction of another national court. Otherwise, it argued, one state would be judging another state's ability or willingness to prosecute without either Security Council or General Assembly approval. This line of reasoning is highly problematic, as it is in practice an action of judicial review of the decisions of foreign courts. In effect, the Guatemalan court disagrees with the Spanish court's interpretation of Spanish law. In addition, the GCC finds that extradition is improper for other reasons: both Spain and Guatemala prohibit the extradition of nationals. However, this is not strictly speaking true: Article 27 of Guatemala's Constitution allows the extradition of nationals where the crimes are based on treaties and conventions with regard to crimes against humanity or international law.[58] The GCC reads this reference, though, as limited to surrender to international courts like the ICC, the ad hoc international criminal tribunals, or even the Inter-American Court of Human Rights (which has no criminal jurisdiction).

In dicta, the GCC finds that the crimes alleged are common crimes connected to political crimes because they are connected to the armed conflict, and that the constitution holds that citizens cannot be extradited for political crimes.[59] This is legally incorrect: the Genocide Convention's Article VII specifically states that "genocide and the other acts enumerated in Article III shall not be considered as political crimes for the purpose of extradition".[60] The GCC may have been signalling that it would consider these crimes in any domestic

57 Tratado de Extradición entre España y Guatemala and Protocolo Adicional aclarando su articulo VII, fn 44 above.

58 Guatemala Constitution, Art 27. The court adds that extradition of nationals is also improper because there is no reciprocity, but this is also not strictly speaking true: where a treaty requires it, Spain will extradite its nationals. Art 1, Ley 4/1985, de 21 de Marzo, de Extradición Pasiva. Available online at http://noticias.juridicas.com/base_datos/Penal/l4-1985.html.

59 Sentencia del 12 de Diciembre de 2007, fn 5 above, pp 22–23 and 54.

60 Convention on the Prevention and Punishment of the Crime of Genocide, Art VII. See also Inter-American Convention on Forced Disappearance of Persons (1994), Art V, ILM, vol 33, 1529 ("The forced disappearance of persons shall not be considered a political offense for purposes of extradition"). The UN and Inter-American Torture Conventions also require that torture be considered an extraditable offence. Convention against Torture and Other Cruel, Inhuman or Degrading Treatment or Punishment (1984), General Assembly Resolution No 39/46, UN Doc A/39/51, Art 8(1) (1987) (torture must be extraditable offence). See also Inter-American Convention to Prevent and Punish Torture (1985), OAS Treaty Series No 67, Art 13 (1987).

prosecution as subject to the Guatemalan Law of National Reconciliation, which grants limited amnesty to persons who have committed political crimes and common crimes connected to them.[61] But Articles 4 and 8 of that law specifically exclude the type of crime alleged in the Spanish request.[62] Along the same lines, the court characterizes the context of the case as a region-wide civil conflict over political and economic models, with external support on both sides and which pitted ethnic and indigenous people against each other. By so labelling the conflict, the court implicitly rejects the charge of genocide.[63]

Finally, the court recognizes the obligation of the Guatemalan courts to investigate and prosecute under the principle of *aut dedere aut judicare* (extradite or prosecute) if extradition is denied and invites the complainants to submit their evidence to the Public Prosecutor. This is a bit disingenuous, since the judges know perfectly well that charges on these crimes had long been filed with the prosecutor and had gone nowhere. However, the GCC's recognition that the domestic system needs to prosecute is important. Now they need to follow through.

As a result, the court finds that the suspects' constitutional rights have been violated and orders the arrest warrants quashed. While technically the judgment should only apply to the two defendants who appealed, they make it extensive to all of the other suspects as third-party interveners. There can be no appeal from the decision.

The GCC's decision was clearly a setback for the complainants and for international law. It exemplifies some of the limits of a transnational litigation strategy. In a climate of intimidation where judges are routinely bribed or threatened into submission, where the legal system has been repeatedly criticized for its ineffectiveness and for allowing rampant impunity, and where some (but not all) of the defendants still hold power,[64] the defensive tone and negative outcome of the case may have been inevitable. The willingness of the lower courts to go forward, the obvious errors and omissions of the GCC's judgment, and even the length of time it took for the GCC to rule on the arrest warrants despite several earlier opportunities to do so, are reasons for hope that there are some cracks in the façade of impunity. After all, early cases in the Chilean and Argentine courts also featured more open lower courts, followed by conservative decisions rejecting international human rights law obligations

61 Ley de Reconciliación Nacional, fn 16 above.

62 Ley de Reconciliación Nacional, Arts 4 and 8.

63 Sentencia del 12 de Diciembre de 2007, fn 5 above, p 50.

64 Efraín Ríos Montt, e.g. was elected to Congress in 2007, in part as a stated attempt to gain immunity from prosecution. As a Congressman, he has immunity for criminal acts committed while in office, but that immunity does not preclude investigation by the Spanish courts. See Inés Benítez, *Ex-Dictator on Rocky Road to Congress—and Immunity*, IPS (23 May 2007). Available online at http://ipsnews.net/news.asp?idnews=37871. As to the other defendants, one strategic consideration here is that they may have less current ability to influence outcomes or to threaten participants than other, lower-ranked former officers who may be more active in current criminal and intelligence networks.

at the highest levels.[65] Both the Chilean Supreme Court and the Argentine Supreme Court have now invalidated or limited amnesty laws and approved prosecutions for past crimes based in part on international law obligations.

The Achilles heel of all international justice efforts, whether at the ICC, through hybrid courts or through transnational prosecutions, is the inability to execute arrest warrants against powerful defendants. The ICC, for example, has been hamstrung by the inability to apprehend indicted Sudanese officials accused of crimes against humanity in Darfur, despite the existence of a Security Council referral and numerous resolutions condemning those crimes.[66] The ICTY became effective only when NATO troops began to seek out and arrest suspects.[67] Hybrid tribunals, although theoretically less exposed to this problem because they have the co-operation of the territorial government, have still experienced difficulties: Charles Taylor for many years could not be extradited from Nigeria to the Sierra Leone Special Court.[68] The Special Panels on Serious Crimes in East Timor were similarly unable to prosecute members of Indonesia's high command for atrocities in East Timor because Indonesia refused to extradite them.[69] Transnational prosecutions will suffer from the same weakness when the defendant's presence is sought through extradition: unless he leaves his country and travels to a third state willing to execute the arrest warrants, the defendant will be beyond the reach of the foreign court.

9.7 Aftermath and current prospects

Reaction to the GCC decision was not long in coming. International human rights groups uniformly criticized the holding and the reasoning. European civil society groups began pressuring their governments and EU institutions to question the Guatemalan Government's commitment to human rights,[70] a particularly sensitive point given the installation of a new government in January 2008 as well as ongoing negotiations for an EU-Central American

65 For description and analysis, see Roht-Arriaza, N and Gibson, L, "The Developing Jurisprudence on Amnesty", *Human Rights Quarterly*, vol 20, 1998, pp 843 ff.

66 UN News Centre, "UN War Crimes Prosecutor Calls for Arrest of First Darfur Suspects" (7 June 2007). Available online at www.un.org/apps/news/story.asp?NewsID=22826&Cr=sudan&Cr1=; Security Council Resolution No 1593, S/Res/1593/2005, 31 March 2005.

67 The two most wanted suspects at the ICTY long evaded capture. See Scheffer, D, "The Least Wanted Most Wanted Man", *Foreign Policy*, 2 June 2011.

68 "Liberia Seeks End to Taylor Exile", BBC News, 17 March 2006. Available online at http://news.bbc.co.uk/1/hi/world/africa/4817106.stm.

69 David Cohen, "Seeking Justice on the Cheap: Is the East Timor Tribunal Really a Model for the Future?" *Asia Pacific Issues*, no 61, East-West Center, August 2002, p 1. Available online at www.eastwestcenter.org/fileadmin/stored/pdfs/api061.pdf.

70 See, e.g. CIFCA (Copenhagen Initiative for Central America and Mexico), *Urgente: Guatemala Anula el Proceso de Espana Contra los Militares Acusados de Genocidio* (15 January 2011) (on file with authors).

Association Agreement.[71] Above all, human rights and humanitarian lawyers pointed out that if Guatemala was not going to extradite the suspects, it had an international legal obligation to try them at home. That obligation was explicit under the UN and Inter-American Conventions against Torture and Enforced Disappearances as well as the Genocide Convention.[72] It was also, quite obviously, not being fulfilled.

Most spectacularly, Spanish Judge Pedraz also responded to the GCC decision. On 9 January 2008, he issued his own ruling condemning Guatemala's lack of co-operation and abandonment of its responsibilities under international law.[73] In strong language, the judge complained about the complete lack of collaboration on his requests for rogatory commissions and lambasted the GCC decision as ignoring Guatemala's conventional and customary law obligations to extradite or to prosecute, which the judge traced back as far as Grotius, as well as the extradition treaty.[74]

Judge Pedraz also recalled that genocide is a crime in international law that cannot be labelled a political offence and found that Guatemala was also violating an international treaty and customary law obligation to prevent and punish the crime of genocide against the Mayan people. He concluded:

> This resolution of the Constitutional Court, issued by the maximal judicial authority, in light of the above-referenced facts and of the advanced age of the accused, together with the well-known fact that the level of impunity for lesser crimes in Guatemala is among the world's highest, confirms the state's intention not to investigate these crimes and bring those responsible before the courts. This gives clear backing to impunity, ignoring the above-referenced international law and, therefore, placing Guatemala in the sphere of countries that violate their international obligations and disdain the defense of human rights.[75]

71 The European Union and the Central American countries were then engaged in negotiation of a comprehensive Association Agreement, which is to include both political and economic components including a free trade agreement. As part of those negotiations, on 15 December 2003, the parties concluded an EU-Central America Political Dialogue and Co-operation Agreement, which states in Art 1(1): "Respect for democratic principles and fundamental human rights, as laid down in the Universal Declaration of Human Rights, as well as for the principle of the rule of law, underpins the internal and international policies of the Parties and constitutes an essential element of this Agreement." CE/AM-CENTR/en/1. Available online at http://ec.europa.eu/external_relations/ca/pol/pdca_12_03_en.pdf. For information on the negotiation process and goals, see *The EU's Relations with Central America: Overview*. Available online at http://ec.europa.eu/external_relations/ca/index.htm (accessed on 15 March 2011).

72 Ley de Reconciliación Nacional, fn 16 above, Arts 4 and 8.

73 Auto dejando sin efecto las comisiones rogatorias a la Republica de Guatemala, Juzgado Central de Instrucción No 1, Audiencia Nacional, Diligencias Previas 331/1999-10, 16 January 2008. Available online at www.derechos.org/nizkor/espana/doc/pedraz1.html (in Spanish).

74 Auto dejando sin efecto las comisiones rogatorias a la Republica de Guatemala.

75 Auto dejando sin efecto las comisiones rogatorias a la Republica de Guatemala, s 6 (translation by authors).

Nonetheless, the judge wrote, the GCC decision showed the continued need for Spanish judicial authorities to investigate the alleged crimes. However, he would no longer rely on the Guatemalan courts, but would bring witnesses to Spain to testify.[76] In addition, he called on anyone—victims, witnesses, or others—having information about the case to bring it directly to him through the proper channels.[77] He thus opened up new possibilities for evidence gathering by victims' groups, complainants' lawyers and others around the world.

In February 2008, witnesses began arriving at the Spanish court. They included experts, journalists and eyewitnesses from some of the areas of the country where, according to the CEH Report, acts of genocide were committed. The eyewitnesses detailed massacres, rape, torture, bombings and persecution of massacre survivors, destruction of crops and livestock, and targeting of Mayan religious practices and community authorities. They also named specific military officials, including the defendants, and specified their role in these crimes.[78] The witnesses spent a full week telling the judge their story. This in itself can have reparatory effects.[79]

The continuing political pressure and what is expected to be an ongoing parade of witnesses will no doubt keep the issue in the public eye in Guatemala. Whether this translates into effective change in the attitude of Guatemala's prosecutors and judges is, at this point, unknown. It is of course more difficult for such change to happen without at least a modicum of physical security for all those involved.[80] However, the pressure already apparently had some result: on 25 February, Guatemalan President Álvaro Colom announced that he would order the military to open up its archives from the armed conflict period and turn them over to the Human Rights Ombudsman.[81]

76 In another innovation, the Spanish Public Prosecutor designated some of the eyewitnesses as witnesses for the Spanish Crown, which allows Spain to pay their travel expenses. Given the modest economic status of almost all of the witnesses, this made it possible for them to testify. Unpublished decision of Public Prosecutor, Audiencia Nacional.

77 Unpublished decision of Public Prosecutor, Audiencia Nacional. The proper channels for submitting additional information or evidence presumably would include Spanish consulates throughout the world.

78 Ortíz, G, "Declaran en España por Genocidio", *La Hora*, 5 February 2008. Available online at www.lahora.com.gt/notas.php?key=25579&fch=2008-02-05.

79 There is extensive literature on truth-telling and its potential salutary effects for some victims. See, e.g. Hayner, P B, *Unspeakable Truths: Confronting State Terror and Atrocity*, New York: Routledge, 2001. On the other hand, there is a risk that victims will end up frustrated by the continued inability to acquire custody over the defendants and thus to proceed to full trial and sentencing. The witnesses were well aware of that possibility and chose to testify nonetheless.

80 On 5 March 2008, unknown assailants shot at the house of the director of the Fundación Nueva Esperanza, Guillermo Chen. The Fundación represents some of the witnesses and complainants involved in the Spanish case. Amnesty International, Urgent Action, Public AI Index 34/006/2008, 7 March 2008.

81 Antonio Ordonez, "Presidente Colom Ordena Abrir Archivos del Ejército", *Prensa Libre*, 25 February 2008. Available online at www.prensalibre.com/noticias/Presidente-Colom-ordena-archivos-Ejercito_0_163783856.html.

In April 2008 the proceedings took yet another turn. Guatemalan trial court judge José Eduardo Cojulún, whose chambers had received Judge Pedraz's repeated requests for a rogatory commission to interview witnesses, decided that he would honour those requests. He reasoned that the GCC's decision had no bearing on his international judicial co-operation obligations, and that, while he could not allow Judge Pedraz to come to Guatemala, he could conduct the interviews himself and forward the results to the Spanish court. He thus set out a demanding schedule of witness interviews, which began on 17 April. When witnesses told him they could not appear because they had no funds to travel to the capital, he agreed to transport them in order to take their statements. He rejected the predictable *amparos* from the defendants.

In any case, along with internal pressure, the Spanish case has already changed the national equation, bringing the issue again to the forefront of national consciousness. Unless the GCC changes its mind or one of the named defendants (or other defendants named in the future) leaves the country, the case may never come to trial; Spain does not allow trial *in absentia*.[82] Nonetheless, the judge will continue taking testimony and eventually, if the evidence is sufficient, is expected to issue individualized indictments (*autos de procesamiento*) against these and, perhaps, other defendants. These indictments would set out the evidence that the charged crimes were committed and that the defendants were responsible, and at a minimum, they would serve as a valuable historical record and a validation of the witness testimony. The indictments would also serve as a powerful tool for lawyers, victims groups and even, if it so chose, the Executive Branch in Guatemala to pursue new avenues of investigation and prosecution.

9.8 Pushing from the present: the international commission against impunity in Guatemala

The Spanish litigation is not the only attempt to overcome the legacy of impunity in Guatemala. As noted at the beginning, this impunity extends beyond the former military and security force officials responsible for past human rights violations to encompass present common crime, including (and especially) that committed by powerful networks of drug traffickers, smugglers of all sorts, extortion gangs and car theft rings. In part, these are the same people: many of the military intelligence and security force networks involved in human rights violations transformed themselves, under weak civilian

82 In 2009 Spain reformed its universal jurisdiction law, narrowing its applicability to cases involving Spanish victims or defendants, cases where the defendant is found in Spain, and those where Spain has a relevant connection. The reform also requires a showing that the case is not being adequately prosecuted elsewhere. The reform does not change the Spanish court's ability to hear the Guatemalan case, which has both Spanish victims and relevant connections. See, generally, "Las ONG Afirman que la Reforma de la ley es un paso hacia la impunidad", *El Mundo*, 29 June 2009.

governments, into criminal networks.[83] So impunity for past crimes and impunity in the present are inextricably bound together.

The result is a pervasive sense of insecurity, an almost completely dysfunctional prosecution service, intimidation and corruption of judges and prosecutors, and many powerful people with a vested interest in maintaining the system in its current ineffective form. Most crimes are never even investigated; only 2 per cent are ever resolved.[84] Even in the few cases where convictions are won, the defendants are often freed by mobs, mysteriously disappear before serving time or are allowed to run rackets in prison.[85]

On 16 January 2003, NGOs together with the Guatemalan Human Rights Ombudsman (*Procurador*) Sergio Fernando Morales Alvarado proposed the creation of a Commission to Investigate Illegal Groups and Clandestine Security Organizations (CICIACS). The proposal responded to "the clamor which has been caused by the assassinations, threats and kidnappings of human rights defenders, judges, magistrates, politicians, lawyers, Congressional advisers, political leaders, journalists, priests, indigenous representatives and other people".[86] The president presented a bill to Congress creating CICIACS, but an agreement between the government and the United Nations to establish CICIACS was torpedoed when the GCC found it unconstitutional because the Guatemalan Constitution reserves a prosecutorial role for the Public Prosecutor alone.[87] It took another two years to modify the plan to meet those objections, but on 11 December 2006 the revised agreement between the United Nations and the Guatemalan Government creating a new version of CICIACS, known as CICIG, was signed. The agreement was ratified by the Guatemalan Congress in August 2007 and entered into force on 4 September 2007.[88]

From the United Nation's perspective, the commitment to help end impunity at the national level in this manner is an innovation. CICIG is "not a truth commission, nor a special international tribunal, nor a classical technical

83 E.g. the Bush administration revoked the visas of two former chiefs of military intelligence because of their links to drug trafficking. Smyth, F, "Guatemala, Home of Powerful Drug Runners", *Nieman Watchdog*, 20 November 2005. Available online at www.niemanwatchdog.org/index.cfm?fuseaction=ask_this.view&askthisid=00152.

84 Daniel, F J and Rosenberg, M, "Crime-Ridden Guatemala Divided in Vote", *Reuters*, 4 November 2007. Available online at www.reuters.com/article/latestCrisis/idUSN03610855.

85 E.g. Captain José Antonio Solares was convicted of ordering a massacre in Río Negro, but has never been "found" even though he continues to reside at home in plain sight. See *ADIVIMA pide que se cumpla la ley y se ejecute la orden de aprehensión dictada contra el Capitán José Antonio Solares por asesinato y genocidio* (October 2004). Available online at www.derechos.net/adivima/es/reports.htm.

86 Garretón, R, *CICIG: An Innovative Mechanism*, Human Rights First (2007). Available online at www.humanrightsfirst.org/wp-content/uploads/pdf/07730-hrd-garreton-article-translation.pdf (unofficial translation).

87 Garretón, fn 86 above; GCC, decision of 8 May 2007, Expediente 791-2007.

88 "Secretary-General Appoints Head of Probe Into Illegal Armed Groups in Guatemala", UN News Centre, 14 September 2007. Available online at www.un.org/apps/news/story.asp?NewsID=23820&Cr=guatemala&Cr1=.

assistance programme, but rather is fashioned to respond to critical needs not always met by those kinds of measures".[89]

CICIG is to "determine the existence of illegal security groups and clandestine security organizations, their structure, forms of operation, sources of financing and possible relation to state entities or agents and other sectors that threaten civil and political rights in Guatemala, in conformity with the objectives of this Agreement",[90] collaborate with the state in the dismantling of these groups, promote the investigation, criminal prosecution and punishment of those crimes committed by their members, and recommend the adoption of public policies for eradicating such groups and preventing their re-emergence.

To accomplish its goals, CICIG cannot directly prosecute crimes, but can initiate criminal complaints, provide information to the Prosecutors' Office and act as a complementary prosecutor (*querellante adhesivo*) in criminal cases.[91] It can subpoena documents, hire its own staff of investigators, file disciplinary complaints against public servants, guarantee confidentiality to witnesses and publish its results. On the other hand, the Commission is weakened by its inability to compel testimony directly and by its dependence on the Public Prosecutor, who is the only person who can actually take the cases to court. It also depends on the Guatemalan courts to act once the cases are being prosecuted.

CICIG has proven important in investigating some notorious cases and in unravelling some of the connections among political elites, narco-traffickers and large-scale corruption. It has also played an important political role: when President Colom attempted to appoint a new Attorney General with alleged links to child-smuggling rings, then-CICIG Commissioner Carlos Castresana resigned in fury. His public resignation prompted the courts to invalidate the appointment, and eventually Colom appointed a new Attorney General drawn from the small number of human rights lawyers in Guatemala.

In its current form, CICIG will not focus on past crimes arising from the 1970s and 1980s, although there is no explicit limitation in the mandate. However, to the extent the organizers and leaders of illegal security groups and clandestine security organizations are connected to, or one and the same as,

89 CICIG, *Background, Nature and Objectives of CICIG* (2008) (unpublished document on file with authors). See also ONU en Guatemala, *La CICIG Está Oficialmente Instalada en Guatemala*, available online at www.onu.org.gt/.

90 Agreement between the United Nations and the State of Guatemala on the Establishment of an International Commission against Impunity in Guatemala, 12 December 2006, Art 1. Available online at http://cicig.org/uploads/documents/CICIG_AGREEMENT_EN.pdf. These groups are defined as those that:
(i) commit illegal acts in order to affect the full enjoyment and exercise of civil and political rights; and
(ii) are linked directly or indirectly to agents of the state or have the capacity to generate impunity for their illegal actions. Art II, para (1)(a).

91 Agreement between the United Nations and the State of Guatemala, fn 90 above.

former military officers implicated in human rights violations or genocide, the Spanish investigation and CICIG's work may end up overlapping.

9.9 Epilogue: the cases in the United States and Canada

As the case in Spain continued, in May 2010 a new set of cases showed yet another aspect of the complexities of international justice. The US Government arrested Gilberto Jordan, a member of an elite fighting unit of the Guatemalan army (known as the *kaibiles*), on charges of lying on his application to become a US citizen. Jordan, who had settled in southern Florida, was tried and convicted of failing to disclose his military service and participation in a massacre in the hamlet of Dos Erres. In December 1982, members of the kaibiles stormed Dos Erres and systematically killed over 200 men, women and children. Soldiers bludgeoned villagers with sledgehammers and threw them down a well and raped women and girls before killing them. Jordan admitted to throwing a baby down the well. He was sentenced to 10 years in prison.

The case demonstrates a new determination by the United States to prosecute cases of human rights offenders found in the country. The investigations were carried out by the Immigration and Customs Enforcement's Human Rights Violators and War Crimes unit, and prosecuted by a unit in the Justice Department that in the past focused on hunting Nazis. The decision to prosecute on fraud charges constitutes a vast improvement over past US practice, which was to deport quietly human rights violators found in the United States, without any concern for whether they would be prosecuted in their home countries. In a few more recent cases, the US Government has co-ordinated with local prosecutors before returning deportees accused of rights violations, but the practice has not been consistent.

Still, while a 10-year conviction for Jordan is a significant step forward, it is not based on a conviction for the underlying crimes, but only for fraud. This has very different moral implications, even though the practical result may be initially similar. The US law allows for criminal prosecution of those found in the United States for torture or genocide, no matter where committed.[92] However, US authorities have been reluctant to use these authorities to deal with crimes committed in the 1980s, presumably on grounds that doing so would violate the principle of legality (no *ex post facto* prosecutions). This may be incorrect from the perspective of international law,[93] but may make sense from the perspective of risk-averse criminal prosecutors also no doubt concerned about potential prosecutions of US officials abroad.

92 18 USC § 1091 (2007) (genocide); 18 USC § 2340 (1994).

93 See, e.g. International Covenant on Civil and Political Rights, Art 15; and European Court of Human Rights, *Kononov v Latvia*, Application No 36376/04, Grand Chamber Judgment of 17 May 2010.

Thus, when another of the accused in the Dos Erres massacre, Jorge Sosa Orantes, turned up in Canada in January 2011, the United States asked for him to be extradited to the United States to stand trial on fraud charges stemming from his naturalization proceedings—he too had neglected to mention his participation in the massacre. Advocates began clamouring for him to be tried in Canada on the underlying charges rather than returned to the United States to be tried on charges that would, at most, result in a sentence like that faced by Jordan. And in March 2011, lawyers in the Spanish litigation asked the judge for an arrest warrant for Sosa, to be followed by an effort to extradite him to Spain. The Canadian Government will have to sort out the different possibilities, based on a calculus that includes the nature of the underlying charges, the ties to the forum states and the international legal obligations of each possible venue.

In Guatemala, the Dos Erres case has been before the courts since 1994, when the bodies were exhumed. Continued inaction led the families to bring the case to the Inter-American Court, which in 2009 ordered the government to put an end to dilatory tactics and bring the case to trial.[94] The Guatemalan Supreme Court then ruled that the prosecutors' office should proceed; however, a month later the investigation was again halted due to yet another series of motions for *amparo* filed by the defendants and accepted by the Constitutional Court. At this time, therefore, the possibilities of moving the case forward at home—especially against those who gave the orders, not just those who carried them out—will depend on continued outside pressure.

9.10 Conclusion

Impunity remains a core problem of post-conflict state building. Guatemala exemplifies the process by which impunity for the crimes of the past begets more impunity in the present; the two are linked. Early efforts to combat impunity worldwide focused largely on the creation of new global institutions like the ad hoc international criminal tribunals and the ICC. As the limitations as well as the strengths of those institutions have become clearer, a more diversified and complex set of responses, grounded in the particular realities of each state, have begun to proliferate. In particular, hybrid courts, with explicit goals that include strengthening domestic legal systems and training local lawyers in international criminal law, have emerged. Transnational prosecutions can serve many of the same functions as these hybrid tribunals, although they suffer from the same weaknesses as other international criminal justice mechanisms in being able to apprehend suspects.

Moreover, international investigatory commissions and transnational prosecutions, like those discussed here with respect to Guatemala, can play

94 Inter-American Court of Human Rights, case of the *"Las Dos Erres" Massacre v Guatemala*, Series C No 211, Judgment of 24 November 2009.

complementary roles in catalyzing changes in domestic ability and the will to investigate and prosecute the powerful. The success of these mechanisms, like that of international prosecutions more generally, should be measured not only (or even principally) by how many convictions they secure, but at how well they succeed in changing the possibilities for justice at home.

As this book went to press, Guatemalan Public Prosecutor Claudia Paz announced an arrest warrant for retired Hector Mario López Fuentes on charges of genocide. López Fuentes was named in the original complaint filed in Guatemala in 2001, and, as Rios Mott's chief of staff, was involved in military planning, especially in the Ixil highlands region. One reason the Prosecutor's office may have chosen to focus on López Fuentes is that his name appears in a military document called "Operación Sofía" detailing killings in the highlands. That document, in its complete version, was first introduced into evidence in the Spanish case, and from there sent to Guatemala. Thus, although there is no simple cause and effect relationship between the Spanish case and the new domestic efforts, the two will continue to support and enrich each other as the fight against impunity moves to a new stage.

10 The criminal investigation and its relationship to jurisdiction, extradition, co-operation and criminal policy

Susan Kemp

10.1 Introduction

The transnational nature of criminal activity throughout history has ranged from piracy and slavery to complex organized crime networks, which harness the modern ease of global travel, communication and technological innovation. It has demanded a correspondingly transnational approach from a plethora of domestic, regional and global law enforcement bodies. Practical advances have been accompanied by legal developments to further international co-operation in the investigation and prosecution of the crimes of concern to all states. Vast progress has been achieved in interstate action against narcotics trafficking, money laundering and the range of offences encompassed loosely by the term "terrorism".

The sphere of human rights and humanitarian law has been no exception. The Geneva Conventions' grave breaches provisions were ground breaking, creating a system that requires the mandatory exercise of criminal jurisdiction by states regardless of their connection to the offence or the offender. Nonetheless, the fields of international criminal and human rights law have perhaps been somewhat slow in creating many of the practical and legal frameworks necessary to make the many innovative treaty provisions effective in practice. It may be no coincidence that it is in these fields that one often finds instances of states themselves and their agents in the role of the accused party. Nonetheless, victims and their representatives are becoming increasingly aware of the opportunities to approach various criminal jurisdictions particularly in Europe as well as using the traditional routes of claims to human rights organs and raising civil actions. Practice is in some cases overtaking the creation of suitable legal and policy frameworks. The experience of recent years has highlighted many areas in which law, policy and practical considerations urgently require to be addressed to respond adequately to the increasing uptake of the possibility for "extraterritorial" prosecutions. Among these, many relate to the criminal investigation stage, which shall be the topic of this chapter.

Choices and decisions made at the investigative stage (such as whether to investigate, and which crimes, suspects, geographic area and time frame to focus on) obviously have a great impact on any criminal case. These challenges are all the more exacting for states emerging from armed conflict or repressive rule. Aside from the institutional, infrastructural and political challenges that may exist, conceptual confusion may damage overall criminal policy if the goals of prosecution are not clearly debated and understood. Answering the basic questions that are posed after a common crime occurring in peacetime can take on a whole new complexity and significance when it comes to prosecuting international crimes during a period of "transition": Who to prosecute? When? Where? What to charge? How to undertake the investigation? Which cases to prioritize? And, most crucially, why prosecute at all, if discretion exists? The response to each of these questions can change radically depending on the policy aim. It is worth going through the process of answering these questions in a given transitional situation based on a policy aim for prosecuting international crimes of, say, "deterrence through combating impunity", and then repeating the exercise if the policy aim of the prosecutions is to achieve peace, democracy or "national reconciliation".[1]

In situations where several states have extended their laws to provide for criminal jurisdiction over the same acts when it comes to the enforcement of these laws logically the impact of their answers to the basic questions listed above may differ and can multiply the legal challenges felt beyond their national borders. Notwithstanding judicial independence, transnational justice also implies added complications rooted in interstate relations generally, and not only between states that have been involved in the same armed conflict. Colonial ties or animosities, trade and development and other considerations may also be affected, though these are beyond the scope of this comment.

Three major legal issues that are likely to be affected by decision-making at the investigative stage are the exercise of jurisdiction, the conduct of extradition proceedings and co-operation (both judicial and in relation to international aid). All of these issues in turn have consequences for criminal policy within post-conflict or post-repressive states where such acts occurred. The challenge is for all the relevant bodies in each state and those regional and international players involved to manage these issues in a coherent and co-ordinated way in order to avoid paralysis or limitations on the available forums in which victims can seek redress. The following analysis seeks to examine the ways in which the criminal investigation affects these larger themes: section 10.3 will deal with jurisdiction, section 10.4 with extradition, 10.5 with co-operation and 10.6 with overall criminal policy. In each section, suggestions will be made of practical ways in which the investigation stage can not only function more efficiently in situations of concurrent jurisdiction but also actively benefit decision-making in all of the areas discussed.

1 Division between immediate and ultimate policy goals does not always solve this conundrum.

10.2 Key aspects of the investigation for multiple forums

10.2.1 Universe of cases

The "universe" of crimes and, therefore, possible criminal cases, that a national jurisdiction will have to deal with will necessarily differ in scale (the difference, say, between a state in whose territory large-scale offences occurred over a protracted period of conflict, compared to a state that receives sporadic complaints from victims of individual offences committed in a foreign conflict over which its domestic laws extend jurisdiction). In addition, while as a matter of law or policy there is no agreed quantitative point at which a state having a duty under national or international law to investigate particular crime types can be said to have discharged that duty,[2] it is generally true to say that states under such an obligation will face a larger "universe" of crimes than those states having merely the option to exercise jurisdiction if they wish.

In certain systems both national and international, prosecutorial authorities that are faced with an overwhelming level of criminality may have the discretion to select cases for investigation and prosecution. In other systems, on receipt of information regarding commission of the crime, the authorities may be required to investigate every single reported crime. In all systems, however, the potential will generally exist for the authorities to organize investigations in such a way as to prioritize cases, connect facts and accused into group cases and/or sequence investigations and prosecutions strategically, for example to build up evidence incrementally against higher level accused, to make progress as their resources come on stream or as security improves.

In any event, a minimum amount of reliable information from credible sources should first be gathered to map the overall "universe" of crimes before decisions are made to select time periods, geographical areas, crime types, incident types or perpetrator profiles for more in-depth investigation. Those selections and any decisions to prioritize, connect or sequence investigations must be transparent and defensible.

It is at this early stage in the investigative process that such criteria and decisions begin to shape the future direction of criminal proceedings. Decisions, for example, to prioritize one or two high profile or notorious incidents or perpetrators, certain types of conduct, or certain victim groups will of course be reflected in the focus of initial evidence gathering. Taking a narrow focus at too early a stage can be just as distorting and obstructive for the investigation and prosecution process as deciding to investigate simultaneously hundreds of thousands of reported incidents at once. Whatever is decided, the first concrete impact will be for the hypotheses of the crimes around which initial evidence-

2 See further Kemp, S, "Alternative Justice Mechanisms, Compliance and Fragmentation of International Criminal Law", in Stahn, C and van den Herik, L (eds), *Fragmentation and Diversification in International Criminal Law*, University of Leiden Grotius Centre for International Legal Studies (forthcoming).

gathering plans will be organized, and which will be continually tested during the investigation.

10.2.2 Hypotheses of conduct and responsibility

At the commencement of an investigation, a hypothesis will generally be formed regarding the circumstances of the crime(s), which will form the basis of investigation planning. Thereafter, by way of the cycle of collection and analysis of information, that hypothesis will be tested and refined throughout the investigation stage. Clearly, the scope and nature of a criminal investigation will determine a prosecutor's subsequent options for the legal classifications of the *actus reus*, potential accused and the possible modes of criminal responsibility. Such classifications will emerge in applications for arrest, extradition, formal charging and decisions on pre-trial conditions such as property embargo. The legal and practical implications are discussed in more detail in the following sections. However, it suffices to highlight that the classification of conduct can trigger the potential application of norms of international law (including, for example, state obligations to investigate and prosecute, obligations under extradition treaties or otherwise to provide mutual assistance, and the applicability of human rights treaty obligations or norms regarding state responsibility)[3] and relevant national law (such as the law relating to the arrest and extradition/transfer of the alleged offender, laws relating to impeachment and pre-trial detention). Classification of the offence may also trigger the competence of military jurisdictions, the rules in relation to which may differ markedly in terms of procedure, forms of criminal responsibility, penalties and extradition.

It is imperative to caution, however, against squeezing conduct into inappropriate legal classifications in order to trigger the applicability of specific laws, such as those permitting the exercise of extraterritorial jurisdiction. To follow the advice often attributed to Einstein, "if the facts don't fit the theory, change the facts", is certain to lead to problems later in the proceedings and possibly to definitions that are at odds with international law.

10.2.3 Circumstantial elements of crimes

It is of central importance that those within national criminal authorities who are viewing the basic information about the universe of crimes are mindful of leaving open options for classification of crimes and linkage to other potential perpetrators when directing evidence-gathering efforts of their staff.

3 Also note the relevance of concepts of attribution in international human rights law. For the issue of attribution under the law of state responsibility generally, see International Law Commission, Draft Articles on the International Responsibility of States for Wrongful Acts, adopted at the 53rd session of the Commission in 2001. The document is reproduced in annex to UNGA Res 56/83, A/RES/56/83, adopted on 10 December 2001.

Once again, decisions at this early stage have later ramifications. For example, if decisions are made to investigate the acts as common crimes, information will not be collected during the investigation about circumstances such as the existence (and type) of armed conflict and any link between the offences and that conflict, the nature and circumstances of a generalized attack on the civilian population, the ethnic, racial, religious, national or other characteristics shared by the victims, whether an overall plan or policy lay behind the violence and so whether a link can be made between the crime and individuals in higher positions of military or civilian authority, how the entire institutions or groups alleged to be behind the violence functioned. All of these facts could offer much wider charging possibilities later in the process, with multi-jurisdictional implications to which we shall now turn.

10.3 Jurisdictional issues

10.3.1 Bases and principles of jurisdiction

It is important to clarify from the outset that prescriptive jurisdiction concerns the question of to whom and in relation to which events can a state extend its laws,[4] and enforcement jurisdiction to the application of the public (including criminal) laws of one state in another, with the latter's consent. Therefore, while the extension of laws of some states such as Spain to cover serious crimes committed outside their territory may be based on any of the accepted principles of prescriptive jurisdiction, the *enforcement* of that law by another state (say, by surrendering a suspect to Spain) may only proceed with the consent of that other state. Of course, treaty obligations between two states in relation to such matters may already exist and can be applied to the situation in question.

As to principles (or types) of jurisdiction,[5] these may be described as connecting factors originating in international law which link the conduct and the state. Those having the longest and most widely accepted legal history are the territorial and national (personal) principles. In terms of criminal law, the latter relates to the nationality of the perpetrator.[6]

4 A state does not have complete freedom to extend its prescriptive jurisdiction in the absence of any express prohibition. Sovereign equality requires rather that there is no presumption in favour of the legality of such an action. See Lowe, V, "Jurisdiction", in Evans, M (ed), *International Law*, Oxford: Oxford University Press, 2003, pp 334–336 (commenting on the judgment of the Permanent Court of International Justice in the *Lotus* case (*France v Turkey*), no 9, on 7 September 1927).

5 For a review of the law of jurisdiction, see, e.g. Akehurst, M, "Jurisdiction in International Law", *British Yearbook of International Law*, vol 46, 1972–1973, pp 145–217; Jenning, R and Watts, A (eds), *Oppenheim's International Law*, 9th edn, Harlow: Longman, 1992; and Brownlie, I, *Principles of Public International Law*, 5th edn, Oxford: Oxford University Press, 1998.

6 It is sometimes referred to as the "active personality" principle.

Others that have come into use more recently are the protective principle and universality principle.[7] Finally, treaty-based jurisdiction, particularly in the area of terrorism and organized crime,[8] often relies on a combination of the territorial, national and protective principles. Although technically not meeting the standard for universal jurisdiction *strictu sensu*, as they only apply between States Parties, some of these treaties can have a similar effect to universal jurisdiction by requiring all Member States to establish jurisdiction over offenders found in their territory whatever their link with the offender or offence if it does not extradite them.[9] The Convention against Torture (1984)[10] and the Inter-American Convention on Forced Disappearance[11] require States Parties to establish their jurisdiction on the basis of the territorial and national principles and provided the option to do so on the "passive personality" basis. The Genocide Convention[12] and Inter-American Torture Convention[13] require states to assert territorial jurisdiction.[14]

7 More controversial bases such as "passive personality" (nationality of the victim) have no solid establishment in international custom, but are occasionally asserted and seen in some international treaties.

8 1963 Tokyo Convention on Offences and Certain Other Acts Committed on Board Aircraft; 1970 Hague Convention on the Suppression of the Unlawful Seizure of Aircraft; 1971 Montreal Convention for the Suppression of Unlawful Acts against the Safety of Civil Aviation; 1972 UN Convention on the Prevention and Punishment of Crimes against Internationally Protected Persons; 1979 Convention against the Taking of Hostages; 1980 Vienna Convention on the Physical Protection of Nuclear Material; 1984 UN Convention against Torture and other Cruel, Inhuman or Degrading Treatment or Punishment; 1988 Vienna Convention against Illegal Traffic in Narcotic Drugs and Psychotropic Substances; 1988 Rome Convention for the Suppression of Unlawful Acts against the Safety of Maritime Navigation.

9 For treaties containing within them systems of *aut dedere aut judicare*.

10 Convention against Torture and Other Cruel, Inhuman or Degrading Treatment or Punishment, UNGA Res 39/46, adopted on 10 December 1984 (Torture Convention of 1984).

11 Inter-American Convention on the Forced Disappearance of Persons, adopted on 6 September 1994 (Inter-American Forced Disappearance Convention of 1994).

12 Convention on the Prevention and Punishment of the Crime of Genocide, UNGA Res 260 (III) A, adopted on 9 December 1948 (Genocide Convention of 1948).

13 Inter-American Convention to Prevent and Punish Torture, adopted on 12 September 1985 (Inter-American Torture Convention of 1985).

14 Some confusion remains, however, about the nature of treaty-based jurisdiction. See, e.g. the Colombian Constitutional Court stating that universal jurisdiction is "explicitly enshrined" in the Genocide Convention of 1948 and the Torture Convention of 1984, Constitutional Court (Colombia), case of *Jaime Enrique Lozano, demanda de inconstitucionalidad contra los artículos 25 y otros del Decreto 2550 por el que se expidió el Código Penal Militar*, no C-358/97, Judgment of 5 August 1997. The case is discussed in Due Process of Law Foundation, *Digest of Latin American Jurisprudence on International Crimes*, Washington DC: Due Process of Law Foundation, 2010, xxviii and xxx. Available online at: www.dplf.org/uploads/128586 1527.pdf.

10.3.2 Mandatory and optional extension of prescriptive jurisdiction and exercise of enforcement jurisdiction

Clearly, in relation to certain crimes, some states have a range of legal duties under treaty obligations with jurisdictional implications. Obligations to criminalize certain conduct and provide penalties under national law,[15] to search actively for persons accused of the conduct and bring them before national courts,[16] to take alleged offenders found on their territory into custody,[17] and to investigate, prosecute or to extradite are well documented in treaty and customary international law.[18]

Outside of treaty regimes, the reliance on mandatory as opposed to optional exercise of enforcement jurisdiction shifts somewhat. In relation to the genocide and torture conventions, it might be argued that their provisions on the obligatory exercise of certain types of jurisdiction have passed into customary international law and so apply to non-members; however, any assertion that these treaties "codified" existing custom relating to jurisdiction is contradicted by the fact that states have tended not to consider themselves bound to assert jurisdiction over crimes committed before they became members of these treaties. If the conduct may be shown to have constituted "an international crime", there is evidence to suggest that the optional exercise of universal jurisdiction in such a situation would not be unlawful under international law.[19]

15 e.g. Genocide Convention of 1948, Art V; International Convention on the Suppression and Punishment of the Crime of Apartheid, UNGA Res 3068 (XXVIII), adopted on 30 November 1973, Art IV (Apartheid Convention of 1973); Torture Convention of 1984, Art 4; Inter-American Torture Convention of 1985, Art 6; and Inter-American Forced Disappearance Convention of 1994, Art 1(b).

16 The Four Geneva Conventions, adopted on 12 August 1949: Convention I, Arts 49–51; Convention II, Arts 50–52; Convention III, Arts 129–131; and Convention IV, Arts 146–148.

17 See, for instance, the Torture Convention of 1984, Art 6(1).

18 For a useful up-to-date review covering customary international law (ICL) duties and relevant human rights obligations, see Ratner, S, Abrahams, J and Bischoff, J, *Accountability for Human Rights Atrocities in International Law*, Oxford: Oxford University Press, 2009. Clear obligations can be found in treaties such as the Genocide Convention of 1948, Arts I, IV and VI, 78 UNTS p 277, and Convention on Torture of 1984, Arts. 4–7; Apartheid Convention of 1973, Arts I, III and IV; and treaty provisions reflecting customary norms: the Four Geneva Conventions of 1949 and their grave breaches provisions: e.g. Convention Relative to the Protection of Civilian Persons in Time of War of 1949, Arts 146–148. For a summary of the customary law position, see Robinson, D, "Serving the Interests of Justice", *European Journal of International Law*, vol 14, 2003, p 481; and Fleck, D, "International Accountability for Violations of the *ius in bello*: the Impact of the ICRC Study on Customary International Law", *Journal of Conflict, Security and Law*, vol 11, 2006, p 179.

19 See International Court of Justice, case of *Arrest Warrant* (*Congo v Belgium*), Judgment of 14 February 1992, separate opinion by Judges Higgins, Kooijmans and Buergenthal, para 45: "That there is no established practice in which States exercise universal jurisdiction, properly so called, is undeniable. As we have seen, virtually all national legislation envisages links of some sort to the forum State; and no case law exists in which pure universal

As to "mandatory" universal jurisdiction, the idea of there being a customary "international duty to prosecute using universal jurisdiction" is largely unfounded:[20] A state may decide to exert jurisdiction and would be considered to be acting legitimately in doing so under customary law in relation to crimes under international law such as piracy, genocide, crimes against humanity and war crimes.[21] However, aside from the grave breaches regime,[22] which requires all states to search for accused persons and bring them to justice and which may be considered to have become part of customary international law, customary law[23] cannot be said to impose any *obligation* on all states to apply universal jurisdiction over all acts of piracy, genocide, crimes against humanity and other war crimes. This is the case whether or not an offender is found on their territory.[24]

jurisdiction has formed the basis of jurisdiction. This does not necessarily indicate, however, that such an exercise would be unlawful." The case currently before the Spanish authorities relating to genocide and other crimes in Guatemala is one example, but the instances of such cases are few.

20 The mistaken belief that all states have the duty (rather than the legal possibility) to exercise universal jurisdiction to prosecute certain crimes such as genocide, and even that such a duty is non-derogable, has arisen in some quarters: see, e.g. the decision of the Spanish Constitutional Court, case of *Guatemalan Genocide*, STC 237/2005, Judgment of 26 September 2005. This appears to have arisen through a misunderstanding of the nature of a *jus cogens* norm of international law. States cannot derogate from the norms prohibiting the commission of genocide, war crimes and crimes against humanity and thereby hope to avoid being liable for committing an internationally wrongful act.

21 The law is still unclear as to the exact scope of violations of international humanitarian law which would authorize a claim of universal jurisdiction; however, at a bare minimum it would include grave breaches of the Geneva Conventions and, almost certainly, the commission in non-international conflicts of the conduct that would constitute a grave breach had it occurred in an international conflict. An argument may also be made that "freestanding" torture (i.e. acts of torture not constituting an act of genocide, a crime against humanity or a war crime) may be a basis for an assertion of universal jurisdiction. See, e.g. the views of an expert group published as *The Princeton Principles on Universal Jurisdiction, Princeton Project on Universal Jurisdiction*, Princeton, NJ: Princeton University Press, 2011. Available online at http://lapa.princeton.edu/hosteddocs/unive_jur.pdf. The Princeton Principles include both slavery and torture.

22 The matter is considered to be still unsettled and untested judicially by Judges Higgins, Kooijmans and Buergenthal, International Court of Justice, the case of *Arrest Warrant* (*Congo v Belgium*), Judgment of 14 February 1992, Separate Opinion, paras 28–32.

23 Whether states have treaty obligations to assert jurisdiction on a number of bases is a different issue, and can easily be determined. Although in practice the regimes of some treaties dealing with international crimes create good systems to ensure "no safe haven" among their parties, requiring them to exercise jurisdiction over persons found on their territory in the absence of any traditional jurisdictional basis, for example, Convention for the Suppression of Unlawful Acts against the Safety of Civil Aviation, adopted on 23 September 1971, p 1151. In these circumstances, the treaty itself functions as the legal basis of jurisdiction, although in essence jurisdiction is universal in the sense that no link between the state and the crime exists.

24 While such an obligation may arise in the future, the current position is stated quite succinctly by Lord Bingham in House of Lords, Opinions of the Lords of Appeals in the case of *Jones & Others v Kingdom of Saudi Arabia* [2006] UKHL 26, para 27: "There is no

The status of "crime under international law" brings with it the ability for any state legally to assert universal jurisdiction over that crime (that is, where it has no link whatsoever to the crime, perpetrator or victim). That status does not provide a legal basis in customary law for an obligation on all states having no such link to use universal jurisdiction to prosecute that crime. Neither is the peremptory nature of the norm prohibiting the criminal conduct definitive here. Such a norm may be *jus cogens*, but this fact does not create a separate customary *jus cogens* norm requiring the exercise of universal jurisdiction.[25] It simply means that the norm outlawing the crime is hierarchically superior to any other conflicting norm in international law (if one could be identified) and that this norm cannot be derogated from on the grounds usually available in international law such as necessity or impossibility. Likewise, the duty not to commit genocide and other international crimes may also be owed by all states to all states (*erga omnes*), but, once again, while the moral imperative may be overwhelming, this is not a sufficient legal basis for the existence of a duty on all states with no other jurisdictional basis to respond to the harm by exercising universal jurisdiction to prosecute it.

Of course, situations will arise where there are different opinions circulating prior to and during an investigation between victims, NGOs, prosecutors, UN agencies and even the media about whether the underlying conduct amounts to a crime which would trigger optional or mandatory jurisdiction. The organization of investigations must not only be done in an impartial manner, but must ensure that the evidence gathering will result in sufficient information to allow the authorities to determine whether or not the conduct prima facie meets the requirements of the elements of "international" crimes or crimes for which domestic law permits extraterritorial (including universal) jurisdiction.

evidence that states have recognised or given effect to an international law obligation to exercise universal jurisdiction over claims arising from alleged breaches of peremptory norms of international law, nor is there any consensus of judicial and learned opinion that they should." If such an obligation did indeed exist, one would be faced with the illogical result that all states not attempting to prosecute the offender or to have him extradited and brought before its authorities would be in violation of international law and as such in theory open to suit. Likewise, all states that have created in their legislation certain requirements for the exercise of universal jurisdiction, such as presence of the offender on their soil, would be in continual breach of international law as would those states that in effect exclude universal jurisdiction for crimes and offenders with no other jurisdictional link. Recent legislative changes put Spain in this category.

25 Whether the creation of such a norm in the future is desirable is outside the scope of this chapter. It may be useful, however, to analyze the scenario in which all states of the globe except those with another basis of jurisdiction were to comply with such a *jus cogens* norm and be forced to open concurrent investigations into every incidence of international crime worldwide. This is obviously impractical. The other logical corollary is that all such states are currently in violation of international law if they are not commencing investigations into those crimes. States' responses to grave breaches allegations since 1949 are surely instructive in this regard.

Crucially this helps decision-makers defend their decision to the relevant parties involved.

10.3.3 Concurrent jurisdiction: methods for determining the forum

The particular situation of interest to this discussion is one in which two or more states have extended their criminal laws over the same facts and persons.[26] As noted above, there will be situations in which one or more of these states may have the legal *obligation* to do so. Guidance may be gained from procedural rules and substantive law developed by the international human rights and international criminal laws and institutions as to the evaluation of investigative efforts in national states and the standards to be applied. However, before turning to those issues, the preliminary question must be answered whether national jurisdictions—and essentially we are talking about judges—will have competence to enter into such evaluations at all.

If proceedings have already begun in another state, domestic courts may be required to stay proceedings. Some systems apply the principle of *lis alibi pendens* (or *lis pendens*), a procedural tool in situations of concurrent jurisdiction allowing a court to refuse to proceed because the same claim is being dealt with before another competent legal forum. It is a "first come first served" notion, designed to avoid the situation where two competent courts come to different judgments about the same issue, and is a corollary of the *res judicata* principle. To trigger the application of *lis pendens* it must be established that the same claim has been presented in another jurisdiction, by and against the same parties, concerning the same facts and having the same objective. The presentation by a victim of a criminal complaint may suffice, although this will be a matter for judicial determination. However, the court has no locus to look behind the existence of proceedings and assess, for example, how appropriate the other forum will be for dealing with the matter.

In other jurisdictions such as the United Kingdom and the United States, a defendant might plead *forum non conveniens*, a procedural tool originally from Scotland,[27] which can have the same effect. A court can stay proceedings if it

26 This comment does not address the jurisdiction of human rights bodies, although decisions on the exercise of criminal jurisdiction (by states or international or internationalized criminal courts) can have consequences for admissibility to those organs. In addition, if a state decides that it cannot act in relation to serious crimes (say because its infrastructure is destroyed, or security or resource reasons make it impossible) but actively co-operates with the authorities of another jurisdiction to investigate and prosecute crime, can this be considered a discharge of its obligations under a human rights treaty regime to provide a remedy?

27 It was later developed in the United States and replaced the older rule of *lis pendens* from English law through the decision of the House of Lords, case of *The Atlantic Star* [1974] AC 436 (on appeal from [1973] QB, see pp 381–388; *MacShannon v Rockware Glass Ltd* [1987] AC 795, conforming the place of *forum non conveniens* in English law in 1984 in the case of *The Abidin Daver* [1984] AC 398.

determines that another forum is more appropriate, taking into account factors that are related to the private interests of the parties[28] and the public interests of the state. A useful outline of the approach can be found in the UK House of Lords decision *Spiliada Maritime Corp v Cansulex Ltd*:[29] judges will decline jurisdiction where a trial elsewhere is more suitable for the interests of all parties and the benefit of justice. These terms are of course fairly vague and so factors to be taken into account in determining "suitability" were fleshed out somewhat by Lord Goff including the availability of witnesses, the law applicable, the residence of the parties or place where they carry on business, the possibility to obtain justice in the foreign jurisdiction and any special competence or expertise that a particular court has which would be relevant. In a later case, Goff emphasized that the availability of *pro bono* legal representation is irrelevant, and the personal or judicial advantage for an individual plaintiff of one system over another is not decisive: only if it can be established that "substantial justice cannot be done" in a more appropriate forum will the court refuse to stay the proceedings.[30] The *onus* is on the person asserting the plea of *forum non conveniens* to show that another more suitable forum is available, and decisions are made on a case-by-case basis.

The major difference between the two tools is crucial for this discussion: *forum non conveniens* builds in a discretionary element for the judge, *lis pendens* does not. It is submitted that, notwithstanding the legal certainty provided by the *lis pendens* rule, its drawbacks and the advantages of the *forum non conveniens* approach justify a compromise position, but one which allows a stay of proceedings[31] (which can later be lifted if necessary) rather than a final declination of jurisdiction. Such an approach, if applied to situations of multiple jurisdiction claims over acts constituting international crimes or serious human rights abuses, would be beneficial and in harmony with current international law.

First, in the sphere of international criminal law and more so in the field of international human rights law, the issue of the quality of criminal proceedings and not their mere existence is a live one. Not only do human rights treaties protect the substantive rights of victims to remedies that are "effective", their admissibility systems embrace the application of standards to domestic remedies on offer. While conceptually the principle of *forum non conveniens* does not address effectiveness among the factors to be weighed, the approach (judicial discretion

28 In criminal matters, it might be argued that the parties include not only the accused, but also the victim(s).

29 *Spiliada Maritime Corp v Cansulex Ltd* [1986] 3 WLR 972, 3 All ER 843, [1987] AC 460.

30 *Connelly v RTZ Corp* [1998] AC 854 at 872. See Kennett, W, "Forum non conveniens in Europe", *Cambridge Law Journal*, vol 54, 1995, p 552, and the useful review of recent developments by Pistis, M, "Forum non Conveniens", in Judicium, *Civil Procedure in Italy and Europe*, available online at http://judicium.it/news/pistis01.html.

31 An analogous concept exists in Scotland, where a prosecutor can ask the court to desert proceedings *pro loco et tempore* (as opposed to *simpliciter*) and can later be reactivated at another time and/or place.

based on applying a range of relevant factors and working on a case-by-case basis) is likely to coexist more appropriately with international human rights law and an emerging system of complementarity in international criminal law.

Secondly, it may be said that the policy aim states are advancing when they extend their jurisdiction extraterritorially over crimes of the utmost seriousness to the international community has been to fill gaps that have allowed those responsible for such crimes to evade justice in the past. The effect of jurisdictional decisions therefore goes far beyond avoiding contradictory judgments and preservation of *res judicata*. Declining jurisdiction under the *lis pendens* rule presupposes that there will be a judicial resolution of the matter in the other forum. However, as practice has shown, states whose own agents are accused of such acts may never complete criminal investigations and trial proceedings against certain persons, thereby leaving the issue unresolved. The discretion to suspend proceedings temporarily pending progress by another state, and reactivate them should no such progress be evident, is a clear advantage, all the more so in cases where one or more states may have a continuing international obligation to investigate.

The Guatemalan case has not yet resolved the question of the procedural life-span of concurrent investigations. At the moment, both Guatemalan and Spanish authorities continue to investigate the same crimes.[32] It remains to be seen, for example, what attitude the Spanish authorities will take if the national prosecuting authorities in Guatemala, under the newly appointed Attorney General,[33] can make significant progress in prosecuting these same crimes. The return of Argentine accused Ricardo Cavallo from Spain to stand trial in Argentina may offer guidance and indicates the need for flexibility in states seeking to apply universal and extraterritorial jurisdiction to changes of circumstances in the territorial state rendering prosecution there feasible. Indeed, independently of the arguments of international comity, in situation of transition it is all the more important that if the national state can deal with such cases, then it should do so. The demonstration of action against former powerful human rights abusers can have a dramatic effect on building local confidence and strengthening institutions.[34] This is sensible, and as noted above, positively beneficial in a transitional situation if, as in Argentina, the courts can function adequately at a future date.

32 On 16 January 2008, the *Audiencia Nacional* decided to continue its criminal investigations related to the Guatemalan genocide. See Audiencia Nacional, Juzgado Central de Instrucción no 1, Diligencias Previas 331/1999, Auto Decision of 16 January 2008.

33 Claudia Paz and Paz Bailey, appointed in December 2010.

34 Judges from the Democratic Republic of Congo commented on the positive effects in the local population's confidence in the judiciary following even the very first detentions of leaders of armed groups for minor common crimes in Ituri. See Human Rights Watch, *Making Justice Work: Restoration of the Legal System in Ituri*, New York: DRC Human Rights Watch, 2004, pp 4–5.

The application of such a flexible approach would be enhanced if courts were required *ex propio motu* to consider competing jurisdictional claims,[35] rather than the issue being dependent on the accused, prosecution or civil party entering a preliminary plea. Failing this, such pleas should be admissible only up to a specified procedural event.

Thirdly, the factors to be taken into account in applying a *forum non conveniens* approach reflect a very different idea of court proceedings than would be ordinarily relevant in a civil law jurisdiction, for example the location of witnesses and other evidence and the costs of transporting these to a foreign jurisdiction. However, the emerging system of international criminal procedure, which draws on all legal traditions, adopts an accusatorial character at the trial stage and takes an approach to evidence which favours the presence of witnesses, physical and documentary evidence in court. The participation of victims and families in the criminal process including at investigative stage, and their presence in court, is increasingly considered as a necessary component of war crimes trials.

Finally, the type of discretionary power implicit in *forum non conveniens* is also more akin to international human rights and criminal procedure. Procedural rules on the exhaustion of domestic remedies before a case can be admitted for consideration by human rights organs require judges to assess the adequacy of legal avenues of recourse open to victims. Such discretion is echoed to an extent in the Rome Statute rules of admissibility,[36] albeit in relation to a decision to decline jurisdiction for reasons not relating to jurisdiction, but to overriding reasons for not proceeding, even where no alternative forum is being offered.

In terms of formal regulation of an approach to use in situations of concurrence, resources are few. Even those treaties dealing specifically with jurisdiction, such as the Torture Convention of 1984, offer little guidance where more than one state has a treaty-based ground of jurisdiction over the same event and suspect. To date, developments in general mutual assistance treaties in Europe on civil and commercial matters seem to have formalized the use of a *lis pendens* approach rather than *forum non conveniens*,[37] although those develop-

35 Such as in the commencement of the trial phase.

36 In addition to situations where there is an insufficient legal or factual basis to seek a warrant or summons, or where the case is inadmissible under Art 17 of the Rome Statute (another state is investigating or prosecuting or has legitimately decided not to prosecute, where the person has already been tried or the case is of insufficient gravity), the prosecutor may decide nonetheless that a prosecution is not in the interests of justice. The Pre-Trial Chamber may review such a decision and if it decides to review, is the ultimate arbiter of the issue.

37 See in particular Arts 27 and 28 of European Council Regulation (EC) No 44/2001, On Jurisdiction and the Recognition and Enforcement of Judgments in Civil and Commercial Matters, 22 December 2000, which entered into force in March 2002 and followed the Convention on Jurisdiction and the Enforcement of Judgments in Civil and Commercial Matters, adopted on 27 September 1968, and the Convention on Jurisdiction and the Enforcement of Judgments in Civil and Commercial Matters, adopted on 16 September

ments relate only to jurisdictional overlap between EU Member States. In the criminal sphere of mutual assistance no guidance has been formalized: regional and international treaties leave matters to the national jurisdictions to determine,[38] although bilateral treaties on extradition can have the effect of creating a pre-eminence for one jurisdiction in cases of concurrence such as, for example, the controversial treaty between the United Kingdom and the United States, which entered into force in 2003. Moves towards incorporating *forum non conveniens* approaches into the *lis pendens* principle can, however, be seen in the proposed Hague Convention on International Jurisdiction and Foreign Judgments in Civil and Commercial Matters (draft Hague Convention).[39] The draft convention states that courts shall take into account factors such as inconvenience to the parties, nature and location of evidence and procedures for obtaining it, limitation or prescriptive periods, possibility and recognition and enforcement of decisions on the merits. It is hoped that this tendency will be welcomed as a useful approach to dealing with domestic prosecution of international crimes. Some courts are already taking the first steps in that direction.

The approach taken by the Spanish courts in the *Guatemalan Genocide* case, as well as in the cases concerning Chile and Argentina, is of particular interest. The criminal chamber of the *Audiencia Nacional* in its decision of 27 April 2000 adopted something of a "wait and see" approach, ostensibly giving the territorial state an opportunity to act.[40] One of the reasons given was that, contrary to the prevailing positions in Chile and Argentina, Guatemala's legislation expressly allowed for the prosecution of the international crimes, including genocide. Furthermore, the court noted that the complainant's case was first presented in

1988. Section 27 of the Council Regulation of 2001 relates to proceedings involving the same cause of action and same parties and offers no discretion to the judge: "any court other than the court first seized *shall* of its own motion stay its proceedings until such time as the jurisdiction of the court first seized is established"; and "where the jurisdiction of the court first seized is established, any other court . . . *shall* decline jurisdiction in favour of that court" (emphasis added). Section 28, dealing with "related" proceedings (those so closely connected that it is expedient to hear and determine them together to avoid the risk of irreconcilable judgments) offers discretion: "any court other than the first seized *may* stay its proceedings" (emphasis added), but does not offer guidance on how to exercise that discretion.

38 Neither the European Convention on Mutual Assistance in Criminal Matters, Council of Europe ETS No 030, adopted on 20 April 1959; nor the UN Model Treaty on Mutual Assistance in Criminal Matters, UN Doc A/RES/45/117, adopted by the UN General Assembly on 14 December 1990; subsequently amended by Mutual Assistance and International Co-operation in Criminal Matters, UN Doc A/RES/53/112, adopted by the UN General Assembly on 20 January 1999, opt for a particular method of priority among concurrent jurisdictions. The Inter-American Convention on Mutual Assistance in Criminal Matters and Asean Treaty on Mutual Legal Assistance in Criminal Matters, adopted by the OAS General Assembly on 23 May 1992, equally make no provision on the matter.

39 Available online at www.hcch.net.

40 Audiencia Nacional, Juzgado Central de Instrucción no 1, Auto Decision of 27 April 2000.

Spain based on facts that had been made public only some months earlier and in any event was not accompanied by any prior judicial decision from Guatemala rejecting the case. Aside from the questionable grasp of the facts behind this reasoning,[41] the approach would seem to be partially positive in that it suggests that the jurisdiction first seized of the matter does not necessarily have pre-eminence if undue delay or legislative impediment can be demonstrated. It is submitted, however, that the requirement of a formal judicial rejection renders the overall formula unacceptable,[42] since impunity would be guaranteed simply through interminable delay with no formal procedural endpoint.[43]

The Spanish Supreme Court and Constitutional Court both discuss the approach of the *Audiencia Nacional* and the "subsidiarity principle".[44] Aspects of the *Audiencia Nacional* approach resemble something akin to the Rome Statute idea of complementarity, although applying lower thresholds of ability and willingness. In considering the complainants' appeal, the Spanish Supreme Court unfortunately rejected the application of universal jurisdiction in the case and required linkage with Spain. It takes a view (similar to that which it adopted shortly afterwards in the case of the *Peruvian Genocide*)[45] rejecting the subsidiarity approach and pointing out that it requires Spanish courts to judge the actions of their foreign peers with the attendant diplomatic and political consequences. Instead, it opts for a seemingly logical idea of "necessary judicial intervention". This prioritizes the territorial jurisdiction unless the inactivity or ineffective nature of the proceedings in the territorial state is demonstrated (again, akin to a complementarity test).[46] To the extent that it treats universal

41 The facts of the major incidents had been known in the public domain internationally since at least the mid-1980s, and state prosecutors have a duty to open investigations *ex oficio* for the types of crimes involved. The delay and inactivity can certainly be demonstrated to have been excessive. See, e.g. Falla, R, "Genocidio en Guatemala: Visión del pueblo indígena de genocidio que sufre", in *Tribunal permanente de los pueblos, Sesión Guatemala, Madrid 27 al 31 de enero de 1983*, Madrid: Iepalam, 1984. See also the AAAS full name background source list. Available online at http://shr.aaas.org/guatemala/ciidh/qr/english/part7.html.

42 Likewise, any requirement that the complainant has the burden of proving the impossibility of future prosecution in the territorial state.

43 In this particular case the Guatemalan authorities obliging with a Constitutional Court ruling in December 2007 rejecting outright Spain's claim to jurisdiction as a legal basis for enforcement acts has only served to increase the legitimacy of a continuing Spanish investigation.

44 See Tribunal Supremo, Sala de lo Penal, STS 327/2003, Judgment of 25 February 2003 and Tribunal Constitucional, STC 237/2005, Judgment of 26 September 2005.

45 Tribunal Supremo, Sala de lo Penal, STS-345/2005, Judgment of 18 March 2005.

46 Given the lack of positive guidance from international instruments or customary rules, reference has been made instead to scholarly pronouncements. These are said to favour a complementary relationship with other jurisdictional bases. See, e.g. Institute of International Law, *Universal Criminal Jurisdiction with Regard to the Crime of Genocide, Crimes against Humanity and War Crimes*, 17th Commission, Krakow session, Res III 2005, adopted on 26 August 2005, available online at www.idi-iil.org/idiE/resolutionsE/2005_kra_03_en.pdf.

jurisdiction in practice as a "last resort", there would appear to be very little daylight between this and the way in which the *Audiencia Nacional* seem to define "subsidiarity".

The Constitutional Court rejected the lower courts' requirements of linkage on the basis that domestic statute[47] does not expressly exclude the application of universal jurisdiction,[48] but the discussion on the principle of "subsidiarity" in the Guatemalan case surfaced again.[49] The Supreme Court minority had taken the view that the "principle" was unknown in domestic law, absent from the Genocide Convention of 1948 and in any case incompatible with the concept of universal jurisdiction if the goal of avoiding impunity was to be achieved. Instead, the dissenters favoured concurrence as the guiding principle of the application of universal jurisdiction. While indicating a preference for "concurrence", the Constitutional Court fails to spell out what that would entail, save for the guidance that what is not prohibited in domestic legislation is therefore lawful. This only serves to bolster the need for some *forum non conveniens* type of criteria, and begs two questions. Until what moment can concurrent proceedings continue and on the basis of which criteria can one of them be halted? Should a parallel investigation take place to obtain information to enable the court to apply those criteria?

The Spanish Constitutional Court does not give a sufficiently fleshed out answer merely stating that, in applying the concurrence principle,[50] and to avoid duplication of efforts, priority should be accorded based on legal policy considerations. However, it does go on to restate the issue of inactivity, this time as a criteria for prioritization: "Serious and reasonable indications of judicial inactivity that would demonstrate an absence of will or capacity to effectively prosecute the crimes."[51] How would a court apply the Spanish Constitutional Court's test as it relates to inactivity due to lack of will or ability? Is inactivity without sufficient explanation prima facie linked to lack of will or ability?

The move towards a complementary approach is, at least, a positive step.[52] The criminal investigation must therefore be accompanied by information gathering regarding the procedure and context of the foreign proceedings. Judges will then be required to weigh that information as evidence of inactivity

47 *Ley Organica 6/1985 del Poder Judicial* (Organic Law on the Judicial Branch), 1 July 1985, Art 23.4.

48 It unfortunately repeats the confusion regarding the *jus cogens* nature of customary norms on universal jurisdiction, but this does not interfere with its legislative interpretation.

49 Tribunal Constitucional (Second Chamber), STC 235/2005, Judgment of 26 September 2005.

50 Concurrence is not so much a principle (in the sense of a guiding maxim) as it is a legal situation: more than one state may lawfully assert jurisdiction over crime and perpetrator.

51 Author's translation of original text: "indicios serios y razonables de la inactividad judicial que viniera a acreditar una falta ya de voluntad ya de capacidad para la persecución efectiva de los crímenes".

52 See section 10.4 below on extradition.

and whether it demonstrates lack of will or capacity. It is important to note that application of criteria for exercise of universal (or extraterritorial) jurisdiction, or for the prioritization of proceedings where concurrence exists, does not mean that courts are determining the competence of foreign (or international) courts and authorities in their domestic decision-making in the sense of legal competence,[53] but it may require them to evaluate their professional competence and good faith. Is there a less controversial option?

10.3.4 Towards criteria for prioritization between concurrent jurisdictions

The ongoing work by the International Law Commission's Working Group on the issue of *aut dedere aut judicare* will be of crucial guidance.[54] In the meantime, an interesting approach suggested by Canadian courts[55] to resolve choices of treaty-based "extradite or prosecute" might usefully be adapted and extended to encompass situations of concurrent national jurisdictions for the crime types discussed here. In theory at least, these objective criteria, while not absolutely value-neutral, may offer a less politically charged test than requiring a domestic bench (as opposed to an international judge ruling on the system of a state party who has signed up to a complementarity system)[56] to reach a finding that a foreign legal system is unwilling or unable to prosecute. According to this approach factors[57] to be taken into account would be:

- where was the impact of the offence felt or likely to have been felt;
- which jurisdiction has the greatest interest in prosecuting the offence;
- which police force (or other legal authority) played the major role in the development of the case;
- which jurisdiction has laid charges;
- which jurisdiction has the most comprehensive case;
- which jurisdiction is ready to proceed to trial;

53 It is quite clear that the issue of *kompetenz kompetenz* remains with the national court in question, a point made clear in the Mexican proceedings against Cavallo. See Suprema Corte de Justicia de la Nacion (Mexico), *Appeal on Constitutional Remedy*, Ricardo Miguel Cavallo, Case No 140/2002, 10 June 2003, Dissenting Opinion: MP Humberto Román Palacios.

54 See further www.un.org/law/ilc/.

55 Court of Queen's Bench of Manitoba (Canada), case of *Swystun v United States of America*, decision of 30 October 1988, 40, CCC (3d) 222, at 227–228, cited by Plachta, M in "Contemporary Problems of Extradition: Human Rights, Grounds for Refusal and the Principle Aut Dedere Aut Judicare", Visiting Experts Paper of the United Nations Asia and Far East Institute for the Prevention of Crime and the Treatment of Offenders (UNAFEI), 114th International Training Course, *Resource Material Series No 57*.

56 Or making such a determination on non-state party with the weight of a Security Council referral.

57 Additions in parenthesis are the author's.

- where is the evidence located;
- whether the evidence is mobile;
- the number of accused involved and whether they can be gathered together in one place for trial;
- in what jurisdiction were most of the acts in furtherance of the crime committed;
- the nationality and residence of the accused; and
- the severity of the sentence the accused is likely to receive in each jurisdiction.

To these, extradition expert Michael Plachta adds:

- whether the prosecution would be equally effective in the other forum given its domestic law and international instruments for co-operation in criminal matters.

One might also add to this, particularly in a transitional justice context if there is a need to reconstruct trust between state and citizen:[58]

- the nationality and residence of the victims and their families.

The factors applied in this *forum non conveniens* type approach already include several that are objectively ascertainable and directly related to the investigative phase: the availability of witnesses and documents, the nature and location of evidence and procedures for obtaining it. That said, some factors are more general and potentially controversial, such as "which jurisdiction has the greatest interest in prosecuting the offence". Other factors not listed above, but sometimes applied in this approach, could require the examination of the capacity and willingness of a foreign jurisdiction depending on how they were interpreted, for example "any special competence or expertise" that a particular court has, and the possibility that "substantial justice cannot be done".[59]

10.3.5 Incorporating the likelihood of an "effective investigation" as a factor?

One of the factors listed above is effectiveness. More precisely, it is a comparative effectiveness, consisting of comparing the two or more jurisdictions seeking to prosecute the case. Should a foreign court incorporate such a factor how might it reduce the sensitive nature of a ruling that its own

58 This will not always be the case. In a transition from war to peace between states, or between a state and rebel movement, the civilian population of each country may have been victimized not by their own state, but by the forces of the opponent.

59 See *Spiliada Maritime Corp v Cansulex Ltd* [1986] 3 WLR 972, 3 All ER 843, [1987] AC 460; and the Hague Convention.

system is likely to produce a more effective investigation than that of another country? One point worth making is the need to avoid any presumption that greater experience in the investigation and higher quality of skill is necessarily concentrated in developed countries (or in the international rather than national prosecutions bodies).

The goal of improving international co-operation in the prevention and prosecution of crimes of concern to the international community as a whole, and the principles governing relations between states would demand that any such judicial enquiry into the adequacy of criminal investigations in a foreign jurisdiction be made on the basis of legitimate and transparent criteria. Bearing that in mind, as to standards of "effectiveness", various sources of guidance may be offered, among them:

(a) The International Criminal Court (ICC) "admissibility standard". In other words, this would mean equating unwillingness or inability with ineffectiveness. Domestic proceedings under way to investigate or prosecute a case may only be found inadequate by the court where the state carrying them out is "unwilling" or "genuinely unable" to do so. The complementarity system may be said to set a very low bar for domestic systems to meet. Since, to demonstrate unwillingness, it must be demonstrated that the national proceedings or decision was intended to shield the person from criminal responsibility, that there has been such an unjustified delay that it is inconsistent with an intention to bring the person to justice, or that the proceedings are or were not conducted independently or impartially to an extent that this again was inconsistent with an intention to bring the person to justice. To demonstrate inability, it must be shown that the state cannot obtain custody of the accused or the evidence and testimony required because its legal system has suffered a total or substantial collapse or is otherwise unavailable.[60] Inability due to lack of resources or training where there is no system collapse would not meet this test.

(b) A human rights law admissibility standard. For example, the exceptions to the requirement for exhausting domestic remedies as set out in Article 46.2 of the American Convention on Human Rights and later developed in the case law of the Inter-American Court: (i) the domestic legislation of the state concerned does not afford due process of law for the protection of the right or rights that have allegedly been violated; (ii) the party alleging violation of his rights has been denied access to remedies under domestic law or has been prevented from exhausting them; or (iii) there has been an unwarranted delay in rendering a final judgment under the aforementioned remedies. European[61] and American

60 Rome Statute of the International Criminal Court, adopted on 17 July 1998, Art 17.

61 In relation to exhaustion of domestic remedies under Art 26 of the European Convention on Human Rights, the European case law takes a similar stance, e.g. there is no obligation to have recourse to remedies which are inadequate or ineffective. In addition, according to the "generally recognised rules of international law" to which Art 26 makes reference, there may be special circumstances that absolve the applicant from the obligation to exhaust the domestic remedies at his disposal. The rule is also inapplicable where an

human rights organs concur that a domestic remedy must be suitable to address an infringement of a legal right[62] and "effective" that is, capable of producing the result for which it was designed.[63] Judges make determinations on a case-by-case basis.

(c) A human rights law standard for substantive or procedural violations. The human rights organs in their determinations on the merits of cases before them have defined a much more thorough and detailed range of requirements for an effective remedy as a stand-alone human right[64] and for procedural violations of the right to life and freedom from torture[65] (the implied duty to investigate alleged violations of this type encompassed in the general obligation to guarantee respect for protected right).

In terms of the case law on procedural violations, the bar set for domestic proceedings is a much higher one than, for example, the ICC admissibility test. An "effective investigation" must meet certain standards. The European Court of Human Rights jurisprudence (reflecting broadly agreed international

administrative practice consisting of a repetition of acts incompatible with the Convention and official tolerance by the state authorities has been shown to exist, and is of such a nature as to make proceedings futile or ineffective. See the above-mentioned ECtHR, case of *Akdivar and Others*, App 21893/93, Judgment of 16 September 1996, paras 66 and 67; ECtHR, case of *Aksoy v Turkey*, App 21987/93, Judgment of 18 December 1996, para 46; and ECtHR, case of *Yaşa v Turkey*, App 22495/93, Judgment of 2 September 1993.

62 IACtHR, case of *Velásquez Rodríguez v Honduras*, Series C No 4, Judgment of 29 July 1988.

63 *Velásquez Rodríguez v Honduras*, para. 66. When it is shown that remedies are denied for trivial reasons or without an examination of the merits, or if there is proof of the existence of a practice or policy ordered or tolerated by the government, the effect is to impede certain persons from invoking internal remedies that would normally be available to others. In such cases, resort to those remedies becomes a senseless formality. Ibid, para 68.

64 e.g. Arts 8 and 25 of the American Convention on Human Rights and Art 13 of the European Convention on Human Rights.

65 Implied within Art 1(1) of the American Convention and Arts 2 and 3 of the European Convention on Human Rights. A substantive violation occurs when actions of omissions attributable to the state directly cause the prohibited conduct or prevent the enjoyment of a right. A procedural violation relates not to the state's responsibility for causing death or injury, but for failing to prevent it or failing to respond adequately afterwards. ECtHR, case of *Ireland v UK*, App 5310/71, Judgment of 18 January 1978, para 118; ECtHR, case of *McCann v UK*, App 18984/91, Judgment of 27 September 1995, para 161; ECtHR, case of *Osman v United Kingdom*, App 23452/94, Judgment of 28 October 1998, para 128; ECtHR, case of *Kaya v Turkey*, App 22729/93, Judgment of 19 February 1998, para 105; ECtHR, case of *Orhan v Turkey*, App 25656/94, Judgment of 18 June 2002, para 348. In relation to procedural violations, the European Court of Human Rights places the burden on the state to show that has carried out an adequate investigation. See ECtHR, case of *Ireland v UK*, App 5310/71, Judgment of 18 January 1978, para 118. In the Inter-American system, see IACtHR, case of *Barrios Altos v Peru*, Series C No 75, Judgment of 15 March 2001, para 43: "In the light of the general obligations established in Articles 1(1) and 2 of the American Convention, the States Parties are obliged to take all measures to ensure that no one is deprived of judicial protection and the exercise of the right to a simple and effective recourse, in the terms of Articles 8 and 25 of the Convention."

standards[66] relevant for the present discussion) requires that for an investigation to be effective:

i. state authorities themselves, and not families or victims, initiate the investigation as soon as the alleged violation comes to their attention;[67]
ii. the persons who carry out and/or are in charge of the investigation must be not only hierarchically but practically independent from those alleged to have been responsible;[68]
iii. the investigation must be *capable of* identifying and punishing those responsible, which means that the authorities must have taken reasonable steps available to them to secure evidence, including eye witness testimony and forensic evidence,[69] and the investigation should seek to determine whether any pattern or practice may have brought about the death;[70]
iv. the investigation must be begun promptly and carried out within a reasonable timescale[71] even if obstacles prevent progress due to the situation; and finally

66 The European Court of Human Rights and Inter-American Court of Human Rights refer in this regard to the Principles on the Effective Prevention and Investigation of Extra-legal, Arbitrary and Summary Executions, ECOSOC Resolution 1989/65, adopted on 24 May 1989, principle 9; and the UN Manual on the Effective Prevention and investigation of extra-legal, arbitrary and summary executions. Model Protocol for a Legal Investigation of Extra-legal, Arbitrary and Summary Execution ("Minnesota Protocol"), UN Doc E/ST/CSDHA/.12 (1991). See, e.g. ECtHR, *McKerr v UK*, App 28883/95, Judgment of 4 May 2011; and IAComHR, *Victor Hernandez Vasquez v El Salvador*, case 10.228, Decision of 13 April 1999, Report No 65/99, CHR, OEA/Ser.L/V/II.95 Doc 7 rev at 512 (1998).

67 ECtHR, *Shanaghan v UK*, App 37715/97, Judgment of 4 May 2001, para 88.

68 ECtHR, *Güleç v Turkey* (54/1997/838/1044), Judgment of 24 April 1998, Reports of Judgments and Decisions 1998-IV, paras 81–82.

69 ECtHR, *McKerr v UK*, App 28883/95, Judgment of 4 May 2001, para 113; and ECtHR, *Kaya v Turkey*, App 22729/93, Judgment of 19 February 1998, Reports of Judgments and Decisions, 1998-I, p 324, para 87.

70 *McKerr v UK*.

71 In IACtHR, case of *La Cantuta v Peru*, Series C No 162, Judgment of 29 November 2006, para 149: "The right to justice includes assurance within reasonable time of the right of alleged victims or their relatives to have every necessary step taken to know the truth and punish those responsible for the events", citing IACtHR, case of the *"Mapiripan" Massacre v Colombia*, Series C No 134, Judgment of 15 September 2005, para 216; IACtHR, case of the *Serrano-Cruz Sisters v El Salvador*, Series C No 131, Judgment of 1 March 2005, para 66; and IACtHR, case of *19 Tradesmen v Colombia*, Series C No 109, Judgment of 5 July 2004, para 188. In relation to timescale, the court points out that three aspects must be taken into account to determine the reasonableness of the time within which a case is carried out: (a) the complexity of the matter; (b) the procedural activities carried out by the interested party; and (c) the conduct of judicial authorities, in IACtHR, case of *Vargas-Areco v Paraguay*, Series C No 155, Judgment of 26 September 2005, para 102; IACtHR, case of *Ximenes-Lopes v Brazil*, Series C No 149, Judgment of 4 July 2006, para 196, and IACtHR, case of *García-Asto and Ramírez-Rojas v Peru*, Series C No 137, Judgment of 25 November 2005, para 166. Similarly, ECtHR, case of *Wimmer v Germany*, App 60534/00, Judgment of 24 May 2005, para 23; ECtHR, case of *Panchenko v Russia*, App 45100/98, Judgment of 8 February 2005, para 129, and ECtHR, case of *Todorov v Bulgaria*, App 39832/98, Judgment of 18 January 2005, para 45.

v. the investigation must be open to a sufficient degree of public scrutiny and must involve the victim's next of kin in the procedure to the extent necessary to safeguard their rights.

In terms of a substantive violation of the right to an effective remedy (or judicial guarantees in the language of the Inter-American Convention),[72] the European Court position is that the remedy must be capable of enforcing the substance of the Convention rights and freedoms in whatever form they might happen to be secured in the domestic legal order. In relation to remedies for breaches of the right to life and personal integrity, such a remedy would require payment of compensation where appropriate, and a thorough and effective investigation.[73] The requirements of an effective remedy are therefore broader than procedural obligations to conduct an effective investigation.[74] They are not a complete solution to judges' reticence about assessing foreign legal systems, but do provide a point of departure that is based in existing law and practice.

Since decisions about criminal jurisdiction will often occur at the beginning or early stage of the investigative phase, it would be more appropriate to apply (b), an admissibility-type test, than hold the national system to the full range of required standards of an effective investigation or the wider right to an effective remedy applied by human rights organs in determinations on the merits. A jurisdictional test necessarily has a prospective element to it, that is to say, it involves a judicial determination of appropriateness of aspects of future proceedings, rather than an *ex post facto* examination of circumstances that have already occurred. It is to be hoped that further developments (whether legislative, judicial or diplomatic) will lead to broad agreement among states as to the approach and types of standards to be applied to jurisdictional conflict.

10.3.6 Other procedural questions

Classifications of crimes start to appear and to have legal and practical effects relatively early in the process, for example in initial complaints lodged by victims or investigations opened *ex propio motu* by the state, later in arrest warrant, extradition and interim liberation proceedings. A jurisdictional determination in a foreign state (or decisions relating to extradition requests, as discussed below)

72 Note that while the right to these guarantees in the American Convention is non-derogable, while the right to a remedy is not among the non-derogable rights in the European Convention on Human Rights and the International Covenant on Civil and Political Rights.

73 See ECtHR, case of *Anguelova v Bulgaria*, App 38361/97, Judgment of 13 June 2002, paras 161–162; ECtHR, case of *Assenov and Others v Bulgaria*, App 90/1997/874/1086, Judgment of 28 October 1998, para 114; and ECtHR, case of *Süheyla Aydın v Turkey*, App 25660/94, Judgment of 24 May 2005, para 208.

74 See ECtHR, case of *Orhan v Turkey*, App 25656/94, Judgment of 18 June 2002, para 384; and ECtHR, case of *Khashiyev and Akayeva v Russia*, Apps 57942/00 and 57945/0, Judgment of 24 February 2005, para 183.

may take place at a stage at which the authorities of another state investigating the matter have not yet formalized a charge and the only description of what crime the conduct might amount to appears in a victim's complaint.

Timing is also crucial since jurisdictional determinations domestically can have a dramatic effect on how investigations proceed, and vice versa. Taking an example from the purely national sphere, the criminal complaints in the *AJR Guatemalan Genocide Cases*[75] related to individual criminal participation of high-level perpetrators alleged to have occurred in the state and military headquarters in the capital city, leading to massacres all over the country. They were presented to the capital city authorities. At one stage in the proceedings, the investigative judge decided to deal with the complaint as a series of separate crimes, the *locus* of each being the village where the massacre took place. He promptly tried to divide the complaint accordingly and send its constituent parts to a range of local prosecutors and judges making for a fragmented approach to investigation and huge co-ordination hurdles. Actions of this type reduce the likelihood of indicting a crime of scale (particularly one with arguments of knowledge and intent based partly on inferences from the fact patterns) and the chances of proceeding against persons involved at the highest levels. Jurisdictional decisions can therefore be a means to impede investigations, sometimes deliberately.

The ease with which a foreign jurisdiction can obtain evidence may emerge as a key factor for timing and for classification of crimes. Perhaps the case of the *Guatemalan Genocide* is indicative of a similar tendency in territorial states. Rather than the official authorities proactively investigating the crimes, reliance is placed primarily on information from local NGOs that have gathered and presented evidence domestically.[76] As well as investigating genocide, Guatemalan NGOs[77] had compiled evidence of crimes of disappearance throughout the conflict.[78] Foreign states may be loath to dedicate scarce resources within their justice sector

75 Two complaints were lodged in 2000 and 2001 before the national authorities by the *Asociación de Justicia y Reconcilación*, survivors from over 20 indigenous villages against former presidents, ministers of defence, chiefs of staff and junta members of the Lucas Garcia and Rios Montt military regimes. They alleged genocide, crimes against humanity and war crimes as included in the 1973 Guatemalan Criminal Code and were legally represented by a group of lawyers from the local NGO, the *Centro para Acción Legal en Derechos Humanos* (CALDH) of which the author of this chapter was a member.

76 Since 1997 CALDH had been gathering evidence on a sample of over 20 massacres, identifying, locating and interviewing eyewitnesses to the central crimes of the 1981–1983 period. Prior to giving statements in Madrid, Guatemalan eyewitnesses and other survivors of the massacres had already made formal statements to national prosecutors giving their evidence of the killings, torture, rape and property destruction suffered by them and their families. CALDH also commissioned expert reports for the Guatemalan authorities on a range of issues and requested out-takes from documentary film footage taken during the period.

77 Particularly the *Grupo de Apoyo Mutuo* and *Familias de los Desaparecidos de Guatemala*.

78 Although the complaint (*querella*) presented in Spain covers the crimes of the entire conflict period, it is on these samples of crimes already well documented by local groups that the Spanish authorities are focusing their follow up and investigation strategy.

budgets to such cases. The case illustrates the successful cross-jurisdictional use of evidence obtained by national civil society groups in both countries and successful co-operation between these and foreign judges.[79]

Quandaries may also arise at the procedural stage as to whether the proceedings in a foreign jurisdiction consists of the same *actus reus* and may lead to the indictment of the same individuals. Recent developments from the ICC in relation to admissibility opt for a useful formulation in defining "case" as consisting of specific accused and a specific *crime* within the jurisdiction of the court. The court points out that for the purposes of determining admissibility, it would only decline jurisdiction if the national system is investigating or prosecuting the same accused for the same *conduct*. However, it is not necessary that the charge be identical. The conduct may be charged in other terms. By extension, it would appear logical that the impossibility in one national jurisdiction of charging the conduct as an international crime such as a war crime, rather than, for instance, murder, would not be a legitimate factor. Not so the form of responsibility if, as happens in some states, domestic law does not cover the kind of participation involved (for example, command responsibility).

10.4 Extradition

Requests for extradition will ordinarily be issued only once any jurisdictional issues have been resolved. However, in the requested state, judicial examination of jurisdiction may occur for the first time on receipt of such a request, or an accused once extradited may challenge the jurisdiction of the court before which he is brought. In any case, the classification of the conduct is once again a key factor, not only triggering claims based on treaty provisions of "extradite or prosecute", but also with potential impact for issues of extradition law rules such as the application of existing treaties or requirement to negotiate ad hoc arrangements, the application of a political offence exception, pending claims of refugee status,[80] application of statutes of limitation and amnesty laws and general due process issues such as legality (*nullum crime sine lege*), double jeopardy (*ni bis in idem*) or the likelihood of the death penalty being imposed.

Tactically, unless there is a clear risk of the accused absconding, making an extradition request at a stage where the investigation is advanced may increase the possibility of classifying the conduct as an international crime (for example, if time is invested in gathering evidence of a widespread or systematic attack

79 In this case the US organization Center for Justice and Accountability.

80 Given the terms of Art 1F excluding applicants from the Convention Relating to the Status of Refugees of 1951 if they have committed a crime against peace, a war crime, or a crime against humanity, a serious non-political crime or have been guilty of acts contrary to the purposes and principles of the United Nations.

within which the conduct took place). This may bring its own benefits in terms of limiting options for challenge such as prescription or prior amnesty. On the other hand, if one's objective is speedy arrest and prosecution, resources are scarce and national laws or treaties do not provide a suitable extradition framework, classification of conduct as a common crime may be advantageous, subject to any overwhelming evidentiary hurdles.[81]

Unlike the jurisdictional question, extradition is in most states an issue ultimately decided by the Executive unless the courts have determined that it is illegal to extradite.

The "extradite or prosecute" principle, which might be considered a general principle of international law but not yet a customary norm,[82] was intended primarily to cover situations where the suspect is not in the country in which the crimes were committed or of which he is a national. The principle was intended to assist territorial and national states to obtain custody. An issue outside the scope of this chapter, but worth a brief mention, is whether extradition and prosecution are equal obligations. If the obligations are not equal, it may be argued that the territorial state's duty to prosecute has primacy, with the effect that if the offender is in foreign territory the requested state has no choice, and simply must extradite him on request from the territorial state. The treaties containing such systems do, however, appear to give some choice to the state on whose territory the suspect is found. If so, a state having one or more bases of jurisdiction which then receives an extradition request from a foreign state can choose to decline jurisdiction in favour of the requesting state for any range of reasons (economic, security, political), or without stating a reason at all. However, if the accused or the victim objects, then questions arise regarding which test the court should apply and the criteria it will use, as discussed above.

10.5 Co-operation

10.5.1 Linking co-operation strategies to investigations

In situations where the criminal investigation involves an extraterritorial element, the importance of planned, organized and efficient co-operation cannot be underestimated. Whether requests are made to states, international organizations, individuals or NGOs, more progress in information-gathering and higher quality analysis can be gained when the investigation plan is constructed

81 Such as a requirement to examine the crime scene (where faced with a non-co-operative territorial state), requirements to produce a body to support a homicide charge or medical evidence for a rape charge.

82 There is no customary law duty to extradite in the absence of a treaty, as pointed out by Plachta, fn 55 above, citing also Wheatons, H, *Elements of International Law*, 5th edn, New York: Stevens and Sons, Ltd, 1916, p 188. Also see the ongoing work of the ILC, fn 54 above.

together with a co-operation strategy. In practical terms, involving and consulting with officials engaged in mutual co-operation issues with specific states or other information providers and who would channel requests for rogatory visits or other forms of co-operation increases the efficiency of an investigation, and allows for forward-planning of resources and time requirements; it also, crucially, can reduce the potential for unnecessary friction that can result from unannounced ad hoc requests for co-operation to a receiving state. Bearing in mind that territorial states may face hostile public opinion and, more seriously, security threats and infiltration, unless the strategy is based on a surprise filing, preparing the ground diplomatically for judicial co-operation requests can offer many advantages.

Non-judicial co-operation strategies operating in parallel can also be of great benefit in strengthening the capacity of states to assume their obligations to investigate. A range of information management, analysis and trial preparation systems and software are now widely available at reasonable cost to assist investigators and prosecutors who in the past were faced with mammoth tasks. Dr Gil Lavedra, contributing a chapter in this book, experienced such a task in the Military Junta Trial in Argentina covering hundreds of crimes, as did the Italian authorities in the Maxi Trial of over 400 accused.[83] This is one example among many of the benefits of sharing the cross-disciplinary expertise and techniques that are used in peacetime efforts to combat organized crime and applying them where possible to armed conflict and repression-era crime.

10.5.2 Simultaneous or sequential use of evidence in multiple forums

Prior to a ruling where two jurisdictions are simultaneously gathering evidence (perhaps even in competition with one another),[84] holders of information may receive multiple requests. Even after resolution of jurisdictional issues, various states and organs may require the same contextual evidence, although they are investigating different individuals and different conducts. So-called "macro evidence", evidence showing the existence and character of an armed conflict, or of a widespread or systematic attack against a civilian population, may be central to concurrent prosecutions relating to different incidents or perpetrators but sharing the same larger fact and context-base. This generally refers to documentary[85] or visual evidence[86] and evidence from expert witnesses, which

83 The so-called Maxi Trial, which took nearly two years beginning on 10 February 1986 and ending on 16 December 1987, involved 474 indictments, of which 360 were convicted and 119 *in absentia*.

84 e.g. in situations involving the ICC, where a national state is eager to demonstrate the inadmissibility of a case before the court due to ongoing national proceedings.

85 e.g. truth commission reports, humanitarian organization statistics, international organization reports, NGO reports, country or thematic expert papers.

86 e.g. aerial photographs and satellite images.

may be commissioned or is already published as open source analyses of the circumstances. Evidence demonstrating the civilian character of victims, or the national, religious, racial or ethnic characteristics of groups attacked, or a characteristic of victims which was a discriminatory basis for attack also falls into this category. Likewise, evidence regarding the grand strategy, strategy, tactics and detailed functioning of groups or institutions to which the accused belonged is of cross-jurisdictional importance.

Subject to protecting the personal security of sources, mechanisms are required to allow this kind of macro information to be supplied to several criminal authorities in different jurisdictions and the parties to proceedings, as well as to human rights organs who are dealing with the same facts. Evidential hurdles may exist, for example whether live testimony is required in place of *affidavits*, whether certified copies and not original documents are sufficient, whether physical evidence must be produced and so on. Contradictory opinions from different courts as to the credibility of these sources or the reliability of the information they provide cannot be avoided; however, pooling of information and resources may be possible. Bilateral or multilateral agreements between jurisdictions and the individuals, states or organizations providing information may offer a practical framework. Direct co-operation is the ideal, but failing this it may be possible for independent organs to function as repositories of information that may serve as evidence in more than one jurisdiction.

Much efficiency can also be gained from promoting the use of "minutes of agreement" between prosecution and defence on the circumstantial elements of the crime which this macro evidence can help to establish (although clearly this tool is perhaps much more at home in adversarial systems or international tribunals). If, for example, factual elements can be agreed such as the existence of an international or non-international armed conflict, or the ethnic characteristics of a certain group, then, subject to the requirements of judicial acceptance of the evidence, considerable time and expense can be saved.

More problematic is the issue of cross-border and cross-institutional co-operation in relation to insider witnesses or other witnesses whose security is at issue. Witness protection is a related and particularly overlooked issue in extraterritorial prosecution of war crimes, crimes against humanity and genocide. These aspects are perhaps the most crucial to the success of investigations and prosecutions and they are also areas where the biggest wealth of experience exists in the field of international organized crime. Much is to be gained from urgently bringing this expertise to the field of prosecuting other international crimes.

The problems are not limited to the practical sphere. A jurisdictional determination does not extinguish relevant legal obligations of other states. It may be that jurisdictional determinations trigger obligations in relation to witness protection, for example. However, human rights obligations will persist for states on whose territory a witness is found. Obligations are necessarily shared where witnesses are travelling to foreign jurisdictions to testify but must return home thereafter. While having no obligations on the matter, as a matter of policy a foreign jurisdiction might be expected to seek assurances from a witness's home state that adequate security measures shall be in place on their return before involving them in the criminal investigation. Likewise, victims' representatives should take such steps as they can and demand that official protection frameworks are in place before advising them to testify, or facilitating their participation in criminal proceedings abroad. Additional legal issues must be addressed as early as possible in the investigation stage, and incorporated into the co-operation strategy. There are markedly different approaches between legal systems on the benefits that can be offered to insiders in exchange for collaboration. Moving and protecting witnesses requires dealing with legal issues of data protection, identity documentation, and immigration and asylum.

The links between the kinds of politico-military structures that exist during armed conflict or authoritarian regimes and powerful organized crime structures in operation post-conflict or regime-change, for example in countries as distant from each other as Guatemala and Serbia, also suggest the advantage of having a cross-disciplinary approach to co-operation by law enforcement bodies dealing with past human rights abuses and current crime.

10.5.3 Sequencing and connection of investigations

Within one jurisdiction, even in circumstances in which the authorities have no formal discretionary power in the sense of case selection from a universe of crimes, some latitude may be possible in the prioritization of investigations and grouping of incidents and accused. Argentina has made great progress with this strategy when dealing with a large caseload and range of crimes including torture. This prioritization might relate, for example, to focusing early on in the investigation on lower level alleged perpetrators, and/or patterns of crimes, in order to encourage insider testimony as well as build up a range of objective information from which inferences can be drawn about the existence of plans and the role and knowledge of hierarchical superiors (both political or military).

Sequencing and connection of investigations can, if the requisite will to co-operate exists, be expanded to a cross-border approach. Sequencing investigations may result in producing the type of evidence that can later be used in prosecutions in other domestic or international jurisdictions. Progress abroad in gathering evidence, particularly insider testimony, may have an impact beyond the legal sphere sending an important signal to victims, the justice system and alleged perpetrators alike that the "impossible" can be possible, thereby encouraging more demand for justice domestically and perhaps encouraging more witnesses and sources of documentary and physical evidence to come forward. However, it may also involve challenges of co-ordination on the timing of cross-border co-operation in relation to organized crime during and after demobilization, such as the extradition of Colombian paramilitary leaders to the United States to stand trial for drugs offences in the middle of a complex domestic criminal investigation process into crimes against humanity and war crimes.[87] The scope of the investigation, the methods to be used and the level of public profile of an investigation can clearly have a great effect on the potential for co-operation, both positive and negative. This is particularly the case if the investigation focus is towards the very highest level of military and state leadership.

Decisions about which crimes and persons to investigate (or, at least, which to focus on initially) will also form the basis for non-judicial co-operation, that is to say, programmes of assistance and aid from governments, international or private bodies aimed at strengthening the capacity of institutions to carry out investigations and prosecutions. Bodies providing this kind of assistance to a territorial state facing security issues and weak institutions can encourage inter-change. Likewise, very tightly focused technical assistance in parallel to extraterritorial investigations with a clear aim of increasing the chance that a state could demonstrate ability to proceed at a later stage (providing it is procedurally possible in terms of jurisdictional determinations) can encourage that state to take over investigation and prosecution of remaining cases. In the case of some territorial states, offering this type of focused assistance can, at the least, help to remove the fig leaf of the lack of resources and capacity so often used to mask unwillingness.

10.6 Criminal policy

A few final words are required about the implications of the above for overall criminal policy, especially in a transitional situation. It is always worth reiterating that the overall objective of international human rights and criminal jurisdictions is the successful protection of human rights and prosecution of offenders domestically. This is the rationale behind the admissibility provisions of all of the major human rights organs and of the ICC. It is the overall vision that should be the compass guiding policy-makers who face the challenges of extending criminal jurisdiction extraterritorially and the judiciary that is required to make it work in practice.

Demand and supply may wax and wane in this area. An initial rush of complaints lodged by victims and NGO representatives to foreign jurisdiction will be tempered by the reality of the time and expense required to pursue complex investigations and criminal procedures through to their conclusion. The experience of parties before organs like the Inter-American and European Courts of Human Rights are instructive in this regard. Countries like Spain and Belgium receive a steady flow of criminal complaints requiring complex investigations overseas and face similar resource challenges to that of the ICC. Investigations on various continents, thematic and linguistic expertise, systems of witness protection, evidence management and forensic and logistic

87 For more information on the Colombian case, see also Chapter 11 by Alejandro Aponte in this book.

capabilities have unfortunately led states to turn to legislative efforts to stem that flow. Political considerations are also relevant, but while the time and expense cannot be underestimated, the "international community" might take the opportunity to analyze the benefits of assisting the efforts of states that take on the difficult and honourable task of investigating and prosecuting these crimes, one might say on behalf of the community of nations.

Such foreign systems, if their legal principles allow, could adopt a policy stance like that of the current prosecutor of the ICC, and focus on a certain type of crime or perpetrator.[88] It is the hope of victims, the public and many justice operators in territorial states that the use of extraterritorial criminal jurisdictions will help to fill the so-called Impunity Gap—of perpetrators who fall through the net. Unless practicable solutions are offered to states about how to divide labour in the pursuit of accountability on behalf of these victims, the unfortunate reality may well be that non-prosecutorial mechanisms will continue to have to be found for the majority of perpetrators in those situations where tens of thousands were involved in criminality. Therefore, it is advisable for national jurisdictions with extraterritorial reach to give themselves enough flexibility in their criminal policy to respond to specific situations. For example, focusing on the most responsible in those countries where disarmament, demobilisation and reintegration (DDR) regimes or alternatives to prosecution (such as operated in East Timor) are in action for the rank and file, and in other situations leaving open the possibility of larger-scale prosecutions in future where they are currently impossible.

Finally, the dilemmas of international prosecutors will most certainly land at the feet of national systems pursuing extraterritorial prosecutions of crimes of this nature, and especially where high level accused are involved. No prosecutor works in a political vacuum and although domestic law enforcement and judicial systems may be created to separate firmly political from legal considerations, the effect of investigating and prosecuting in physically and politically difficult and often dangerous circumstances demands an appreciation on the part of policy-makers and justice operators of each other's objectives and obligations.

10.7 Conclusion

The opportunities brought by the recent trend for an internationalization of justice clearly challenge the spheres of jurisdiction, extradition, co-operation and criminal policy. Cross-border co-operation in law enforcement and the cross-fertilization of legal norms from national to international and vice versa are inevitable and states around the world have already embraced this. State action in relation to human rights abuses within another state's borders is and

88 On the unintended negative consequences of a policy to prosecute the "most responsible", see Kemp, fn 2 above.

will remain an extremely delicate legal and political challenge for states. In order to create a positive climate in which to develop norms of international law that favour the internationalization of criminal justice responses to massive human rights abuses, these norms must be seen to work in practice. The criminal investigation is the "petri dish" where good planning and collaboration between victims, NGOs, investigators, prosecutors and judges can be tested and successes demonstrated so as to facilitate judicial and political decision-making on jurisdiction, extradition, state co-operation and overall transitional justice policy issues. The experiences of Spain and of the many countries of Latin America grappling with these issues will surely enhance that climate of discovery and development.

11 Colombia as a sui generis case

Alejandro Aponte

11.1 Introduction

This chapter seeks to contextualize the unorthodox Colombian case within the general international framework of discussion about transitional justice.[1] Out of the broad range of legal and practical challenges that Colombia and its courts are facing in the process of giving effect to the different principles and mechanisms associated with transitional justice, the present study focuses on three themes which are believed to be especially perplexing, and in need of attention at this moment. To begin with, it will examine the influence of the government in the mentioned process, both within its legislative dimension and in the context of legal enforcement. Secondly, it will direct attention to the difficulties encountered in the prosecution of massive violence within a limited legal system. The third theme in focus, finally, relates to the political corruption associated with the activities of the actors involved in the massive and systematic commission of international crimes in Colombia.

11.2 A sui generis case?

From the outset, it is important to emphasize the heterodox, different and specific character of the Colombian case, compared with others. In fact, the particular features of the Colombian case have led to divisions inside the domestic judicial community as to whether it makes sense, at all, to approach the process in Colombia through the prism of transitional justice. On the one hand, some express scepticism towards the claim that Colombia is under an *authentic* process of transitional justice. This perspective is especially evident in titles of studies that reveal the complexity of the Colombian case, such as, for

1 This chapter recollects reflections developed in the meeting of the Latin American Study Group on International Criminal Justice held in Valparaíso, Chile, in March 2008. The reports of the group have been published in Ambos, K and Malarino, E (eds), *Justicia de Transición*, Montevideo: Georg August Universität Göttingen/Konrad Adenauer Stiftung, 2009. Available online at www.kas.de/wf/doc/kas_15990-1522-4-30.pdf?090629220310. The author appreciates the assistance of Diana Dajer Barguil in the revision of this chapter.

example, "Transitional Justice without Transition?"[2] The supporters of this position insist on the need to focus on the real effects that different transitional justice mechanisms are meant to have on the normal functioning of a democracy, and to assess whether it is actually possible to detect any such effects in Colombia.

Other more optimistic points of view, on the other hand, affirm that Colombia is, indeed, experiencing an authentic process of transitional justice. Yet, a fact that must be stressed in this context is that the Colombian Constitutional Court and the criminal justice system as a whole recognize the Justice and Peace Law (JPL), adopted in July 2005, as a special law that entails procedures and mechanisms distinctive of a transitional justice process.[3] In fact, in numerous cases, the Criminal Chamber of the Supreme Court of Justice has affirmed that its provisions must be interpreted in the light of objectives and standards of transitional justice. Furthermore, national courts have been very active in the process of implementing the JPL. One illustration of their central role is the massive review of the JPL that was undertaken by the Constitutional Court in May 2006, and which resulted in a revision of several provisions related to the rights of the victims so as to adjust them with transitional justice standards.[4] In addition, the Office of the Prosecutor, which has a central character in the application of the cited law, has also understood its nature against the backdrop of transitional justice. Indeed, all those who participate in the implementation of the JPL and its mechanisms, such as the participants in the process of disarmament, demobilization and reintegration, understand the purpose of its mechanisms in the light of transitional justice.

However, there is also an intermediate position in the debate about the nature of the Colombian justice and peace process, which recognizes its complex character given that it uses formulas and mechanisms of transitional justice, but without actually converting itself into a transitional justice process.[5] Still, from the standpoint of legal practitioners and public institutions in the domestic realm, the cited law, including its different mechanisms, must be interpreted in the light of the objectives of transitional justice.

The claim about the *heterodox* nature of the Colombian case centres on the fact that the country is not experiencing an orthodox transition from a de facto and

2 Uprimny, R (ed), *¿Justicia transicional sin transición? Verdad, justicia y reparación para Colombia*, Bogotá: Centro de Estudios de Derecho, Justicia y Sociedad, De Justicia, 2006.

3 Law no 975 of 25 July 2005.

4 Constitutional Court of Colombia, Case No C-370, Judgment of 18 May 2006.

5 This is e.g. a conclusion made by Pablo de Greiff, one of the scholars who has worked the most on this theme from a comparative law standpoint. His conclusions were expressed in the context of the international conference about transitional justice on 19–21 June 2007 organized by the International Center for Transitional Justice. See de Greiff, P, "La contribución de la justicia transicional a la construcción y consolidación de la democracia", in Bleeker, M et al (eds), *El Legado de la verdad: Impacto de la Justicia Transicional en la construcción de la democracia en América Latina*, Memoria—Conference Papers 3/2007, available online at www.ictj.org/es/news/pubs/index.html.

anti-democratic regime to a democratic form of government, as was the case in, for instance, Argentina and Chile. For this reason, it does not seem correct to understand the Colombian case as an effort to overcome the past, but rather to "overcome a conflictive present". Indeed, in my opinion, the latter expression seems to illustrate better the nature of the situation in focus.[6] Certainly, mechanisms that are designed to overcome a conflictive past have been developed in Colombia both historically and nowadays; however, as suggested in this chapter, the concept that better captures the ongoing process is that of *overcoming a conflictive present* which is characterized in terms of endemic violence.

As I have suggested in previous studies, the relation between war and law, and, ultimately, the very dynamics of war, determines the actual contents of relevant international legal instruments, such as the Rome Statute of the International Criminal Court.[7] Moreover, the dynamics of war also give specific meaning to the relevant jurisprudence about criminal prosecution of international crimes and, certainly, to the transitional justice mechanisms that have been adopted in Colombia. In fact, these mechanisms have been created at the horizons of a degraded conflict that has produced and continues to produce immense economic and social costs, and which generates crimes against humanity and war crimes committed against innocent persons and disarmed civilians on a daily basis. It is against this background that the arguments in this chapter will be developed.[8]

As has already been mentioned, numerous mechanisms have been employed in Colombia, not only to overcome a conflictive past, but also to tackle a conflictive present. Indeed, amnesties, self-amnesties, the use of *ius gentium* as a regulating mechanism of the armed confrontations in the country, as well as the crimes of rebellion and sedition as bases for political offences are all instruments that have been, and continue to be, frequently relied upon in this context.

6 This expression was employed in Ambos and Malarino, fn 1 above.

7 In the cited scenario, "humanization" of international humanitarian law has been a jurisprudential aim in Colombia, in the context of criminal prosecution of international crimes, especially the crime of homicide of a protected person. This is a similar process to those that some authors, with great critical and historical sense, have today called the (further) "humanization" of international humanitarian law. For instance, Tamás Hoffmann asserted that the decision of the Appeals Chamber of the International Criminal Tribunal for the Former Yugoslavia in the case of *Tadić* was a vehicle to *humanize* international humanitarian law by extending the regulatory framework of international armed conflicts to non-international armed conflicts. See Hoffmann, T, "The gentle humanizer of humanitarian law—Antonio Cassese and the creation of customary law of non-international armed conflict", in Stahn, C and van den Herik, L (eds), *Future Perspectives on International Criminal Justice*, The Hague: TMC Asser Press, 2010, pp 58–80. See also Aponte, A, "Criminal Prosecution of International Crimes: The Colombian Case", *International Criminal Law Review*, vol, 10, no 4, 2010, pp 549–569.

8 See Aponte, A, "Estatuto de Roma y procesos de paz: reflexiones alrededor del 'proyecto de alternatividad penal' en el caso colombiano", in Ambos, Malarino and Woischnik (eds), *Temas actuales del derecho penal internacional. Contribuciones de América Latina, Alemania, España*, Montevideo: Fundación Konrad-Adenauer, 2005, pp 117–150.

Hence, the Colombian resort to amnesties and pardons is by no means a novel method of seeking peace; indeed, it has been used in relation to guerrillas that have existed historically with the aim of incorporating them into civil life. The same or similar instruments have also been utilized, although in a more exceptional manner, in relation to drug dealers. Moreover, when the government has not resorted to direct amnesties or pardons, it has employed criminal justice models which, from a comparative law perspective, can be defined as a kind of *privileged criminal justice*. One example of the latter is the *Ley de Sometimiento a la Justicia* ("Law of Compliance to Justice"), adopted in November 1993, which, throughout the 1990s, afforded special benefits to drug dealers and members of paramilitary groups with the aim of dismantling their war machines.[9]

Nonetheless, the mechanisms that were traditionally used in Colombia to incorporate illegally armed actors into civil life were only used in relation to the guerrillas. The activities of the guerrillas were seen as amounting to political criminality, and its members were considered to be political offenders. For this reason, unlike in the case of ordinary criminals, the state could enter into dialogue with them. In other words, the state perceived the guerrillas as an *Überzeugunstäter*, to use the term of Gustav Radbruch, or as a "delinquent by conviction". Meanwhile, other actors, such as the drug dealers or the members of the paramilitary groups, were not perceived as political delinquents and, therefore, the state did not enter into negotiations with them (at least not in an open manner).

The distinction made between different kinds of actors or criminals in the Colombian case is similar to that introduced by Johan Huizinga in his classical book *Homo Ludens*, in which he distinguishes between the "enemy of the game" and the "false gambler".[10] Whereas the former is an actor who in principle stands outside the economic, political and juridical game, and who in this sense is a political offender, the false gambler, in contrast, is an actor who threatens the game in general. Even though the latter does not oppose the game as such, he or she is constantly seeking a better position within the game through the means of violence, crime and all kinds of illegal methods. While from an empirical and a normative perspective this distinction is nowadays seen as outdated, this study suggests that the debate about the character of different actors continues to be important, not least in the Colombian case. Indeed, with the adoption of the JPL, for the first time in Colombian history, members of paramilitary groups are treated in a way similar to the guerrillas and, in the context of the governmental decision-making, as political offenders. In fact, Article 71 of the original JPL recognized a political character to the paramilitary groups, even though both the Constitutional Court and the Criminal Chamber

9 Law no 81 of 2 November 1993. The law in question took into account a range of norms that were developed in Italy in the 1980s and 1990s to combat the mafias and neutralize their impact.

10 Huizinga, J, *Homo Ludens*, Hamburg: Vom Ursprung der Kultur im Spiel, 1997, p 20.

of the Supreme Court of Justice thereafter rejected this understanding in a systematic manner.[11]

The classification of different actors in the armed conflict has created considerable animosity between the judicial and executive branches of government.[12] The "power of definition" operates constantly in this context, and its connotative and explanatory values are more fundamental today than ever. However, the dispute between the judicial and the executive branches of government about the proper classification of the different actors to the conflict is part of the Colombian tradition. Also part of that tradition is the disagreement as to whether there is an armed conflict at all: while the judiciary maintains that there is such a conflict, which must be regulated, the executive branch has rejected this understanding.[13] That being said, the adoption of the JPL means that advancements have taken place, not only with regard to the mechanisms employed to diminish the devastating effects resulting from the dispute concerning the actors, but also in terms of consolidating and applying transitional justice norms in Colombia.[14] In particular, the JPL counterweighs the benefits awarded to the perpetrators of war crimes and crimes against humanity in terms of reduced sentences with another dimension of justice that is of fundamental importance from the standpoint of transitional justice: the benefits in terms of truth, justice and reparation which are owed to the victims.

11.3 Mechanisms to overcome a conflictive past and present

11.3.1 The JPL and the role of criminal justice

The JPL was adopted in July 2005 following an intense debate in Congress and several governmental attempts to promote the adoption of a different law more similar to the *Proyecto de Alternatividad Penal* (Bill of Criminal Alternativity), discussed in 2003. The latter lowered the prison terms to a minimum and also

11 See, for instance, Constitutional Court of Colombia, Case No C-370, Judgment of 18 May 2006.

12 For an account of this issue in the context of the prosecution of international crimes in Colombia, see Aponte, A, *Persecución penal de crímenes internacionales: diálogo abierto entre la tradición nacional y el desarrollo internacional*, Bogotá: Pontificia Universidad Javeriana, Fundación Konrad-Adenauer, 2010.

13 See, e.g. a study conducted by the author of the present chapter in which he reconstructs the jurisprudential tendency in the last two decades as manifested in the case law produced by the Criminal Chamber of the Supreme Court in relation to the issue of armed conflict. Aponte, A, "Civiles y conflicto armado en la jurisprudencia de la sala penal de la corte suprema de justicia", *Revista de Derecho Penal y Criminología*, Madrid: Universidad Nacional de Educación a Distancia (UNED), January 2007, pp 79–111.

14 See Ambos, K, *El marco jurídico de la justicia de transición*, Bogotá: Temis, 2008, p 2. The author of this book, which makes several references to the Colombian case, advocates the use of the expression "justice in societies in transition" with regard to societies that experience conflict or post-conflict situations. This expression is included in the more basic concept "transitional justice".

substituted them for alternative penalties. However, as a result of international pressure, the attempts to adopt that kind of law failed. Indeed, it is possible to uphold that the content of the JPL was influenced by the international community insisting upon the inclusion of a set of minimum international standards and rules concerning truth, justice and reparation. In previous legal initiatives, the rights of the victims had not been recognized in an explicit manner and had been extremely fragile. However, in addition to international pressure, the recognition of the rights of the victims in the JPL was only possible because of the intense debates in Congress, and the radical intervention by the Constitutional Court in the process.[15] In relation to this process, Hernando Barreto Ardila has asserted, in a synthesized manner, that the JPL:

> Is meant fundamentally to establish a procedure that permits the reincorporation into society and the reconciliation of illegal armed groups, who have committed crimes that are not necessarily political or have connection to them, whenever there is a significant and efficient contribution to the implementation of national peace, and the rights of the victims to truth, justice and reparation are assured.[16]

Since the adoption of the law in focus, numerous decrees have been issued, some of which have been criticized for contradicting the basis of the JPL, as established in the jurisprudence of the Constitutional Court.[17] Later on, the process reached a critical phase when the "free declarations" (*versiones libres*) began, and which refer to oral hearings where the version-givers (that is, the paramilitaries that have been subjected to the law) confess their crimes. In this phase, the darkest stories of Colombian armed conflict are brought to the surface; stories which bear witness of a period of Colombian history that is characterized by the most horrible and systematic commission of all kinds of crimes, of attacks against the minimum standards of dignity of innocent persons, of dark complicities between different illegal actors and all classes of officials, and collaborations of multinationals and foreign businesses in the crimes. The statement-giving process has revealed that, for years, the state was privatized in broad regions of the country and substituted by private and criminal agents.

Furthermore, since the beginning of 2008, national efforts have been made to strengthen the Office of the Prosecutor, which has faced an enormous number of narrated events with the presence of victims—in rooms made available in addition to the chamber for the hearings—and difficult encounters between the victims and the victimizers. There have been occasions where a version-giver alone has confessed more than 100 crimes; one statement only has involved

15 Constitutional Court of Colombia, Case No C-370, Judgment of 18 May 2006.

16 Barreto Ardila, H, "La Ley de Justicia y Paz frente a la Corte Penal Internacional", *Revista del Instituto de ciencias penales y criminológicas*, vol 27, no 81, Bogotá: Universidad Externado de Colombia, May/August 2006, p 55 (unofficial translation).

17 Constitutional Court of Colombia, Case No C-370, Judgment of 18 May 2006.

the confession of several homicides, acts of torture and disappearances. It is an exercise without precedents in Colombian history. Therefore, the number of prosecutors has increased.

In addition, some members of the guerrillas are now being prosecuted under the JPL. Even though the cited law initially focused on the demobilization and disarmament of paramilitary groups, its application has thereafter extended to members of other organizations, such as the guerrillas. In this regard, the justice and peace process recently reached a critical phase when, in spite of the considerable challenges faced, the *Sala de Justicia y Paz del Tribunal Superior de Distrito Judicial de Bogotá* (Justice and Peace Chamber of the Superior Court of Bogotá) handed down its first decisions in response to the first incidents of integral reparations of the victims. These decisions were made in June 2010 and concerned members of the *Bloque Montes de María* and the *Frente Canal del Dique* of the *Autodefensas Unidas de Colombia* (AUC), Edwar Cobos Téllez, "Diego Vecino", and Uber Enrique Banquez Martínez, "Juancho Dique", and in December 2010 against the former commander of the *Frente Fronteras* of the *Bloque Catatumbo*, Iván Laverde Zapata, "El Iguano".[18]

In this context, it is also important to consider a precedent of the JPL: Law no 782 of 2002 on Pardon, because of its impact on the legal classification of the actors involved in the Colombian justice and peace process. In pursuance with the Law on Pardon, amnesty or pardon may be given to individuals who belong to armed groups, but limited to those who have committed a political offence or crimes connected to such offences (that is, simple crimes connected with the political ones, such as the illegal transport of weapons, the illegal utilization of uniforms or signs, or the instigation to commit such a crime). In the light of this law, it is not difficult to understand the significance of the national discussion about the meaning and scope of political offence and, in particular, if it can be applied directly to persons belonging to paramilitary groups. A wide interpretation of what counts as political offence would mean that an immense number of common soldiers belonging to paramilitary groups would be pardoned. However, the Criminal Chamber of the Supreme Court of Justice has rejected this understanding, although its rejection generated additional confrontations with the executive branch.[19]

Through the adoption of the Law on Pardon and the JPL, the Colombian Government is seeking to ensure respect for international standards of transitional justice, above all, with regard to the rights of victims to truth, justice

18 For more information about the implementation of the justice and peace process until September 2010, see Aponte, A, *El proceso penal de Justicia y Paz desde la práctica cotidiana: síntesis y diagrama de flujo, Observatorio Internacional de DDR y Ley de Justicia y Paz. Tercer informe*, Madrid-Bogotá: CITpax, September 2010, pp 18–57. Available online at www.toledopax.org/uploads/Tercer_Informe_CITpax_Observatorio_DDR_Ley_Justicia_Paz_septiembre_2010.pdf.

19 For the most significant decision in this context, see Supreme Court of Justice of Colombia, Criminal Chamber, Case No 26945, Order of 11 July 2007.

and reparation. Also, the hope is to advance efficient forms of reparation that go beyond restitution and compensation and include others, such as symbolic reparation, rehabilitation, satisfaction and guarantees of non-repetition.[20] Considering the gravity of the crimes that the JPL is meant to address, it is clear that international standards of transitional justice focus on the rights of victims, oblige and entitle the state to investigate the crimes committed by the illegal armed groups, and to impose sanctions upon those who are responsible for them. For this reason, in a lead to justify the JPL, the High Commissioner for Peace in Bogotá has stated that the benefits granted to the members of the paramilitary groups are reasonable and minimal in comparison with the benefits obtained in terms of democratic institutionalization and the dismantling of these "machines of death". For these reasons the benefits are fully justified within the framework of the peace process.[21]

11.3.2 The extraditions and the JPL: the law absorbed by politics

In the final stages of an extradition, the Criminal Chamber of the Supreme Court of Justice must deliver an opinion (which is not binding for the executive branch if it is favourable to the extradition). Thereafter, the government decides, with full discretion, whether or not to extradite the requested person.[22] Under the previous government, several persons were extradited to the United States. In this manner, it used its power to extradite those who have been demobilized and requested from the United States. The possibility of extradition has been used to exert pressure on persons who have been demobilized to participate in the justice and peace process. One example is the extradition of the demobilized paramilitary chief named Macaco (his alias). Macaco is a former paramilitary chief who had over 6,000 men under his command, and who became, in the initial stage of the process, a major concern in terms of ensuring respect for the minimum conditions imposed by the JPL. According to the government, he was responsible for the commission of crimes while in prison, especially drug dealing, a charge which from the outset was denounced by several legal practitioners. For this reason, once all of the foreseen instances had been exhausted, the Colombian Government ordered his extradition to the United States.

Macaco's extradition became the upshot to an important discussion about the fate of those who had been victims of the activities by this paramilitary

20 A current challenge facing the judges concerns the right to reparation of the victims. See Área de Justicia, *El proceso penal especial de Justicia y Paz: alcances y límites de un proceso penal concebido en clave transicional*, Observatorio Internacional de DDR y Ley de Justicia y Paz, Madrid-Bogotá: CITpax, February 2011. Available online at www.toledopax.org/uploads/Proceso_penal_Justicia_y_Paz_febrero_2011_CITpaxObservatorio.pdf.

21 High Commissioner for Peace, "Balance de un Proceso", in *Simposio de evaluación y balance: dos años de la Ley de Justicia y Paz*, Bogotá: Universidad Santo Tomás, 25 July 2007 (unofficial translation).

22 Law no 906 of 31 August 2004, Arts 490 to 514.

chief. In fact, victims' associations immediately questioned the decision to send him to the United States since his confession would become truncated, and the victims would not know the truth about the thousands of crimes that occurred under his command. However, Macaco promised to give information about many of the events that were mentioned in the free declarations, which took place before he was extradited. Also, the associations questioned that the harms and sufferings of the victims would not be repaired in an effective manner, as the paramilitary chief would be faced with other processes in the United States.

The Criminal Chamber of the Supreme Court of Justice supported the initial criticisms set forth by the victims' associations. Its most important opinion on the matter was delivered on 10 April 2008 and concerned a similar case also concerning an extradition request.[23] In its decision, the judges of the Supreme Court of Justice maintained that a subject of the JPL can be extradited as long as he or she has submitted to the requirements forestalled in this law in an effective manner. Furthermore, when the chamber considered the case, it interpreted all of the relevant provisions in the light of the goals of transitional justice announcing that the Colombian Government, prior to meeting a treaty obligation to extradite a crime suspect, especially of drug dealing, must assure that the rights of the victims, that is, the rights to justice, reparation and truth (or information), are guaranteed.[24]

The opinion on extradition delivered on 10 April 2008 was the first in Colombian history to recognize that, when combating drug dealing, priority must be given to the fate of the victims and their rights. The Supreme Court thus resolved the tension between the interests in punishing drug dealers (supported by the United States) and the interest in punishing international crimes in favour of the latter. The concerns behind the opinion were expressed by a judge in the following way: "One does not understand the motives of the executive for giving priority to the investigation of a crime of drug dealing, when nothing has been done to investigate or sanction the grave crimes committed for years in our country."[25] But the government's response did not wait. It criticized the judiciary for its opinion and began to work on the basis of a regulatory norm that gave the possibility of excluding a demobilized person from the JPL.[26] At the moment, the justice and peace process is facing the challenge of implementing hearings from the United States of the free declarations of extradited paramilitaries who are being judged under the JPL. Furthermore, since February 2010, the Criminal Chamber of the Supreme Court

23 Supreme Court of Justice, Criminal Chamber, Case No 29472, Order of 10 April 2008.

24 Daniel Pastor asserts the necessity of understanding the notion of truth as a right to information, given the arbitrary management and accommodation of political interests surrounding what is called the truth. Pastor, D, "¿Procesos penales sólo para conocer la verdad? La experiencia argentina", *Jueces para la Democracia*, no 59, July 2007, pp 95 ff.

25 Montaña, M I, "Gobierno impugnó fallo que suspendió temporalmente extradición de 'Macaco'", *El Tiempo*, 22 April 2008.

26 For an analysis of these issues, see Área de Justicia, fn 20 above.

of Justice has denied, in a consistent manner, the possibility of extraditing persons who are being judged under the JPL.

11.3.2.1 The political gamble against the JPL and social expectations

Undeniably, one of the most pertinent discussions in the Colombian justice and peace process concerns the exclusion of a subject altogether from the application of the JPL. As it is established in the JPL, the government must present a list of those who are subject to this law. Thus, in the initial stage of the process, the government intervenes in the evaluation of the requisites of eligibility. However, the remainder of the process belongs to the judicial system, that is, to the prosecutors and the judges of the Justice and Peace Chambers. This means that the government cannot intervene in this part of the process, at least not in a direct manner, for the purpose of excluding a subject. Only the prosecutor may do so following a request of the competent judge.

In the light of these rules of the game, rules that the government itself had established, something absolutely unexpected occurred on 13 May 2008, which brought the government into an especially awkward and complex situation. That day the country woke up in surprise with the news that the government, without any prior announcement, had extradited the 13 most important paramilitary chiefs, together with a simple drug dealer, to the United States. However, just prior to this extradition, the government had dictated the Regulatory Decree no 1364 of 25 April 2008, which recognized a title for the executive branch to withdraw demobilized subjects from the JPL if it considers that the demobilized have failed to comply with their obligation not to commit new crimes. Even if the decree in question seemed contrary to what was deemed to be logical within the JPL framework, permitting, as it did, differential treatment of the paramilitary chiefs compared to other subjects of the JPL, it was nevertheless assumed to be consistent with the legality principle.[27] The extradition on 13 May 2008 provoked a discussion related to the possibility of withdrawing the initial list of possible beneficiaries of the JPL if such beneficiaries failed to conform with their obligations (and not, as it would have been reasonable to expect, whether the decree actually excluded in a direct manner certain persons). In reality, however, this discussion was nothing but a game of words, as the executive branch had, indeed, excluded members of the paramilitary groups and, according to its own declarations, continues to do so de facto.

Because of the extradition on 13 May, it became unclear whether the paramilitary chiefs would continue to participate in the statement-giving process, and reveal to victims the whereabouts and final destiny of their family members. Certainly, it raised outstanding concerns. An aggravating factor that illuminates the political game of the government is that the chiefs were the

27 Irrespective of the final objective of this decree, the extradited chiefs have not been sent back to Colombia.

persons who had initiated the so-called "parapolitical scandal", that is, the disclosure of the connections between politicians and paramilitary groups.

11.3.2.2 Applying the peace and justice process at a distance?

Given the apparent impossibility of an eventual prosecution of international crimes committed by members of the paramilitary groups, the Colombian Government announced that it was negotiating with the US ambassador to ensure that the goods owned by those who had been extradited would be remitted to Colombia, and that the chiefs may eventually be brought back to Colombia to be prosecuted for crimes against humanity. However, up until now this has not happened, and the independence of US judges indicates that they are not in any case obliged to follow the outcome of diplomatic negotiations. As a matter of fact, from a legal perspective, an agreement between the Colombian Government and the US ambassador can be understood as amounting to a recommendation at most

In an attempt to give endurance to the justice and peace process, Colombian prosecutors have travelled to the United States to continue with the "free declarations" of the paramilitary chiefs, although it has turned out to be a complex task, full of technical difficulties. The victims of grave crimes in Colombia have consistently argued that the extraditions to the United States manifest that there will be no truth, justice and reparation.[28] The government, in contrast, maintains that the drug dealers have been subjected to "exemplary punishment". For months the government was aware of the continued commission of crimes by paramilitary chiefs. Against this background, one may ask: why did the government wait for so long before reacting? Which factors finally led it to act? One thing is certain and that is that in war the political decision about who the enemy is prevails notwithstanding his or her concrete acts.

11.4 The limits of law in scenarios of extreme conflict

So far, this study has focused on the factual details of the political game of those who govern in Colombia. However, for the argument in this chapter, it is essential to also direct attention to the more general problem of prosecuting international crimes in times of transition, given the limited possibilities of law in situations characterized by particularly extreme and persisting conflicts.[29]

28 The incidence of these extraditions over the rights of the victims can be found in the study composed by the Área de Políticas Públicas, *La extradición de los comandantes de las AUC y sus implicaciones en el proceso de Justicia y Paz, Observatorio Internacional de DDR y Ley de Justicia y Paz, Segundo informe*, Madrid-Bogotá: Citpax, November 2009, pp 137–164. Available online at www.toledopax.org/descargarfichero.php?fichero=CITpax_Segundo_Informe_Observatorio_DDR_Ley_Justicia_y_Paz_Colombia_noviembre_2009.pdf.

29 See Aponte, A, *Guerra y derecho penal de enemigo. Reflexión crítica sobre el eficientismo penal de enemigo*, Bogotá: Universidad de los Andes, Facultad de Derecho, Centro de Investigaciones Socio-Jurídicas (CIJUS), 2006.

11.4.1 "Pure violence" and its relations with law

In 1921, Walter Benjamin published his essay "Critique of Violence" in which he analyzes a range of complex themes, including the relation between law and violence.[30] According to Benjamin, there are different kinds of violence. One of them is "pure" and is situated outside the legal realm. In his view, this form of violence could also be thought of as "divine", and can be contrasted with "mythical violence", which is directly related to the legal domain. In his own words: "Mythical violence is bloody power over mere life for its own sake, divine violence is pure power over all life for the sake of the living. The first demands sacrifice, the second accepts it."[31] This is why this type of violence exists outside the law. In this context, Benjamin also introduced a further distinction between the sort of violence that is foundational to the law (*rechtssetzende Gewalt*) and the violence that sustains or maintains it (*rechtserhaltende Gewalt*). However, between the lines of his text, it is possible to detect a third kind of violence which is "pure" (*reine Gewalt*) and outside the law.[32]

The Italian philosopher Giorgo Agamben understands pure violence as referring to an "anomic zone" that is present in human communities.[33] But what is the proper approach to this anomic zone? Can the law absolve it, at least in a minimalistic manner? The recognition of the existence of pure violence, which is latent and threatening, implies that there is a grey or obscure zone in the relation between law and violence, which is characterized by "undecidability".[34] Yet, Carl Schmitt and Walter Benjamin disagree about the nature of this zone. While Schmitt seeks to maintain this zone *within* the law (denominating it as a "state of exception"), for Benjamin, pure violence is situated outside the legal realm. In his concluding remarks in "Critique of Violence" (while more concerned about the threat of violence that is required to preserve the law), he holds that the undecidability, or incapacity of law in relation to pure violence, reveals that there is something that is *rotten*

30 According to contemporary linguists and authors, in general, Carl Schmitt read and responded to this text, albeit in a cryptic manner.

31 Benjamin, W, "Critique of Violence", in Benjamin, W, *Reflections: Essays Aphorisms, Autobiographical Writing*, translated by Edmund Jephcott, New York: Schocken Books, 1986, p 297.

32 An allusion which is not meant to be denigrating, but as stressing the fact that Benjamin says more in the dusk prevailing between the lines than in the concrete phrases.

33 See Agamben, G, *Stato di Eccezione*, Torino: Bollati, 2004, pp 68–70. With historical facts, Agamben reconstructs in a concise manner the imbrications (not always explicit but clear in some epistolary quotations of Carl Schmitt) between Benjamin and Schmitt in relation to the question of what to do with primitive violence.

34 Jacques Derrida has made notable contributions to the discussion about this zone as initiated by Walter Benjamin. See, e.g. Derrida's debate on the basis of Walter Benjamin's text concerning violence: Derrida, J, *Gesetzkraft: Die Mystische Grund der Autorität*, Frankfurt: Suhrkamp, 1991.

in the law: the law, all law, in its attempt to extinguish violence, not merely fails in doing so, but even reproduces it with greater vehemence.[35]

Furthermore, faced with the claim about the destructive nature of pure violence, Benjamin, in a consistent and almost metaphysical scepticism, asserts that: "To this extent it is justifiable to call this violence, too, annihilating; but it is so only relatively, with regard to goods, right, life, and suchlike, never absolutely, with regard to the soul of the living."[36] His brilliance lies in his ability to discern, in an impeccable manner, that the pure and naked violence is inherent: it belongs to the spirit of all life, is confused with life and goes further. From this perspective, he drew one of his most insightful conclusions about the social role of violence: "Divine violence, which is the sign and seal but never the means of sacred execution, may be called sovereign violence."[37]

11.4.2 "Pure violence" and the banalization of evil

When analyzing the Colombian experience in the light of these philosophical underpinnings, the narrations given in the "free declarations" that have taken place in the justice and peace process until now—loaded with cynic details and surrounded by a prosaic context of thousands of crimes—may be interpreted in the words of Hannah Arendt as an exercise of the "banalization of evil". The declarations concern pure, massive and primitive violence, which in principle are situated outside the civil language and the rational pretensions of the legal language. It is a kind of violence that covers an immense anomic or grey zone. Thus, the question set forth by Benjamin and Schmitt remains critical: is it possible to comprise the violence within the limits of the law? In other words, can law (not only criminal law, but law in its totality) address this kind of massive and permanent violence, which is "pure" in its most primitive sense, and place it at the horizons of the law? Can the law use this violence in favour of a future state of peace or security, which would be characterized in terms of its absence?

11.4.3 The state of exception and the Colombian case

As mentioned in the previous subsection, the notions of "state of exception" or "state of emergency", introduced by Carl Schmitt, finds a place for "pure

35 Carl Schmitt's argumentative sequence can be observed in his text. See Schmitt, C, *Politische Theologie. Vier Kapitel zur Lehre von der Souveränität*, München-Leipzig: Duncker und Humblot, 1993.

36 Benjamin, fn 31 above, p 297.

37 The divine violence ("pure violence") is inherent to the human condition. It is prior to all regulation and not an instrument; the law does not intervene to regulate it or to judge it. It is the spirit of the living. For this reason it governs. Thus, it is not a coincidence that Benjamin makes a reference to Schopenhauer. In Benjamin's cryptic writings, it is possible to find his pessimism or scepticism of the permanent will as the essence of all life.

violence" within the legal domain.[38] From this perspective, one may perceive the JPL as an exceptional law, even if it has not been publicly recognized as such. In other words, it is possible to think of the JPL mechanisms, which are now being perceived in terms of public policies, as a great vehicle of assimilation of pure or primitive violence. Its adoption implied a political determination of the form in which the pure violence of paramilitarism was relevant to the law. At the same time, it is also possible to maintain, as Benjamin did, that the law, all law, is incapable of accommodating such violence. In other words, according to him, pure violence goes further than the law and is undecided. Its undecidability can be expressed in some way in terms of the *divine* character that Benjamin assigns to pure violence, because of its precarious rationality. In essence, the anomic zone is a zone in which the human action is placed outside the law.[39]

If Benjamin is correct in his understanding, all Colombian attempts to integrate violence into its legal domain will inevitably fail even if it would not result in a total failure such as an institutional or social collapse.[40] The failure might instead become manifest when observing a single paramilitary chief narrating hundreds of crimes in front of public officials who are bravely taking note of them, and observing that one single narration is crystallized into hundreds of similar ones. These are events that bear witness not only to the crude nature of human action, but also to its massive and constant character. Indeed, there is a sense of real impotence when these events are articulated within the limited language of criminal law. In practice, the task amounts to the investigation and prosecution of an entire private state which is parallel to the state; of thousands of actions committed in defiance of all law by actors who are attached to the massive dynamics of that parallel state.

At the same time, the real sense of impotence is mediated by an extraordinary effort by the legal practitioners of the Colombian justice system, and certain administrative authorities, to carry out the process of affording moral and economic reparations of the victims. But even if they were to succeed, the question remains whether criminal law and the entire legal order which, in essence, are restricted to take account of endemic violence, would be capable of creating a framework of minimum expectations expressed in terms of authentic and renewed social pacts, of true foundational pacts, which would require a profound reconstruction of a minimum basis for peaceful coexistence. Sadly, the real outlook is not reassuring. One challenge is the state of affairs of the Congress of the Republic, which was shown to be illegitimate in 2008 as the result of the co-optation of a significant percentage of illegal groups forming part of the logic of endemic violence. Indeed, everyone who hoped for progress

38 It is important to note that Carl Schmitt has in mind the real chaos, which is close to the total negation of law and not to any kind of emergency that can be approached through administrative means.

39 Agamben, fn 33 above, p 78.

40 All crises in Colombia are in principle superseded. There are ways in which socially minimum expectations are always stabilized. The question is always the same: for how

in the field of transitional justice has serious concerns about the corruption inside the legislative branch, but there is no sign of serious action. Congress is one of the institutional mechanisms that cowardly preserve the violence derived from corruption. Considering the natural scepticism and the structural conditions that accompany the Colombian process, the idea of new pacts and true alliances is a real gamble.

11.5 Recuperation of the victims for the society and the law

A central objective of a transitional justice policy is to ensure respect for the rights of the victims. By now, a range of mechanisms has been established in Colombia for the purpose of repairing, in economic and moral terms, the harms done to the victims in the conflict. However, with regard to the victims, an additional question surfaces in times of transition, namely, how to recuperate the victims for law and society? How to convert victims into citizens? How to construct (or, as the case may be, reconstruct) a sense of confidence between the state and its citizens?[41]

The institutions have a central role to shoulder in the demobilization process, since they must, in the words of Max Weber, mediate the tension between the "ethics of conviction" and the "ethics of responsibility".[42] Traditionally, in this process, emphasis has been placed on amnesties and peace agreements, which seek to establish peace as a condition for a functioning legal system. Nonetheless, attention must also be paid to the victims. But how can the establishment integrate the victims into the legal system and the social institution of citizenship?

The dilemma came to the surface in a conversation that I had with a mother who was a victim of the Colombian armed conflict when she said: "As a citizen, I must accept the laws and this law of justice and peace; therefore, I must even *forgive*, if this is the case. Yet, as a mother I will never do it." Indeed, it is not possible to oblige someone to forgive considering that it is an individual gesture of benevolence that is established in the internal sphere of the human being. However, the mother, by virtue of her status as citizen, must perform this

long? Even in relation to private states parallel to the state, and in the spirit of the thought of Luhmann, one may also ask: can the terror be a way of stabilizing social expectations? For how long may this kind of stability last?

41 This is the argument put forth by Paul Seils in Chapter 12 of this book. According to him, all transitional justice mechanisms build upon the necessity of constructing or reconstructing confidence between the state and the citizens. It coincides with the notion of citizenship related to the condition of the victim discussed in this chapter. The state is distant from the persons and when it intervenes it does so in an arbitrary or chaotic manner, and this is a fact that is connected to the alternative private states of authority which it is necessary to avoid.

42 Weber, M, "Der Beruf zur Politik", *Soziologie. Universalgeschichtliche Analysen. Politik*, Stuttgart: Kröner, 1973; and Weber, M, *Politik als Beruf*, Berlin: Duncker und Humblot, 1919.

gesture nevertheless. Therefore, the question is at what point the internal expression of the human being becomes external? Can the inner perceptions become exteriorized revenges? It is a precarious equilibrium given that the dilemma cannot be resolved through the cold claim for reparation, but requires the authentic reconstruction of social fabrics that were destroyed or which have never existed at all, as well as the creation of a minimal principle of confidence as an elemental condition for a functioning legal system, including an authentic solidarity in front of the pain of others.

The ethics of a sceptic, such as Arthur Schopenhauer, may illustrate what is meant by authentic solidarity. His definition of *mitleiden* does not refer to mere *compassion* (which is a central concept in the Spanish language because of its relation with the Catholic tradition), but rather refers to an authentic exercise of "suffering with the other", and of recognizing that the other is made of the same material and unceasing fire as oneself. The pain of the other must be true because it coincides in the base and substance with what we are all made of. This understanding appears to be an ingenuous reflection when listening to the narrations about the killings and abuses that have taken place for so many years in Colombia. Still, the point of departure for such narrations is the sinister spectacle of horror and the pain that threatens all of us. Because of this commonality one may speak of a kind of solidarity that is not merely discursive and hypocrite or which dissolves itself into pure rhetoric. While the notion of humanity, which is present in "crimes against humanity", is a normative and discursive construction, an ethics of shared suffering is a (irrational) foundation that is prior to such construction.

The idea of a transitional justice process that has been agreed upon is solely a technical term: from the human standpoint, such process will not function without pacts and alliances or authentic solidarity constituting the deeper basis for all political and judicial decision-making.[43] The idea of transitional justice is not about false promises, but nor is it about making the fundamental principles of criminal law, such as the principles of legality and the prohibition against retroactivity, more flexible. Transitional justice is not about creating false criminal law categories or using existing ones to fit certain behaviours so that the state can punish in the name of the victims in a manner that does not make any sense. Rather, the idea of transitional justice is about transforming victims into citizens and of constructing authentic confidence in the legal system that has been adverse to them, and in the public institutions that have not only been contingent, but also entirely opposed to the victims.

The actual panorama seems disheartening, especially since the extraditions in May 2008. However, the incapacity of the JPL to repair the damages done by the paramilitary groups has become a pertinent issue. In its judgment on 29 June 2010 against members of the *Bloque Montes de María* and the *Frente Canal del Dique* of the *Autodefensas Unidas de Colombia* (AUC), Edwar Cobos

43 See, e.g. Ricoeur, P, *Finitud and Culpabilidad*, Madrid: Taurus, 1982.

Téllez, "Diego Vecino", and Uber Enrique Banquez Martínez, "Juancho Dique", the Justice and Peace Chamber of the Superior Tribunal of Bogotá manifested concern about the lack of resources for the effective reparation of the victims.[44]

Another dilemma that has deepened the scepticism in the judicial community is the management of the property and goods that are meant to serve as reparation. In the third week of May 2008, a senator initiated a debate about the effects of the JPL (three years on) in which the following conclusions were drawn: until now, there are 9,000 million pesos (US $4.5 million) in the Reparations Fund. Thus, if the government will issue reparation through administrative means, which in practice will amount to between 13 and 18 million pesos per person, the money is going to be generated from the national treasury and not from the immense fortunes of the paramilitaries.[45] The management of property generates several problems considering that the administration of justice receives goods the debts of which have not been paid or which turn out to be owned by someone who is claiming their property. In addition, as held by the Justice and Peace Chamber of the Superior Court of Bogotá in the judgment on 29 June 2010, the disposable goods are not enough to repair the totality of victims who are registered in the Office of the Prosecutor. In other words, the losers in this story will be the same as always: the victims.

11.6 Subversion of procedures and the illegitimacy of the parliament

An especially problematic issue that arises for societies in transition is the depuration of state institutions from agents attached with the generalized politics of human rights violations. A critical challenge for Colombia in this regard is what has been defined as the "parapolitics", that is, the generalized relation between politicians and paramilitary groups. In July 2008, more than 70 Congress members were involved and the Criminal Chamber of the Supreme Court had already sanctioned some of them. The Chamber is investigating not merely the existence of connections between politicians and paramilitary groups, but also how the former have benefited from such connections in terms of gaining illegal political opportunities. Some politicians are also being investigated for involvement in atrocious crimes committed against their political enemies.

From Niklas Luhmann's perspective, the decisions of the modern state are legitimated through the following set of procedures. According to him, there are no prior truths and, therefore, the decisions ensuing from the proper procedures will be regarded as true. Thus, the question about the legitimacy of

44 Tribunal Superior de Bogotá, Tribunal Superior de Distrito Judicial de Bogotá, Case No 110016000253200680077, Judgment of 29 June 2010.

45 Revista Semana, "Las que pierden siempre", *Justicia y Paz*, Bogotá, 21–28 April 2008, p 45.

the procedures as such becomes fundamental. However, in Colombia, as revealed by the many cases that by now have been disclosed, at least 40 per cent of former Congressmen were connected, in some way or another, with paramilitary groups. Considering that such a significant percentage of Congressmen did not conduct their affairs in a lawful manner, it seems difficult, if not impossible, to hold that the decisions taken by Congress were legitimate.[46] A majority of the former Congressmen responded to the accusations in a superficial and cynical manner. Additionally, some members of Congress who were elected in March 2010 have also had connections with paramilitary groups and local traditional illegal powers in some Colombian regions. This situation indicates that there is no political will to end the privileges that emanate from corruption and other illegal activities in Colombia.

The legitimacy problem is a fundamental concern since it indicates the existence of what Trutz Von Trotha has defined as a "form of parallel state organization of the violence", which is perceived as an authority. In other words, there is a parallel state that is controlled by illegal groups with territorial dominium that exercise authority, administrate resources and collect taxes.[47] Indeed, in the Colombian case, the historical fragility of the state, which has failed to ensure the minimal conditions to promote peaceful coexistence among its citizens, has led to its replacement with private authority: an unforgiving, cruel authority without normative ties.[48]

46 See Luhmann, N, *Legitimation durch Verfahren*, Frankfurt am Main: Suhrkamp, 1983. The reference to Luhmann is merely illustrative.

47 Von Trotha, T, „Ordnungsformen der Gewalt oder Aussichten auf das Ende des staatlichen Gewaltmonopols", in Nedelmann, B in collaboration with Koepf, T (eds), *Politische Institutionen im Wandel*, Cologne: Kölner Zeitschrift für Soziologie und Sozialpsychologie, 1995, p 130. Sociologists use four criteria to analyze parallel states within the framework of the crisis of the Western notion of state monopoly over the exercise of violence: the role of violence in the administration and politics, the "juridical domestication or the ground rules of the central power", the "culture of violence" and the degree of urbanization of societies. All of these criteria converge in the Colombian case. There has been a predominant role of *reine Gewalt* (pure violence), a domestication of violence in enormous territories, a chaotic urbanization in diverse cities and a generalization of the paradigm of recourse to violence to resolve all conflict. However, the author of this chapter does not agree with some authors who refer to the "culture of violence" in Colombia as well as its generalization. Instead, I prefer to refer to the generalization of the paradigm of self-defence and self-protection in the face of the precarious presence of the state or its chaotic and deinstitutionalized presence. People themselves furnish a lasting exercise of self-defence and self-protection and transfer their protection to illegal armed actors.

48 The war usually takes place in areas of the country that still experience weaknesses similar to the ones categorized by Gabriel Almond and Lucian Pye as "crisis of integration" and "crisis of penetration". The origin of these crises is the state's inability to uphold a national bureaucracy adequate for the collection of taxes and the development of common political projects. In the legal context, these crises lead to the absence of the effective implementation of the law throughout the territory. See Almond, G A, Powell, B G Jr, Strom, K and Dalton, R J, *Comparative Politics: A Theoretical Framework*, 4th edn, New York: Longman Publishing Group, 2003; and Pye, L W, *Aspects of Political Development: An Analytic Study*, Boston: Little, Brown and Company, 1966.

The parallel state in Colombia was preceded by contingent institutionalism, which was almost purely formal in enormous parts of the country's territory. The parallel state took advantage of public resources and was the real authority in these territories. Hundreds of politicians benefited from this situation. The result was the creation of a parallel state with its own proper rules, which exercised all kinds of violence, and utilizing resources from the paramilitary groups. In this scenario, the question that was put in the beginning of this chapter resurfaces: Is it possible for the legal practitioners involved in the justice and peace process to eliminate this kind of deinstitutionalized and parallel violence, which in principle is situated outside the legal realm, through the law itself? This is the real challenge facing transitional justice efforts in Colombia.

11.7 Colombian transitional justice mechanisms and the International Criminal Court

Does the International Criminal Court (ICC) have competence to prosecute international crimes committed in Colombia? This question must be answered in the light of the JPL, although, as Kai Ambos notes, it is not reasonable to maintain that this law on its own could activate the prosecution competence of the ICC.[49] The JPL must also be contrasted with previous legislative initiatives, such as the Bill of Criminal Alternativity of 2003, which was mentioned earlier on in this chapter. That being said, however, the JPL has generated an extensive discussion about the "substantial impossibility" of the Colombian state to prosecute international crimes under this law. In this discussion, the Office of the High Commissioner for Human Rights in Colombia has insisted that the JPL amounts to a particular form of generalized pardon, which is prohibited by the Rome Statute. The international community, on the other hand, has argued that since the Colombian law does not formally exclude the criminal justice system from the justice and peace process, and that the process has not failed in general, it is pivotal to consider the prevalence of a true will to resort to the judicial process in relation to those who commit international crimes. Neither does it follow from the judgment of the Constitutional Court on 18 May 2006 that the prosecutorial competence of the ICC could be activated.[50] In the end, the practical application of the JPL, and the results of the justice and peace process, as a whole, will be decisive to an eventual activation of the ICC competence.[51]

49 Ambos, K, *The Colombian Peace Process and the Principle of Complementarity of the International Criminal Court*, Berlin: Springer, 2010.

50 Constitutional Court of Colombia, Case No C-370, Judgment of 18 May 2006.

51 For an analysis of the complementarity test of Art 17 of the Rome Statute in the Colombian Case, particularly in the "Justice and Peace Process", see Ambos, K, *Procedimiento de la Ley de Justicia y Paz (Ley 975 de 2005) y Derecho Penal Internacional*, Bogotá: Temis, 2010, pp 149 ff. Available online at www.department-ambos.uni-goettingen.de/index.php/en/Forschung/friedensprozess-in-kolumbien-aufgrund-des-gesetzes-975-v-2272005.html. For a shorter English version see Ambos, fn 49 above.

In this context, it is important to stress the judicial independence of the Colombian judicial system. Indeed, the judges and the prosecutors have demonstrated a capacity to apply the criminal law in an independent manner in spite of the pressure exerted by the executive branch in an extreme situation of armed conflict and vulnerability. A particularly troublesome incident related to judicial independence occurred in 2007 when the Criminal Chamber of the Supreme Court refused to apply the category of political crimes to acts of members of the paramilitary groups, and to assimilate the crime of sedition to the crime of collaboration to commit crime. The former President of the Republic used all means to manifest his objection to the decision of the Supreme Court in this case and also accused the judges of policy-making, blocking ongoing processes and impeding the work of the executive branch. Even so, the pressure has not paid off.

In general, there is a fierce contest among the actors who participate in the justice and peace process with its source in the *power of definition*. In particular, there is a contest about the capacity to award the status of delinquent to different persons and categories and to establish what kind of delinquent it is. The international community must pay attention to this contest, not least ICC officials, because of the fact that the extreme selectivity of the criminal justice system is also a source of impunity. The political and selective application of criminal law means that some actors end up not contributing to peace in an effective manner in spite of the fact that peace is a basic condition for the proper application of the JPL.

As revealed by the incident between Colombia and Ecuador in March 2008, which amounted to a military operation of the Colombian armed forces and the police on Ecuadorian territory, and leading to the intervention of President Chávez in Venezuela, there is still a lack of general knowledge of the basic provisions of the Rome Statute. The advisers and the group of lawyers who are now being questioned for their lack of competence advised the Colombian President to denounce President Chávez to the ICC for assisting and developing genocide (because of his recognized connections with the FARC guerrillas). As is evident, there is still confusion about these themes, even within the highest authorities. This advice was never followed, but serves as a reminder of the improper use of fundamental issues related to the Rome Statute. Indeed, public officials even considered the possibility of denouncing the Venezuelan President for collaboration with terrorist activities, etc and, thus, also failing to recognize the limited range of crimes upheld in the Rome Statute.

11.8 Conclusion

As a final reflection, it may be noted that the complexity of the Colombian case can be understood in terms of paradoxes: the paradox of war and law, of war and politics, of violence and democracy, of violence and legitimacy. It can also be seen as reflecting other great tensions, such as illustrated in the claim about the prevalence of limits to the humanitarian conscience in situations of horror, or in reaction to the commission of crimes against humanity and war crimes. From a global standpoint, there is an obsession to impose punishment and to do justice on the basis of absolute and non-negotiable values and assumptions. Preference is given to the delimitation of the humanitarian conscience through punishment and to fight the impunity that is rampant in extreme situations of social and political violence. The problem in Colombia is that militarily unconquered enemies would be the basis for such limits. Faced with this dilemma (the tension between the universalist requirement to punish and the real war situation), Iván Orozco Abad holds that:

> While from a political-punitive perspective of the democratic state of law and of globalized human rights, on universalist and abstract logic, the amnesties might be thought of as simple and hateful impunity and as the expression of a policy that is the other and even the opposite to law, from a political-military perspective, in contrast, the correlations of the real political forces must be represented, in contextual and international pluralistic logics, as part of the factors that inform a sense—responsible—of justice, and the amnesties and the transitional pardons as institutions fully in line with law.[52]

The Bill of Criminal Alternativity, discussed in 2003, was permanently criticized for amounting to a pardon in disguise. While the current process that is evolving within the framework established by the JPL is not criticized in such harsh terms, it includes certain privileges that could be interpreted as "transitional pardons". To cite some reflections of Orozco Abad:

> The great danger encompassing the universalistic visions of the democratic state of law and human rights on a global scale is that of the excessive submission of politics and the domestic political organs to an international judicature committed to values and with the fair punishment of criminals, but little preoccupied by issues such as the failed peace processes in the periphery of the world.[53]

These possible failures and the drama in the periphery are the upshot to studies that, with comparative references to the Chilean, Argentinean and the El Salvadorian cases, analyze the "limits to the humanitarian conscience", and, with them, the "dilemmas of peace and justice in Latin America".[54]

52 Orozco Abad, I, *Combatientes, rebeldes y terroristas. Guerra y Derecho en Colombia*, Bogotá: Temis, 2006, p 26 (unofficial translation).

53 Orozco Abad, fn 52 above, p 27 (unofficial translation).

54 Orozco Abad, I, *Sobre los límites de la conciencia humanitaria. Dilemas de la paz y la justicia en América Latina*, Bogotá: Temis, 2005. It is noteworthy that several public officials have used this book as a kind of Bible to understand aspects related to the objective of transitional justice mechanisms.

The sense of paradox is also present in the limits between "the pardon and the wall".[55] In the light of this tension, Angelika Rettberg explores the questions and dilemmas of transitional justice in a country that is debating critical themes from that perspective. The borders of war and peace constitute our own "geometry of transitional justice".[56] Furthermore, the possible impact of the transitional justice mechanisms that are now being implemented is also subject to a paradox that was mentioned in the beginning of this chapter: "transitional justice without transition?"[57]

In addition, it is appropriate to ask if the process that has been set in motion by the JPL creates a social expectation about the possibility of peace. This expectation and the risk of deception must be assessed in the light of the conflict, social violence and degraded politics that still prevail in large parts of Colombia. The failure of living up to this created expectation, together with deception, will generate more violence. However, the more specific relation between created expectations and possible deceptions must be analyzed with regard to each specific mechanism, such as the application of international criminal law in the domestic context, or the application of ordinary criminal law violations of human rights and humanitarian law. In my view, the real capacity of criminal law to contribute to peace and generate authentic results in terms of transitional justice is extremely limited, and its usage is merely symbolic. The irresponsible propaganda about its great effects and the unfulfilled promises created because of the limits to law generates more violence and less social impact, as well as more precariousness with regard to the effective criminal prosecution of international crimes. The great demands of justice always exceed the regulative capacity of law and even more so if the demands have substantive weight from an evaluative perspective. For this reason, it is of significance that a real political will is present in the mobilization of an adequate and massive number of transitional justice mechanisms.

One conclusion seems simple and expresses a claim to which the entire society ought to be committed: that the reconciliation in function of a possible peace is the effective result of the sum of diverse transitional justice mechanisms. It must be recognized that this claim has a utopian flavour, but such flavour is always present, even in the most terrible dilemmas that are repeated time and again in Colombia and which have been repeated globally: What to do with the killings of the past, faced with the possible killings of the present and the future? Should the dynamics of the punishment around those who are not here prevail over the prevention of future killings?[58] Finally, what is the scope of a

55 Wall is traduced in Spanish as "paredón", a word that refers to an imaginary place of execution.

56 Stahn, C, "La geometría de la justicia transicional: opciones de diseño institucional", in Rettberg, A, *Entre el perdón y el paredón. Preguntas y dilemas de la justicia transicional*, Bogotá: Universidad de los Andes, 2005, p 81.

57 Uprimny, R (ed), *¿Justicia transicional sin transición? Verdad, justicia y reparación para Colombia*, Bogotá: Centro de Estudios de Derecho, Justicia y Sociedad, 2006.

58 Arendt, H, *Eichmann en Jerusalén. Un estudio sobre la banalidad del mal*, Barcelona: Lumen, 2003.

possible pardon (conceptualized in the form of privileges, concessions, gifts with conditions), and what is the scope of promises based on authentic pacts in which the rights to truth, justice and reparation would be a reality? Should the public policy be looking backward or forward? What is the proper solution for the victims who did not have a right to select among philosophical possibilities? In times of transition, in the middle of a conflict, there are many puzzles that must be rethought time and again. In any case, if the process fails, for whatever reason, Colombia would once again be faced with the fate of the circularity of an unfinished conflict and degrading violence.

12 Restoring civic confidence through transitional justice

Paul Seils

12.1 Introduction

A mature reflection on the role of the courts in transitional justice largely depends on a clear understanding of the general purposes of transitional justice. Therefore, a considerable part of this chapter stakes out an argument of how those purposes should be understood. Secondly, the chapter argues that among transitional justice mechanisms, criminal justice occupies a special place. Again, this is a controversial claim, as many scholars and practitioners will argue that criminal justice is simply one mechanism among many, and moreover, one which might often be prudently delayed in favour of prioritizing others.[1]

The argument for the privileged position of criminal prosecutions is a legal one more than a practical one, and certainly does not necessarily demand that criminal prosecutions must take place first. It cannot be pretended that the role of the courts and the timing of their action are unrelated, but this matter can only be dealt with to some degree superficially here. However, the Rome Statute and the position adopted by the prosecutor have made the timing issues significantly more complicated and, at least for the time being, have reduced the space in which states might previously have been able to manoeuvre.

In conclusion, I argue that the role of criminal justice in times of transition is partly about providing a degree of justice to victims directly and indirectly affected by the crimes of perpetrators, but perhaps more significantly about the restoration of a concept of civic trust in the key state institutions which are required to guarantee a new era of genuine respect for fundamental rights and values.

1 See, e.g. the views of various authors, including Alex de Waal and Graeme Simpson in Wadell and Clark (eds), *Courting Conflict*. Available online at www2.lse.ac.uk/internationalDevelopment/research/crisisStates/download/others/ICC%20in%20Africa.pdf.

12.2 The principal aim of transitional justice: reconstituting confidence of state institutions

As a working definition, we can take transitional justice to refer to the application of a variety of mechanisms applied to mass crimes and human rights violations that have taken place in the context of conflict or political repression.[2]

There is a tendency nowadays to use the term to refer to any attempt to address large-scale violations of human rights without any apparent connection to a change of regime or political order. For example, in Colombia, the government, courts and civil society all refer to the processes related to the demobilization of paramilitary groups as a transitional justice process. It may well be the case that the "transition paradigm" was exhausted some time ago, but there is little value in entering upon what is likely to be a sterile definitional debate.[3] What is interesting, however, is the reality that many of us who have worked in transitional justice for a long time have often observed: it is a fundamentally unsatisfactory term and even more so when translated into Spanish. A proper discussion on these matters requires a comprehensive exposition on a theory of transitional justice, which is not possible here.

If a qualifying term is to be given to the kind of justice in question, my preference would be to talk of "reconstitutive justice". The term, while hardly euphonic, captures the central element of the aim of justice in the contexts we are talking about: the reconstitution of bonds of trust and confidence between citizens and institutions that have been fundamentally ruptured in the context of mass violations of human rights.[4]

The material consideration is not whether a political order has changed, but whether the norms and institutions protecting fundamental values have been so radically attacked (and substantially defeated) that a particular kind of effort is required to restore the trust necessary to make those norms and institutions efficient again. In this sense the concept is qualitative: the application of

2 See the summary of transitional justice adopted by the UN Secretary General in his report to the UN Security Council, *The Rule of Law and Transitional Justice in Conflict and Post-Conflict Societies*, UN Doc S/2004/616, 23 August 2004.

3 See for instance, Carothers, T, "The End of the Transition Paradigm", *Journal of Democracy*, vol 13, no 1, 2002, pp 5–21.

4 Seils, P, "Reconciliation in Guatemala: The Role of Intelligent Justice", *Race and Class*, vol 44, no 1, 2001, pp 33–59. At that time, I spoke more of reconstruction. I now prefer the term "reconstitutive" precisely because of the constitutionalist concepts it suggests. At the same time, it raises an uncomfortable question about where the goal of dignity restoration of victims fits. Part of the canon of transitional justice virtues has always been to pursue a victim-centred approach, and has been one I have strongly advocated. In truth proceedings, the aim of satisfying victims' rights has to be subordinated to a broader goal or the reconstitution of trust to which I refer. This does not mean we should not be sensitive to victims' needs or that transitional justice must lose the aspect of vindicating a rights-bearing culture for victims, but it does mean in practical terms that massive violations will result in an extremely imperfect form of justice for the direct victims of abuses and this should be recognized honestly.

transitional justice mechanisms makes sense when the degree of damage is such that core confidence needs special efforts to restore it.

In some circles this view of criminal justice as aiming at something beyond the protection of certain legal rights is seen as controversial if not extreme. What has to be understood is the context in which the discussion is located. Where there is sufficient confidence in the institutions of justice, it may well make some sense to say that at least the immediate aim of criminal justice is to ensure the effective protection of certain basic rights. However, to suggest that this is the aim in the context of crisis and rupture is like telling a patient who needs triple bypass surgery that he needs to keep doing 30 minutes' exercise every day. If the system is working more or less well, its daily effective functioning might be compared to such an exercise regimen, but if there is a chronic failure, something more and something of a different qualitative order is required.[5]

12.3 Reconciliation as a product of transitional mechanisms

It is generally suggested that there are four principal mechanisms: criminal prosecutions, reparations, institutional reform and truth seeking.[6] It is sometimes suggested that reconciliation forms a core element of transitional justice either as a mechanism or as a goal.[7]

The inclusion of reconciliation as an end of transitional justice is unconvincing for three reasons. First, the meaning of reconciliation is so contested that the discussion almost always ends up being about definitions rather than actions. Secondly, the experience of the term, especially in Latin America, has tended to be a politician's and perpetrator's code for impunity. It is made even less attractive by the tendency to place a burden of forgiveness on victims rather than to require contrition and reparation of perpetrators. Thirdly, if it means anything at all it seems to be best understood as the collective result of successful transitional justice efforts rather than as a programme similar to prosecutions, reparations, truth commissions or institutional reform. One cannot exclude the possibility that criminal justice or transitional justice have the ability to promote something that some people might recognize as reconciliation.[8] The

5 The difference between reconstitution and maintenance is a significant one and is one reason why the arguments that transitional justice should be seen as simply a form of ordinary justice are misplaced.

6 See Report of the UN Secretary-General, fn 2 above.

7 e.g. the International Centre for Transitional Justice began to endorse explicitly this position around late 2001, which can be found in their presentation in their own website. Available online at: www.ictj.org.

8 Furthermore, it is possible of course to have a programme that seeks to have, e.g. town hall meetings or even more ambitious efforts between previously opposing communities, and to call these "reconciliation mechanisms". As commendable as such efforts may be, they are, in empirical terms, an almost non-existent component of transitional justice programmes.

best description of this is a concept of reconstitution of civic trust, rather than reconciliation.

12.4 A working definition of confidence or civic trust

If transitional justice aims at the reconstitution of civic trust and is in this sense distinguished from the concept of reconciliation as it would ordinarily be understood by most people, there still remains a need to explain more clearly what kind of trust we are talking about and how it can be achieved.

Fundamentally, this conception of transitional justice is a practical and modest one, even to the point of being minimalist. The history of efforts in the last 20 years indicates that the optimism that permeates the body politic at times of transition often inflates the expectations beyond what is reasonably possible in the light of resources and capacity. While to suggest that "where there's a will, there's a way" may be the stuff of motivation handbooks, it is no basis upon which to run a transitional justice policy.

The reconstitution of civic trust in the context of transitional justice should be taken to mean effective efforts the results of which create in a critical mass of the citizenry an adequate sense of confidence that the key institutions charged with protecting fundamental human rights are both willing and able to do so. This working definition excludes a number of concepts. It conceives of civic trust in the short term in a more or less binary fashion between certain institutions of the state and the citizens of the state. A triangulated concept might suggest that civic trust must also include the relationships of citizens to one another as well as to institutions of state. In the longer term, this is an important concept, but in terms of priorities must be secondary to the binary relationship mentioned before. In the aftermath of systemic failure in the protection of fundamental rights, it is only natural that people will look first towards institutions to offer protection, and not to fellow citizens who may be the very ones from whom they have something to fear.

The working definition is also modest in its expectations. It seeks only adequate confidence among a critical mass of the population. A critical mass of the population does not necessitate in the short term an overwhelming majority, nor even necessarily a majority, but certainly something very close to it to meet a basic standard. The measurement of such confidence is extremely complicated, and serious judgment on levels of confidence has to go beyond superficial analysis presented through *vox pop* surveys. While these may be important in some regards, they are far from being sufficient. Furthermore, adequate confidence means that the critical mass does not expect the institutions of state to work perfectly in all regards, nor for there not to be the occasional serious lapse.

This does not mean that they should be abandoned, but it seems like something very close to spin to pretend that they form a genuine mechanism compared to prosecutions, truth commissions, reparations programmes and institutional reform.

Such failures can be seen in the most stable and developed of democracies. Adequate confidence means that there is a belief that the institutions of state are in the vast majority of cases regulated by enforceable laws and that those charged with enforcing them in the police, prosecution and judiciary are able to do so without fear or favour. This of course is a different matter from guaranteeing convictions, for example.

12.5 The developing appreciation of a holistic strategy in transitional justice

Before addressing the central theme of the role of the courts, a few additional reflections on the development of the field of transitional justice may help to situate the following reflections.

Up until a few years into the new millennium, there was a perception among many lawyers involved in the human rights field that transitional justice was little more than a sophisticated way of avoiding criminal justice.[9] A significant element contributing to this view may have been the prominent role played by the South African Truth and Reconciliation Commission in many people's thinking about transitional justice. That Commission is sometimes criticized (extremely simplistically) as a means of providing immunity to serious criminals. It is certainly true, however, that in reading many comments of key players in the Truth and Reconciliation Commission, there appears to have been a perception that not only was criminal justice inadequate in the circumstances, but that it was also somehow inappropriate.[10] This perception has changed in the last 15 years. Most people working in the field now recognize that a comprehensive approach offered by the range of transitional justice mechanisms has a better chance of meeting the objectives than relying on one or two elements.[11]

9 See Roht-Arriaza, N, *Transitional Justice in the Twenty-First Century: Beyond Truth versus Justice*, Cambridge: Cambridge University Press, 2006. In particular, the introduction and the chapter written by Reed Brody. See also the article of Reed Brody concerning the role of truth commissions as an obstacle to the delivery of justice: Brody, R, "Justice: The First Casualty of Truth?", *The Nation*, 30 April 2001.

10 Desmond Tutu, the Chairman of the South African Truth and Reconciliation Commission, explains the reason for its creation this way: "While the Allies could pack up and go home after Nuremberg, we in South Africa had to live with one another." See Mpilo Tutu, D, *No Future Without Forgiveness*, New York: Doubleday, 2000, p 21.

11 There are some who would go further than me on this issue and consider that an adequate understanding of the theory of transitional justice always requires a comprehensive application of the principal mechanisms in order to ensure that it contributes as meaningfully as possible to the reconstitution of trust. I am doubtful about this and believe that the scale and scope of the efforts needed depend to a large extent on pre-existing infrastructural capacities (including intellectual, political, economic and bureaucratic). If one takes the example of post-Franco Spain where the only recognizable form of transitional justice was very significant institutional reform, it is difficult to argue that it was not a very meaningful contributor to the reconstitution of trust in the protection of fundamental rights.

12.6 The re-emergence of the importance of criminal justice

An article published in early 2008 about the work of the International Criminal Court (ICC) in Uganda argued that it was essential to understand that criminal justice was simply one of a range of options that did not necessarily have to be privileged over others; that we had to be creative in terms of timing so that we could be sensitive to the pursuit of peace.[12]

A strong moral and practical defence of this position can be made, but there is a strong risk that it ignores the direction in which transitional justice is now headed. It is not necessary here to rehearse in detail the well-known jurisprudential and legislative events that have described a clear trend in establishing a duty on national authorities to prosecute certain kinds of crimes. The jurisprudence of the Inter-American Commission and Court of Human Rights in particular and to a slightly lesser extent the European Court of Human Rights developed in a way that supported this view throughout the 1980s and 1990s. The ad hoc International Tribunals for the Former Yugoslavia and Rwanda contributed importantly to the development of the recognition of such obligations. The preamble to the Rome Statute talks explicitly of the duty of states to exercise their criminal jurisdiction in relation to the proscribed crimes. One of course should be careful about reading too much into matters contained in preambles to treaties, but without going into exactly what this reference means in terms of legal obligations, one can admit quite easily that it is significant evidence of a continuing trend. Most crucial of all is the principle of complementarity enshrined in the Rome Statute. Whatever the meaning of the language in the Preamble, one can understand the simple concept that if national authorities do not prosecute, the ICC will.

This is the current legal reality. From a moral and practical perspective this may be an entirely unsatisfactory position for many people. Recent debates on the possibilities of the UN Security Council delaying ICC action under article 16 of the Rome Statute raise very legitimate questions about the role of the Court in the context of peace efforts. One can make a respectable practical argument that the ICC ought not to enter into investigations in ongoing conflicts or in the context of peace negotiations. But one immediately comes up against two conflicting arguments. One rests on the unproven expectation that the threat of prosecutions can act as a brake on atrocities and push forward the cause of negotiation. The other is the legal requirement established under the Rome Statute that in order to be genuine, investigations and prosecutions must take place within a reasonable time.

Exactly what amounts to a reasonable time will surely depend on the facts and circumstances of each case. However, perhaps the example of Colombia is

12 See Simpson, G, "One among Many: The ICC as a Tool of Justice during Transition", in *Courting Conflict*, fn 1 above, pp 73–79.

instructive in this regard. The Rome Statute entered into force for Colombia in November 2002. Efforts to pass legislation offering a deal to paramilitaries who demobilized took three years to pass and its implementation did not begin in earnest until 2007. Taking into account the complexity of the situation, it would appear that at least under the current prosecutor, as long as there appears to be some serious activity towards prosecutions, it will be enough to postpone a decision to open an investigation. In those circumstances, it may well still be true that a sensible structuring of efforts that do not necessarily entail prioritizing criminal prosecutions could still prosper without the intervention of the ICC.

There would appear to be two preconditions to such structuring of procedures. It would have to be sufficiently evident to the prosecutor that the steps being taken were not intended to and did not in fact inhibit the prospects of future prosecutions. Secondly, that the efforts being taken in the interim were justifiable given the complexity of the circumstances and that all things considered might be seen as enhancing the prospect of justice rather than precluding it, albeit at a later stage.

It has been suggested that a truth commission might be considered an investigation within the meaning of Article 17 of the Rome Statute and that, as such, the preparation and execution of a commission could be enough to prevent an investigation being opened by the ICC.[13] This matter is addressed in more detail later on in this chapter. It is possible that certain models of truth commissions could meet such a test, although to date only Argentina's in 1983 is likely to meet that standard. To be considered an investigation, there must be a direct procedural and institutional connection to that activity and the prospect of prosecution.

12.7 Priorities, structuring and sequencing

While the prosecutor has sometimes suggested that he does not consider sequencing a relevant concept in the deliberations of the ICC, he has at least certainly been prepared to give a very considerable margin of appreciation to the Colombian authorities, including in terms of time, so that they can deal with prosecutions of serious criminals.[14] While doubtful, it is not inconceivable that circumstances could emerge in a situation where, if carefully crafted, a structured approach that did not prioritize criminal justice could still prosper. The key in any such approach would be in presenting arguments indicating that the delay in prosecution is justified under those circumstances.

13 See, e.g. Robinson, D, "Serving the Interests of Justice", *European Journal of International Law*, vol 14, no 3, 2003, pp 481–505.

14 See the speech of the ICC Prosecutor in Nuremberg in June 2007 as an example of his view that justice in Uganda could not be "sequenced". Available online at www.icc-cpi.int/NR/rdonlyres/4E466EDB-2B38-4BAF-AF5F-005461711149/143825/LMO_nuremberg_20070625_English.pdf.

The arrival of the ICC does not mean that criminal justice is the only game in town. It does not even necessarily mean that it must be the aspect upon which a state concentrates the majority of its financial resources. What it does mean is that it is privileged in the following two senses. First, there is simply no alternative to prosecution at some point: for States Parties, there must be prosecutions. Secondly, they cannot be delayed indefinitely while other deals are negotiated and mechanisms take place. The current Prosecutor of the ICC has indicated that there has to be an adaptation to the reality that there is not only no impunity, but that criminal responsibility has to be dealt with as a matter of urgency. If states delay unreasonably, the ICC will act. An interesting example is that of Kenya. The Office of the Prosecutor wrote to the government and other bodies there. It is almost certain that the ICC action in this regard was a significant catalyst in driving forward the creation of the special court that has now been set up. (It might be reasonably said, however, that the example of Colombia, the longer time goes on, presents a serious challenge to this concept.)

The second way in which criminal justice is in a sense different from the other mechanisms is that the margin of appreciation afforded to states in meeting relevant obligations is narrower in respect of criminal justice than it is in respect of truth, reparations and institutional reform.[15] This is largely because the substantive and procedural context in which criminal justice can take place will have been established before the violations took place and for the processes not to violate human rights norms they will have to conform significantly to those established norms and procedures.

There is an additional aspect to this consideration: there is an element of recognition or expectation on the part of the public with regard to criminal justice. The institutions of justice represent the frontline in the defence of fundamental norms and values. The public look to and expect such protection. On the other hand, reparations schemes, truth commissions and reform programmes in the aftermath of mass violations are necessarily ad hoc and do not respond to the same kind of recognition and expectation generated in the context of the permanence of the institutions of justice.

15 I have argued previously that truth commissions do not provide justice in the sense required by the provision of an effective remedy under relevant human rights, but represent a contribution towards that goal. This does not mean that they do not provide a means of meeting the obligations of states in respect of the right to truth, but they should not be confused as simultaneously satisfying the right to justice. See Seils, P, "The Limits of Truth Commissions in the Search for Justice: An Analysis of the Truth Commissions of El Salvador and Guatemala and Their Effect in Achieving Post-Conflict Justice", in Bassiouni, M C (ed), *Post-Conflict Justice*, New York: Transnational Publishers, 2002.

12.8 The role of the courts in reconstructing confidence

12.8.1 The false dichotomy of retributivism and restoration

A frustration in reading transitional justice literature discussing criminal justice is the frequent reference to criminal justice as retributive justice. Then, in almost all cases this understanding is compared unfavourably to restorative justice. This approach is philosophically confused, empirically wrong and practically damaging.

In the first place, one must make a distinction between the philosophical justifications for imposing punishment and the policy objective in doing so. The two classical justifications for imposing punishment are those of retributivism (generally associated with Kant and premised on the basis that an individual as a free moral agent can be punished on account of the actions he or she has voluntarily engaged in) and deterrence (from the classical utilitarianism school of Bentham) where the moral justification is that punishment can be justified, since it stops others committing crimes and thereby contributes to the greatest happiness of the greatest number.

However, almost none of the discussion on criminal justice in the context of transitional justice relates to arguments about philosophical justifications for punishment. Rather, wittingly or not, it is about the policy goals. In this context, when people talk about retribution, they mean something very close to a form of judicialized vengeance, and generally also mean that this is on the whole a regrettable idea that reflects the weakness of criminal prosecutions. The retributive goal is compared to the restorative goal, with the latter generally being seen as somehow not possible within the context of criminal justice and preferable in the context of certain kinds of violations or cultural contexts.

In empirical terms, we know that the policy aims of criminal justice are much more complicated than simple retribution. It may be the case that retribution is a very strong feeling on the part of victims, or indeed of broader elements of society, but it is quite clearly only one of a number of aims in terms of state policy.

Almost all modern approaches to criminal punishment identify at least five possible objectives in criminal punishment: incapacitation through incarceration to stop offending; specific deterrence aimed at stopping the person who has been punished from offending again (after release); rehabilitation, where the punishment is aimed at helping to reform the offender's behaviour and general deterrence, where the punishment of offenders sends a message to society at large of the risks of offending. One may add retribution to this list, but it is by no means the dominant aspect of most criminal justice policies in modern societies. One can also add a different concept that is sometimes referred to as positive deterrence (promoted notably by the German theorist Jakobs) or a slightly different concept of persuasion. This sees the purpose of the effective functioning of prosecutions and the courts not simply in the negative deterrence of putative offenders, but, more positively, sees the role of the courts as formally upholding and affirming the underlying values of society adhered to by its vast majority. In this sense most people are not resisting crime because they fear the risk of detection and punishment, but because it does not accord with their moral values and because they see that their moral values are, broadly speaking and at a certain functional level, those upheld by the institutions of the state.[16]

The lazy assimilation of criminal justice to retributive justice is damaging because it undermines the multiple effects it should and does have in any society. It is a reductionism that misrepresents the real value of criminal justice and, more damagingly still, pretends that its ad hoc replacements can fill the gaps it is alleged to have.

12.8.2 The policy goals of criminal justice in transitions

If we accept that in the most ordinary of times the pursuit of criminal justice is a complex mix of policy objectives, how should we describe them in the exceptional context of transitional justice?

In relation to criminal justice, the particular context of mass atrocities does not affect the role of the courts or the purpose of criminal prosecution. It does not matter if the conflict or repression that led to massive crimes against civilians was on the basis of ideology, ethnicity or resources; they all result in the chronic weakening of the institutions of the state, in their ability to support and protect the values that bind the state.

It is for this reason that the best way of explaining the purpose of criminal justice in transitions (and transitional justice generally) is in terms of reconstituting the necessary conditions for confidence. A successful criminal justice programme after mass atrocities should be able to say that the worst kinds of crimes have been identified; the most egregious patterns of abuse and attacks on fundamental norms underpinning the society have been exposed. Those with the responsibility for creating and directing the criminal plans of the organizations involved should have been held to account; the relevant institutions—above all the prosecuting and judicial authorities—should be able to say that they have acted efficiently and impartially; and the citizens at large should be able to say that the fundamental values of the society have been reaffirmed and that the institutions charged with protecting them deserve our confidence once again.

12.8.3 The role of the courts in connection with other transitional justice mechanisms

It is almost certain that criminal justice in itself will not restore confidence among the population at large after mass violations and chronic system failure.

16 The idea of persuasion set out here is taken largely from the approach set out by de Greiff, P, "Deliberative Democracy and Punishment", *Buffalo Criminal Law Review*, 2002, vol 5, no 2, pp 373–403.

In particular, the mechanisms of institutional reform will be of vital importance to ensure that whatever gains are made by specific trials be consolidated and long lasting. What relationship do other transitional justice mechanisms have with criminal justice?

The principal difference between the pursuit of criminal justice in transitions and the other mechanisms I have already mentioned is that the exercise of criminal jurisdiction is the only element whose form is both required and legally defined. There must be criminal trials subject to the laws of criminal procedure and evidence. There may be a significant margin of appreciation in terms of precisely what crimes are prosecuted and who the targets should be, but the form and nature of the obligation are established. Furthermore, the other three mechanisms by their nature are ad hoc mechanisms with ad hoc institutions. Even if the criminal justice mechanisms had ad hoc features, such as a special tribunal, it still takes place within established institutions with pre-established rules of evidence and procedure. It has a different nature from the other mechanisms.

The jurisprudence of the Inter-American Court on the issues of the right to truth and reparations is a matter of some interest. Some people argue that the duty to prevent crimes recurring puts a duty on the state to carry out institutional reform, but whether citizens have a correlative right to institutional reform seems to be more problematic. It is true that all three of these mechanisms by their very nature leave states a very wide margin of appreciation. The question is how these mechanisms should relate to criminal justice.

It is clear that in Latin America, in the past the issue of criminal justice has not only not been privileged, but has been conspicuously ignored either by de iure or de facto amnesties, the most notable examples of de iure amnesties coming from Chile and El Salvador, with perhaps the most obvious de facto example being that of Guatemala. Times have changed, however. The new millennium has brought a clear recognition of the changed landscape. The decision in the case of *Barrios Altos*[17] has had an important impact both on the issue of prescription and amnesty. Similarly, the entry into force of the Rome Statute, even if not binding on all states, has had a marked effect on changing the nature of the discourse on the relevant obligations. Until the situation of Colombia, it is arguable that the only transition in Latin America that has the issue of criminal prosecutions as central in the transitional justice programme was that of Argentina. Chile, El Salvador, Guatemala and Peru had no genuinely comparable elements.

12.9 Prosecutions and truth commissions

The Truth and Reconciliation Commission in Peru had a unique characteristic in that a special team was set up (called the *equipo de judicialización*), which was

17 IACtHR, case of *Barrios Altos v Peru*, Series C No 75, Judgment of 14 March 2001.

meant to investigate specific crimes with a view to passing that information on to the Prosecutor Office (*Ministerio Público*).[18] The idea was positive, but undermined by the lack of legislation requiring the *Ministerio Público* to take any account of the work done by the Truth and Reconciliation Commission team. It depended ultimately on good faith. The relations between the two institutions were not good and in the event the Prosecutor General (*Fiscal General*) at the time showed no interest in the work of the Commission.

The idea of the *equipo de judicialización* offers one interesting idea about the possible ways in which truth commissions and criminal justice might work in the future. The idea of the *equipo* was unique in the context of truth commissions, but was not entirely original in another sense. There are a number of entities in different countries which have the power to carry out investigations and pass these on to national prosecuting authorities. Those authorities are then obliged to make a decision on whether to proceed with a criminal investigation and their decisions are subject to public scrutiny. Two examples of such bodies are the Police Ombudsman's Office in Northern Ireland and the Ugandan Human Rights Commission.

This thought is not relevant for the past in Latin America, but it may be helpful for the future. It offers three potential advantages: it means that the resources put towards criminal investigation at that time do not detract from the resources of the ordinary law enforcement and prosecution (or at least would do so to a much lesser degree); in addition, it ensures a certain degree of independence and transparency in the initial investigation, and it gives institutions the time to improve their abilities and reputation before being tasked with carrying out the criminal investigation and prosecution.

The need and desirability of such a mechanism will depend on the circumstance of each situation, but it is certainly something that deserves serious consideration. Such a power increases significantly the already valuable role that truth commissions can play in addressing massive crime.

It is impossible and *in purely practical terms* perhaps even undesirable to prosecute all of the crimes that may have been committed. We all recognize that truth commissions have a huge value in exposing the truth about many cases that would never get to trial, in allowing victims to bear witness to their suffering and to offer the prospect of acknowledgment and dignity. Truth commissions can cover the sweep of criminality, and go into more detail about the social and historical causes. Nonetheless, one should be wary of over-stating the capacity of any historical study including truth and reconciliation commissions, to establish a definitive truth. Circumstances are rarely apt for such results, and less so in the immediate aftermath of repression. Michael Ignatieff's

18 While I was employed by the International Center for Transitional Justice (ICTJ) from 2001 to 2004, I carried out work with the Peruvian Truth and Reconciliation Commission in this area. The reflections here are personal and do not necessarily represent the views of the ICTJ.

more modestly stated notion that commissions may "narrow the range of permissible lies" seems a much wiser framing of a commission's ambition.[19]

12.10 Prosecutions, history and case selection

If truth commissions limit the field of permissible lies, what should be the relationship of the courts to history? In short: very limited. The role of the courts is to establish the guilt or innocence of the perpetrators, not to tell the history of the nation. They are fundamentally ill-equipped to tell complex historical dramas and attempts to do so will inevitably bring into question the legitimacy of the exercise.

Having said that, courts should not be entirely blind to the historical reality. Even if they are not well equipped to write history, their decisions clearly can have a huge historical impact. One needs only to look at Nuremberg, Eichmann and the Junta trials to prove the point.

Therefore, an important and minimal standard in case selection might be called "historical fidelity".[20] By historical fidelity I mean establishing a minimal test which requires that criminal prosecutions in transitional contexts do not distort the broad historical realities of what went on during conflict or repression. This is essentially a method of guaranteeing the legitimacy of the processes. For example, if it was reasonably clear that 80 per cent of all serious violations that had taken place in a conflict were by one party, but a prosecutions programme sought to prosecute both sides for one massacre each, one might have serious difficulty if criminal trials appeared to establish that both sides were equally responsible for atrocities. This does not mean that those who committed the lesser number should not be prosecuted. It means that prosecutions have to be brought in a way that demonstrates the nature of the criminal organizations and the crimes they committed, and with a degree of proportionality. Historical fidelity does not mean that the courts should tell the history of a conflict, it means that prosecution strategies should not distort the broad realities of responsibility for atrocities committed in conflict or repression.

12.11 The numbers issue: how many should be prosecuted?[21]

There are differences in the appropriate prosecution strategies of international courts, extraterritorial courts and national courts in times of transition. The Office of the Prosecutor at the ICC has made it clear that he will pursue those most responsible for serious crime and that this will normally only result in a small number of prosecutions in any given situation. The ICC is a court of last resort. Its aim is to ensure that if national authorities are unwilling or unable

19 Ignatieff, M, "Articles of Faith", *Index on Censorship*, vol 25, no 5, 1996, p 113.
20 See Seils, fn 4 above.
21 Seils, fn 4 above. See also Robinson, fn 13 above, pp 493–495.

to prosecute, the ICC will do so. In a sense, its role is to provide a credible threat against impunity, but it cannot prosecute everyone. The ICC's role is not the same as national authorities in a time of transition. If the national authorities fail, the ICC will step in, but it cannot, by its own nature, restore the confidence in national institutions. The ICC is part of a global system of justice. It can play a crucial role in affirming those global values and in showing other states that if they also fail, those bearing the greatest responsibility will be brought to account. In this sense, the ICC is also about more than simple retribution: it is also about affirmation of universal values, the prevention of crime and the dignity of victims.

The narrow and limited policy of the ICC may not be as justifiable in the context of national prosecutions. If the aim is to reconstruct relationships of confidence, there will have to be a critical balance achieved that gives a sense that it is not only scapegoats that have been pursued, but that the criminal proceedings have managed to expose the criminal nature of the systems or institutions that have been responsible for the crimes.

This does not necessarily require that hundreds of people be prosecuted. The very limited prosecutions that took place in Argentina prior to the Full Stop and Due Obedience laws were in many ways sufficient to re-establish confidence in the institutions of justice within the concept of the working definition I proposed earlier—a critical mass of the population having adequate confidence that the institutions of state were willing and able to protect fundamental rights without fear or favour. What numbers are to be prosecuted cannot be determined in the abstract, but limited resources will strongly incline the choice towards less rather than more.

One notes the current situation in Colombia, where more than 3,000 people have been put forward by the government as eligible for the special benefits under the Justice and Peace Law. The number is huge and is presenting important logistical difficulties while, at the same time, it almost certainly represents a small percentage of alleged perpetrators.

The issue of whether it is permissible to proceed against only a limited number of accused presents a real challenge in terms of human rights norms. Some people might argue that each and every perpetrator has to be tried in order to address the right to an effective remedy.

The requirement that all perpetrators are tried is clearly not required by the relevant human rights norms: the fact that in certain jurisdictions a deal for non-prosecution can be made in exchange for crucial information that may lead to a conviction indicates certain limits on what is required. A strong argument can be made that prosecuting those with the greatest responsibility for crimes can go a very long way to meeting the international obligations of states. At the same time, it cannot be pretended that each and every victim will receive an effective remedy. In those circumstances, a national prosecution programme should only be considered legitimate if the crimes which it does prosecute can be said to pursue those with the greatest responsibility, and to illustrate the general systems or patterns that led to the atrocities.

The concept of the most responsible is not a legal concept, but a practical one.[22] It requires an understanding of the kinds of crimes that have taken place. If, as is likely, large numbers of serious crimes have been committed in a widespread or systematic way, it is probable that such activities responded to a degree of planning and organization. The efforts of selection and investigation should be directed towards identifying the structures or organizations involved in such systematic or widespread crimes. Having identified those structures or groups, the aim should be to prosecute those people who actually participated in the planning, ordering or instigation of those crimes *before* prosecuting low-level perpetrators. That is to say, we are not talking about strict liability or presuming that those at the top of structures necessarily hold criminal responsibility. The evidence must show that such people acted criminally.

There are three key reasons for such an approach. In the first place, if one wants to restore confidence in the institutions of state, there has to be a clear perception that it is those at the top of such structures and groups who will be held responsible and that they will not be allowed to avoid responsibility by laying the blame on scapegoats. Secondly, if only limited numbers can be prosecuted, aiming at those responsible for multiple crimes at a higher level is preferable to prosecuting those who carried out the orders in individual cases. Thirdly, in purely practical terms, obtaining relevant evidence to ensure a conviction requires allowing some degree of co-operation with insiders or informants. Many Latin American systems now include some degree of "effective collaboration" mechanisms. While to be effective these should not exclude high level people, at the very least they ought to provide a way for investigators to obtain crucial information about planning, ordering and instigation that will often be able to come from medium ranking and lower levels.

12.12 Extraterritorial prosecutions and restoring confidence

The role of extraterritorial courts in transitions is obviously complex. It is important to establish to what extent such courts are actually operating in transitional contexts at all. If the proposition is correct that transitional justice has the aim of restoring destroyed confidence in the way already described, it is reasonable to say that the transition is over when that confidence has been adequately restored among a critical mass of the population. Obviously, this will depend on the facts and circumstances of each situation. One would have no real hesitation, for example, in saying that Argentina has completed its transition. I am inclined to think of the processes that are going on now as much more related to normal justice processes designed to maintain, not restore, confidence in the institutions of state.

22 See, for instance, the comments of the ICC Appeals Chamber on the subject of whether the ICC Prosecutor was legally obliged to pursue those bearing the greatest responsibility. *Prosecutor v Bosco Nataganda* case, Appeals Chamber Decision, 13 July 2006, paras 73–79.

On the other hand, one can, unfortunately, be equally confident that Guatemala has actually barely begun its transition in terms of confidence restoration. There has been almost no justice and what has come has come at a terrible price. The fact that the war finished 12 years ago has nothing to do with the stage of its transition. Indeed, the creation of the International Commission against Impunity by the United Nations and the Guatemalan Government is an abject testimony to chronic failure.

I therefore think that the role of the Spanish courts in relation to Guatemala is quite different from their role in relation to Argentina. It is clear that Guatemalan authorities are broadly unwilling or unable to prosecute the mass atrocities of the conflict. The Spanish courts cannot restore confidence in Guatemalan institutions, but they can play a role similar to that of the ICC in ensuring that there is a credible threat of prosecution in the light of Guatemalan failure. They cannot prosecute everyone, and the efforts should be strategically aimed at those most responsible. The degree to which extraterritorial prosecutions are necessary or prudent in the context I have set out will depend on the circumstance in the country that has gone through or is going through transition.

12.13 Conclusion

The foregoing reflections seek to present an overview of the place that criminal justice should occupy in the framework of transitional justice. The field itself has undergone some significant changes in the last 10 years or so, with a growing realization that the mechanisms in question may be of great value in circumstances where there is no real transition to speak of. In this light, it begins to make much more sense to see the role of such mechanisms as a means of confidence restoration more than being bound to a particular political transition.

While awkward and in some quarters no doubt an unwanted truth, criminal justice has returned to the centre of such mechanisms, not least as a result of the entry into force of the Rome Statute. Sophisticated efforts to sequence transitional justice mechanisms that also delay criminal justice, despite the positions publicly taken by the ICC Prosecutor, cannot be ruled out. They will have to be presented, however, in a way that recognizes the non-negotiability of criminal justice if they are to have any success, and such justice cannot be postponed indefinitely. The suggestion to tie truth commissions into a quasi criminal investigation requiring decisions from the prosecuting authorities on further action is potentially useful in this context, albeit it would perhaps have some kind of chilling factor on those prepared to come forward to speak the truth.

But the issue is no longer simply a matter of moral or political debate. Whether we like it or not, the law has moved on. Strategies must be guided towards the most effective form of prosecutions in all of the circumstances, and such processes must take place within a reasonable time.

13 The International Criminal Court

Possible contributions of the Rome Statute to judicial processes in transitional societies

Elizabeth Odio Benito

13.1 Introduction

During the second half of the twentieth century, Latin America was the scene of serious armed conflicts that resulted in hundreds of thousands of victims of very grave mass violations of basic human rights. Women and men of all ages, classes and ethnicities, making up the social fabric of many of our countries, suffered, and are still suffering, from abuses of power by political groups that indiscriminately violate people's right to life, freedom, dignity and physical integrity.

Experts in various disciplines coined the concept of "societies in transition" for countries that have experienced serious conflicts with violations of international humanitarian and human rights laws and are still striving to repair the harm done to victims and to democratic institutions and processes. Others are still in the midst of conflict. In transitional societies, the role of justice and the rule of law are essential in achieving social reconstruction, consolidating truly engendered democratic institutions and strengthening the judiciary. Judicial relief alone is insufficient, therefore, making opportunities for survivors to rebuild their lives essential. This will only succeed if all victims of the conflict are involved, or at least duly represented, in all decision-making, consolidation and social reconstruction processes. However, this condition has not materialized for the majority of women, whose exclusion from political decision-making has been detrimental to their interests and also to the other half of humanity.

There is a constant reiteration that the primary objective of national and international criminal justice systems is to combat impunity long enjoyed by those bearing the greatest responsibility for the most serious human rights violations. Nowadays, a further stated objective of these systems is to grant victims the right to obtain reparations and to participate in judicial proceedings and administrative or non-judicial processes dealing with past or present serious violations suffered by them and their families.

Against this background, the purpose of this chapter is to examine some possible contributions of international criminal justice, primarily of the 1998 Rome Statute, to the work of national courts, whether officially established courts or transitional justice systems in transitional societies. The core themes are twofold: the categories of international crimes under the Rome Statute and the rights of the victims of such crimes whose status is recognized for the first time in international criminal justice with the adoption of the Statute. The focus will also be on the crimes of sexual violence.

13.2 Crimes within the jurisdiction of the ICC

The idea of having a permanent international criminal court was not a novel one; indeed, it was not even novel when the First World War came to an end and (unsuccessful) attempts were made to put Kaiser Wilhelm II on trial. However, when the Second World War ended and the victors opted to try some of those who bore the greatest responsibility for the massacres that had been perpetrated during the conflict (instead of shooting them directly, as Churchill proposed), the political decision of creating the Nuremberg Tribunal clearly paved the way for unprecedented developments of international humanitarian law, international human rights law and, finally, international criminal law. This decision permanently transformed relations between member states of the international community and relations between the state and women, men and children in each country.

As a result of the gradual development of all branches of international law from 1945 to 1998, the prosecution of international crimes, which, since 2002, has been the mandate of the International Criminal Court, has benefited from the important precedents, case law and contributions of the military courts of Nuremberg and Tokyo (1945), the ad hoc international tribunals for the former Yugoslavia (1993) and Rwanda (1994) as well as the experience of the hybrid courts, such as Sierra Leone, Timor Leste and, more recently, Cambodia.[1] The Rome Statute's Preamble sets forth two concrete objectives: to prosecute and punish the perpetrators of international crimes and to put an end to impunity as a means of preventing further crimes.[2] It also refers to the victims of "unimaginable atrocities that deeply shock the conscience of humanity", and recognizes that these crimes "threaten the peace, security and well-being of the world".[3]

1 This chapter does not include international references or commentaries which, as from 1948, created international crimes such as genocide and torture, and with them, universal criminal jurisdiction. However, the importance of such instruments and their application by the national and international courts and, of course, in the drafting of the Rome Statute of the International Criminal Court, is clear.

2 Rome Statute of the International Criminal Court, adopted on 17 July 1998, preamble, paras 4 and 5.

3 Rome Statute of the International Criminal Court, paras 2 and 3.

The reference to victims and the recognition of a relationship between the commission of international crimes and the threat to international peace and security may well be seen as reflecting mere aspirations. Stating (as some authors and civil-society organizations have done) that another objective of the court should be to contribute to world peace and security by putting some criminals on trial places too much responsibility on what can be achieved by laws and their implementation alone. While the administration of justice is certainly a fundamental requirement for attaining peace, it must not be forgotten that without any transformation of the social and political power structures, the "peace" attained will be an engendered one and so will also be the kind of justice delivered. For example, gender violence crimes are still barely mentioned or recognized in national judicial systems, whether in formal proceedings or in so-called transitional justice proceedings. And yet, sexual violence committed predominantly against women and also a significant number of men and which constitute, within the context of international criminal justice, a crime against humanity, is integral to conflicts, and also to so-called "peacetimes". It is also known that after "conflict-resolution", sexual violence against women peaks again.[4]

When the multilateral treaty incorporating the statute for a permanent international criminal court, an international criminal code, international criminal procedures and an international co-operation treaty were ratified in Rome on 17 July 1998, it marked the successful—almost miraculous—culmination of an arduous political process of tough negotiations. The most important issue within that process, and also the most politically difficult, and hence most contentious point of the Rome negotiations was, in the opinion of Professor Claus Kress, the delimitation of the jurisdiction of the future court.[5] Others, me included, hold that the most contentious point was the introduction of the term "gender" into the Statute.

The potential impact of the Court on judicial processes in transitional societies can be gauged from the types of crimes within its jurisdiction. What is, I hope, indisputable, is that the international crimes falling within the scope of its jurisdiction are acts that are particularly serious, unlawful and punishable.[6] It is important to note that the Statute does not provide a general definition of international crimes. Indeed, no international convention does. However, it does enumerate the acts considered to be genocide, crimes against humanity and war crimes. Legal scholars have recognized that Articles 6, 7 and 8 of the Rome

4 For an argument about the importance of a gender-perspective when repairing human rights violations, see, for instance, Rubio Marín, R, *The Gender of Reparations. Unsettling Sexual Hierarchies while Redressing Human Rights Violations*, Cambridge: Cambridge University Press, 2010.

5 Kress, C, "Jurisdicción y cooperación en el Estatuto de la CPI: principios y compromisos", in Ambos, K (ed), *La nueva justicia penal supranacional, desarrollos post-Roma*, Valencia: Editorial Tirant Lo Blanch, 2002, p 299.

6 Rome Statute, Arts 5.1(a), 5.1(b) and 5.1(c).

Statute represent an enormous international achievement, as they represent the codification of what had until that point been customs in international humanitarian law and international law. Once part of treaty law in pursuance with the treaty approving the Statute, they are models that national laws must follow and apply under the principle of universal jurisdiction.[7] As a matter of fact, years before the Statute was approved in 1998, the ad hoc international criminal tribunals for the former Yugoslavia and for Rwanda and some national courts had already been working, on the basis of this *jus cogens*, in this manner with considerable success. As a result of the case law developed by the ad hoc tribunals, serious sexual violence committed primarily, but not exclusively, against women, was established as war crimes, crimes against humanity and genocide. The valiant struggle in Rome by hundreds of NGOs, with many women at the helm, assisted greatly in incorporating the jurisprudence of these ad hoc tribunals into the Statute.

Article 6 of the Rome Statute mirrors exactly Article II of the Convention on the Prevention and Punishment of the Crime of Genocide, which was adopted by the UN General Assembly in 1948.[8] Some very important criteria concerning the concept and elements of genocide in international criminal law have evolved from the case law of the ICTR, including crimes of sexual violence and gender crimes, some of which were not taken into account in the Rome Statute, but may be considered in the Court's future work. For example, in the *Akayesu* judgment, mass rape of women was considered to be one of the elements of genocide.[9] Moreover, the concepts arising from the analysis of the UN Commission of Inquiry on Darfur[10] and the judgment of the International Court of Justice in the case of *Bosnia and Herzegovina v Serbia and Montenegro*[11] will be relevant in the Court's future analysis of situations where genocide potentially has been or is being committed.

Article 7 of the Rome Statute concerning crimes against humanity is a fundamental contribution to all branches of international law. It has also great significance at national levels as it contributes to the adoption of domestic legislations that incorporate the Rome Statute being especially vital in transitional justice process systems. By including these crimes, the Rome Statute has

7 Meron, T, "Crimes under the Jurisdiction of the International Criminal Court", in von Hebel, H et al (eds), *Reflection on the International Criminal Court: Essays in Honour of Adriaan Bos*, The Hague: TMC Asser Press, 1999, p 48.

8 Adopted by the General Assembly in Res 260 A (III) of 9 December 1948. Entered into force on 12 January 1951, in accordance with Art XIII.

9 International Criminal Tribunal for Rwanda, *The Prosecutor v Jean Paul Akayesu*, Case No ICTR-96-4-T, Judgment of 2 September 1998, paras 706–707.

10 United Nations, *Report of the International Commission of Inquiry on Darfur to the United Nations Secretary-General pursuant to Security Council resolution 1564 of 18 September 2004*, 25 January 2005.

11 International Court of Justice, case concerning the Application of the Convention on the Prevention and Punishment of the Crime of Genocide (*Bosnia and Herzegovina v Serbia and Montenegro*), Judgment of 26 February 2007.

become the first and most comprehensive treaty in defining and setting out which acts "when committed as part of widespread or systematic attack directed against any civilian population" are classified as crimes against humanity. The chapeau of Article 7 of the Statute confirms that, like genocide, the category of crimes against humanity is applicable in national or international armed conflicts. Given the widespread and systematic grave human rights violations perpetrated in the Latin American region throughout the second half of the last century, the codification of such crimes is without a doubt a fundamental contribution of the Rome Statute. However, the contribution is not measured simply in terms of listing criminal acts, but also because it opens the possibility of prosecutions of non-state actors. In various forums in the region, there is already talk of the application in national courts of the concept embodied in paragraph 2(a) *in fine* of Article 7 of the Rome Statute, according to which these crimes may be committed pursuant to or in furtherance of a state or organizational policy to commit such attack.

It is extremely important that Article 7 of the Rome Statute includes crimes of sexual violence in the light of the fact that crimes against women have always been seen as spoils of war, and thus excluded from international humanitarian law. Such crimes were also forgotten in Nuremberg, and were omitted from the ICTR and ICTY Statutes, even though sexual violence was used, inter alia, as an element of ethnic cleansing in both situations, a fact that was widely documented, for example, by the Bassiouni Commission,[12] and known worldwide. Thus, the struggle to include crimes of sexual violence and a definition of gender that went beyond sexual difference was historical. Political, ideological (and always misogynistic), cultural and religious arguments were advanced, in vain, to reimpose the traditional silencing of these crimes and the lack of recognition that gender involves social construction.[13]

According to Article 8 of the Rome Statute, the Court shall have jurisdiction in respect of war crimes, "in particular when committed as part of a plan or policy or as part of a large-scale commission of such crimes". This statement sets the limits of the Court's jurisdiction rather than the profile or definition of war crimes. However, the wording "in particular" leaves a margin of interpretation as regards the framework in which these crimes may be committed. The provision in question sets out four major categories of war crimes: (i) grave breaches of the four Geneva Conventions of 1949 (known as Geneva Law);

12 UN Final Report of the Commission of Experts Established Pursuant to Security Council resolution 780 (1992), S/1994/674, 27 May 1994.

13 It can be concluded from the final reports of Truth and Reconciliation Commissions such as those in Guatemala and Peru (to name but two) that, also in conflicts in our region, sexual violence has been widespread, systematic and indescribably cruel, principally against women. Even so, since a normal judicial situation has not yet been restored in these countries, hope remains that transitional justice will follow the parameters of the Rome Statute. In the Peruvian report, the Commission included a gender perspective which may well be adopted when legislating on these crimes and issuing the corresponding judgments.

(ii) other serious violations of the laws and customs applicable in international armed conflict (known as The Hague Law and the additional protocols); (iii) in the case of an armed conflict of a non-international character, serious violations of Article 3 common to the four Geneva Conventions; and (iv) other serious violations of the laws and customs applicable in armed conflicts of a non-international character.

In order for the judges to determine whether or not international crimes (including war crimes, of course) have occurred, Article 9 of the Rome Statute refers to the Elements of Crimes that were drafted and approved by the States Parties to "assist" judges in the interpretation and application of the provisions in question.[14]

In the context of Article 8 of the Rome Statute, the transitional provision of Article 124 of that Statute grants a moratorium of seven years on the jurisdiction of the Court with regard to war crimes to those states that opt to implement that clause when becoming a State Party. This is very important, since it applies to war crimes committed in the territory of that state or by its nationals. As such, it may play a key role in the social reconstruction processes in transitional societies. Colombia has already taken recourse of this mechanism. The importance of survivors' involvement in the decision-making progress will be a key element in its successful completion of the task at hand.

Whether countries include, exclude or make inadmissible amendments to Articles 6, 7 and 8 of the Rome Statute when adopting them into their national legislation will be a real measure of states' political will—or lack thereof—to prosecute, punish and prevent the commission of international crimes in their own territories and by resorting to their own courts, according to the complementarity principle. This issue will undoubtedly have to be studied carefully by the judges of the ICC when considering issues of admissibility pursuant to Article 17 of the Rome Statute. It is noteworthy that a significant proportion of such exclusions or amendments made by some countries in their complementary legislations relate to sexual violence and gender crimes.[15]

13.3 Notes on the ICC jurisdiction

The duty to prosecute the international crimes set out in Articles 6, 7 and 8 of the Rome Statute is founded on the decision adopted in the Rome Conference to grant the Court automatic or inherent jurisdiction over those crimes. How and when the Court's jurisdiction is exercised is regulated by the provisions of Articles 12 and 13 of the Rome Statute, known as the trigger mechanisms.

14 Elements of Crimes, adopted by the Assembly of States Parties of the International Criminal Court, ICC-ASP/1/3, 9 September 2002.

15 For more information about such legislations, see Kress, C and Lattanzi, F (eds), *The Rome Statute and Domestic Legal Orders. General Aspects and Constitutional Issues.* Vol 1, Baden-Baden: Nomos Verlagsgesellschaft, 2000.

Furthermore, Article 17 governing the principles of admissibility of cases attempts to balance states' sovereignty in exercising criminal jurisdiction with the international community's historical interest in putting an end to impunity for international crimes. The role of the Prosecutor of the Court is crucial within the framework of such jurisdiction trigger mechanisms. At present, the Court is working on the five following situations (and a number of cases in each): Democratic Republic of the Congo, Northern Uganda, Darfur, Central African Republic and Kenya.

These situations and cases have been brought before the Court in the manner indicated, but the strategy set out by the ICC Chief Prosecutor Luis Moreno Ocampo from the beginning of his mandate has undoubtedly played, and continues to play, a decisive role. To explain this strategy briefly, the prosecutor has stated in his reports that his objective is to investigate and prosecute the most serious crimes, including crimes of sexual violence, and the perpetrators who bear greatest responsibility for the crimes.[16] For societies in transition, this prosecutorial policy means that national judicial systems and mechanisms have an essential role to play in the administration of justice. If the ICC deals with only some of the most serious crimes and prosecutes only those persons (civilians or militaries) alleged to bear greatest responsibility in the national domain, the domestic courts will obviously have to become an essential instrument of the international criminal justice system.

In the case of gender crimes, the role of the national courts and transitional justice systems is vital in preventing, at least to some extent, situations where women who are survivors of rape are forced to live within the same communities and walk the same streets as their alleged rapists. Under the premise that the ICC will deal with those who bear greatest responsibility for atrocities (who are not usually the direct perpetrators), the principals of sexual crimes must be brought before the national courts. For many women who have been raped, one thing that justice means is punishment of the direct perpetrator and therefore for them they are "big fish".

Finally, as regards the work of the prosecutor, it must be noted that the interests of justice clause contained in Article 53.1(c) of the Rome Statute provides additional means to exercise prosecutorial discretion, albeit subject to the supervision of the Pre-Trial Chamber through the checks and balances conceived by the States Parties for judicial oversight over the prosecutor's powers.

13.4 Victims' rights to participate in judicial proceedings and obtain reparations

The second paragraph of the preamble to the Rome Statute acknowledges the existence of millions of children, women and men who have been victims of

16 International Criminal Court, Office of the Prosecutor, "Paper on Some Policy Issues before the Office of the Prosecutor", September 2003.

"unimaginable atrocities that deeply shock the conscience of humanity". Since the Second World War, the majority of these millions of human beings have been innocent civilians caught up in armed conflict. Accordingly, the provisions of the Statute grant victims the rights to protection, to participate in proceedings and to receive reparations. This is the first time in the history of international criminal law that these rights have been recognized as such in an international treaty.

All conflicts—whether large or small, national or international—leave a profound impact on and cause extensive, often irreparable, damage to the entire system of institutions aspiring to democracy. The impact on survivors is also devastating. All states which have attained or are striving towards the rule of law and which are experiencing or have survived such conflicts have had to take up the challenge of rebuilding all of their constitutional, judicial, social and material institutions and structures and to care for those who survived. The hope is that they will be rebuilt in societies truly democratic for women and men. Rebuilding discriminatory laws and practices is no gain to the planet. However, those who have tirelessly devoted themselves to studying the processes and mechanisms designed to combat this inhuman legacy can attest to the fact that, until relatively recently, the victims (especially women) of such atrocities were seldom taken into account by either traditional or transitional justice.

The pioneering work of the Inter-American Court of Human Rights is fundamental to the reconstruction processes in transitional societies in Latin America. The Court's judgments have already recognized the rights of direct and indirect victims to truth, justice and reparations. Its work must continue, but it must have an essential gender perspective (all too often barely noticeable in the texts of judgments) to become a truly progressive force in social reconstruction. Indeed, thanks to the work of that Court, we now hear more and more talk of restorative justice combined with retributive justice. Justice for all, I add.

Despite these undeniable advances in the development of principles and rules of law contained in the Rome Statute and judgments of regional courts, various social stakeholders in societies plagued by conflicts frequently pose a peace versus justice dichotomy where the needs of the former require compromises in the latter. In other words, there is a trade-off between peace and justice. Needless to say, the majority of the victims are excluded from this decision-making process. My own experience in the area of international criminal justice has taught me that international criminal courts are unlikely to meet the restoration of peace as one of our specific and attainable goals. "Judicial" justice must be accompanied by social and economic justice on an equitable basis for women and men. I do not think that this seems possible as a result of our actions. However, I do believe that our mandate of trying those responsible for international crimes, or at least some of them, is an essential contribution to the struggle against impunity. It is based on a conviction that there can be no lasting peace without justice and those solutions which seek to guarantee impunity for those responsible for massacres and widespread, systematic human rights violations do not help transitional societies or societies in general. The volcano continues to simmer slowly underneath until the next rupture. Additional restorative mechanisms may help to improve the living conditions of victims, but impunity for those bearing greatest responsibility for international crimes cannot, and must not, be one of these mechanisms.

Let us now briefly examine what international criminal justice has offered thus far to victims who have sought, and continue to seek, justice in courts of law. This international experience may or may not contribute to the recognition of the rights of victims of international crimes committed in Latin America.

First, we are aware of the fact that despite the fundamental work done by the ICTY and ICTR courts in advancing modern-day international criminal law, their proceedings gave no opportunity for the victims of these grave conflicts to claim their rights, voice their concerns or defend their interests. An attempt was once made to amend their respective statutes to offer this opportunity for survivors, but the Security Council rejected it on the ground that it might violate the rights of the accused to a fair and expeditious trial. The ICTR, for example, has failed to deal, however minimally, with the dire consequences of the widespread and horrendous sexual violence suffered by women and girls during the genocide. There are numerous reports documenting the physical, social, psychological and medical consequences of these survivors. As victims of HIV/AIDS (between 70 and 80 per cent of survivors suffer from this disease and transmit it to their children), they have received little assistance or reparations. Too many to count are now dead, leaving a legacy of orphans who are also in dire need of assistance. The situation of women of all ages who were victims of sexual violence in the war in the former Yugoslavia is no different. Many of them live in poverty today and it was not until recently that they were recognized as war victims with the right to a pension which most of them consider insufficient to survive. It is also fair to say that no victims of the other international crimes committed in the war in the former Yugoslavia received any reparations or compensation either; however, many of these women lost their husbands and partners and poverty also has a distinct differential impact on men and women.

This awareness led the drafters of the Rome Statute to include specific provisions offering those victims the opportunity to be heard not only as witnesses, but also as victims in an international criminal court. Articles 68 and 75 of the Rome Statute expressly grant victims the rights to protection, to participate in judicial proceedings and to obtain reparations. With regard to reparations, Article 75 of the Statute and the definition of victims contained in rule 85 of the Rules of Procedure and Evidence are fundamental provisions.[17]

Individual victims and groups of victims will come before the ICC. Their individual interests will be considered according to the universal legal rights that are violated through the commission of international crimes. The

17 International Criminal Court, Rules of Procedure and Evidence, ICC-ASP/1/3, adopted on 9 September 2002.

procedures set out in the Statute and the Rules have only just started their judicial course. However, the Pre-Trial Chamber, the Trial Chamber and the Appeals Chamber have already issued rulings on victims' rights to participation. These decisions have clarified some concepts and determined the scope of some provisions. Little by little, we will see how victims' access to justice will be guaranteed, their voices heard and a fair balance struck between their interests and the rights of the accused.

In conclusion, there is no doubt that the current outlook for victims in general and, in particular, for victims of the current unprecedented sexual violence in Sudan, the Democratic Republic of the Congo, the Central African Republic, Uganda and in various countries in our Latin-American region—in short, in all societies which have been or still are victims of conflicts, which are, or soon will be, in transition—is more encouraging compared to what international criminal justice had afforded them hitherto. We must stop pretending that sexual violence only occurs during conflict and that there is a "post" for women in conflict resolution. Rape must be seen as preventable and as such it must be approached. As far as democracy is concerned, we must work towards an engendered one free and with hopes for all where justice is neither incomplete (that is, fixated on criminal and judicial aspects alone) nor the exclusive preserve of men for men.

14 Conclusion

Jessica Almqvist and Carlos Espósito

The increasing influence of the canon of criminal law within the concept of transitional justice is present in every part of this book. The canon has been defined as referring to a set of principles or conduct rules for judges and prosecutors, mandating the investigation and prosecution of all crime, including war crime, genocide and crimes against humanity, without any exception. In our view, the *Junta* trial in Argentina may represent a first attempt to translate this claim into judicial action. A more mature understanding of this canon is now reflected in the law, jurisprudence and institutions of international human rights and criminal justice. As former judge Ricardo Gil Lavedra explains, the canon is by now a customary international rule, for him even a peremptory norm, which means that there are no exceptions that can be legitimately invoked to avoid investigating and prosecuting grave crime; as a consequence, a "different and flexible approach in international law to the legality debate" is required.

We believe that the idea of the canon is also present in the concept of "true crimes of state" as upheld by Judge Antônio Cançado Trindade in his contribution to this book. Under this concept, the international responsibility of the state and the international criminal responsibility of the individuals concerned are complementary. The recent cycle of cases concerning massacres in Latin America has brought the issue to the forefront of the international legal discussions. As noted by Judge Cançado Trindade, "segments of contemporary legal doctrine still try to circumvent the issue, but, with the awakening of human conscience, and the disclosure nowadays of atrocities which in the past did not reach international justice, it becomes increasingly more difficult for those petrified by state sovereignty to deny the existence and repeated occurrence of crimes of state". The process of jurisdictionalization of the cycles of massacres in Latin America manifests the right to the realization of justice itself as an imperative of law, and should be accompanied by full respect for the right of direct access of victims to courts, both national and international.

Also the argument of Paul Seils developed in this book is telling of the existence of a canon that is binding upon states and their institutions in the context of transitional justice. As Seils puts it, from a legal standpoint, criminal prosecutions have a privileged, but not exclusive, position in transitional justice.

While certainly not insisting that prosecutions must be carried out prior to any other transitional justice measure, his claim implies that decisions related to prosecutions are no longer in the hands of politicians and subject to discretionary judgment, but must be transferred to the courts. He stresses that the argument about the privileged position of criminal prosecutions is a legal and not a practical one. At the same time, he directs attention to morally flavoured arguments in support of this claim. According to Seils, it is "partly about providing a degree of justice to victims", but perhaps more significantly about "the restoration of a concept of civic trust in the key institutions which are required to guarantee a new era of genuine respect for fundamental rights and values".

While endorsing the idea of the canon and its increasing influence in different judicial settings, it must be acknowledged that it usually takes time before local courts are capable and willing to investigate and prosecute serious human rights violations or grave crime on a massive or considerable scale. The time issue is clearly present in every case, either because a transition has not actually taken place, as shown by Alejandro Aponte in the case of Colombia, or because too many years have passed between the commission of the crimes and the transition itself. Even when a transition has taken place in the sense that a previous dictatorial or authoritarian regime has left power and democratic elections have been held, a new constitutional moment has taken place, and the most remorseful laws associated with the previous regime have been abolished, the courts may well remain passive in relation to serious violations and grave crimes committed in the context of the previous regime for years, even decades, to come. Indeed, such judicial inactivity may last for so long that the perception that it is "too late" for courts to assume a role becomes true, at least in the sense that the perpetrators of the violations and crimes have passed away. In such contexts, it is important to make a distinction between, on the one hand, the conduct of criminal investigations and, on the other hand, prosecutions and sanctioning. As evinced in the Spanish case, even if many of the principal perpetrators of the violations and crimes associated with the dictatorship are by now dead and can thus not be actually prosecuted, it may still be important to consider the possibility of conducting criminal investigations. Javier Chinchón Álvarez emphatically claims that such investigations might have a real significance from the standpoint of family relatives to women, men and children who suffered "enforced disappearances" and whose final destiny or whereabouts are still unknown. This is, however, a contested claim, as shown by the insightful arguments of Alicia Gil Gil, who insists on marking the limits of criminal law to achieve the goals of truth, justice and reparations in cases singled out by the passage of time.

Indeed, the importance of at least conducting criminal investigations for the purpose of localizing the human remains or whereabouts of disappeared persons, which include the identification of perpetrators, is felt throughout the cases. The idea that courts can contribute in a critical manner to the establishment of the truth of what happened to the disappeared persons came to the forefront in the amicable solution that was reached between the Inter-American Commission on Human Rights and Argentina in the case of *Aguiar de Lapacó*, decided on 4 May 1999. The Commission pronounced in this case that the Argentinean Government must exhaust all means to reveal the truth in the sense of establishing the facts related to the circumstances of the enforced disappearances. Argentina agreed to adopt laws that recognized competences of its Federal Courts to perform this task. Such proceedings were thereafter carried out in La Plata, Córdoba and Bahía Blanca, organized in an informal manner and extending to oral hearings, numerous testimonies and the transmission of reports. The judicial decision on 18 October 2008 by *Audiencia Nacional* in Spain and taken by Judge Garzón to open criminal investigations in response to allegations related to crimes of enforced disappearances that took place during the Francoist dictatorship could be seen as inspired by the idea of "truth proceedings", that is, to carry out criminal investigations to establish the truth of what happened to the disappeared persons and to localize their remains or to find out about their current whereabouts. This judicial attempt resembles truth proceedings, although, as we have seen, that attempt was met with ferocious opposition and led to the suspension of Judge Garzón, who is now accused for having breached his duty as a judge as a result of the decision he took to open these investigations.

The real significance of criminal investigations is also unveiled in the debate concerning the "objective" versus the "subjective" character of the Chilean amnesty law decree, as only the latter interpretation of the character of that law would allow criminal investigations to be conducted until the perpetrators have been identified. From this standpoint, while criminal investigations in the context of transitional justice are nearly always seen as "second-best" solutions, that is, the best to hope for in the actual circumstances considering the legal or de facto impossibility of prosecutions, in reality such investigations are of great worth from the standpoint of the family relatives of persons who have disappeared in a lead to establish the truth. Finally, in the Colombian justice and peace process, emphasis is placed on the role of courts as providing mechanisms through which the truth about certain crimes can be unravelled. Of particular importance is the organization of oral confession hearings in which paramilitaries provide "free declarations" (*versiones libres*) of their crimes.

In any case, and as mentioned in the outset of this conclusion, the process of shouldering the burdens of criminal justice, which extend to the holding of proceedings and the imposition of criminal sanction in response to past serious violations and grave crime takes time. It takes time because of the great array of obstacles and impediments that tend to stand in the way and hinder courts from opening criminal investigations or prosecuting such violations and grave crimes. The different contributions in this book have revealed that some obstacles are especially evident and recurrent in the aftermath of transitions and it may be useful, by way of conclusion, to provide a concise summary of each of them. Before doing so, however, it is important to acknowledge that what is an "obstacle" and what is not, whether a given obstacle is intolerable or permissible according to domestic or international law, morally desirable or deplorable, or politically necessary or inconvenient, are matters that are still the object of heated debates and disagreement among the judges, political leaders and civil society actors.

That being said, for the purpose of this conclusion and in the light of the contributions of the different authors of this book, we believe that it is possible to identify a number of legal obstacles that tend to be especially recurrent in discussions on the role of the courts in the aftermath of transitions and which have come to be coined by Professor Yván Montoya Vivanco as "impunity mechanisms". These include amnesty laws; the legality principle; the prohibition against the non-retroactive application of unfavourable criminal law; and statutory limitations. In what follows is a brief account of what is meant by each of them and their recurrence in the different cases under consideration.

One of the perhaps most evident obstacles to local criminal justice that has been and, in some cases continues to be, most acutely felt in Argentina, Chile, Peru and Spain is the existence of amnesty laws. Whereas some of these laws were drafted by the military dictatorships while still in power (self-amnesty laws), others were democratically adopted in the aftermath of transition and still remain intact. The case of Uruguay, although not in focus in this book, deserves special mention in this context, as its amnesty law was adopted on the basis of popular referenda. In more recent years, in response to the evolution of international human rights and criminal law and jurisprudence that condemn amnesties, renewed efforts have been made to create different incentives for members of the armed forces, whether regular or not, who gave or executed the orders to commit grave violations or serious crime, to accept a change of regime, or a peace agreement. Thus, the utility of other legal mechanisms are explored, such as in the Colombian justice and peace process. Unlike amnesty laws, the Colombian legal measure meant to create an incentive does not block the investigation or prosecution of grave crime altogether; rather, it contemplates the promise of a mild sanction as creating an incentive for the perpetrators of the atrocities committed in this country to demobilize, reintegrate into society and submit their conduct to the courts for trial. For many, however, this is an unacceptable compromise, which goes against the canon of criminal justice.

A second obstacle refers to the legality principle and the related prohibition against the retroactive application of criminal law to the detriment of the accused. Indeed, in most of the cases dealt with in this book, a common counter-argument against the holding of proceedings or in defence of an accused of serious violations or grave crime is that such conducts had not been criminalized at the time of their commission. To the extent that the principle of legality is meant to guarantee basic legal security in social relations, which includes a significant degree of "foreseeability" and, thus, a real possibility of avoiding criminal sanction, the law's addressees must know, in advance, the range of actions that are criminal and therefore subjected to criminal sanction. Now, all of the national criminal codes in force in the countries under consideration evidently prohibit common crimes, such as "murders", also at the time when the commission of the serious human rights violations or grave crimes took place. However, criminal law categories introduced in international law, such as "torture" and "cruel and inhuman or degrading treatment or punishment", "enforced disappearances", "extrajudicial, summary and arbitrary executions" and "massacres" or, more generally, "crimes against humanity", are more recent and may not have existed at the time when the violations or crimes were committed or had not yet been incorporated into these penal codes.

To be sure, the lack of incorporation into domestic penal codes of these international criminal law categories have not necessarily impeded national judges from investigating and prosecuting the violations and crimes in focus under other headings that were indeed included in the domestic penal code at the time of their commission, such as murder, illegal detention, injuries, etc. Furthermore, in the absence of suitable domestic criminal law categories, the judges of some national jurisdictions have also come to develop additional arguments in the light of international conventions that define certain conduct as amounting to serious human rights violations or violations of the laws of war, sometimes even invoking the Martens Clause of 1899. However, not all constitutions recognize a right for the domestic courts to apply international law in a direct manner, particularly not general international law, and especially not for the purpose of defining the objects of criminal investigations and prosecutions. In addition, the strong dominance of legal positivist thinking among judges in countries such as Spain, Chile and Peru have meant that the arguments on the possibility of relying upon general accounts of human rights violations as defined in different conventions have been perceived as deeply problematic and in violation of the legality principle. From their standpoint, it is not enough that a given human rights convention was adopted or even ratified by their state unless some additional legislative measure has been adopted for the purpose of incorporating the relevant provisions of that convention into the domestic penal code. In this sense, path-breaking international legal developments, such as the London Charter of the International Military Tribunal (in Nuremberg), adopted on 8 August 1945, although actually defining the notion of "crimes against humanity", have little or no bearing upon what counts as applicable law in a given local jurisdiction at a given time, unless the notion of crimes against humanity has been made part of domestic law. Evidently, from this perspective arguments about the existence of peremptory norms defined as *ius cogens* which prohibit certain conduct without any exception at all times and in all places, even if not written down and posited in domestic law, are particularly difficult to muster as providing legal bases for conducting criminal investigations and prosecutions against persons who have violated these prohibitions.

A third obstacle, closely connected to the legality principle, refers to statutory limitations. As already mentioned, it usually takes a considerable amount of time before courts are able and willing to act and often it takes so long that statutory limitations enter into play. Indeed, the crime of enforced disappearance—thought of as composed of the common crimes of kidnapping, illegal detention and murder—was construed in a lead to overcome this obstacle. The Argentinean judges argued that as long as there is no certainty as to the final destiny or whereabouts of the persons who were kidnapped and illegally detained by the military dictatorship, the crimes persist in time until these persons or their remains have been found and identified. Meanwhile, the crime has not been consumed and the calculation of time limits has not even begun. The power of this line of argument is evident and has been relied upon by lawyers and judges in Chile, Peru and Spain. Still, as shown in the chapter of Alicia Gil Gil, the argument about statutory limitations still has considerable force, both in criminal law theory and practice.

The extent to which each of the legal obstacles are perceived as insuperable barriers to the conduct of criminal investigations and/or prosecutions in domestic judicial contexts depends, to a significant extent, on existing power relationships between the executive and judicial branches of government. For example, according to Roberto Garretón, the transition to democracy in Chile in 1990 did not change the close affinities between the courts and the executive that had been built up and guaranteed throughout the dictatorship. In spite of the transition, no judges were ever removed and the composition of the courts is now changing only as a result of inter-generational changes, retirements and the entry of young judges. In Argentina, the military *Junta* trial was made possible in great part due to the fact that the military dictatorship had lost some of its credibility and thus power because of the Falkland Islands war. However, as we suggest, it obviously also depended upon the existence of individual prosecutors and judges, such as Ricardo Gil Lavedra himself, who were committed to open proceedings against military *Junta* members as a matter of principle at a time of uncertainty as to how the armed forces would actually react. The democratic transition in Spain in 1975 was similar to those in Chile and Argentina, as well as Peru, inasmuch as no measure was ever adopted to remove judges who had supported (or were still supporting) the Francoist dictatorship.

Whereas the military *Junta* trial that was held in Argentina in 1985 demonstrates that it is possible, at least in certain circumstances, to open criminal investigations and prosecutions in the transitional period, most of the cases under consideration indicate that court action is greatly facilitated by the development of international human rights and criminal law, tireless efforts to voice demands for justice by civil society actors and improvement of judicial independence. The most commonly cited factor in all of the contributions is the significant evolution of international human rights and criminal law that has taken place, especially since the beginning of the 1990s. This development is owed, in great part, to the judges of the Inter-American Court of Human Rights and their progressive interpretations of the Inter-American Convention on Human Rights as well as general international law in responding to complaints ensuing as a result of local judicial inaction in the face of serious human rights violations. The path-breaking judgment that was delivered by this Court in the case of *Barrios Altos* on 15 March 2001, and which pronounces the obligation of states to investigate, prosecute and sanction serious human rights violations, is cited in all of the country studies in this book, including in the case of Spain even if formally not within the jurisdiction of this Court. Thereafter, more judgments in a similar spirit have followed and, most recently, in relation to Uruguay and its amnesty law in the *Gelman* case decided on 14 February 2011. And, as Judge Cançado Trindade notes in the opening chapter of the book (after the introduction), the court has been particularly concerned with the multiple massacres committed in Latin America and upheld a prominent role for the local courts in response to them. Furthermore, as noted by Felipe Gónzalez Morales, the Inter-American Commission on Human Rights has also performed a crucial function in this regard. At first moving with caution and drawing a distinction between self-amnesty laws and amnesty laws that had been democratically adopted, it thereafter changed its mind on amnesty laws and came to uphold a general prohibition.

Much of the international human rights law, including the pertinent international jurisprudence that has been cited in the preceding chapters, evolved and matured after many of the serious violations and grave crimes in focus in this book had taken place. Perhaps the most critical case in this regard is that of Spain, whose amnesty law was adopted in 1977 at a time when no international court or international procedure, such as the UN Human Rights Committee, upheld an understanding of international human rights law as encompassing a prohibition against amnesty laws. In addition, to the extent that the violations and crimes considered took place prior to the incorporation of new international legal developments into domestic penal codes, the problems posed by the legality principle and the prohibition against the application of retroactive law unfavourable to the accused remain pertinent counter-arguments that local courts cannot simply ignore. At the same time and as indicated in the Peruvian case, it is by no means evident that the legality principle poses an insuperable obstacle to investigations and proceedings. In fact, the Peruvian judicial experience demonstrates that it is perfectly possible to mediate the tension between the legality principle and the obligation to investigate, prosecute and sanction serious human rights violations in favour of the latter. In this sense, it provides a critical alternative to the doctrinal view on this matter and which is dominant in the Spanish judiciary, as shown in the chapters dedicated to the Spanish experience.

A somewhat similar question that crops up is how to tackle statutory limitations and whether the international rule of non-applicability of such limitations with regard to war crimes and crimes against humanity could be upheld as a counter-argument. The international rule in question was codified as a result of the adoption of the Convention on the Non-Applicability of Statutory Limitations to War Crimes and Crimes against Humanity on 26 November 1968. This Convention was ratified by Peru in 2003 and Uruguay in 2011; however, Argentina, Chile, Guatemala and Spain are still not States Parties. In the light of the fact that so far only 54 states have ratified the Convention, the claim that the rule is part of customary international law is not evident; furthermore, even if it was, it remains unclear at what point this new rule can be said to have originated and which states it binds. Because of the uncertainty that prevails on how to reason about these matters, the way in which local courts respond to the question about the applicability of statutory limitations in cases involving war crimes and crimes against humanity will most likely contribute to the advancement and refinement of international law. It is of special interest how courts of non-States Parties to the Convention or courts that are investigating and prosecuting crimes committed prior to the entry into force of the Convention in relation to their state have responded. Again, the way in which the Peruvian courts have dealt with this issue provides a crucial counterpoint to the position of their Spanish counterparts.

Besides the evolution of international human rights and criminal law, attention must also be paid to the role of civil society actors, especially international and local human rights NGOs and defenders acting in the countries concerned. And, as Professor Naomi Roht-Arriaza and Counsel Bernabeu make evident in their examination of the Guatemalan case, such NGOs now operate in a transnational environment, exploiting the possibility of turning to foreign courts with universal jurisdiction competences when the judicial avenues at home fail. Also of significance in the Chilean and Peruvian cases are the Catholic Church and religious congregation, although this positive influence is contested in other countries, such as Argentina. Additionally, the ability of the victims to organize themselves has turned out to be crucial. The rise of international institutions of human rights and criminal justice that exert pressure has meant that victims can rely on them and no longer depend on spontaneous and informal initiatives alone.

Finally, consideration must also be given to the importance of independent judiciaries and judges. Taking into account the proximity that is usually built up between the executive branch of government, the armed forces and the courts during a dictatorship, it seems evident that even if a transition has taken place, the loyalty of the courts to the previous regime may subsist. This background explains the resistance of local courts—especially military tribunals—to investigate, prosecute and sanction crimes perpetrated by army officers, generals, admirals, etc. The Peruvian, Argentinean and Chilean cases are especially telling of the tendency of military tribunals to shield the armed forces in their respective countries from convictions and severe penalties rather than holding them to account. The adoption of deliberate policies aiming at the removal of judges most evidently enmeshed with the previous regime is missing. More common has been to restrict the competences of military tribunals over the cases concerned. Nevertheless, as the study of the Chilean case so clearly demonstrates, judicial independence is difficult to accomplish: even if the majority of the judges at the Chilean Supreme Court now uphold the sentences issued by lower courts against perpetrators of grave crimes committed during the Pinochet regime, that majority is still vulnerable to the occasional substitution of judges.

The evolution of the law and organs of international human rights and criminal justice, the strengthening of judicial independence of local courts and the existence of civil society actors are critical factors that explain why court actions have multiplied in the Latin American region in the last decade, and have even led to the opening of cases involving crimes from the Francoist period and the Spanish Civil War before Spanish courts. The same factors also explain the recent judicial developments in other countries, such as Colombia and Guatemala, two substantially different cases in which, however, no traditional transitions have taken place. Indeed, these cases are either characterized by conflicts which have not come to an end or judiciaries that have not taken the lead in the process of delivering justice. The role of extraterritorial investigations and prosecutions, or threat of such investigations and prosecutions, experienced in such cases renders it essential to treat the question about the role of courts separately in these scenarios.

Returning to the key time issue, it is important to underscore that the establishment of the Rome Statute framework has meant that local courts whose states are parties to the Statute are required to investigate and prosecute grave crimes "without an unjustified delay in the proceedings" (Article 17.2.b of the Rome Statute). In the light of this provision it seems evident that the grace period given to local courts obliged to act in response to the perpetration of massive crime is shrinking. Indeed, as a result, most situations before the ICC are characterized by conflict that has still not been brought to an end. At the same time, the fact that the ICC Prosecutor is still "examining" the situation in Colombia indicates that, as a matter of international criminal justice policy, there may be a considerable grace period as long as local governments and courts demonstrate some ability to deal with the situation. At the same time, the patience of several human rights organizations and scholars with the "wait and see" approach seems to have run out. A similar sense that the grace period is shrinking is strengthened when considering the decisions of the Spanish courts to open criminal proceedings in relation to the genocide committed in Guatemala. From the outset, the principal question for the Spanish courts was whether the Guatemalan courts had been given sufficient time to investigate and prosecute the genocide. The Spanish Constitutional Court, in contrast, upheld that the Spanish and Guatemalan courts have concurrent jurisdiction in relation to the Guatemalan genocide, thus, endorsing an interpretation of the universal jurisdiction doctrine that avoids the time issue entirely.

In spite of the notable differences between the cases of Colombia and Guatemala, on the one hand, and those of Argentina, Chile, Peru and Spain, on the other, with regard to the nature of the obstacles facing local courts, the performance of the former tend to be assessed in the light of the standards and objectives of transitional justice. Both Alejandro Aponte and Paul Seils express doubts about the accuracy of this approach to Colombia. Aponte highlights what could be seen as legitimate doubts expressed by scholars and practitioners engaged in the Colombian justice and peace process. Especially prevalent is the question of whether Colombia is actually undergoing a transition in the traditional sense. However, as he also points out, the Colombian courts have endorsed an understanding of the Justice and Peace Law adopted in 2005 as a legislative initiative the efficacy of which must be evaluated within a transitional justice framework. Also, Professor Roht-Arriaza and Counsel Bernabeu seem to have reservations against adopting the transitional justice approach when analyzing the Guatemalan case at least when considering the role of Spanish courts therein. Roht-Arriaza and Bernabeu, whose primary focus is on how foreign courts become an option because of the environment at home, introduce the notion of "transnational justice" to capture the nature of contemporary judicial developments. In their view, this notion better captures the hybrid nature of the judicial processes that have developed in reaction to these crimes and the transnational character of the civil society actors and lawyers' teams that have pushed for this development. According to Paul Seils, however, even if "extraterritorial prosecutions", whether carried out by the Spanish *Audiencia Nacional* or the ICC, are no doubt a welcome development, such prosecutions cannot restore confidence in local institutions, but only ensure that there is a credible threat of prosecutions. In this sense, foreign courts cannot achieve what in his view is the goal of transitional justice.

The multiplication of human rights trials in the Latin American region over the last decade strengthens the perception of a real possibility of giving effect to the canon of criminal law in transitional and post-transitional settings. With the emergence of a more globalized system of international criminal justice and, thus, the opportunity of selecting among different judicial forums, new practical questions must be addressed. This new scenario, which is of central concern in Susan Kemp's chapter, requires the development of investigative and prosecutorial strategies that carefully consider how choices at an early stage of investigation, including crime classification, collection of evidence and mapping, will influence the selection of judicial forum and the likelihood of sound judicial settlements. But also substantial concerns still need to be addressed seriously. As Judge Elizabeth Odio Benito so convincingly reminds scholars and practitioners in the field of transitional justice, gender-specific crimes, although recognized in the jurisprudence of the ICTY and other international criminal tribunals as well as endorsed in the Rome Statute, remain marginal.

Index

Printed in the USA/Agawam, MA
January 7, 2013

571697.094